West Virginia's
LOWER TYGART VALLEY RIVER: PEOPLE AND PLACES

by: CAROLYNN FORTNEY HAMILTON

A long time in the making but its finally here —

Carolynn Hamilton

West Virginia's
LOWER TYGART VALLEY RIVER: PEOPLE AND PLACES

by

CAROLYNN FORTNEY HAMILTON

copyright ©2004 Carolynn Fortney Hamilton

All rights reserved. No part of this publication may be reproduced or transmitted in any other form or for any means, electronic or mechanical, including photocopy, recording or any information storage system, without written permission from TVR Press and Headline Books, Inc.

All photographs not labeled as provided by someone else are the sole property of the writer. No portion of this book may be reproduced without the express permission of the author.

To order additional copies of this book or for book publishing information, or to contact the author:

Headline Books, Inc.
P.O. Box 52
Terra Alta, WV 26764
www.headlinebooks.com

Tel/Fax: 800-570-5951 or 304-789-5951
Email: chamilton@headlinebooks.com

Published By:
TVR Press
P.O. Box 57
Colfax, WV 26566

ISBN 0929915321

Library of Congress Control Number: 2003114185

PRINTED IN THE UNITED STATES OF AMERICA

DEDICATION

I dedicate this book to my mother, Ila Fortney, who provided mounds of historical information and gave me the inspiration to continue research and to my son, Rob, who built me my first computer. Without it, this book may never have been written, and to the rest of my family for their love and understanding of my goal.

Acknowledgements

During the eight years of researching material for this book, I visited numerous libraries and will be forever grateful to the many staffs whose assistance were so willingly and generously given as well as were that of the clerks in the Marion County Courthouse.

My heartfelt thanks and appreciation to Peggy and Tom Fortney for their exceptional talent in editing this book. Local historians and genealogists who had documented past events were a special gift. Having lived all my life on the river, I was already acquainted with some of the older families, and met many new ones through interviews and by their sharing of family histories and events. Visits with friends and neighbors were a delight and I came away more inspired than ever. Recollections were sometimes conflicting but all were taken into account during the actual writing.

Thanks to the people at the following; US Army Corps of Engineers, Pittsburgh, PA; National Archives, Washington DC; West Virginia State Archives, Charleston, WV; WVU Library Archives, Morgantown, WV; Waynesburg College Library Genealogy Dept., Waynesburg, PA; Taylor County Historical Society, Grafton WV; Westmoreland County, PA Historical Society, Greensburg, PA; Patricia Tolliver, United Methodist Archives at WV Wesleyan College, and the people at Carpenter & Ford Funeral Home, Fairmont, WV.

Preface & Introduction

This book is the result of my wanting to know and document as much about the history of Colfax as I could discover. I soon realized I could not possibly stop with just my hometown. Colfax is so connected with surrounding communities that I realized the Tygart Valley River, including the B&O Railroad, was really my subject. In certain areas I could not succeed as well as I had hoped. Time had caused some events to fade like old photographs but that was compensated for by discovery of new information.

In the past, the history of the Tygart Valley River in Marion County, WV has been only lightly touched upon. Beneath the main events that took place here, there are yet some great untold stories. Almost every family on the river has a story to tell and each has a role to play in the culture of the river. Some of those stories are moments in time that otherwise might be lost forever. Documents and records back up most of the experiences encountered in this writing. The research became an unforgettable educational experience. Come with me to examine these tales and truths, so we can pass them on to future generations. My heartfelt thanks to those who contributed their time, stories, knowledge and pictures.

Carolynn Hamilton
Colfax, WV

Table of Contents

Dedication 3
Acknowldegements 4
Preface & Introduction 5

Chapter One   **THE RIVER** 11
    INDIANS 12
    HOW THE RIVER GOT ITS NAME 13
    NEW COUNTY 14
    THE TRIBUTARIES 15
    WOOD'S BOATHOUSE 25
    TYGART DAM 27

Chapter Two   **THE B&O RAILROAD** 33
    THE BEGINNING 34
    FETTERMAN/GRAFTON 36
    IRISH IMMIGRANTS 37
    TRESTLES 39
    COMPLETION 41
    STEAM ENGINES 41
    COLFAX TRAIN DEPOT 43
    LOCAL WORKMAN FOR THE RAILROAD 45
    TELEGRAPH OPERATORS 50
    The Watchman's Ghost 52
    TRAIN WRECKS IN THE VALLEY 52
    SELECTED SHORT SUBJECTS 61
    CSX 62
    1902 THE BUCKHANNON AND NORTHERN RAILROAD 63

Chapter Three   **RIVER COMMUNITIES** 65
    THE WILDERNESS OF VIRGINIA 67
    MILLERSVILLE 70
    PLEASANT VALLEY 70
    KINGMONT 77
    BENTON'S FERRY 85
    WHITE HALL 94
    COLFAX 105
    VALLEY BEND 148
    LEVELS 151
    GOOSE CREEK 157
    POWELL 158
    HAMMOND 170
    QUIET DELL 173
    ROCK LAKE 178
    VALLEY FALLS 181

Chapter Four **CHURCHES ON THE RIVER** 197
    RELIGIOUS FREEDOM ON THE FRONTIER 198
    1800's EARLY CHURCHES IN MARION COUNTY 198
    THE CIVIL WAR and Places of Worship on the Tygart Valley River 200
    1804 QUAKERS 201
    PLEASANT HILL CHURCH OF THE BRETHERN 202
    1856 MILLERSVILLE/PLEASANT VALLEY 202
    1858 CALVARY BAPTIST CHURCH 204
    1861 BENTON'S FERRY 204
    1812 LEVELS 205
    1875 LAWLER METHODIST EPISCOPAL SOUTH CHURCH 206
    1894 COLFAX 207
    1905 NAIN 214
    1911 ST. ANTHONY 215
    1914 KINGMONT 216
    1914 SARIETTA 216
    1920 QUIET DELL BAPTIST CHURCH 217
    1949 JEHOVAH'S WITNESSES 218
    1964 FIRST SOUTHERN BAPTIST 220
    1971 GALILEAN BAPTIST CHURCH 220
    1985 PLEASANT VALLEY CHURCH OF CHRIST 221
    1990 FAITH REFORMED PRESBYTERIAN CHURCH 222

Chapter Five **CEMETERIES** 223
    GRAVEYARDS 224
    TOMBSTONES 224
    BURIAL TRADITIONS 226
    COFFINS 226
    CEMETERY HISTORIES AND LISTINGS 227
        1852 SAM LINN CEMETERY 227
        1961 REST HAVEN MEMORIAL GARDENS 237
        1836 JOHN LINN CEMETERY 237
        1885 VINCENT CEMETERY 243
        1850 DODD CEMETERY 243
        1816 COLFAX CEMETERY (Nuzum No. 2) 244
        1841 BOYCE-CLARK CEMETERY 248
        1866 VANDERGRIFT CEMETERY 249
        1840 LITTLE CEMETERY 250
        1903 SMALLWOOD CEMETERY 252
        1814 SHRIVER CEMETERY 253
        1814 NUZUM NO. 1 256
        1972 TAYLOR CEMETERY 266
        1860 NUZUM NO. 3 267
        1808 WILLIAM LINN CEMETERY 268
        1823 SAMUEL LINN CEMETERY 270
        1875 LAWLER CEMETERY 271

Chapter Six	**LOCAL CIVIL WAR STORIES**	275
	THE BLUE AND THE GRAY	276
	THE SLAVE AUCTION	277
	A GHOST STORY	278
	THE RAIDERS	279
	THE BLOODY SIX	282
	VINCENT'S ESCAPE	282
Chapter Seven	**ORIGINAL LOG CABINS**	283
	ORIGIN OF LOG CABINS	284
	SAM LINN LOG HOME	285
	"THE LOG"	286
	CLELLAND LOG CABIN	287
	THE HONEYMOON CABIN	287
	THE TUCKER CABIN	288
	OTHER INTERESTING LOG HOMES.	289
	BIBLIOGRAPHY	292
	ARTICLES	293
	INDEX	294

Chapter One

The Tygart Valley River

*The source of our river
Begins near Valley Head.
Here it flows northward,
Where David Tygart had his homestead.*

*Mountains high on both sides,
It hugs the valley floor.
Whitewater and boulders always in view,
With honeysuckle scent I adore.*

*The rains can be fierce,
When Mother Nature makes her call.
It makes the tributaries roar.
Then floods the lowlands all.*

*The covered bridge at Philippi crosses over,
With many stories to tell.
From there the Tygart Dam awaits,
All the water that it can dwell.*

*At Valley Falls the gorge gets rough,
The elevation drops might quick.
But soon smoothes out with islands,
Where the fish have always been thick.*

*Down river past the riffles,
The West Fork comes in sight.
Here they merge to form the "Mon,"
Oh, what a beautiful sight.*

C. Fortney-Hamilton 1999

West Virginia's Lower Tygart Valley River

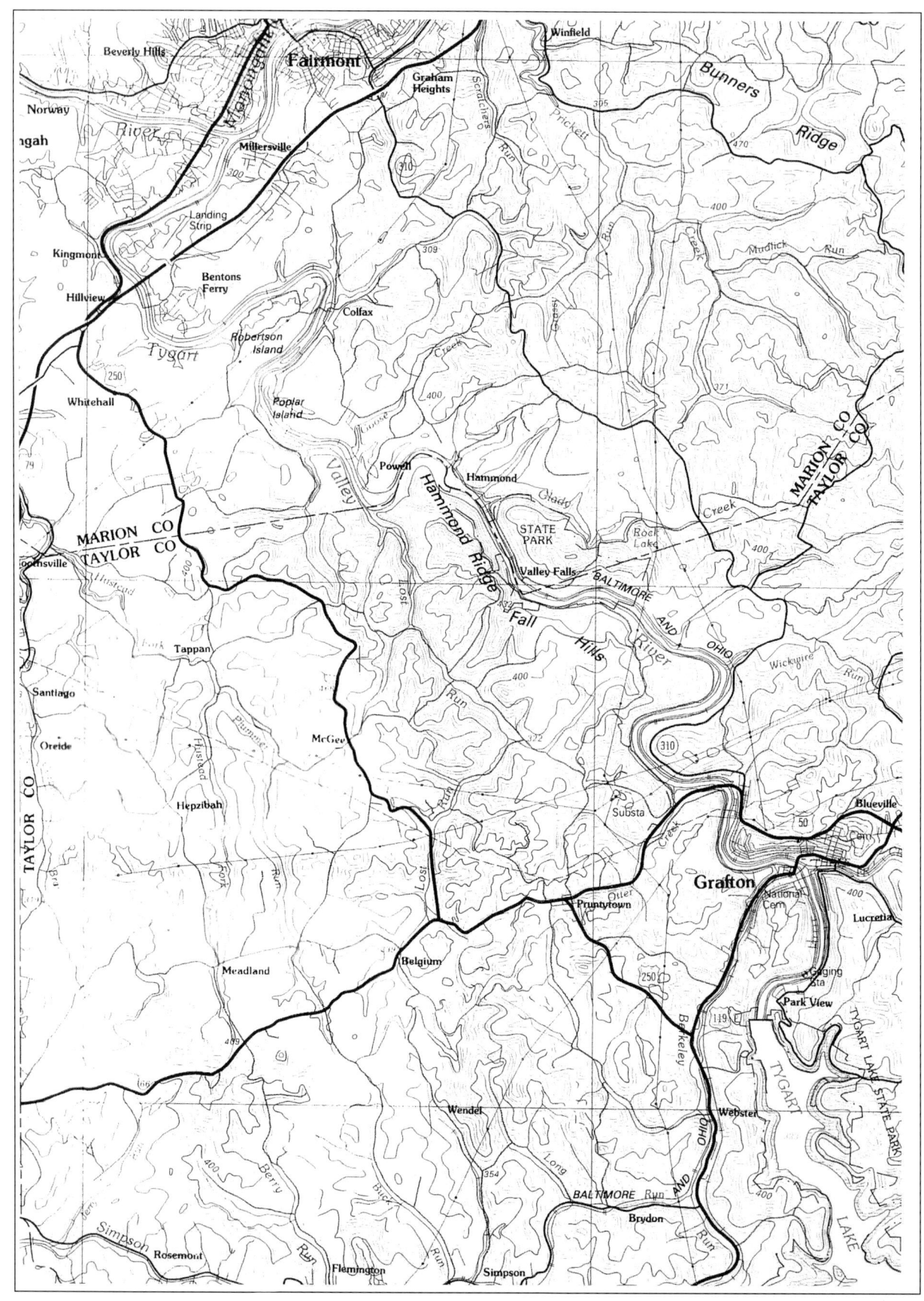

Map of the Tygart Valley River from the Grafton Dam to the West Fork River. The river distance is 23.1 miles.

THE RIVER

Geologists assure us that far back in time there was a broad trough perhaps 500 miles wide running through what is now the Eastern shore of North America. For millions of years, this trough was filled with water and was a part of the Atlantic Ocean. Rivers, were formed pouring sediments into this trough. Those sediments gradually rose to a height of eight miles above sea level. Through millennia, the shallow sea became a fresh water swamp where dead plants piled up to form the coal of the distant future.

Enormous forces within the earth's crust created mountains that slowly heaved upward. Geologists claim they probably compared to the Swiss Alps. Erosion wore them down to almost nothing. However, again movements in the earth produced uplifts in the old mountains, squeezing them from the original 500-mile wide syncline to 300 miles. In a time span of a half-a-billion years the Appalachian Mountains, as we know them today, were created.

The melting of snow and rain on the mountain tops created networks of streams which began to cut waterways in the landscape. That kind of erosion formed the basin of the Tygart Valley River. That process is ongoing yet today. The lower portion of the Tygart Valley River is the setting for my story.

Road sign on the Colfax Bridge.

Geologically the lower part of the Tygart Valley River is very different from the upper portion where it originates. Those of us who have been born, raised and live on the river know its everyday rustic beauty. Whether the river is at normal or high-level stage; ice-covered or flooding, it captures our attention. Knowing the strength and power of this river instills the respect that it amply deserves.

Getting to know the river—learning its secrets—means close observation that takes almost a lifetime. It has been said, "A river can the closest of friends. You must love it and live with it before you can know it." Fishing, swimming, boating, tubing, snorkeling or just plain wading are all great avenues for exploring those secrets. It is one of the most beautiful rivers and one of only a handful in the United States that flows north.

Much of what is now known as West Virginia once had water connections with the Great Lakes. Before the Ice Age, the predecessor of today's Monongahela River flowed northward across western Pennsylvania to Lake Erie. Pennsylvania State Route 18 closely follows this ancient stream, but this changed with the coming of the Kansan and Wisconsin glaciers. The huge icebergs blocked the flow of streams and forced new rivers to develop. Although glaciers did not reach as far as West Virginia, they changed our land patterns.

About 10,000 years ago, the Monongahela River was naturally dammed to form a huge lake that extended from Pittsburgh, Pennsylvania to 150 miles south in present-day Lewis County, West Virginia. The Monongahela Lake, as it is called by geologists, and the Allegheny River formed the Ohio River, which eventually drained southward. The drainage patterns in West Virginia changed forever as the waters then fed into the Mississippi system to the Gulf of Mexico.

Left: Aerial view of the conjunction of the Tygart Valley (left) and West Fork (right) rivers, which form the Monongahela River.

The Tygart Valley River is formed at an altitude of 4000 feet from a spring coming out of the side of Cheat Mountain in Randolph County. At this point, it is a mere brook which meanders down the mountainside northward towards Upper Mingo, WV. Unlike most, this river is unusual in that it flows northward as it runs gently down the valley. It can be seen from State Route 219. The road follows it south of Huttonsville where it is still so narrow that one could easily throw a stone across it. As it makes its way northward, it widens greatly as tributaries pour into it. By the time the river reaches Elkins, our pioneer forefathers would have had difficulty crossing it. Magnificent boulders dominate the riverbed from Belington to Philippi, and there are roaring waterfalls in between. After the Buckhannon and Middle Fork rivers empty into the stream, the volume of water gets intense. At Valley Falls the elevation is 998 feet and drops drastically to 938 within two miles. A spectacular series of natural falls result from this decline in elevation. The Tygart Valley River flows 131 miles to join the West Fork River in Marion County, where the two rivers merge to become the Monongahela. At Pittsburgh, it joins the Allegheny to form the great Ohio River.

INDIANS

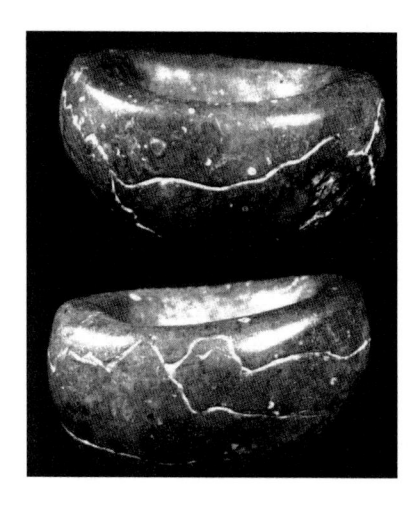

Left: Flint bowl found by Joseph Jolliffe in 1854. The bowl was traded to Joseph Parkinson in 1878, under the direction of W.F. Horn, who came to this area for an archaeological excavation. *Permission to reproduce by Lori Gerkin.*

Right: The etching on the outside of the bowl matches the drainage of the Tygart Valley River to the headwaters of the Monongahela River.

Among the earliest of Indian cultures (500 B.C.) along the Tygart and Monongahela Rivers were the Late Adena (or Mound Builders, as they were often called). It is believed the early Adena Culture was made up of the last of the Mound Builders, who mysteriously disappeared. To this day even the experts can't agree on what happened to them.

They left no written record to tell who they were and why they abandoned the country. Excavation sites near the Tygart have revealed they were indeed once here and buried their dead. Remains and artifacts have been found at excavation sites near Palatine Knob in Fairmont; at the confluence of the West Fork and Tygart rivers; at White Hall's Red Roof Inn; on the old Monongah Road near the Industrial Park; near the site of Hoult School, and at the Trinity Assembly of God Church site at Eldora.

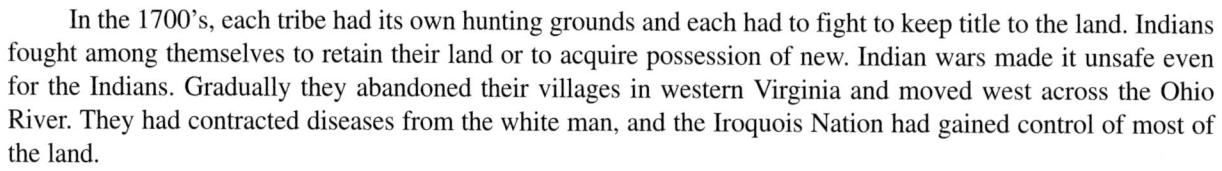

In the 1700's, each tribe had its own hunting grounds and each had to fight to keep title to the land. Indians fought among themselves to retain their land or to acquire possession of new. Indian wars made it unsafe even for the Indians. Gradually they abandoned their villages in western Virginia and moved west across the Ohio River. They had contracted diseases from the white man, and the Iroquois Nation had gained control of most of the land.

Many natural spots in West Virginia were named by the Indians, such as the vast mountain range of Ap-pal-ach-ia, meaning "the endless mountains." They clamored over the mountains so long covered in snow they called them the "Alle-ghe-ny," implying "the place of the foot." The Delaware Indians named the Mo-non-ga-he-la River, because it was "the river of caving banks". Even the Ohio Valley and the Ohio River was named by Indians calling it the "river of blood" because of the many Indian wars fought trying to gain control of it.

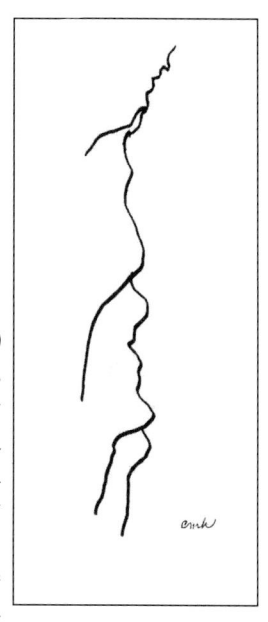

In the early 1700's when the white man came down the Monongahela River and its tributaries, the Indians used this portion of the state as their hunting grounds. According to Glenn Lough's book, *Now & Long Ago* they were members of the Six Nations of western Pennsylvania. Among them was the Iroquois Nation, consisting of the Mohawks, Onondagas, Senecas, Oneidas, Cayugas and the Tuscarawas. Some accounts say the early Massawomees, one of the branches of the Algonquin Indians, were also thought to have occupied western Virginia. It is believed the Massawomees included the Delaware's, Shawnees and Mingos, who claimed territory north of the Great Kanawha and west of the Alleghenies. East of the Ohio River, they considered the land to be their territory and used it as their hunting grounds. It is believed that each tribe respected the invisible boundary lines of the others.

To the Indian, the Tygart Valley River was called "The Muddy," so named because the banks were continually falling in and making the water muddy and murky on the river's edge. At that time, it was considered a branch of the Monongahela River. The Indians followed the river, and made camp in many places. In our area, they did not have horses until our pioneers brought them across the mountains in 1769. Until then, travel either was by canoe or on foot.

Indian trails have been discovered on both sides of the Tygart from Valley Falls to the bend in the river at Colfax and at Benton's Ferry. There were Indian trails on the hillsides, one still detectable, which led down to the main trail along the river. Today some of those trails have become roads. The Seneca Trail near the headwaters of the Tygart Valley River leads into the Catawba Trail, which follows the river north.

Walter Balderson wrote in his book *Fort Prickett Frontier and Marion County* that the Cherokee Indians once had a village at Valley Falls. Explorers and traders reported that the friendly Cherokee who made their camp there called the falls the "Cherokee Falls" and the valley the "Cherokee Valley." This was documented by Jacob Horn. In recent years, though, the idea of Cherokee Indians being this far north has been questioned. Whatever the true facts are, it is hard to believe that the local tales and folklore surrounding the Cherokee are based on myth. They explain why so many local pioneer families have Cherokee ancestry.

HOW THE RIVER GOT ITS NAME

In the early 1700's, the Tygart Valley River was considered the East Branch of the Monongahela River. It was nameless. The West Fork River was the West Branch of the Monongahela. Indians traveling up and down the rivers laid claim to them. Both the French and Indians savagely raided local white settlements during the French and Indian War. They destroyed the Eckarly (Eckerlin) brothers settlement at Dunkard's Bottom on the Cheat River and other families along on the Monongahela, the Potomac and all the lands between to the New River. The Indians ruled.

In 1753, the first white men arrived on the river near present-day Beverly in Randolph County. Little did they realize that they had settled in the pathway of the local Indians. David Tygart (perhaps spelled Taggart) and Robert Files (perhaps spelled Foyles) brought their families south from the South Branch of the Potomac to settle on the headwaters of the East Branch of the Monongahela River. Here there was virgin timber, fertile land and plentiful game. David Tygart and Robert Files were brothers-in-law as well as very good friends. Robert was married to the fair-haired Elizabeth Tygart.

Robert (born 1715) and Elizabeth Files (born 1717) had six children. They built their cabin on an elevated point on the river at the mouth of what is now called Files Creek near Beverly. One family history, by Margaret Files of Cleveland, Texas says "The Files cabin stood about 50 yards, a little North of West, from Stark L. Baker's Mill, on a high point of land which at that time was washed on one side by what has since been named Files Creek." The course of the creek has changed. Although it has filled in with soil, its former course can still be seen. Files Creek empties into the Tygart Valley River.

David Tygart and his family built their cabin about two miles upriver from the Files' cabin. They cleared the land and planted crops but they did not plant enough to sustain them through the winter. Their remoteness made it difficult to obtain supplies. This factor and the lack of military protection made the two families think seriously of returning over the mountains. They had found the local Indians unfriendly and discovered they had settled near their trail along the river.

But they had waited too long. In October of 1753, a passing band of Indian savages swooped down upon the Files' cabin and savagely

Highway marker in Beverly, WV.

> **BEVERLY**
> Settled about 1753 by Robert Files and David Tygart. Files' family was massacred near by. Site of Westfall's Fort, 1774. In Mt. Iser Cemetery are the Union trenches and graves of Confederate soldiers killed in Battle of Rich Mountain.

massacred Files, his wife and five of their children—the youngest being only ten. Only their eldest son, 14-year-old John, who was in the forest across the creek at the time, escaped with his life. Hearing the screams from the cabin, he ran to see what was happening. He hid in the brush and watched as his entire family was massacred. Realizing that he alone could not save them, he ran to his uncle's cabin. David Tygart quickly gathered his family together and escaped, taking the Files boy with them. The river and the valley were named after this family.

Two months later, a band of friendly Indians related their discovery of the victims to a 21-year-old George Washington who had volunteered to carry a message from Virginia Governor Robert Dinwiddie of Virginia to the French, who were moving into the Ohio country. The message asked the French to leave the valley territory claimed by Britain's King George III. Washington was accompanied by Christopher Gist, Jacob Van Braam and Half-King, an Indian chieftain who was their guide. This historic mission took them to Ft. Le Bouef on the site of present-day Waterford in Erie County, Pennsylvania.

On their return journey, they traveled by raft down the Allegheny River where Gist and Washington were thrown overboard. They spent the night on an island in wet clothes. According to *Washington's Diaries Vol. I*, dated December 23-31, 1753, they were camped at a trading post at the mouth of Turtle Creek on the Monongahela River on the east end of what is now Pittsburgh, Pennsylvania. The Indian told George what happened. "The cold was so extremely severe that Mr. Gist had all his fingers and some of his toes frozen, and the water was shut up so hard that we found no difficulty in getting off the island on the ice in the morning and went to Mr. Frazier's. We met here with 20 warriors, who were going to the Southwest to war, but coming to a place upon the head of the Great Cunnaway, *(the river above the mouth of the Buckhannon River was referred to as the headwater of the Great Cannaway)* where they found seven people killed and scalped, all but one woman with very light hair. They turned about and ran back for fear the inhabitants should rise and take them as the authors of the murder: They reported that the people were lying about the house and some of them much torn and eaten by hogs; by the marks that were left, they say they were French Indians of the Ottaway Nation, Ect. that did it." According to the Files family history, Major Washington never forgot that the Indians did not scalp the fair-haired woman.

When Washington returned to Virginia in February of 1754, he gave his journal to Governor Robert Dinwiddie who used the report of the massacre to persuade the Virginia House of Burgesses to provide more protection for the brave people who were trying to settle the frontier. During Dinwiddie's plea, he described the murder scene in gory detail. But even with additional protection, it was 18 years before anyone tried to settle in the area again. During those years, the East Branch of the Monongahelia River had begun to be referred to as the "Tyger's" Valley River. That name can be found on various early land transactions. Today, a stone marker in the center of the town of Beverly commemorates the Files and Tygart families for their struggle in developing the area.

According to one account, the Tygart family moved back across the mountains to present-day Hampshire County taking young Files with them. Today in Romney there stands a house, called the Taggart House, built in 1795 which gives proof some of the Tygart (Taggart) family remained in the area. Other family members settled along the Roanoke River in Roanoke County, Virginia.

Young John Files married Mary Catherine Manley in 1759. They had five sons before they moved to Abbyville, South Carolina. This move came about because John was awarded two land grants by King George III in 1769 and 1770. When the Revolutionary War started in 1776, John Files enlisted as Lieutenant and later became Captain. Three of his sons also joined the army and fought in the same regiment as their father. In 1781 the Indians and Tories captured Captain Files. He was tortured and killed, thus meeting the same fate as his father before him.

NEW COUNTY

In 1634, our valley belonged to the vast territory of Orange County, Virginia, named for the Prince of Orange. It remained so until 1738, when this area, which was considered the wilderness west of the mountains, became known as Augusta County, Virginia. It was created out of the western portion of Orange County and named in respect of Augusta, a companion of the Prince of Wales.

In 1714 Governor Alexander Spottswood of Virginia and his party made the first attempt to penetrate the mountain wilderness. He never made it beyond what is now Harpers Ferry. The next effort was made in 1740, when traders and adventurers began working their way into the interior to trade with the Indians.

In 1730, the craving for more land for settlements increased, so the Colony of Virginia began offering 1,000 acres of land to anyone willing to stake a claim—providing that any claimant family was from outside of the Commonwealth. This resulted in several different nationalities making claims. The Scotch-Irish, German,

People and Places

Dutch, English and French emigrated to the wilderness. The combination of their unique personalities and customs were the beginning of the Appalachian culture.

Prickett's Fort was built in 1774. Two years later Monongalia County was formed from West Augusta and Augusta Counties. Some historians think the spelling of the name was a misspelling of the name of the Monongahela River. Morgantown became its county seat. The new county included all the lands drained by the Monongahela River.

Eight years later in 1784, a new county called Harrison was formed from Monongalia County. It was named after Benjamin Harrison who was then Governor of Virginia. (His son, William Henry Harrison, later became the ninth President of the United States). Clarksburg became Harrison's county seat. The formation of this county brought its borders to the banks of the Tygart Valley River in what is now Grant District in Marion County.

It remained so for 58 years until 1842, when Marion County was formed from Harrison and Monongalia Counties. Both shores of the Tygart then fell under the jurisdiction of the new county. Taylor County was formed in 1844 by taking portions of land from all three counties.

THE TRIBUTARIES

The first of the major tributaries below the dam is **Three Forks Creek** which begins in Preston County where Field Creek, Lick Run and Squires Run join forces to form a larger body of water in Lyons District. Located at the headwaters of the Three Forks Creek is the site of the old Fortney's Mill. It ground corn and had an "up-and-down" saw that cut wood. Three generations of Fortneys owned and operated the mill. The rustic beauty of this stream is marred from the acid mine drainage in the area. It flows into the Tygart near the train yards in Grafton. **Wickwire Run** originates in the northeastern part of Taylor County very near Route 119 north. Once known for great fishing, the stream meanders for several miles in the countryside before finally emptying into the Tygart. The stream is named after John Wickwire, Sr., who had a farm on the stream in 1774. Wickwire ran a ferry on the Tygart Valley River at the mouth of the run. In 1784, the new county of Harrison ordered "a bridle path to be opened from Clarksburg to Wickwire's ford." Near Wickwire Run, the river is a stunning site to behold with its huge ancient boulders and native Mountain Laurel shading the stream. **Plum Run** is the next small stream downriver. No information could be found on the naming of this stream.

The tributaries flowing into the Tygart Valley River in Marion County below Valley Falls are all very special in their own unique way. Just outside of the Valley Falls State Park boundary line in Union District is the legendary stream of **Glady Creek.** The stream originates near the border of Taylor County in an area called Upper Glady Creek. It flows through Rock Lake then drops 400 ft. in elevation very quickly to form a set of beautiful falls close to where it meets the Tygart Valley River. The Glady Falls is on private property outside the boundary of Valley Falls State Park and can only be seen by hiking to them. It is commonly known as 27 Foot Falls. Rugged terrain surrounds the falls, which is 27 feet high and is partially enclosed with native Rhododendron and rugged to reach. Very seldom running dry, the stream provides a panoramic view the average tourist does not see. Not far below the falls is a second set but the drop is much smaller. It is called Twin Falls. The stream empties into the Tygart in what is known as the gorge below Valley Falls. The gorge is a wonder of nature and

Winter scene of "27 Foot Falls" on lower Glady Creek in the early 1900's. *Courtesy of FSC Folk Life Collection; Donated by Buddy Myers.*

27 Foot Falls as it looks today. *Courtesy of Sharon Linn.*

15

Twin Falls below 27 Foot Falls on lower Glady Creek

Nuzum's Run at the Hammond Railroad trestle showing the road underneath the trestle.

picture postcard perfect. Huge rocks and boulders prevent boating here and the river is dangerous for the angler looking for that big catch.

Below Glady Creek, downriver about 200 yards, is **Burnt Cabin Run.** It flows from the Quiet Dell community near East Grafton Road into the Tygart just above the ghost town of Hammond. In 1767, Richard Falls ran a Shawnee Indian trading post here. According to legend, there was once a log cabin that Indians torched somewhere alongside the stream, hence the name. Burnt Cabin Road is a small road leading off East Grafton Road. It used to follow the stream all the way to the river but it now branches off and comes to a dead end. In the 1860's, the road led to Tunnel Hollow where it was used to take cannel coal to Nuzum's Mill (Hammond) for shipment.

Not far downstream from the mouth of Burnt Cabin Run is what used to be the town of Hammond. Here **Nuzum's Run** meanders down the hillside and flows beneath the railroad trestle before emptying into the Tygart. It shares the trestle with the old county road leading into Hammond. The property now belongs to the Tygart River Mine. The stream suffers from pollution from an "unidentified" source which makes the stream run red. The property is posted and not available to the public. About 100 yards upriver is a nice sandy beach on the river's edge, once bustling with activity from the town of Hammond. The beach lies in a little cove of still water ideal for swimming or fishing. Today the property is posted and no longer available for public use. Directly across from the mouth of Nuzum's Run is an island of solid rock in the middle of the river. It floods over during high water, as does another very small unnamed island less than a half-mile downriver. Neither is habitable. Swift, shallow rapids surround the islands.

Downriver on the Taylor County side, opposite the present Tygart River Mine, is **Lost Run.** It originates close to Pruntytown, WV and flows several miles before **Meetinghouse Run** joins it and then pours into the river. Meetinghouse Run begins near Lawler Church, used in the early days as a meetinghouse. The run flows through private property and is not open to the public. Having obtained permission to research the area, I was able to see where the old log tram road from Valley Falls came downriver to the landing beside the river. Before the Grafton Dam was built in 1939, the river was much shallower than it is today especially at this point. At the mouth of Lost Run there was a time when a person could wade across the river. During high water in the early 1800's, a ferry was in operation here.

In pioneer days, as this story goes, a Taylor County man went to Cumberland twice a year to get a load of salt for himself for a winter's supply and to sell to others. In those days Cumberland was the nearest place to get this valuable commodity. Upon his return from one of his trips, with six oxen pulling the heavy wagon, he had to ford the river at an angle at this point. One of the wagon wheels got lodged between rocks in the middle of the river. Before he realized what was happening, the wheel broke and he lost his cargo in the river at the mouth of what later became known as Lost Run. Discouraged by his loss, he decided to dig his own salt well where he had seen wildlife licking the rocks. He dug for days, finally hitting what he thought was salt but it turned out to be mostly sulfur. He abandoned the well and began making the long trek back to Cumberland for salt before winter set in again. It is thought Lost Run was named in the early 1800's.

People and Places

The following land transaction is located in what is now Taylor County near the mouth of Lost Run: John Booth, Heir at Law to James Booth is entitled to two hundred acres of land in Monongalia County on the south side of the Tiger Valley River [sic] opposite Forsheys Level to include his improvement made thereon in the year 1771 in the right of Preemption.

A short distance downriver from Lost Run, across the stream in Union District, Marion County, is **Goose Creek**. It originates up on the flats beyond the community of Levels. The stream gets its name from the many geese that ran loose on the farms in the early days. The old Liberty Mine, abandoned in the 1920's, was very close to this stream. Over the years since its closure, it had been slowly seeping two-to-three gallons per minute of bad water into the stream. On April 14, 1998 the seepage had increased to over 400 gallons per minute. Martinka Mine, as the Tygart River Mine was formally called, had cut into the Liberty Mine several years before but the seepage hadn't increased much until the mine pool rose when the mine closed and the water was shut off at the treatment ponds on Guyses Run at Colfax. The water level had risen to the point where it flowed into the old Liberty Mine. Pressure from backed up water finally made it pop like a cork. Water came gushing out of the mine and into Goose Creek. When it emptied into the Tygart, there was a black plume from coal dust, which was in the water for weeks. It left a black sediment on the bottom of the river to beyond Colfax. Tygart River Mine was cited for the violation. It treated the Liberty flow with soda ash before it was discharged into Goose Creek. Incidents such as this are one of many that still plague the Tygart Valley River.

Unnamed island at Hammond. It is solid rock and is the first of a chain of islands in Marion County. *Photo by C. Hamilton*

Aerial view of Lost Run as it meets the river with the Tygart River Mine tipple on the left.

Scout Island with Martinka Mines gob pile on the right. *Photo by C. Hamilton*

17

View of the cable swinging bridge across the Tygart on the west side of Poplar Island as it looks today.

Almost within sight of Goose Creek downriver is **River Run** in Grant District. It got its name from the merger of two smaller creeks, the South Fork and the North Fork, forming the much larger run that drains into the river. Both forks originate at an altitude of 1200 feet and run together at 1000 feet. When the run finally reaches the river, the altitude is 900 feet above sea level. River Run Road follows the shady stream down the hill where native rhododendron grows in abundance. The road comes to a dead end before the stream meets the river. Not so long ago, the road went all the way through to Sarrietta but in the past several years it has not been maintained for traffic.

Scout Island is located at the mouth of River Run. The island is long and narrow and encompasses ten acres. The highest point of the island usually escapes floodwater. At one time, a suspension footbridge was used to get to the island but it deteriorated over the years, eventually fell down and was never replaced. Today there is only one camp on the island. The only way to get to it is to drive through the shallow water or wade over. Scout Island got its name when Charles W. Vandergrift sold the island to Boy Scouts of America Troop 4 of Mountaineer Area Council in Marion County in 1920. Now owned by Pizatella Realtors, Scout Island can easily be seen from the Poplar Island Road. According to an old John Wood map of 1820, this island was once called Pine Island.

Immediately below Scout Island, the river gets very shallow with riffles. Here one can wade across at low-water stage. The late Delbert Smith of Colfax, who was 93 when we talked, recalled how he drove a coal wagon with a team of horses over this natural crossing in the river back in 1920. Today there's a buried gas line there but it doesn't affect the crossing.

Poplar Island, a landmass of about eight acres, is very close downriver to Scout Island. It has a long history of being a summer fun spot. According to an 1820 John Wood map, it was once called Sycamore Island. In the early 1900's, when the first camps were built, it was renamed Poplar Island. At that time, it boasted virgin stands of poplar trees.

A young, energetic Russell Nichols from Colfax and an unknown partner built six camps on the island starting in 1905. They eventually plotted off 12 lots. Three of the camps names were Bide-e-Wee, Windsor Camp and Tarazell. Guests from town were a regular occurrence on weekends. They arrived by train from the railroad landing on the east side of the river. Poplar Island is 9.3 miles from Fairmont by rail. The Glenn K. Little Store at the railroad landing offered supplies for the islanders. G. K. Little was the son of Helen (Linn) and Zimri Little. Russell married Pearl Hawkins, daughter of William "Peg" and Susan Hawkins of Colfax in 1913.

Sometime around 1919, a suspension walking bridge was erected from the landing on the east bank to the island. When automobiles became widely used another much larger suspension bridge was erected on the west side of the river to get to the island. Visitors and property owners then parked their cars on the shoreline and walked across the footbridge. The landowners on the island pay for suspension bridge maintenance. Electric service was brought to the island in the 1940's and telephone service came later. Individual camp owners have privately owned Poplar Island since its inception.

There are only four of the original summer camps left. Owners still have to cross the west bank suspension bridge to get to the island. The east bank suspension bridge fell down in the early 1940's and was never replaced. All that is left is the tall steel supports. The train platform was taken up not long afterwards. The island was flooded in 1888 but has never been flooded since. A campsite now occupies the place where the store used to be on the east bank. Poplar Island remains the most habitable of the islands in the chain on the Tygart. They are a beautiful sight anytime but especially from the air.

Just below the northern point of Poplar Island, **Fall Run** empties into the Tygart from Grant District. Originating on the old Ed Barnes property, near Route 250 South, Fall Run gets it name from the sudden 25-foot drop where Poplar Island Road crosses over to Sarrietta. The falls is hidden in a deep ravine that is surrounded in the Summer time by lush vegetation. It is so hidden that strangers, as well as near by communities do not

People and Places

Three of the original camps on Poplar Island. Pictures taken in 1922. *Courtesy of West Virginia State Archives, Elizabeth Windsor Collection.*

19

Aerial view of Poplar Island in the center. Tygart River Mine gob pile and Scout Island on the upper right. *Photo by C. Hamilton*

Left: Unidentified people on the west end suspension bridge to Poplar Island in 1922. *Courtesy of WV State Archives, Elizabeth Windsor Collection.* **Right: Footbridge on the west bank as it looks today.**

Fall Run Falls at Sarrietta.

know of its existence. From the falls to the river it descends a total of 61 feet before it discharges into the river.

Fishing in this area has long been an all-season past time. In the early 1960's one of the largest bass ever caught in West Virginia was caught near the mouth of Fall Run. Along the western shoreline and in view of Poplar Island (upriver) and Sandy Beach (downriver) there is a huge boulder the local people call Sunfish Rock. It was so named for the sunfish that can usually be seen swimming around the rock. Many local small tykes learned their first fishing skills here. Fish including perch, catfish, suckers, bass, muskie and pike have all been caught in the deep holes nearby.

At Sandy Beach, on the east side of the river, is **Shrivers's Run**. It originates on Tygart River Mine property. This run is named after John and Mary Shriver, who received a land grant here in 1800. They were one of the pioneer families who contributed greatly to the development of the area (see Cemeteries).

Shriver's Run flows under the railroad trestle at Sandy Beach then empties into the river. The river is very deep at this point and is an excellent fishing hole. The new settling ponds for the Tygart River Mine empties into this stream. Sandy Beach has been a popular local swimming hole for several generations. Its natural sandy shoreline is near the old sand dunes on the original Levels Road. It is unique compared to the rest of the shoreline in the area. It is on private property. The flow from the new Tygart River Mines Water Treatment Plant now empties into this stream.

Further downriver is **Robertson Island**. This island was completely submerged during the 1888 flood. In 1918, Charles W. and Lovie Robertson bought the island from Lawrence Cathers. They were the parents of Agnes (Robertson) Irons of Colfax. Mr. Cathers built the first of two camps ever built on the island. The island encompasses eight and a half acres. Glenn Parrish built the second camp for the Robertson Family.

The only way to get to Robertson Island even today is to wade or ford the river. In 1924, the Robertson's sold an acre of land with one of the camps on it to Russell Meredith and friends. Because it was next to impossible to cross the river during high water, they installed a cable from the west bank to a hugh tree on the island. A two-man cable car was attached to the cable and was operated with hand pulleys.

Right: Aerial view of Robertson Island, Colfax is in the distance.

Overview of the old Little family farm beside Poplar Island, 1940. *Courtesy of WV State Archives, Elizabeth Windsor*

Left: Patty Pyecha standing in the cable car cage that went from shore to shore on the west side of Robertson Island in 1949. *Courtesy of Terry Pyecha.* **Right: One of two camps that used to be on Robertson Island in the 1950's.** *Courtesy of James Priester, Marion County Assessor.*

In 1949, Andy and Betty Jo Pyecha, with son Terry and daughter Patty rented the Robertson camp for the summer. In July of that summer, during high water, Betty Jo was in the cable car crossing the river when the cable snapped. The cage fell into the high muddy river. Luckily, she survived with a broken leg but had back problems thereafter. Due to the incident the cable car was never reinstalled.

In 1952, Ike White and his brother bought the island from the Robertsons except for one acre where the Meredith camp was. For several years during the 1960's Ike, who lived near the island, let people take their cars over to the southern most point to go swimming and picnicking for the day. The rocky, shallow beach was a favorite swimming hole for years, especially for children since it was so very shallow. But the public began to abuse the land and the beach was eventually closed due to safety issues.

Still officially called Robertson Island the camps that were once located there no longer exist. Vegetation has long since taken over and has caused the island to go back to nature. It remains private property and is posted.

Guyses Run in the foreground at Colfax where it empties into the Tygart. "Pebble Beach" is in the bend of the river.

Downriver at the site of the old Colfax Bridge there is a US Geological Survey water gauging station (hydrograph station) used to gather the river's flow data. It is operated in conjunction with the U.S. Army Corps of Engineers. It was built in 1939 with local labor by the Works Projects Administration (WPA) and resembles the Washington monument.

The station gauges the water depth and the flow daily and broadcasts statistics of conditions of the river and Guyses Run some 300-ft. downstream. Daily readings can be found on the Internet.

People and Places

Water gauging station at Colfax. Still in use but computerized.

Colfax gauging station was built by the WPA in 1939 for the Army Corps of Engineers.

At Colfax, **Guyses Run** empties into the Tygart beside the new Colfax Bridge on State Route 66. According to Walter Balderson's book *Fort Prickett Frontier and Marion County,* Guyses Run got its name from a trapper or hermit whose surname was Guyses or Guiser or Gise. The very earliest area maps and deeds refer to the name as Gise's Run. He was supposed to have lived somewhere along the river or run in a cave under a cliff.

Guyses Run begins three miles east of Colfax on East Grafton Road below the city water storage tanks near Crossroads. Several smaller brooks empty into the run before it finally reaches the river. Up until the late 1950's suckers swam up the creek to spawn. Fisherman used to line up along the creek for weeks to catch them. The fish no longer frequent the area.

Upstream on Guyses Run behind the Colfax School, which was closed in 1995, is a completely shaded deep pool of water known locally as the "deep hole." This particular pool of cold water was a favorite fun site for several generations of Colfax-area kids. Some learned how to swim here before they were allowed to go to the river to swim.

The streambed of Guyses Run below the old Tygart River Mine's water treatment plant became polluted with chemical residue after the mine closed in 1995. However, a new treatment plant at Levels has corrected most of the problems with the stream. By 2003 Aquatic biologists from West Virginia University declared the stream healthy.

The upper portion of Guyses Run above the mine's old water treatment plant runs dry most of the time. That area's watershed is undermined and leaks underground. It easily flows with rain run-off. In

Pebble Beach at the mouth of Robinson Run.

23

Turtle Rock in the riffles below the Colfax Bridge.
Courtesy of Charles Fortney.

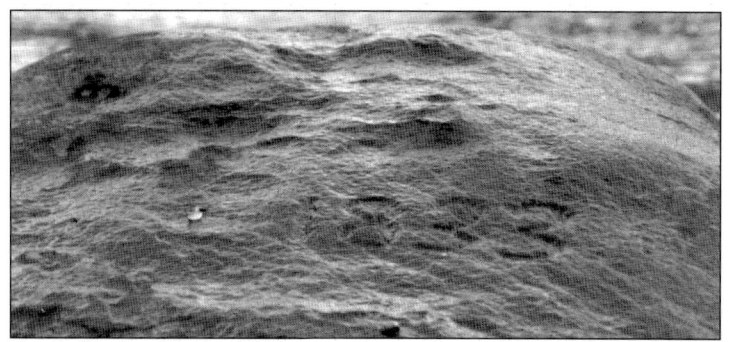

Turtle Rock with the 1833 engraving on it.
Courtesy of Charles Fortney.

2000, Tygart River Mine relined the upper portion of the creek bed with limestone rock.

The riffles at the Colfax Bridge harbor several large rocks in the river. One such rock has been dubbed "turtle rock" because its striking resemblance to a turtle when exposed by low-water level. The rock is significant enough to be mentioned because the date 1833 is engraved on it. At that time Colfax was still referred to as Springer's Bend. The initials H H are also engraved on the rock. Discovered many, many years ago the engravings are not commonly known. Who did the stone engravings? Perhaps it was Henry Hawkins, who owned land at Springer's Bend at that time. The author of the engravings has become one of the river's mysteries. When the river is up, the rock is barely visible, so it could easily spell disaster for a raft or canoe going downstream. During low-water level periods, the riffles and rocks prevent navigation upriver by motorboat. The water is normally very swift, making it difficult to stand or wade it. Canoes or small boats headed upriver have to be pushed.

At the bend in the river below the Colfax Bridge is what is known today as "Pebble Beach," a rock-covered natural beach with water excellent for swimming or wading. Our early pioneers used this natural shallow ford to cross the river. **Robinson Run** enters the river at Pebble Beach as it flows under the railroad trestle. This run originates in the valley below Morris Park and is named after Christopher Robinson, who with Peter T. Barnes, mined surface coal on the hillside in the 1860's and again in the 1950's. This run can be found on very early maps of Marion County. Robinson's Run flows downhill through the shaded canyon of Pinchgut Hollow to the river at 890 ft. above sea level. Navigation on the Monongahela River for large boats ends at this point since the river is much too shallow.

Downriver there are several smaller, unnamed creeks and brooks flowing into the Tygart before they meet up with the West Fork River. Together they add to the beauty of the river, particularly after a heavy rain. Waterfalls from the high ridges cascade down, causing the water level to go up and usually making it muddy. As the river nears Benton's Ferry, the water looks calm but the current is swift beneath the surface.

Black willow and sycamore trees grow along the riverbanks. The sycamores shed leaving white blotches on their tree

Steve Hamilton in 1993 before the tall ghostly sycamore trees were cut down to make way for the new Colfax Bridge.

trunks. The older trees, almost entirely white, provide shade along the riverbanks. The Indians called the sycamore the "ghosts of the forest." Legend has it that they believed the ghostly trees were inhabited by evil spirits. They were careful when passing by them. They believed the evil spirits lived near the trees at the bottom of the river and came to the water's surface to pull canoes down. Apparently their fear of these spirits kept them from felling these trees. The legend passed on to our pioneer ancestors who scoffed at the idea but thought of it when someone got hurt or died near them.

This legend came to mind in 1993 when the huge sycamore trees were being cut down on the riverbank to make way for the new Colfax Bridge. The majestic trees were well over 100 years old when the workmen began to fell them. The treetops were cut first, then the limbs. Things did not go well from the start...every day it was something: uncooperative weather, misplaced tools, or workmen reporting off. The trees began to fall but before the last tree came down, a worker fell from one of the tall ones. He was badly injured; the legend lives on.

Unnamed stream flowing under the railroad trestle at the site of the old Mundell's Ferry.

WOOD'S BOAT HOUSE

In 1938, Paul and Eloise Woods purchased the old water pump station on the west side of the Tygart Valley River from the Virginia-Pittsburgh Coal & Coke Company. Situated near the head of the navigational system, which extends to the Gulf of Mexico. The water here is 12 feet deep. Because of its calm surface, it is ideal for water sports and boating. Paul, a gifted carpenter, converted the pump station into a boat repair and sales business. He built docks along the river for boat rental space and docking. Since navigation for boats on the river ends above Benton's Ferry, it was an ideal location for boat docks. For a short time, the Woods' also had a luncheon business as an added attraction.

Conversion of the Monongah Water Plant's pump station into Wood's Boat House in 1942, *Courtesy of Pat Carr and Wood's Boat House.*

Woods' Boat House after remodeling. *Courtesy of Pat Carr and Wood's Boat House.*

West Virginia's Lower Tygart Valley River

Snack bar inside the main room of Wood's Boat House during the ownership of Paul Woods. Pictured left to right are: John Police and wife, Mary Eloise Wood and Thelma Cross. *Courtesy of Pat Carr*

A home builder by trade, Paul Woods first operated the boathouse as a hobby. By 1960 his love of water and boats became his major interest and he made it his full time business. In the winter of 1962, a flood and ice jam overwhelmed the docks and repair shop and 78 motors were destroyed.

Boat races and regattas enlivened the river before Woods retired. He sold the business to Patrick Carr and Ronald Rowland in 1978. As kids, both were members of a ski club, which met at the docks. They spent most of their summers on the river. Upon purchasing the docks the pair opted not to change the name of Woods' Boat House.

From March to October all size boats (except Jon and fishing boats), pontoons, ski boats, runabouts and personal watercrafts are sold and repaired. Rental space for pontoons and 125 boats are available.

In the off-season from October to March ski equipment is sold. Ski clothing, skis, ski rental and repair are available. In 1987 Pat and Ron put up a lighted Christmas tree in the middle of the Tygart Valley River during the holiday season. The lights and their reflection on the water at night can be seen from U.S. 250 and from I-79. Much to the appreciation of the community, the lighted Christmas tree became an annual tradition.

In 1938, at the opening of Wood's Boat House the late Paul Woods became a dealer for Johnson motors. Today, after 60 years, they can still be purchased there, carrying on the tradition.

Left: Night reflections on the Tygart from a lighted Christmas tree provided by Wood's Boat House during the Christmas season since 1984. *Courtesy of Rob Hamilton.* **Right: The late Paul Woods, past owner of Wood's Boat House.** *Courtesy of Pat Carr and Wood's Boat House.*

TYGART DAM

Flooding was a serious problem in our valley before the Tygart Dam was built. Communities along the river were always threatened when hard rains came. The flooding created a chain reaction downstream, affecting the Monongahela River and in Pittsburgh where two rivers join to form the Ohio River.

In 1852, the Thomas family lived at the mouth of Robinson's Run, three-tenths of a mile from the B&O passenger station in Colfax. They had gone to bed as usual at the end of a rainy day. Sometime during the night, their cat jumped upon the bed and woke them. Mr. Thomas threw the cat off the bed and heard a splash. He told his wife he thought he had thrown the cat into the water bucket, so he got out of bed to step into water up to his knees. This was how he learned that the backwater of the Tygart, coming through the B&O trestle, had flooded their house. Naturally, they vacated the premises.

Early history records a flood in 1832 and the Valentine's Day Flood in 1884, which left 10,000 people in Pittsburgh, miles away, homeless. That flood was not so bad here but did damage to the B&O train

Tygart Dam.

General view of the dam looking upstream. May 14, 1936 *Courtesy of the US Army Corps of Engineers*

bridge at Fetterman. Combined with the West Fork River, which was higher than the Tygart, it caused a chain reaction that was devastating. The Great Flood of 1888 became the most memorable flood the lower Tygart Valley has ever known. The raging waters of the Tygart appeared again in 1912 but were not as devastating as the 1888 flood.

On July 5, 1888 it began to rain and continued through July 10. The eight inches of rain that fell into the small tributaries upriver created a rapid rise in the river. High water came into the streets at Fetterman (now Grafton), far over the railroad tracks. The raging waters swept away their covered bridge (built in 1834-35). Its piers can still be spotted today on Riverside Drive in Grafton.

At Valley Falls, a log boom held thousands of logs behind it. As the water rose, the inevitable happened. All of the logs were swept downstream in a continuous roar. The force of the raging waters destroyed everything in its path. The communities of Valley Falls, Nuzum's Mill (Hammond), Colfax, Benton's Ferry and Kings Station (Kingmont) were hit hard. All but one of the mills on the river were destroyed. The mill at Valley Falls was badly damaged but survived. Nuzum's Mill, the Hall Mill at Sarrietta, the Hayhurst Mill at Kings Station were all swept away. In Colfax, the water flooded the cemetery and carried the old Hawkins house downriver to the bend. The house was later put back on its foundation with the help of the B&O Railroad.

Following another deadly flood on the Monongahela in 1908, the Flood Commission of Pittsburgh was created to study previous flood damage and suggest possible solutions. Another problem the commission wanted to address hinged on the Monongahela's water depth during dry periods. Most of the time, the river was too low for navigation for the barges, which were the primary way supplies and commodities were moved. The Monongahela River needed a constant water supply. In 1912, the commission proposed to construct 17 levees and reservoirs in the Allegheny and Monongahela basins. However, nothing was done and the flooding continued.

In the flood of 1928, youngsters Isaac Knight and Billy Nichols sat on the old Colfax Bridge, dangling their feet in the water which had risen almost to the floor planks of the old bridge and covered the camp road.

Flood control became a reality in 1933, when President Franklin D. Roosevelt signed the National Indus-

Upstream face of the dam. Sept. 25, 1936 *Courtesy of the US Army Corps of Engineers*

trial Recovery Work Act, which provided work for people who found themselves unemployed because of the Great Depression, which began in 1929. This program became known as the WPA. All public works projects across America were built under this program. The Tygart Dam was one of them. In January 1935, the Frederick Snare Corporation of New York City began construction of the dam. By May of that year more than 700 men from in and around Grafton, WV were working at the dam site. At its peak in 1936 the project employed 1,701 men. They earned a set wage of 45 cents per hour for non-skilled labor and $1.10 for skilled labor. The WPA called for a maximum 30-hour work week. Grafton's present-day City Park was the project's main office area for the building of the dam.

Above: Railroad trestle crossing Pleasant Creek along U.S. Rt. 119. Rt. 250 south in Barbour County, in 1937. *Courtesy of US Army Corps of Engineers.*

Railroad trestle as it looks today.

The B&O Railroad was forced to relocate 12.2 miles of its Grafton-Belington branch. The spectacular, tall trestle that crosses over Pleasant Creek along US Rt. 250 south in Barbour County resulted from the move. Cost of the relocation was $3.9 million. Buildings and timber in and around nearby Yates, Stonehouse Hollow, Cecil, Cove Run, Moatsville and Pleasant Creek had to be evacuated or removed because of the intended flooding of the 5,962 acres. Homes and cemeteries also were relocated. Impoundment of water behind the dam began in February 1938.

The Tygart Dam is one of the largest concrete gravity structures east of the Mississippi River. It towers 234 feet above the Tygart Valley River streambed and has eight sluice gates. It was the first of sixteen dam projects built in the Pittsburgh District for flood control. Ten fatalities were recorded from the 3000 employees it took for the construction. The project was completed in February 1938 at a total cost of $18,432,000.

The dam is about 23.1 miles upstream of its junction with the West Fork River at Fairmont. The reservoir is located in both Taylor and Barbour counties.

The dam met its greatest challenge in 1985. Spokesmen for the dam said the water rose ten feet from the emergency spillway behind the dam. It all started the week of Oct. 27, 1985 with the development of Hurricane Juan in the Gulf of Mexico, although three days later, Juan was downgraded to a tropical storm as it slowly came along the Louisiana coast. Rain swept up the Ohio Valley toward Pennsylvania and northward.

According to the weatherman, there was a high-pressure ridge over the eastern seaboard, as well as, a low-level jet stream originating in the Gulf of Mexico. Beginning on November 1, they carried a considerable amount of rain into the upper Ohio Valley. The combination of the tropical storm Juan and the airflow caused heavy downpours on the Tygart Valley watersheds. The storm was so intense and slow moving that the tributaries began to overflow their banks. For the next six days, rainfall totalled between five and ten inches. The rainstorm lasted for two days and caused flooding in the entire Monongahela River basin. Circumstances were bad all over the state, especially for communities along the Cheat, West Fork, Buckhannon and Monongahela rivers. Forty-seven people died. Several bridges were taken out and many people lost their homes and suffered severe losses.

Sept. 2, 1937 *Courtesy of the US Army Corps of Engineers*

There was $55 million in damages. Without the Tygart Dam, the communities on the Tygart Valley River would have been devastated.

The Monongahela Area Office of the US Army Corps of Engineers, Pittsburgh District, is located at the dam site. During the summer months, visitors may take guided tours through the long tunnels that stretch throughout the inside of the dam on several levels. Those of us who live in the valley appreciate the 62-year old dam and feel safe.

Six years after the dam was completed, the U.S. Government deeded the first land to the state for the creation of Tygart Lake State Park. Through the years, additional land was acquired until the park covered a total of 2,134 acres. Three boat ramps were made available for use in the park. Between 200 and 300 boats use the lake and ramps yearly.

In 1949 and again in 1951, the state legislature appropriated a total of $65,000 for additional park development. Improvements made at that time included a bathhouse, picnic area, water systems, roads, a superintendent's residence, service garage, and a recreation hall/park office. A campground was opened in 1953 and in 1955, cabins were constructed. In 1964, the park received another $300,000 for the construction of a 20-room Lodge overlooking the lake. It includes a restaurant, gift shop featuring many WV-made crafts, and a conference room. There is a magnificent view of the marina and lake from the lodge. The five hiking trails are open year round. L E. Elsey is the current Superintendent.

One of the many tunnels inside the dam available for tours during summer months. *Courtesy of the US Army Corps of Engineers*

The dam is designed to hold spring run-off water for release during the dry summer months. According to the Army Corps of Engineers, "The pool of elevation is generally held near 1,030 feet above Mean Sea Level (MSL) range from December through February. In order to provide adequate storage for navigation, the pool is allowed to rise, based on hydrometrical conditions until an elevation of 1,094 ft. is attained in early May. This elevation gradually declines from mid-July to mid-September because storage is being used to augment navigation. Then beginning in mid-September, the lake is drawn to nearly 1,030 ft. by December."

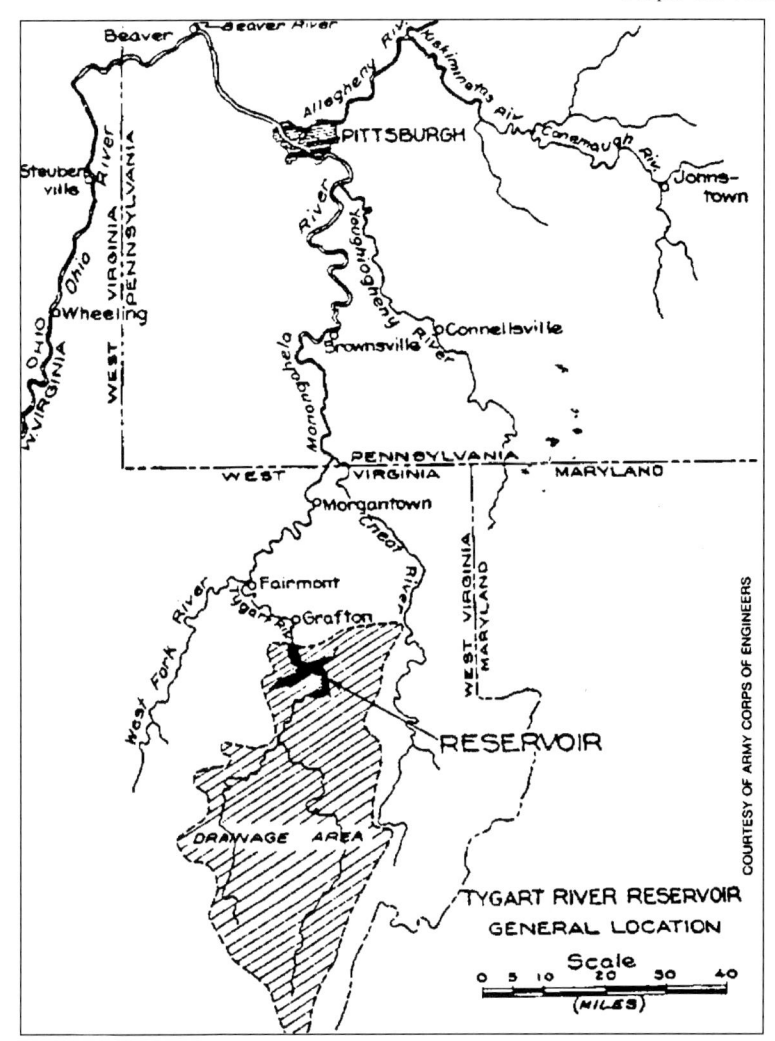

Right: Reservoir and drainage basin of the Tygart Valley River. *Courtesy of the US Army Corps of Engineers*

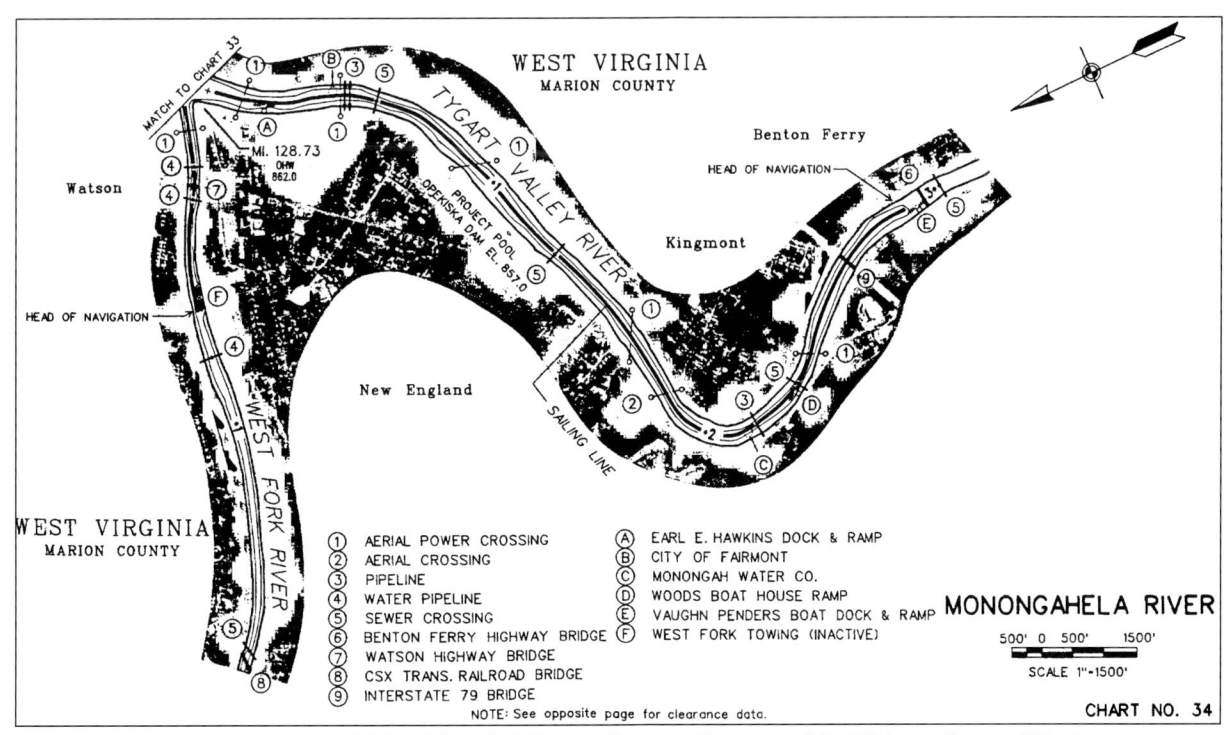

Navigational map of the Tygart Valley River in Marion County. *Courtesy of the US Army Corps of Engineers.*

West Virginia's Lower Tygart Valley River

VALLEY RIVER CAMP COLONY MAKING PLANS

Coming Season Will Be Unusually Active One For Camp Lovers

The Tygart's Valley River colony promises to be unusually active this season and in addition to those who annually frequent this summer resort, others are planning to join the colony.

Before many weeks have rolled around local citizens who own camps there will begin an exodus from the city and will remain there during the heated season.

A survey finds that most everyone who owns a cottage or camp along the river plans to occupy same while a few others will rent their camps, while still others plan to build camps for occupancy.

The season usually extends from about the middle of June until early in September. This permits families having children to occupy the camps as soon as school closes and to return to town when it reopens.

Some, however, do not observe this rule and May 30 probably will see a few families domiciled there. Some see fit to remain there until frost and even later.

The river has had at least one occupant all winter. Mitchell Mills and family have remained in their camp all winter and have enjoyed it.

Last year Dr. C. H. Neill and family remained in their camp, "Bide-a-Wee," until after Thanksgiving and suffered no inconvenience whatever. The Neill cottage, has many of the conveniences not had in many however, which makes it really an all-year-round home.

Walter Smith, who runs a camp near the Neill cottage, may be the first camper to move there as he plans to occupy his cottage about the middle of May.

The Tygart's Valley River is dotted with camps from Colfax to Benton's Ferry and scores of families spend the season there. Most of the camps are privately owned though a few may be rented.

James H. Thomas, it is understood plans to build a cottage this summer and others may follow his example.

Last year the Marion County Court seeing the need of improving the roads leading to the camps, set about these improvements with the result that the roads are all year roads and are in good condition and the camps are therefore, more desirable and easier of access.

Some are predicting that many may join the colony there on account of the high rents and the fact that if one so desires, he may live more economically.

Still others predict that the legalizing of beer may attract others there who may prefer a quiet isolated place in which to satisfy his thirst for the "cup that cheers" and who might find camp life more interesting with his favorite beverage obtainable.

Among the campers that make up the river colony each year are Dr. C. H. Neill, Walter Smith, Alex Riheldaffer, Arthur Frey, Richard Shurtleff, Dr. J. B. Clinton, June Orr, C. E. Mumford, W. E. Johnston, Clyde Morris, Earl Windsor, E. P. Henderson, Dr. C. H. Layman, Michell Mills, Dr. Hustead Brownfield, Joseph Rosier, R. H. Dollison, Clyde S. Holt, W. E. Arnett, Arnett, Jr., Willis Hawley, M. M. Foster, Dr. T. M. Vandergrift, M.

Left: The local daily newspaper. *Fairmont Times*, April 23, 1933.
Right: The local daily newspaper. *Fairmont Times*, July 31, 1936.

VALLEY RIVER TO BE STOCKED

Thousands of Fish to Be Placed in Stream at Proper Time

Certified by the State Health department as adequate for propagating fish, the State Conservation department is making plans to stock Tygarts Valley river between Fairmont and Valley Falls, with the finny tribes which once infested it. In this movement, the aid of sportsmen and other citizens is being solicited.

B. L. Tate, state game protector for Marion county, said yesterday it is the intention of his department to place thousands of fish in the Valley river at the proper periods between the present and next spring. He said that adult bass, three-inch bass, channel cats and crappe would be placed in the stream just as fast as they can be obtained from the state hatcheries and from the government.

Dputy Tate said that the request of citizens for cans of government fish will aid greatly in the stocking of the stream, as it is the policy of the federal government to comply with the requests of tax-payers in a prompt manner. He said that crappe, better known to local anglers as "lake sunfish," and channel cats must be obtained from the government, as the state does not breed them.

Deputy Tate said that it is the policy of the state hatcheries to change the adult bass breeding stock. This will make it possible for him to obtain several hundred large bass to be liberated in the Valley river, he said. He said, with the proper co-operation of citizens, he plans to place more than a car-load of fish in the Valley before the end of next spring.

Twenty years ago, the Valley was the best fishing stream in this section. Bass, pike, salmon, white perch and all kinds of catfish could be caught in the stream in large numbers. All were killed by poison from an over-flowing mine in Preston county in 1912.

Chapter Two

THE B&O RAILROAD

The Good Ole' Days

I love to remember the days gone by....
Of the trains we'd wave and all yell "Hi."

Black soot and cinders filled the air...
But to us kids, we didn't care.

The earth would shake and the valley would roar...
When the engine came by standing at the door.

Quickly it would be gone down the tracks...
Waving to the caboose in the back.

C. Fortney-Hamilton 1999

THE BEGINNING

The railroads running through the small communities along the river is not only a landmark for residents but a way of life. The blow of the whistle may sound different from the old days but the meaning is the same.

As the National Road was being finished in the East, construction of the Baltimore and Ohio (B&O) Rail Road (two words at that time) began with a groundbreaking on July 4, 1828 at Gwynn's Falls near Baltimore, Maryland. It was chartered in 1827 and was patterned after the first steam railroad in England in 1825. That railroad had only 20 miles of completed track. Charles Carroll, the last surviving signer of the Declaration of Independence, placed the cornerstone on a foundation of stones that supported wooden rails. This marked the birth of a rail system that would eventually lead to the western part of Virginia. Little did they know that it would take 24 years to finally reach the Tygart Valley River and on to Fairmont.

On the same day another cornerstone was being laid near Washington DC by President John Adams who presided over the groundbreaking ceremony for the start of construction for the Chesapeake & Ohio Canal, commonly known as the C&O Canal. These two events launched a race to reach the Ohio River.

The age of canals was in progress in 1828, and already traffic on the established Erie Canal was heavy. Coastal state businesses were being jeopardized because the trade was being diverted north bypassing coastal states altogether. Shipping on the Erie Canal was much cheaper. Fearing the doom of their city, a group of shrewd Baltimore businessmen envisioned a railroad that would stretch from Baltimore through western Virginia and on to the Ohio River. By 1834, the C&O Canal was in operation on the Potomac River at Harper's Ferry, Virginia. That was almost two years before the railroad arrived there. It was so successful that Maryland hoped to connect the canal with the Monongahela River, but engineers who inspected the route beyond Cumberland said the plan was not practical. It was dropped.

Seven years later in 1841 tracks had arrived in Cumberland, Maryland. The Iron Horse had reached that city first. The tracks ran parallel to the canal but they weren't handicapped by floods and freezes as the canal was. Besides, the canal could not begin to match the speed and dependability of the railroad.

Marion County was just being formed in 1842 when major decisions were being made about the railroad concerning the mountains. Construction on the railroad ceased altogether due to the tremendous obstacles for chief engineer Benjamin H. Latrobe and

..."**soulless corporation with screeching locomotives which would affect wagon traffic, reduce the price of horse feed, set fire to hay stacks, and frighten to death our hogs and wives.**"

determined railroad officials. It was decided to send out three groups of engineers to survey and find a sensible route over the Appalachian Mountains to reach the Ohio River. Some of the problems to be dealt with were the vast acres of wilderness, steep rugged mountains, rock cliffs, deep ravines and packs of roaming wolves. Officials realized their dream of a railroad could become a nightmare because these were the same reasons the C&O Canal did not reach the Ohio River.

During this stage of development, political problems developed. Neither Pennsylvania nor Virginia seemed willing to grant permission for a Maryland-owned railroad company to lay tracks across their states. Both hoped that someone from among their own citizens would form their own railroad company connecting the west with the east.

In 1847, when Pennsylvania agreed to charter the Connellsville B&O branch, the Virginia legislature authorized the extension of the railroad through Virginia on limited terms acceptable to the company, thus granting permission to cross the western part of its commonwealth. The legislative act specified that construction was to begin within three years and that the project had to be completed within 12 years. The designated route had to be along the mouth of Three Forks Creek and the Tygart Valley River. Surveyors immediately began purchasing property for the railroad.

Thomas Haymond, a Marion County Representative for northwestern Virginia in the Virginia Legislature, made a stipulation to guarantee that his home territory would benefit from prosperity promised by the railroad. He knew the B&O would open up the wilderness as well as provide better travel conditions into the isolated areas. In fact, it would contribute to a new way of life altogether.

At the time, the people of Morgantown opposed having the railroad built near their community. They called it…. "a soulless corporation with screeching locomotives which would affect wagon traffic, reduce the price of horse feed, set fire to hay stacks, and frighten to death our hogs and wives." Note the hogs were listed before the wives! Much later, of course, they regretted their resistance. When the railroad was completed between Baltimore and Fairmont, Morgantown's business and industry slumped badly. Realizing their mistake, they tried many times to get a branch railroad line, but failed. Thirty-two years later, in 1886, the railroad finally did arrive in Morgantown. The coal mines made it necessary.

The coming of the railroad along the Tygart Valley River made living much easier and more comfortable. It brought with it a brand new way of life for the folks in our sparsely-settled region. Rich mineral deposits could be mined. That meant industry, and that meant development and prosperity. Eventually the stagecoaches and long cattle drives to Cumberland over roads that were difficult to travel in the wintertime faded away. Although Mundell's Ferry and Benton's Ferry continued their services for the people who traveled along the Morgantown-Bridgeport Pike for another fifty years.

Engineers estimated that the cost of the railroad would be as high as $10 million — an astounding amount of money for a company to invest in those days. Little wonder financial problems developed. Work on the railroad did not begin again until late in the 1840's when revenues started coming in from the Cumberland coal basin.

When the rails were extended to the half-mile-high summit of present day Terra Alta in Preston County, a new and greater problem loomed. How and where were they going to descend to the Cheat River and climb again to reach the Tygart Valley River? Traversing the valleys and ridges at the right angles required to get over the Appalachians proved to be the engineers' greatest challenge of their careers. Paymasters paid out $200,000 a month in payroll to railroad workers who challenged the mountains.

Major land owners who sold land to the B&O from Kingmont to Valley Falls on the Tygart Valley River:

April	1850	William B. and Rebecca Mundell - (Mundell's Ferry)
April	1850	Abraham and Mary Barnes – (Benton's Ferry)
April	1850	William and Margaret Carpenter – Tygart Valley River
April	1850	Jacob and Ester Davis – (Shriver's Flat)
April	1850	Mathew L. Fleming – Tygart Valley River
April	1850	Richard and Hannah Thomas – Tygart Valley River
April	1850	Isaac Courtney – Tygart Valley River (Pleasant Valley)
April	1850	Sarah Tatterson – Tygart Valley River
April	1850	David Barker- (Shriver's Flat)
April	1850	Elzy Dodd – (Mundell's Ferry)
April	1850	Jesse Miller – Tygart Valley River (Millersville)
April	1850	Jacob Shriver – (Shriver's Flat)
April	1850	Jane Shriver Nuzum – (Shriver's Flat)
April	1850	Margaret Powell – (Powell)
May	1850	Job and Rebecca Springer – Texas (Colfax)
May	1850	Samuel Linn – (Benton's Ferry)
May	1850	Pearcy Phillips Irons – Texas (Colfax)
May	1850	William Linn – Tygart Valley River
May	1850	Reynear Hall – (Benton's Ferry)
May	1850	Charley S. Johnson – Tygart Valley River
May	1850	Charles Irons – Texas (Colfax)
June	1850	Franklin and Jane Davis – (Shriver's Flat)
June	1850	Silas and Sarah Barnes – (Millersville)
June	1850	Richard B. Nuzum – (Nuzum's Mill)
June	1850	Joseph C. Wiseman – Tygart Valley River
August	1850	Andrew Byers – Tygart Valley River
October	1850	Joel Nuzum – (Nuzum's Mill)
June	1852	Richard Thomas – (Texas) for a construction camp.
July	1852	P S. Gallahue – (Shriver's Flat)
January	1854	William B. Powell – (Powell)

November	1857	Zimri Harr – Tygart Valley River
July	1870	John Bradshaw – Valley Falls
October	1871	Rawley Barker – (Shriver's Flat)
July	1915	Samuel Williams – Tygart Valley River

Location in parenthesis reflect the author's personal knowledge of precise locations.

FETTERMAN/GRAFTON

In 1850, the route of the railroad came into the Tygart Valley by way of Three Forks Creek. The village of Fetterman in Taylor County was created when the railroad arrived and named after Sarah B. Fetterman. It was the site of the county's first railroad station and post office built on lands donated by Sarah B. Fetterman. One of the conditions in this transaction was "that the railroad shall establish a first class passenger and freight station at Valley Bridge and maintain the same and that the same passenger and freight station be known as "Fetterman." The family owned all the land on the river from Valley Falls to the middle of what is known today as Grafton. Fetterman was a place where there were already stagecoach connections with the Northwestern Turnpike (today's US Route 50). Within two years of the building of the railroad yards, the railroad needed more land for its various repair buildings in the railroad yards but it did not want to pay the Wall Street prices the Fettermans were asking.

In 1852, as well as the B&O, the Northwestern Virginia Railroad was laying track a few miles upriver through grapevines and blackberry thickets for a railroad towards Parkersburg. The B&O called this area the Parkersburg Junction. So it was here that a river and two railroads created the town of Grafton. There are two theories as to how the town got its name. One theory is that it was named after a man by the name of John Grafton, a civil engineer under Col. Benjamin Latrobe who laid out the route for the B&O Railroad. The other is from the railroad crews who called it "Graftin" from grafting two railroads together. Whichever is correct, one month after the railroad was completed from Parkersburg the B&O purchased the rail line for $5,400,000. That included the work shops. When the sale was complete, the B&O moved its entire equipment from Fetterman to Grafton, which became the terminal for the Piedmont and Parkersburg divisions. It became recognized from the beginning as an important connection point. Trains and travelers came and went 24 hours a day. By 1857, the first Grafton Hotel was constructed. Population was at its peak. It was a respectable place where travelers could get a good meal and a good night's sleep.

Grafton was incorporated in 1856 and 22 years later became the county seat. Prior to that, Pruntytown was the county seat. During the Civil War, Grafton became the prize coveted by both the Northern and Southern armies. Its population in 1860 was 466 white males, 419 white females, 5 colored free males and 1 colored free female making a total of 891 persons. There is no record of slaves.

Displaying an extraordinary example of the Beaux-Arts neoclassical architectural styling the B&O passenger station in Grafton was dedicated on August 11, 1911.
Courtesy of the Hamilton Collection

Sarah B. Fetterman owned most of the land inside the corporate limits of Grafton. She had it plotted off into lots and sold them except for one on Washington St. (named after her late husband Washington W. Fetterman) that she donated to the Catholic Church. It became the first and only church in Grafton at that time and for a while was used by all faiths. It has now been demolished. She also gave land up on top of Grafton's hill (North Western Turnpike/US Rt. 50) for a Catholic Cemetery. Wilford, Gertrude and Francis Streets were all named after the children of Sarah Fetterman.

An Irishman named John T. McGraw (1854-1920) was born in Oakland, Maryland and educated at Yale University where he graduated in law. He opened a law office in Grafton and became the town's Prosecuting Attorney in 1880. He moved to Grafton in the 1870's. In his twenties McGraw learned the cigar and tobacco manufacturing business. He made and sold cigars, stogies and scrap tobacco. His shop had a wide reputation for producing one of the best brands of stogies on the American market. He also took the opportunity to purchase land that later became the location of the railroad shop and buildings which eventually became the major division stop to change engines and crew. McGraw became one of Grafton's earliest outstanding citizens.

In 1911, McGraw was helpful in getting the new, more modern B&O passenger station and hotel on Main Street. He offered to donate land for the passenger station if the B&O would build it. If they did, he agreed to build a hotel next to it since the Hepburn Railway Act (1906) prohibited railroads to subsidize hotels. The deal was decided upon and the new station opened August 22, 1911. With the help of George Whitescarver the hotel was built at the same time. The construction cost was $75,000. Builders of both were J. J. Walsh and Sons from Baltimore, Maryland. The station had its main offices on the second floor and had beautiful marble columns inside. The train station closed to the public in the early 1970's. For a while, it was used by CSX as office space, but has since sat vacant. The original hotel was razed in 1948.

The new hotel was named after Daniel Willard, the President of the B&O Railroad at the time. The Willard Hotel opened on April 17, 1912 and was closed in the early 70's. In an attempt for Grafton to preserve its railroad heritage in recent years, both structures were sold to the Vandalia Foundation and Vandalia Redevelopment Corporation. Restoration of the hotel is currently underway and a railroad museum is planned for the depot in the future.

With the coming of cleaner, more-efficient diesel engines, Grafton eventually experienced a decline in prosperity. The large roundhouse and the railroad offices were removed and although trains still pass through this town, it would be hard to guess at what was once here.

Over time, Fetterman itself lost its identity and was annexed by Grafton in 1903.

IRISH IMMIGRANTS

The fact that the B&O Railroad was financed largely by British capital indicates that perhaps British subjects hoped they could find work in its construction. The need for labor to build the railroad happened to coincide with the time that the Irish were suffering from the potato famine in 1845-47 in their homeland. Fortunately for the railroad, poverty-stricken immigrants came to the U.S. en masse to escape starvation and disease. The railroad company enlisted workers from this eager and needy pool of immigrants.

Construction of the railroad required 5,000 workers before it was finished. They worked seven days a week. Local people also were hired to help accomplish the job, but the work force was largely made up of the Irish. The backbreaking labor all was done by hand using picks, shovels and wheelbarrows. All the drilling was done by hand, too, with charges of "black powder" blasting away the mountainsides for the railroad bed. "Drill, Ye Terriers, Drill" was a folk song written by the drill team workers. Steam drills were not invented until 1870.

Strong and lively, the Irish were thankful to have a job. If any of them got hurt or maimed, it was their problem. They had no benefits. It did not take long for the railroad company to realize the clansmen had also brought their local quarrels and disputes with them to this country. Local residents and area farmers, who were mostly Methodists, found the "new religion," Catholicism, a threat.

Old conservative Virginians were not quite ready for the behavior of the newcomers. Even though the Irish were experienced in building railroads and tunnels from having done so in their homeland, the locals disliked the "Tunnel Irish" and looked down their noses at them. Businesses had signs in their windows which said "HELP WANTED. NO IRISH NEED APPLY." Unperturbed, the Irish would boast that a true Irishman would rather drink than read…and be proud of it! Although after the Civil War, the Irish were eager to see their children educated in the free public schools. Burdened with the ever-present Irish "brogue" in their speech, the Irish students lived up to the name "the fighting Irish."

RIOTS

According to George A. Dunnington's book, *"History and Progress of the County of Marion, WV,"* the Irish were fresh from the bogs of Connaught and the Lakes of Killarny, Ireland. They brought with them all their local feuds and prejudices. They were kept apart while working on the railroad.

During the laying of the track between Tunnelton in Preston County and Fairmont in Marion County, minor labor wars broke out among the Irish workers. One such incident took place near Benton's Ferry while the men were working on the track bed. Irish clansmen, called the Connaugters, were camped on the Tygart Valley River. One morning they decided to settle their disagreements with another clan called the Fardowners, who were working at Ice's Mills, only a few miles away from the west bank of the Tygart. Their purpose was to drive the Fardowners from the country for good. They formed themselves into a band of 200 men armed with pickaxes and shovels and pursued the panic-stricken Fardowners on the tracks. Irish yells could be heard rolling down the hills toward Fairmont where the sheriff was able to bring everyone to a halt. In this scuffle, 88 Irish railroad men were jailed until a B&O foreman could get them out. From that time on the clans were kept far apart.

On the day of the clansmen's trial, Dunnington says they crowded into the courtroom where, since their were not enough seats, they stood around the walls and sat in the windows with their feet hanging out. According to newspaper accounts by Rev. Isaac Barnes, they seemed to be enjoying themselves. Their punishment is unknown and is lost to history. This was the last known conflict among the Irish in Marion County.

Large riots involving the Irish also were reported in Kingwood and Evansdale where the military had to be called to restore the peace.

CONSTRUCTION CAMP

Construction camps were built by the workers at various points along the railroad so they would not have far to go to work. Their temporary housing was usually in shacks or tents. Built in groups, they formed villages of sorts. Usually, they were called "The Irish Patch." One of these villages was located at Kingmont; it was just called "The Patch."

In Colfax, a five-acre construction camp was located at the bend of the river on the east side of the tracks. The Irish workers who built the small camp at first slept in large tents and then a large wooden structure was built for a mess hall. When the rail bed work in this area was finished, the men moved farther downriver and set up another camp. The abandoned camp in Colfax became a B&O storage area. Their old mess hall became a residence for B&O employee families who had free rent over the years.

In 1936, Dale Hunter, a railroad employee and resident of Colfax, dismantled the main building of the camp and reassembled it precisely as it had been for his home on the southern end of Colfax.

The five-acre construction camp was sold in 1947 to William "Willie" Boice. He was by all accounts, a hard-working railroad man who worked on the B&O road gang in Colfax until he

Above: The old mess hall for the B&O construction camp in Colfax. It was dismantled by Dale Hunter to build a house.
Courtesy of Ila Fortney
Left: House built by Dale Hunter from lumber out of the old Mess Hall.

was 72 years old. Don and Mary (Willie's granddaughter) Myers still reside on the property today.

While the B&O buildings and shacks have long since disappeared, it isn't difficult to visualize the boisterous individuals who once lived there. Perhaps if you listen closely in the early morning dawn, you might hear the faint sound of clanging sledge hammers.

After the completion of the railroad, many laborers remained in this vicinity and continued working for the railroad. They became responsible property owners and outstanding citizens. Some of their dialect remains in such words like shenanigans, shebang and smithereens and the tales of the leprechauns.

Descendants of those railroad Irish still live in the area today. Family names like Fluharty, Reynolds, Gallihue, Lee, Murphy, Malone, Boggess, Kirk, King, Morgan, Collins, Bucklew, Burrows, Hickey, Lavell and McDonald are only a few. The next generation of the Irish did not take up the pick and shovel like their fathers. Instead they sought positions in the railroad telegraph communications and operated and regulated the trains over the railroad that their fathers had built. The Irish built the railroad then maintained it and finally ran it.

A LOCAL IRISH YARN

This story was handed down in the Irons family in Colfax and told to me by the late Charles Joe Irons:

Food was scarce for the Irish laborers in the local work camp except for the excellent fish from the river, wild game and vegetables from the local farmers. One day a local farmer's wife was working in her garden when one of the Irishmen came over and asked her if he could have a few eggs that he found in a nest. She told him he could but they were probably spoiled since they had been there for several days.

She saw him again a few days later and asked him if the eggs were all right.

He said, "Yes ma'am, them eggs were real good. They had little baby chicks in them, you know."

The farmer's wife could not have known the Irish considered unhatched eggs a treat. He would have paid double the price if he'd had the money for what was considered such a delicacy back home in Ireland.

TRESTLES

There were 113 bridges, 11 tunnels and numerous trestles from Baltimore, MD to Wheeling, WV on the B&O line. The tunnels were built by the "tunnel Irish." Their knowledge of tunnel building made them famous. The work on the bridges and trestles was contracted out. Hand-cut stone trestles were built in remote areas (like the Tygart Valley was considered) despite the railroad's low budget. They had to withstand floods, ice jams, heavy traffic and tremendous amounts of weight, so they were built properly to begin with because they had to last. These were

High arched ceiling of hand-cut sandstone in the trestle over Guyses Run at Colfax.

The west end of the trestle over Robertson's Run on "Pebble Beach" at Colfax.

West Virginia's Lower Tygart Valley River

Left: East end of the trestle over Shriver's Run showing where it was repaired with bricks from the Colfax brickyard in the 1920's. Right: Another example of the craftsmanship on the west end of the trestle over Shriver's Run at Sandy Beach.

Train bridge crossing the Monongahela River.

Hammond trestle over Nuzum's Run.

the deciding factors for the B&O to build trestles made of stone instead of wood over the streams emptying into the Tygart Valley River.

The trestles from Glady Creek to Colfax were all constructed by the same local master stonemason and from stone quarried in the Hammond and Valley Falls area. John Sertees, who was born in Montreal, Canada and settled at Nuzum's Mill (Hammond) with his family, won the contract. Under the supervision of John Bradshaw for the B&O, the hand-quarried stones were all wedged into place by hand to form the beautiful arched ceilings. It is not known how long it took to build the trestles but it's easy to imagine the amount of hard

East end of the trestle at Glady Creek clearly showing the addition to the trestle when the second set of tracks was added in 1911.

40

People and Places

labor involved. After almost 150 years, they continue to pass strict inspections and can still withstand the heavy weight of the trains.

Mr. Sertees died soon after the completion of the railroad and is buried in the cemetery at the Church of the Brethren up on the hill from Hammond. The largest of the railroad bridges was constructed near Millersville crossing the Monongahela River to Fairmont. The partly wooden structure was 650 feet long and 35 feet above the average water line. It took two years to complete and was said to be the longest in the United States at that time. The cost was estimated at $800,000. The bridge was destroyed on April 30, 1863 by Rebel cavalrymen in the Jones Raid during the Civil War but was replaced within two years (see Civil War Stories).

COMPLETION

The B&O line from Three Forks Creek to Fairmont was completed on June 22, 1852. Trains to and from Cumberland and Baltimore began running immediately. This meant trains were operating daily to Fairmont even though the line was still incomplete to Wheeling. Towns like Grafton, Fetterman, Valley Falls, Nuzum's Mill (Hammond), Texas (Colfax), Benton's Ferry and King's Station (Kingmont) began to emerge along the Tygart Valley River.

Six months and 71 miles later the last spike was driven at Rosbby's Rock, 18 miles east of Wheeling, Virginia (WV) on Christmas Eve 1852. Despite the misspelled name that workers carved in the glacial rock, it marks the end of the line. Rosby Carr, an Englishman, was in charge of construction forces in that area.

Even before the last spike was driven that day, workers already began work on a rail line to Parkersburg. Over all, 1200 horses were used to complete the first railroad in western Virginia. The railroad marked the difference between pioneer and near modern times.

STEAM ENGINES

During the ten years of interruptions while the railroad was being built, the B&O developed much bigger engines. They kept getting bigger, stronger and faster over the next half-century. Towards the end of the 19th century, trains traveled the 379 miles from Wheeling to Baltimore at an average of 23 miles per hour.

The largest part of the steam engine was its water boiler. Underneath was a firebox where the fireman had to keep the fire roaring at all times by shoveling coal or wood into it. The fire boiled the water, which made steam, which, in turn, powered the train.

The huge steam engines called mallets, weighed 250 tons. The B&O had to lay new 110-pound steel track just to accommodate them. Their whistle had a very distinct sound. Mallet-type engines had problems maneuvering West Virginia curves and were involved in several accidents. Eventually they were removed from use in this part of the country but while they were used they had to have 18,000 gallons of water to operate smoothly. This required water being available all along the line. It was stored in what was known as "penstocks" or water storage tanks which stood on stilts high above the siding tracks.

Eastbound B&O passenger train No. 66, running from Connellsville, PA to Grafton, WV. Picture taken in front of the city pump station at Millersville.
Ora Nelson photo; Terry E. Arbogast Collection.

41

The last steam engine eastbound through Colfax on June 5, 1956. *Courtesy of Beverly (Wilson) Irons.*

When an engine needed water it would be driven under the penstock and filled up. There was one at Mason's Landing at Coffman, two miles above Valley Falls, and at Benton's Ferry. The penstocks were dismantled after the diesel engines took over in the 1950's. The more economical diesel engines required fewer workers, eventually creating many lay-offs within the company.

Trains came on a regular basis along the river. I know I'll never forget the steam engines, the wailing whistle and the belching smoke from their smokestacks. Housewives would run to the clothesline to take down the wash. If they didn't, the laundry would have to be re-washed because the black smoke and cinders soiled their white sheets and pillowcases. Conversations waited until the train passed, shaking the buildings and ground as it went through. Senior citizens in the Village of Colfax remember at least 22 passenger trains coming and going 24-hours a day.

Western Maryland engine No. 7548 and two Chessie system diesels as they roll through Colfax, WV in route to Grafton, WV. July 1, 1979. *Courtesy of Terry Arbogast.*

People and Places

Citizens who were young during the reign of the steam engine remember Ol' Engine No. 44. Henry Malone, an engineer from Wheeling, threw candy out to the kids as he went by. Those were the good old days.

Steam engine No. 4618 made the last run from Grafton to Fairmont as usual on June 5, 1956. H. Reid, a reporter from Roanoke, Virginia was assigned to write the story and get photographs for posterity. He chose Colfax as his vantage point. On that Tuesday morning, there was no fanfare and very few people to watch. I think most folks who lived along the river failed to realize that a new era was emerging. C. M. Rush was the engineer. L. Hardman, the fireman and J. R. Puffenbager, was the conductor. That day and a legend on the Tygart Valley River just quietly slipped away.

COLFAX TRAIN DEPOT

Colfax train depot (left) as it looked in 1920. William H. Hawkins operated the store and post office (right).
Photo by Milton Fortney. Courtesy of the Hamilton Collection.

The train station or depot for Texas (Colfax) was first located on the northern end of the community which was then the center of town. Painted red, it had a very small waiting room that was also used for storage.

In 1916, the Colfax depot was relocated to the crossing near the old mill. Sometimes a hobo would spend the night in the depot and then hopped a train when it stopped for passengers. It didn't matter which direction the train was going. People remember hobos knocking at their doors asking for something to eat. Most would work for a meal but others wanted handouts. They were usually harmless and appreciated anything they could get. The depot was closed in the late 1930's and since has been dismantled. A much larger depot was located at Hammond.

A platform was nothing more than wood flooring to make it easier for passengers to board the train. They had no roof and were located at Coffman, Valley Falls, Powell (on both sides of the tracks), Poplar Island, Antioch, and the Knights of Columbus camp at Benton's Ferry and at Kingmont.

Camp owners and their guests in the early 1920's boarding the train at Antioch. *Courtesy of Dale Huey, Jr.*

43

West Virginia's Lower Tygart Valley River

March 24, 1929. The only known photo of the last Colfax depot. Pictured are Charles "Doc" Knight, Gus Wilson and Charles D. Fortney. Train depot (right) and the old mill (left) in the background. *Courtesy of Delbert Smith*

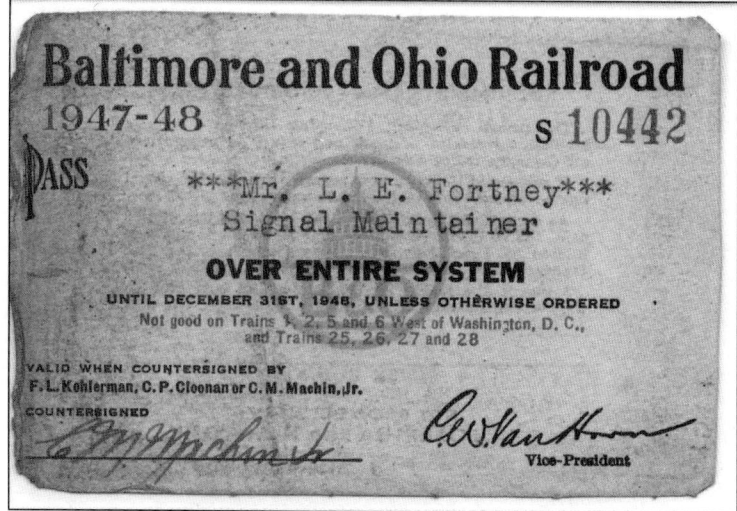

A pass over the entire system meant the holder could ride anywhere the train went. *Courtesy of the Hamilton Collection.*

B&O Railroad bosses had permanent passes on all its lines. They were frequently given out to political figures until the abuse became so outrageous that the U.S. Congress passed a law prohibiting all railroads from issuing passes to anyone except employees and their families. Lots of people took advantage of this because it was the best and quickest way to travel and it cost nothing. Before school buses, kids after the eighth grade went to school in Fairmont and traveled by train. Most of them used a pass.

In the early 1920's Earl Herndon Smith, a local camp owner, persuaded the B&O management to install a train platform for the owners of camps on the river. The platform was located about one and a half-miles downriver from Colfax. Mr. Smith, who owned the camp named "Rockley," named the platform stop of Antioch. On weekends and during the summer, camp owners would board or get off here and then take a boat to the other side of the river to their camp. Visitors arrived the same way. The platform was removed when automobiles replaced the railroad for popular travel. Mr. Smith served in the State Senate.

Some of the older generation recalls the dissatisfaction felt over the way the last accommodation train at night was scheduled from Fairmont to Grafton. Colfax was the last stop of the day at 4:00 PM. The last train to stop at Antioch, 1 1/2 miles away was at 10:00 PM, so any passenger returning to Colfax from town after 4 o'clock had to get off the train at Antioch and walk the dark, lonely track back home. People recall it as a walk they'll never forget.

A wagon road above the railroad tracks used to meander alongside of the hill from Antioch towards Colfax. The road probably started out as an Indian trail. Delbert Smith, who was 92 years old when we talked, remembered hauling coal in a wagon over it in his youth. A landslide made the road impassable and was abandoned but the current landowners opened the road up for private use.

One of the schedules between Grafton and Fairmont before the discontinuation of passenger trains in 1952.

Engine No.		
	43 to Fairmont (westbound)	6:40 AM
	66 to Grafton (eastbound)	1:40 PM
	65 to Fairmont	4:10 PM
	44 to Grafton	10: 10 PM
	(44 was the last train at night. It was bound for Washington, D.C.)	

Competition from buses, planes and automobiles had cut into the trade so much that the B&O started to eliminate the nonprofitable passenger trains in the early 1950's. None of the communities along the river liked being deprived of the convenient service they were used to but they had no say in the matter. It wasn't long before the passenger trains became a memory.

Those living along the railroad tracks for many years learned to read the signals. For instance; approaching a station, one short blow then a stop; leaving the station, two long blows. Most familiar whistle, then and now, is the signal that means a train is approaching a railroad crossing: two longs, a short and two more longs. In September 1981, signal lights were installed on the two major crossings in Colfax due to the increased traffic on the highway to and from Martinka Mines. Even today trains are required to give a warning whistle signal at all crossings. In the early days before the Environmental Protection Agency (EPA) and health safety codes the toilet on all passenger trains flushed out onto the railroad tracks. That was why this sign was above all of the toilets

Unidentified Poplar Island guests at the train platform in 1919. *Courtesy of WV Archives, Elizabeth Windsor Collection*

PLEASE DO NOT FLUSH TOILET
WHILE TRAIN IS IN THE STATION

LOCAL WORKMAN FOR THE RAILROAD

In the early 1900's if a man worked for the railroad, he had a job envied by many another man. Colfax, Kingmont and Benton's Ferry all provided railroad workers in their time. Some started out in their youth and worked till they retired. Some started in minor positions and rose to the ranks of white collar. Railroad workers

Work gang from Colfax. Left to right are (2nd person) Austin A. Satterfield, (6th) William H. Hayhurst, (8th) Pat Irons and (9th) Rufus Satterfield. The others could not be identified. *Picture taken around 1900. Courtesy of Delbert Smith.*

West Virginia's Lower Tygart Valley River

WESTWARD.

Distance from Grafton.	Train Order Stations.	Grafton and Fairmont Sub-Division. TIME-TABLE No. 20. July 12, 1931	Passing Siding Capacity in Cars.	FIRST CLASS.				
				69	43	55	51	
				DAILY	DAILY	DAILY	DAILY	
				A. M.	A. M.	P. M.	P. M.	
0.0	DN	GRAFTON.		S 5.50	S 7.45	S12.55	S 5.35	
1.8		1.8 FETTERMAN.		F 5.53	F 7.48	F12.59		
4.3		2.5 COUNTRY CLUB				F 1.01		
6.1		1.8 COFFMAN		F 6.00	F 7.55	F 1.08	F 5.45	
6.4	DPN	0.3 WINONA.		6.01	7.56	1.09	5.46	
8.0		1.6 VALLEY FALLS.		F 6.04	F 7.59	F 1.13		
9.5		1.5 HAMMOND.		F 6.07	F 8.02	F 1.17	F 5.51	
10.6	DN	1.1 OY TOWER. (End of Double Track.) 0.5	67	6.10	8.05	1.21	5.53	
11.1		POWELL		F 6.11	F 8.06	F 1.22		
12.8		1.7 POPLAR ISLAND		F 6.15	F 8.10	F 1.25	F 5.57	
13.9		1.1 US TOWER.	98	6.20	8.15	1.27	6.00	
14.4		0.5 COLFAX		F 6.21	F 8.16	F 1.28		
15.9		1.5 ANTIOCH		F 6.24	F 8.19	F 1.33		
17.5	DN	1.6 BENTON FERRY. (End of Double Track.) 1.1		F 6.28	F 8.23	F 1.37	6.05	
18.6		KINGMONT. 2.4		F 6.30	F 8.25	F 1.40	F 6.07	
21.0	DN	GASTON JUNCTION.		6.35	8.31	1.45	6.12	
22.1		1.1 FAIRMONT. 1.3		S 6.40 / 6.50	S 8.37 / 8.47	S 1.50 / 2.00	S 6.15 / 6.25	
23.4	DN	WD TOWER.		6.55	8.52	2.05	6.30	
				A. M.	A. M.	P. M.	P. M.	
		Time over Sub-Division Average speed per hour		1.05 21.6	1.07 20.9	1.10 19.9	0.55 25.5	

Passenger trains will not exceed a speed of 40 miles per hour between Grafton and Gaston Junction.
Speed as shown in Special Instruction 5, and such other restrictions as may be in effect, will not be exceeded.

FAIRMONT TERMINAL—WESTWARD.

Train Order Stations.	TIME-TABLE No. 20. July 12, 1931.	FIRST CLASS.					
		Mon.& C'ville Div.	Mon.& C'ville Div.	Mon.& Whg. Div.	Mon.& Whg. Div.	C'ville Div.	Mon.& Whg. Div.
		67	69	43	55	65	51
		DAILY	DAILY	DAILY	DAILY	DAILY	DAILY
		A. M.	A. M.	A. M.	P. M.	P. M.	P. M.
DN	GASTON JUNCTION. (End of Double Track.) 1.1	12.07	6.35	8.31	1.45		6.12
	FAIRMONT. 1.3	S12.15 / 12.25	S 6.40 / 6.50	S 8.37 / 8.47	S 1.50 / 2.00	S 2.20	S 6.15 / 6.25
DN	WD TOWER. (End of Double Track.)	12.30	6.55	8.52	2.05	2.25	6.30
		A. M.	A. M.	A. M.	P. M.	P. M.	P. M.
	Time over Sub Division Average speed per hour	0.23 6.2	0.20 7.2	0.21 6.8	0.20 7.2	0.05 15.6	0.18 8.0

Passenger trains will not exceed a speed of 30 miles per hour.
Speed as shown in Special Instruction 5, and such other restrictions as may be in effect, will not be exceeded.

EASTWARD.

Distance from WD Tower	Train Order Stations	Grafton and Fairmont Sub-Division. TIME-TABLE No. 20. July 12, 1931.	Passing Siding. Capacity in Cars.	FIRST CLASS. 56 DAILY A.M.	52 DAILY P.M.	70 DAILY P.M.	44 DAILY P.M.
0.0	DN	WD TOWER. (End of Double Track.) 1.3		11.00	3.35	9.20	9.40
1.3		FAIRMONT. 1.1		s11.05 / 11.15	s 3.39 / 3.49	s 9.24 / 9.30	s 9.44 / 9.55
2.4	DN	GASTON JUNCTION. 2.4		11.20	3.52	9.33	9.59
4.8		KINGMONT. 1.1		F11.26	F 3.57	.....	F10.05
5.9	DN	BENTON FERRY. (End of Double Track.) 1.6	78	F11.27	F 3.58	9.38	10.06
7.5		ANTIOCH 1.5		F11.31	F 4.01	.....	.....
9.0		COLFAX 0.5		F11.34	F 4.05	.....	.....
9.5		US TOWER. 1.1	104	11.35	4.06	9.45	10.15
10.6		POPLAR ISLAND 1.7		F11.38	F 4.09	.....	F10.18
12.3		POWELL 0.5		F11.41	F 4.11	.....	.....
12.8	DN	OY TOWER. (End of Double Track.) 1.1		11.42	4.12	9.50	10.21
13.9		HAMMOND. 1.5		F11.45	F 4.15	.....	K10.24
15.4		VALLEY FALLS. 1.6		F11.48	F 4.18	.....	.....
17.0	DPN	WINONA. 0.3		11.53	4.21	9.57	10.30
17.3		COFFMAN 1.8		F11.54	F 4.22	.....	.....
19.1		COUNTRY CLUB 2.5		F11.59	.....	.....	.....
21.6		FETTERMAN. 1.8		F12.03	F 4.30	.....	.....
23.4	DN	GRAFTON.		A12.10	A 4.35	A10.10	A10.45
				P.M.	P.M.	P.M.	P.M.
		Time over Sub-Division Average speed per hour		1.10 / 19.9	1.00 / 23.4	0.50 / 28.0	1.05 / 21.6

Passenger trains will not exceed a speed of 40 miles per hour between Gaston Junction and Grafton.
Speed as shown in Special Instruction 5, and such other restrictions as may be in effect, will not be exceeded.

FAIRMONT TERMINAL—EASTWARD.

Train Order Stations	TIME-TABLE No. 20. July 12, 1931.	FIRST CLASS. C'ville &Mon. Div. 68 DAILY A.M.	Whg. &Mon. Div. 56 DAILY A.M.	C'ville Div. 66 DAILY P.M.	Whg. &Mon. Div. 52 DAILY P.M.	C'ville &Mon. Div. 70 DAILY P.M.	Whg. &Mon. Div. 44 DAILY P.M.
DN	WD TOWER. (End of Double Track.) 1.3	5.45	11.00	1.50	3.35	9.20	9.40
	FAIRMONT. 1.1	s 5.50 / 6.00	s11.05 / 11.15	A 1.55	s 3.39 / 3.49	s 9.24 / 9.30	s 9.44 / 9.55
DN	GASTON JUNCTION. (End of Double Track.)	6.03	11.20	.....	3.52	9.33	9.59
		A.M.	A.M.	P.M.	P.M.	P.M.	P.M.
	Time over Sub-Division Average speed per hour	0.18 / 8.0	0.20 / 7.2	0.05 / 15.6	0.17 / 8.4	0.13 / 11.0	10.9 / 7.5

Passenger trains will not exceed a speed of 30 miles per hour.
Speed as shown in Special Instruction 5, and such other restrictions as may be in effect, will not be exceeded.

Previous page and above: B&O passenger train timetable dated July 12, 1931. *Courtesy of the Main Street Grafton Committee.*

West Virginia's Lower Tygart Valley River

Roy Oliver (left) and Elmer Fortney (right) at work on the railroad in their velocipede in front of the MP church parsonage in Colfax. 1912.
Photo by Milton Fortney

were tough and worked hard for a living. In the early days very few had a high school education but the B&O provided a good steady income to men who were willing to work for it.

Names of some of the local railroad workers on the road gangs between Millersville and Hammond; Charles (Gus) Wilson, an Engine Machinist who worked 45 years. Elmer Fortney (my grandfather) 50 years, Signal Maintainer; Vance Hunter and Albert (Abe) Hoffmaster, his assistants (Abe later became Assistant Regional Engineer). Cecil Kinty, who worked for the railroad for a short time and William Cheuvront. Fred Bice, Brakeman (who rode in the caboose). He once fell between two moving coal cars and crushed his ankle. He was thought to never walk on it again but after a long recovery he was able to return to work.

Tom Ruston, Electrician; Johnny and Kenny French, Linn Summers, Car Shop; Track Laborers, Banks Nuzum, Robert and James Carpenter, William Hayes, Robert Hunt, Sr., 42 years; Edsel Goodwin, Ben Hewitt, Track Laborers; L.Eldon (Smuck) Smith, Jacob Bishop, Bill Storms, A C. Hawkins and Michael Hoffmaster, Locomotive Engineers; John Barker, Stores Dept.; Hiram Nichols, Section Foreman; Charles "Huff" Hoffmaster, Dale Hunter, Earnest Efaw, Emmet Schmuck, James "Casey" Reese, Ruse Ford, Brooks "Popeye" Bingman, Kenny Osburn and Mike Lipscomb of Fetterman were all Track Foremen.

The following were all Trackmen or "Paddy Hands" as they were called in the early days: William Hayhurst, Robert Biddle, Oscar Haddix, Boyd Stemple and Isiah (Grandpa) French, Francis Boice, Charlie Holt, Clarence L. (Pop) Lance, Joe Fluharty, Charles Hunt, Richards Burns, Lloyd Linn, George Linn, Gordon Linn, John Barker, Earl Sanders, Mac Knight and William (Willie) Boice (who worked 58 years before retiring). G.K. Little was a conductor.

Today, due to downsizing, the work crew for the railroad along the river has been reduced to the minimum. Maintenance is done by a mere handful compared to the good ole' days. Robert Hunt, Jr. (Pleasant Valley) is the Road Master in this area. In the late 1990's Charles Sayre (Colfax), Tommy Efaw (Colfax) and Benny & Junior Linn (Benton's Ferry) made up the only maintenance crew along the river.

1949-50 motorcar permit. *Courtesy of the Fortney Collection.*

48

Unidentified B&O track gang in the 1890's. They worked the track from Fetterman to Colfax. *Courtesy of Beverly Wilson Irons.*

WATCHHOUSES

After the railroad was up and going, it was necessary to have a maintenance crew in order to keep the tracks in condition. Often the men who had done the grading were retained to maintain the track as permanent employees. They were known as the repairmen. In addition to the repair hands, the B&O employed a watchman on each of the high slopes along the grade. At one time, there were seven watch houses between Valley Falls and Millersville.

Curvature of the tracks as well as heavy traffic on the rails made necessary the 24-hour inspection for any irregularities. For one thing, poor weather conditions caused landslides quite often in the 21 miles from Grafton to Fairmont. Sometimes, too, in dry weather the sparks from the steam engines would start brush fires. The guard was on the alert for any kind of danger, which would possibly disrupt the train schedule. George W. Louden (Colfax) and John Shaver (Levels) were local watchmen.

In the days of steam engines, during very dry weather, flagmen in the caboose had to ride the rear of the train to observe whether hot cinders had been dropped. If so, the train was stopped and the fire extinguished.

In 1903, a brush fire got out of control when the wind kicked up and spread to the Levels Methodist Church and burnt it down. This church was located less than half a mile from the railroad tracks on the Sand Bank Road. The church was rebuilt but burned down yet again from sparks from another engine.

During the late 1920's, the watch houses were discontinued to save money, but steam engines continued to set brush fires until the more modern diesel engines came to town.

The Watchman's Ghost

A local man in the early 1900's lived at Levels and worked for the B&O at one of the watch houses next to Powell. One dark, quiet night he was working at the watch house and got overwhelmingly sleepy. He laid down close to the tracks with his ear to the rail so he could hear if a train came. Instead he fell soundly asleep and did not hear a train coming. His untimely death was later attributed to alcohol.

To this day his ghost is said to roam the railroad tracks at night in that area looking for his head. Being a bit superstitious and living in this valley, I for one would not like to walk the tracks on that part of the railroad at night.

TELEGRAPH OPERATORS

In Colfax, early B&O trains ran on a single track but later a sidetrack was added. Occasionally a train had to pull off on the siding—sometimes for hours—and wait until a train approaching from the opposite direction had passed before it could continue on its way. To cut on waiting time and to prevent head-on collisions, engineers began using a new mode of communication, the telegraph, which used the earth as an electromagnet. Invented in 1844 by Samuel F.B. Morse, reception by sound with audible clicks called Morse Code was developed. It was a fast and reliable method of signaling for the railroad. This type of communication helped with the movement of trains during the Civil War. The telegraph was vital to the Union Army in sending coded messages.

Sometime after the completion of the railroad through Colfax (Texas), a telegraph office was built near the Kinty-Fortney railroad crossing, which was then the center of the community. It had a small railroad depot and nearby post office, store combination operated by the Hawkins family.

In 1902, the railroad company replaced this office with one on the eastern end of Colfax. This telegraph office became known as the US Tower. From it, the operator could switch a moving train from the main line onto the North-South siding to meet and/or pass main line trains without having to stop at the telegraph office. In those days that technique was considered very modern. In 1911, double tracks from Powell to Grafton were put in.

Frank Shorter, telegrapher, at CY in 1946. *Courtesy of Ada Pearl Shorter*

The telegraph towers were designated as Grafton (D), Valley Falls (VF), Powell (CY), Colfax (US) Benton's Ferry (BF), Gaston Junction (GF) and the WD at the Fairmont yards.

Frank Shorter, 1917-1991, a long time resident of Colfax/Levels, worked at the CY (Powell) tower. He was from a large local family that produced five telegraphers. Frank learned the trade from his father, Charles L. Shorter, who also worked many years for the railroad. When Frank was a small boy in 1929, one day he was playing cowboys and Indians with some friends. One of his playmates had a real gun but didn't know that it was loaded. He accidentally shot Frank in the stomach. It so happened that Frank's father was at home at the time, about seven miles by rail from town. Frank's dad knew that the need for medical attention was urgent. He grabbed Frank up in his arms and ran for the railroad tracks. An experienced telegrapher, he knew the precise time the next train was to come through from Grafton to Fairmont. Luckily, one was due.

Mr. Shorter flagged down the train and boarded the freight engine (No. 43) with his son in his arms. With the help of the telegraph operator on duty at the US

US Telegraph Tower in Colfax built in 1903. It was shut down in the fall of 1930 during the Depression and dismantled in 1951. C.L. Shorter was the oldest operator on the line when he was transferred to the BF Tower at Benton's Ferry. *Courtesy of the Hamilton Collection.*

Sat. Sept. 7, 1912

EXTRA TRAIN 12 TAKES TO DITCH IN LOWER B. & O. YARD AT COLFAX

Engineer Instantly Killed and Fireman Perhaps Fatally Hurt in Crach

ENGINE LEAPS SWITCH DERAIL

None of Cars Leaves Track and None of Passengers Is Injured

Front-page article from the *Times-West Virginian* (9-7-12) headline.

Newspaper article from the *Fairmont Times*. (Retyped)

EXTRA TRAIN 12 TAKES TO DITCH IN LOWER B&O YARD AT COLFAX

A terrible railroad wreck occurred at 11:45 Saturday night in the lower Colfax yards, a few miles above this city in which one was killed, one seriously injured and considerable property loss resulted.

THE DEAD - Engineer A. L. Cumpston, aged 30, of McMechen, West Virginia, head crushed and body burned.

THE INJURED - Fireman R. A. Wooten, of Benwood, skull fractured and suffering from shock. At Miners Hospital. Will recover.

Train No. 12, due here at 9:27, was late Saturday evening and as there were many passengers who wanted to make connections at Grafton, a special No. 4 was made up. Engineer Cumpston and Fireman Wooten were in charge of the engine. The train made the trip to Grafton and was returning when the accident occurred. It is supposed the engineer lost his bearings in the darkness and did not know where he was. The train ran into a derail of a switch in the lower Colfax yards and the engine was thrown from the tracks. It is estimated the train was making 60 miles an hour when the wreck occurred. The engine broke from the empty coaches and rolled over the bank to the edge of the Tygart Valley River. Engineer Cumptson was caught beneath the engine. He was held under the engine for nine hours and the body was nearly destroyed by steam and burning wreckage.

The engine was badly wrecked and the track torn up to some extent. The wreck was one of the worst in this section for some time and hundreds visited the scene yesterday.

Clinton's fireman, Frank Baker, had just stepped down from the engine and was standing beside the track to watch the express thunder by. He escaped the fate of his engineer. Clinton was dozing and half-asleep in the cab of his engine and probably never knew what hit him when the flying express crashed into his engine.

Later it was learned that the train left Grafton at 5:45 P.M. and was running 60 miles an hour making up for lost time when it struck the freight train. Both engines were demolished from the impact.

FRIDAY, NOVEMBER 5, 1909

There was a train-related accident that did not involve wreckage of a train but did take a human life. The following article is significant in that it depicts the life of the men in the engine and their duties. The description of the accident is typical of the early 1900's. On Nov 5, 1909, something happened out of the ordinary.

FELL FROM HIS ENGINE—KILLED
****
Exact Manner of Brakeman Kirkpatrick's death will Not Be Learned
****
ACCIDENT AT COLFAX
****
Yesterday Resulted In The Fatally Wounding Of Young Barton Man.
****

A fatal accident occurred at 9:20 yesterday morning at Colfax when B&O brakeman William Kirkpatrick, of the Cumberland Division and working with the crew on engine number 1849 fell from the locomotive and was so badly injured that death resulted a few hours later at the Miners Hospital where the man was removed. The accident cannot be explained as no one saw the man fall and he was not able to tell of the manner in which he met his death.

Kirkpatrick was riding in the engine on the fireman's side of the cab, the fireman at the time being engaged in shoveling in coal. He started out on the engine and was not seen again by the engineer. Later the Engineer and crew of another train on the opposite track called to the crew of 1849 that they had run over their brakeman. The train was stopped and an investigation made. It was found that in some manner Kirkpatrick had fallen from the engine to the track and the locomotive and eight cars passed over his body. He was still living but was terribly injured. The injured man was picked up and hurried to this city and taken to the Miners Hospital. There everything possible was done for the man but from the first it was seen that to be a hopeless case and his death came at 12:45 yesterday afternoon.

The body was badly mangled and cut. A foot was amputated, the right leg broken and the right arm and chest mashed.

Kirkpatrick was a single man. 21 years of age. His home was at Barton, Maryland and it is supposed the body will be taken there for burial. As yet no word has been received from his relatives and pending their orders nothing will be done with the body. Undertaker Cunningham has already prepared the body for burial and is now holding it for the morgue. Kirkpatrick was well known among the railroad employees of this city and was a general favorite with them. His horrible death is greatly mourned by his friends here and was received with great sorrow by his family and friends at Barton.

Fairmont Free Press
FRIDAY NOVEMBER 5, 1909

Today the entire railroad system in the East is run by computerized remote controls from Jacksonville, Florida—all in the name of progress, they say. But in time of an emergency or national disaster, the Morse code tickers could still be a blessing. Telegraphers were a very special breed.

Left: Telegraph message from Gaston Junction to CY Tower in 1978. *Courtesy of Eric Hunter.*

TRAIN WRECKS IN THE VALLEY

Even a big enterprise like the B&O Railroad could not prevent accidents that were just bound to happen as speed, carelessness and rail failures increased. There was a major derailment in front of our house when I was only eight years old. It was an experience I'll never forget. I came to terms with the railroad tracks that day, and have had my respect for them ever since. The unavoidable accidents happened time and again. Here are a few of the them, the first based on information taken from an old newspaper article submitted by Kate Griffith:

SATURDAY, NOVEMBER 14, 1888

The New York-Chicago Express/freighter wrecked at Valley Falls on the night of November 14, 1888. Four railroad employees lost their lives. Edward Dewire, engineer, James Shay, his foreman, and Charles Hall, a postal worker, who were on the express. Oscar Van Loan, a novice in the postal car was learning his duties of clerk at the time. Miraculously he escaped injury. Three tramps, who were seated in the blind (windowless) postal car, were killed instantly.

Dewire applied his air brakes but the distance was too short to hold the train back before he saw the freight train. The postal and baggage cars were destroyed.

William P. Clinton, engineer of the freight train, was parked on the siding at the falls. Both engineers were destined to meet death that night when an incompetent brakeman left open a switch through which the freight train had just sided to let the express pass. William Clinton was a new young engineer from Grafton and was a grandson of William Powell, one of the first settlers and the first postmaster of Grafton.

People and Places

CY signal pool in 1946, Frank Shorter on the tower. *Courtesy of Ada Pearl Shorter*

Tower in Colfax a message was sent to Fairmont's WD Tower and help was waiting for him at the Fairmont Station when they arrived. Frank was taken to the Miners Hospital. The bullet was removed and saved in a glass jar where it is to this day. He survived, of course, due to the quick thinking of his father who knew telegraphy and how it could help save his son's life. Charles "Sallie" Shorter, as he was sometimes called, was indeed his son's hero that day.

"Sallie" Shorter had a brother, Henry, and another son, Cecil all of whom were telegraphers. A nephew, Charles W. Shorter, also took up the occupation.

William Fred Hawkins (1891-1953) was another long-time employee of the railroad who lived in Colfax and was a telegraph operator at the CY Tower near Powell. Since no roads led to the two-story tower, he had the use of a "speeder" car in order to get back and forth to work. It was a three-wheeled handcar and he parked it in his front lawn when it was not in use.

On January 20, 1945, Mr. Hawkins was working when a train derailed right at the tower. A steam engine flipped over and slid down the riverbank. From the force of the rails hitting the base of the tower, it shoved the tower off its foundation, over the bank and into the river. Mr. Hawkins escaped serious injury but never found a gold watch he lost in the river during the incident. Life could indeed be hazardous at times for a telegrapher.

After the derailment debris was cleaned up, the CY Tower was moved about three-quarters of a mile upriver. A taller, more modern tower was built. It had a ground level office. The foundation stones from the old tower were removed and used as a foundation for a garage apartment in Colfax. The CY tower was moved two more times before it was discontinued. Telephones replaced the telegraph, marking the beginning of yet another era.

Russell Nichols (1888-1974) grew up on a farm near Colfax in Grant District and started working for the B&O Railroad in 1907. He became a telegrapher at age 17 and worked at various towers over the next 32 years. He was elected sheriff of Marion County in 1941, County Commissioner, a US Marshal and a member of Marion County's Board of Education. Russell's brother, Harry, was also a telegrapher who worked at CY and Gaston Junction. Both men are buried in the Colfax Cemetery.

Other telegraph operators from the area were Joseph Springer, Lloyd Arnett, Eddie McDonald, Dale Hubert, Dorsey "Slick" Hawkins, L.W. Graham, Harry Robinson, Jr., Bud Davis, Earl Carpenter, and brothers Don and Eric Hunter. During World War II when most men were away fighting for freedom, Doris Durett and another woman whose name is unknown, worked the telegraph at CY.

Railroad signal towers are silent these days. Gone are the clicks and dashes that gave way to the modern telephone. Morse tickers that were depended upon to spread news throughout America are now gathering dust. It's been forgotten how people in the little towns along the railroad rejoiced when the news was posted on their bulletin boards, such as the surrender of General Robert E. Lee to General Ulysses S. Grant at Appomattox, Va.

WD Tower at the Fairmont train yards.
Courtesy of Ila Fortney

April 14, 1918

EARLY MORNING FREIGHT WRECK NEAR COLFAX

ENGINEER F. LINES OF GRAFTON BADLY INJURED, OTHERS SLIGHTLY.

One man was seriously injured and three others were more or less slightly hurt in a head-on freight wreck which occurred near Colfax yesterday morning about 5:30 o'clock. The most seriously injured was Engineer F. Lines, of Grafton, who was cut and bruised and had several bones broken. Other members of the two crews suffered cuts and bruises.

A crew from the G. & B. branch of the Baltimore and Ohio railroad was hauling freight No. 1400 out of the local yards yesterday morning. It is said the crew had not been over the local division for the past twelve years and that it was necessary for a yard engine to bring the train in and take it out of the local yards.

The train was on its way up the river when it crashed into a freight headed this way near Colfax. Both engines were badly demolished and several cars smashed up. The crews of both trains were injured in the wreck.

Immediately upon report of the wreck reaching Fairmont local railroad officials organized a relief train. Dr. Ramage, Dr. Sands and other local physicians were placed on the train and rushed to Colfax. Upon their arrival they treated the wounds of the injured men. Engineer Lines, the most seriously hurt, was able to proceed to his home in Grafton and the other men were also sent to their homes after their wounds were dressed.

The track was tied up for some time following the wreck but was opened for traffic later in the day.

April 14, 1918 *Fairmont Free Press*.

Right: MARCH 22, 1911
Fairmont Free Press

FAIRMONT FREE PRESS
****

MARCH 22, 1911
RAILROAD WRECK

Passenger Train No. 7 Had Rear-End Collision With Freight Train.

Passenger Train No. 71, westbound, due here at 1:25 P.M. was wrecked yesterday afternoon at a point near Benton's Ferry, although the damage was light, and no one was injured.

The train ran into the rear end of a freight train, which was taking the water at Benton's Ferry, but fortunately the engine was bought nearly to a stop before the collision occurred. The engine was slightly damaged and the train was delayed for a few hours.

Some of the passengers on 71 were given quite a little scare.

B. & O. SERVICE TIED UP IN HARD KNOTS

Freight Engine Jumps Track Near Colfax and Piles up Train Badly.

Passenger service on the Wheeling division of the Baltimore & Ohio railroad between this place and Grafton was paralyzed practically day yesterday by a freight wreck which took place just west of Colfax in the morning. Trains numbers 3, 71, 72, 12 and 55 were either abandoned or detoured with much delay.

The accident was caused by a freight engine leaving the rails and dashing down the side of an embankment, piling up its train across the single track behind it. Wrecking crews from Fairmont and Grafton worked all day on the debris to have it cleared at seven o'clock last night.

Train No. 3, carrying the sleeper from Baltimore for Wheeling, was caught behind the accident and was detoured. No. 72, eastbound, was turned back from Benton's Ferry, while No. 71, westbound from Grafton, was abandoned. No. 16, the Baltimore express, was detoured via the M. R. division.

No. 12, east bound, was held for over an hour at the Benton's Ferry tower, passing the scene of the wreck at 7 last evening and a little later No. 55 from the east, got past the accident.

Details of the wreck were not reported to officials here and were not obtainable. There was no injury to members of the crew, so far as could be learned.

Right: Tuesday, June 9, 1914. *Fairmont Free Press*.

NOVEMBER 13, 1920

On the division between Fairmont and Grafton, a freight train loaded with coal cars and pulled by engine # 4808, tipped over not far from Nuzum's Mills. The trouble occurred at a point on the Nuzum's grade when a wheel on one of the cars slipped from the rail bringing several others over with it. Although no one was hurt passenger trains couldn't pass and rail traffic was tied up for some time.

Work crews from both Grafton and Fairmont worked for six hours to clear the tracks. Fairmont workmen who went to the scene said it was one of the worst looking derailments the company had experienced in months.

Huge Locomotive, Thrown From Track By Derail Device, Turns Completely Over Near Colfax

Crew Escaped in Accident at Point Where Engineer Was Killed in Like Occurrence Six Years Ago

---

Times-West Virginian front page headline: December 16, 1920.

THURSDAY, DECEMBER 16, 1920

The sight of a monster B&O freight engine lying with its wheels pointing to the sky, greeted the people of Colfax yesterday morning. The story of the mishap to the locomotive is a thrilling one for it is featured by the fact that none of its crew received the slightest hurt when the engine turned over.

Locomotive 2616, operated in the freight service between Grafton and Wheeling, was on the siding at Colfax awaiting the passing of a passenger train. In front was a Fairmont local train. After the passenger had come and gone, the local pulled out but left the switch in such a way that the derail device was not against the Wheeling engine.

Engineer Wyatt was at the throttle of the 2616 and he did not realize his danger until his huge machine had climbed the derail and had started to tumble over on its side towards the ravine on the other side of the track opposite the river on Pinchgut Road. Wyatt called to his fireman and both leaped from the engine, escaping unhurt, how they do not know.

The engine rolled over on its side and then took another half turn pointing its wheels towards the sky. In this position it remained until late morning.

The tank of the engine met a better fate for its coupling broke before it left the rail and it remained on the track.

Traffic over the division was not interrupted by the accident for the ill-fated engine had rolled clear of the rails so trains passed on as usual during the night and morning.

Wrecking trains from Fairmont and Grafton were sent to the scene to get the huge machine back on its wheels. It was taken to the Grafton shops for repair.

The accident happened at an ill-fated spot where eight years ago, an engineer was killed in an accident identical to that of Wednesday night. The engineer was pinioned under the wreckage and instantly killed.

People and Places

THURSDAY, NOVEMBER 16, 1933

Times-West Virginian article on front page headlined: **TRAIN WRECKS NEAR POWELL.**

Fifteen cars were derailed in a wreck near Benny's cut near Powell at 4:00 P.M. Thursday when a long freight train encountered a broken rail probably due to the cold weather. The cars were loaded with coal and piled up in such a way that there was a car squarely across the track and several others forced over the bank until cars reached almost to a big rock in the Tygart Valley River at that point.

The wreck tore down two telegraph poles and put the lines out of commission. The US tower at Powell was able to reach Grafton by phone and gave the news of the wreck. The foreman of the section was on the train. He had to walk to Colfax to get his men who had a key and a motorcar. It was the first wreck on that section in four years.

The wreck was cleared up by 8:00 Friday morning so the traffic could be resumed but there are still signs of the wreck. The coal cars were wrecked at a place where it is impossible for needy folks to secure the coal, which was likely to go to waste.

WEDNESDAY, MARCH 29, 1950

At 4:55 A.M. just before dawn, five coal cars derailed eastbound in Colfax. Eastbound mallet engine No. 43 cleared a broken rail but the second car from the engine did not. It fell on its side and four others followed it. The cars were tossed over toward the sidetrack and Pinchgut Road.

An older type mallet engine, No. 7169, hauled the long freight train. The conductor was H. R. Huffman and the engineer was Eddie Pierce. Neither man was injured.

Our family lived only 25 feet from the railroad tracks and the sound will be forever etched in my memory. My

B&O officials inspecting the damage on the March 29, 1950 wreck. *Courtesy of Ila Fortney*

mother was awakened by a thudding sound as the engine went by the house. She rushed to the front door in time to watch the drama unfold. In a matter of seconds, tons of coal was spilled on the ground. By some miracle, the cars fell away from the house. My mother called my grandfather, who worked for the B&O and who had a direct telephone line to the Fairmont yards. An older type mallet pulled the coal train. Engine No. 43 was heading eastbound when it cleared the broken rail but the second car from the engine and four others did not. No one was injured in the accident.

A seven-car special passenger train carrying B&O royalty was delayed because of the accident. Coming from Pittsburgh the train was going to Grafton for an inspection tour of the Monongah Division. The train was held up for an hour and a half when it was eventually put on the siding track where it waited until the wreck was cleared.

People from all around came to pick up the scattered coal. Many got enough for their winter's supply. The kids in the neighborhood declared themselves a holiday off from school that day to watch the clean up.

After this accident occurred practically on our doorstep, Ila Fortney was more perceptive of the danger inherent in living so close to the railroad tracks. About a year later, she said she again woke up in the middle of

Another view of the March 29, 1950 train wreck in Colfax.
Courtesy of Ila Fortney

the night feeling something was wrong. She checked us kids and the house and found nothing amiss but still this feeling kept nagging her, so she grabbed a flashlight and went outside. The railroad tracks were the focus of her attention. She walked about 30 feet down the tracks, when she found a rail broken in half lying wide open for about two feet. Again she called my grandfather, Elmer Fortney, who immediately called the WD Tower at the Fairmont yards. Afterwards he went to the railroad tracks to flag down any trains that may have been en route but none came.

Two years later when she was walking up the railroad tracks to work at the post office one morning, she found another broken rail, reported it herself and averted yet one more derailment. This time the railroad rewarded her with $25.00.

As an adult looking back, I think of what might have been and realize it could still happen today.

SATURDAY, APRIL 5, 1952

Left: Steam-driven crane out of Grafton with a work crewman.
Courtesy of James Prahl.

Left: Karen (Knotts) Gregor standing in front of the wreckage.
Courtesy of James Prahl

From the *Times/West Virginian* (4-6-52) headline: **SEVEN INJURED AS B&O PASSENGER TRAIN DERAILS AT BENTONS FERRY.** At 2:30 P.M. passenger train No. 66 derailed at Benton's Ferry eastbound with seven people injured. The steam locomotive and tender turned over on their sides and three coach cars on the local passenger train (baggage-mail car and passenger coach) left the track, apparently when a defective rail gave way under the weight of the engine. Only two passengers were injured.

All the injured were removed immediately after the accident, identified as follows: William Baylor, 60, Connellsville, Pa., engineer, extensively burned by steam. Filbert Tissue, 60, Connellsville, Pa., conductor, lacerations and bad scalp wound. Charles Kunkle, 57, from Connellsville, Pa., 57, was flagman and had a light concussion. Andrew M. Cebraska, 33, Uniontown, Pa., fireman, cuts and bruises. Lora Detamore, 61, Connellsville, Pa., baggage master, bruises and shock. J.E. Martin, 73, Powell, a passenger, treated and dismissed. John Collins, 71, Powell, a passenger, treated and dismissed.

The accident occurred about a quarter mile from the Benton's Ferry station near the home of Mrs. Delia Wood, who immediately telephoned for assistance. Her son-in-law, Jim Weaver, and Mr. and Mrs. Harold McDougal removed three of the injured to the hospital. McDougal was also a B&O employee.

People and Places

West Virginian

Cloudy, Rather Cold With Showers, Snow; Highest 40 to 45

WEST VIRGINIA, SUNDAY MORNING, APRIL 6, 1952.   PRICE 10 CENTS

Seven Injured as B&O Passenger Train Derails at Benton Ferry

ENGINEER IS BADLY BURNED BY LIVE STEAM

Broken Rail Said Cause Of Wreck; Three Crew Members in Hospital

Seven persons were injured, one critically and two others sufficiently to require hospitalization, when Baltimore & Ohio railroad passenger train No. 66 derailed near Benton Ferry, about five miles east of here, at 2:30 o'clock yesterday afternoon.

The steam locomotive and tender turned over on their sides and all the other cars on the local passenger train—a baggage-mail car, a combination baggage car-coach and a passenger coach—left the track, apparently when a defective rail gave way under the weight of the engine.

Only two of the seven passengers aboard the little-used Connellsville-Grafton train, which left here eastbound at 2 p. m., were injured. Both were dismissed after receiving treatment and examination at Fairmont General hospital.

The hospital, to which all the injured were removed immediately after the accident, identified the victims as follows:

Headlines of the *West Virginian* newspaper April 6, 1952.

VOL. 52 NO. 286   WEST VIRGINIA, THURSDAY MORNING, AUGUST 21, 1952   PRICE FIVE CENTS

Two Hurt as Diesel Plows into Rear of Freight Train

WEDNESDAY, AUGUST 20, 1952

Oil Burner Set on Fire, Coal Hoppers Heavily Damaged

Grafton Crew Spotting Cars on Colfax Siding Wh Diesel Plows Into Caboose; Fairmont Firemen Extinguish Blaze in Locomotive

(The *West Virginian* headline)

Taken from the front page of the *Times/West Virginian* (8-21-52) headlined: A diesel locomotive bound for Keyser with a train of 60 loaded coal hoppers, crashed into the rear of a local freight train in Colfax at 3:15 P.M. yesterday. Two members of the crew were injured; C.D. Runner, engineer, and J.J. Aern, brakeman, both of whom were riding in the cab of the diesel. Both men were from Keyser. The injured were taken to Fairmont General Hospital.

Witnesses said that the Grafton local crew had been engaged in spotting cars near the Colfax coal tipple with most of the train on the main line.

Diesel engine after impact at Colfax on August 20, 1952. Web Fleming, right. *Courtesy of Ila Fortney.*

Flagman, H.R. Royce, a member of the local crew, was stationed at a grade crossing some 300 yards from the crash scene. Signal torpedoes had also been placed near the crossing and exploded when the diesel passed over them.

The wreck occurred between the two crossings which are about 400 yards apart. The flagman signaled to stop the train. But the engineer did not have enough time to do so.

The front unit of the engine after it had struck the caboose was derailed and came to a stop at a 90 degree angle on the edge of the road. Fire broke out in the oil burners after the impact, but was extinguished by the Fairmont Fire Department before it reached the main fuel tanks. The Fire Department had to receive clearance from the city before it could go outside the city limits. The city's new "600" pumper engine was used for the first time since its arrival the week before. The emergency car was also at the scene.

Scattered debris from the wooden caboose involved in train mishap August 20, 1952. *Courtesy of James Prahl.*

The derailed second unit and third units of the engine were not damaged heavily but the three derailed coal hoppers loaded with coal was a twisted mass of metal with coal scattered over a wide area.

It was estimated the speed of the train was between 30 and 40 miles per hour. The impact sent the caboose high in the air, tearing out telephone, electric and Western Union lines in the area. Witnesses to the accident were Ann Dodd, Nancy Mowery, Jimmy Harr, William Hostutler and Charles Bittle.

In February, of 1961, West Virginia's Monongah Division absorbed the Wheeling Division, making Monongah the largest division of the B&O as far as track was concerned and second to the Baltimore Division on the gross tons per mile moved. The Wheeling headquarters was moved

Above Right: Fairmont's new "600" pumper fire engine, used for the first time at the scene of August 20, 1952 train wreck. *Courtesy of Ila Fortney.* **Below: Monongah Division**

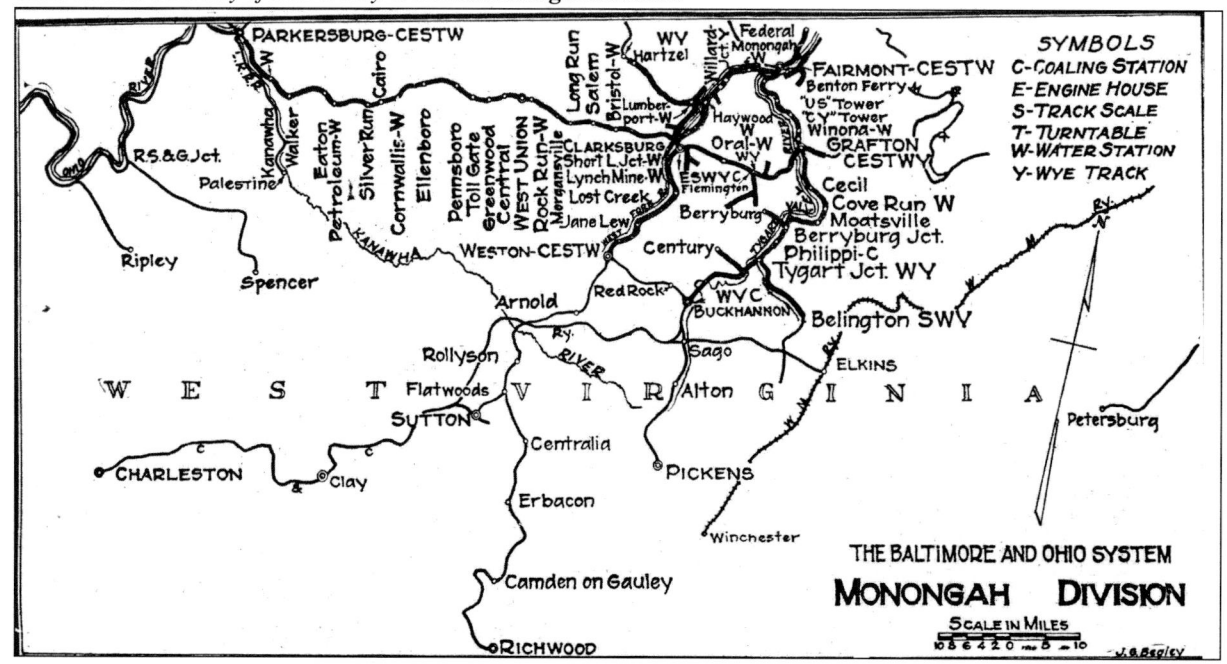

People and Places

to Grafton but five months later 16 positions and all heavy maintenance on diesels were transferred to Cumberland, Maryland. This was a death blow to the Grafton yards. The Railroad Express Agencies also were jeopardized in 1961, then in 1985 the Monongah and Pittsburgh Divisions merged. Pittsburgh became the headquarters.

SELECTED SHORT SUBJECTS

- The speed limit for trains going through Colfax, which has four crossings, is 30 miles per hour.
- When the rail bed was being built the workers blasted through solid rock to lay a section of track just above Scout Island on the Tygart Valley River. This location was called "Benny's Cut" and still is today.
- Colfax lies between the 294-5-railroad mileage marker eastbound from Baltimore and is 7.8 miles from Fairmont.
- In 1981-82 the safer "ribbon rail" (continuous) rail was laid from Grafton to Fairmont, WV.
- In the 1930's, B&O employees Dale Hunter and "Willie" Boyce were crossing guards at the Colfax crossings when President Franklin D. Roosevelt's presidential train came through in the middle of the night. Hunter and Boyce were paid overtime.
- In the early 1900's W. H. "Peg" Hawkins tragically lost his leg after being run over by a train gathering coal in front of his house and store in Colfax. It was replaced by a "peg leg" he made himself. That's how he got his nickname.
- Eldon "Smuck" Smith (1880-1964) from Valley Bend was a locomotive engineer on the Monongah line for years till he retired. He escaped a very bad wreck on that line. He was the father of Delbert Smith of Colfax.
- There were B&O platforms at Kingmont, Benton's Ferry, Antioch, Colfax, Poplar Island, Powell, Hammond and Valley Falls for passengers to get on or off the passenger trains.

**Above: Benny's Cut near Scout Island.
Below: Work crew laying ribbon rail in Colfax during the summer of 1982.**

- Valley Falls is 8 miles east of Fairmont and 7 miles from Grafton by rail.
- Benton's Ferry is 4 miles east of Fairmont by rail.
- Baker's Curve on the railroad line is between Kingmont & Millersville near the old brick kilns.
- Automatic signal lights in Colfax were installed at the two major crossings in September of 1980. Before that there were only railroad crossing signs.
- In the early 1930's the railroad siding track was pulled to the closed Utility Farm Company on the Sand Bank Road at Levels.
- Steam engines spewing hot cinders from their smokestacks were the source of many brush fires along the river.
- Mason's Landing was at Coffman two miles upriver from Valley Falls.
- Eleven years after the completion of the railroad in 1852, West Virginia became a state (1863).
- The original B&O train station in Fairmont was torn down on March 31, 1969.
- The B&O removed the East End Switch on the sidetrack at Colfax near the present site of the post office on March 15, 1960.
- VF Tower at Valley Falls was closed for good in 1912 and moved upriver towards Fetterman.
- Double tracks were laid from Powell to Grafton in 1911. They were removed in 1960.
- There were double tracks from WD Tower in the Fairmont yards to Benton's Ferry.
- In June of 2001, new modern rubberized railroad crossings were put in at Colfax.

VETERAN ENGINEER TO PENSION STEED

An "iron horse" is going on the retired list. He is Prince, owned by "El" Smith, who resides on a farm near Colfax, and 27 years old this spring. He has been doing farm chores for the Smith family since he was a 2-year-old.

Mr. Smith, who is a veteran engineer of the Baltimore & Ohio railroad company, praised the old steed yesterday for his faithfulness.

Laughingly he said he had been driving iron horses on rails for many years, but he had never driven a more faithful horse than Prince.

"We have a day or two more of spring farm work for him to do," said his owner yesterday. "When we complete that, I am putting Prince on an old-age pension, which will consist of plenty to eat, a fine field to romp in and plenty of shelter in inclement weather. He has earned all these and more."

The Fairmont Times **May 5, 1937.**

THE B&O NAME IS RETIRED

Beginning in 1960, the Chesapeake & Ohio Railroad began buying B&O stock shares. By 1964, the C&O owned over 90 percent of the B&O stock, assuming control of the railroad. In 1973, the B&O and the C&O formed the Chessie system. In 1980, a conglomerate composed of ten railroads formed the CSX system. C stands for the Chessie system; the S stands for the Seaboard system and the X represents the corporation. In 1987, despite heritage and tradition the new management decided to drop the term B&O. It was retired and renamed CSX. The name of one of the oldest railroads in America died at the venerable age of 160 years.

In 1999, the Norfolk Southern Corporation and CSX absorbed Conrail with each sharing Conrail's rail lines. Norfolk-Southern maintains about a third of West Virginia's railroad lines. The remainder belongs to CSX. At this writing, West Virginia ranks 23rd in the nation in total railroad miles and ranks 37th in accidents.

Today with all the changes even the caboose has been removed from the end of the train. Modernization eliminated the need for both caboose and brakeman in the early 1990's. No longer needed they say, but I still can't help but watch for it at the end of a train and the friendly wave of the man inside. The caboose was more than just a little red car at the end of the train, it was a piece of history and now only a legend that will never be forgotten. Kids today have to go to a museum to see what one looks like or perhaps visit the one on display in downtown Grafton by the Historical Society. For 150 years they added to the romance of the rails.

1902 THE BUCKHANNON AND NORTHERN RAILROAD

The Buckhannon and Northern Railroad Company (B&N) received a charter dated January 10, 1902 recorded in Marion County in March of the same year. The "Little Kanawha Syndicate" acquired all the B&N Company's stock in March of 1903, and plans were made for construction of a railroad on the west bank of the Tygart Valley River from Grafton to Fairmont. This railroad was intended to connect with the Monongalia Railroad in Fairmont that was organized in 1900.

It was proposed that a new rail bed be built. It was to run from the Pennsylvania-West Virginia state line near Blacksville to Wilmouth's Ford (a point on the existing B&N Railroad line, four and one-half miles from Belington, WV— a distance of 79.5 miles). Early construction work began on the rail bed in Greene County, PA, which is still visible from the highway from Blacksville to Waynesburg. This section was completed in 1913.

The B&N Railroad Company had spent a total of $836,777 for the purchase of land, rights-of-way, grading and masonry. Perhaps a re-evaluation of the trade and traffic was made when the company found that a new rail bed was not merited along the Tygart Valley River. Construction was terminated on the west bank. Another factor for the change of heart could have been the fact that the B&N Railroad had

B. & O. TRAINS RACE FOR BRIDGE

On Parallel Tracks, They Enjoy Five-Mile Contest of Speed, Monday.

Two heavy freight trains, on parallel tracks and running in the same direction, proved an interesting race to those living between the Benton's Ferry Tower and the East End of the Fairmont yards of the Baltimore & Ohio railroad yesterday.

The sight of two trains running side by side on parallel tracks is not often seen on the B. & O. There was a reason for the novelty yesterday. Two huge locomotives were being taken west by the B. & O. The engines were so large that they could not cross the Johntown bride on the west bound track so their train was detoured to the eastbound track. At the same time the second section of the train porceeded on to Fairmont on the eastbound track. Running side by side the engineers had a race for the bridge.

Yesterday was a heavy day on the local divisions, a vast amount of coal being shipped from the local regions. Coal business is picking up daily as the lake trade is heavy, eastern orders increasing and the empty car supply being adequate at all times.

From the *Fairmont Times*. Tuesday, June 9, 1914.

consolidated with the Monongahela Railroad Company in 1915. The B&O Railroad Company owned a one-third interest and it already had a working railroad on the east bank of the Tygart. For whatever reasons, grading stopped in this valley as well as in Greene Co. PA.

At Valley Falls grading had followed the old tramway on the west bank where logs had been hauled downriver. In certain places along the river the grading can still be seen. In 1993, the old Monongalia (B&N) rail bed rights-of-way were sold.

OTHER RAILROADS IN THE AREA

	Date Completed
B&O from Grafton to Parkersburg, WV	1857
B&O from Grafton to Belington, WV	1884
B&O from Fairmont to Morgantown, WV & Pittsburgh, PA	1886
B&O/Monongahela and West Fork Branch	1890
B&O in the Paw Paw District	1902
Rail line from Morgantown to Kingwood, WV	1903
B&N Railroad from Pittsburgh, PA to Lake Erie, PA	1912

Chapter Three

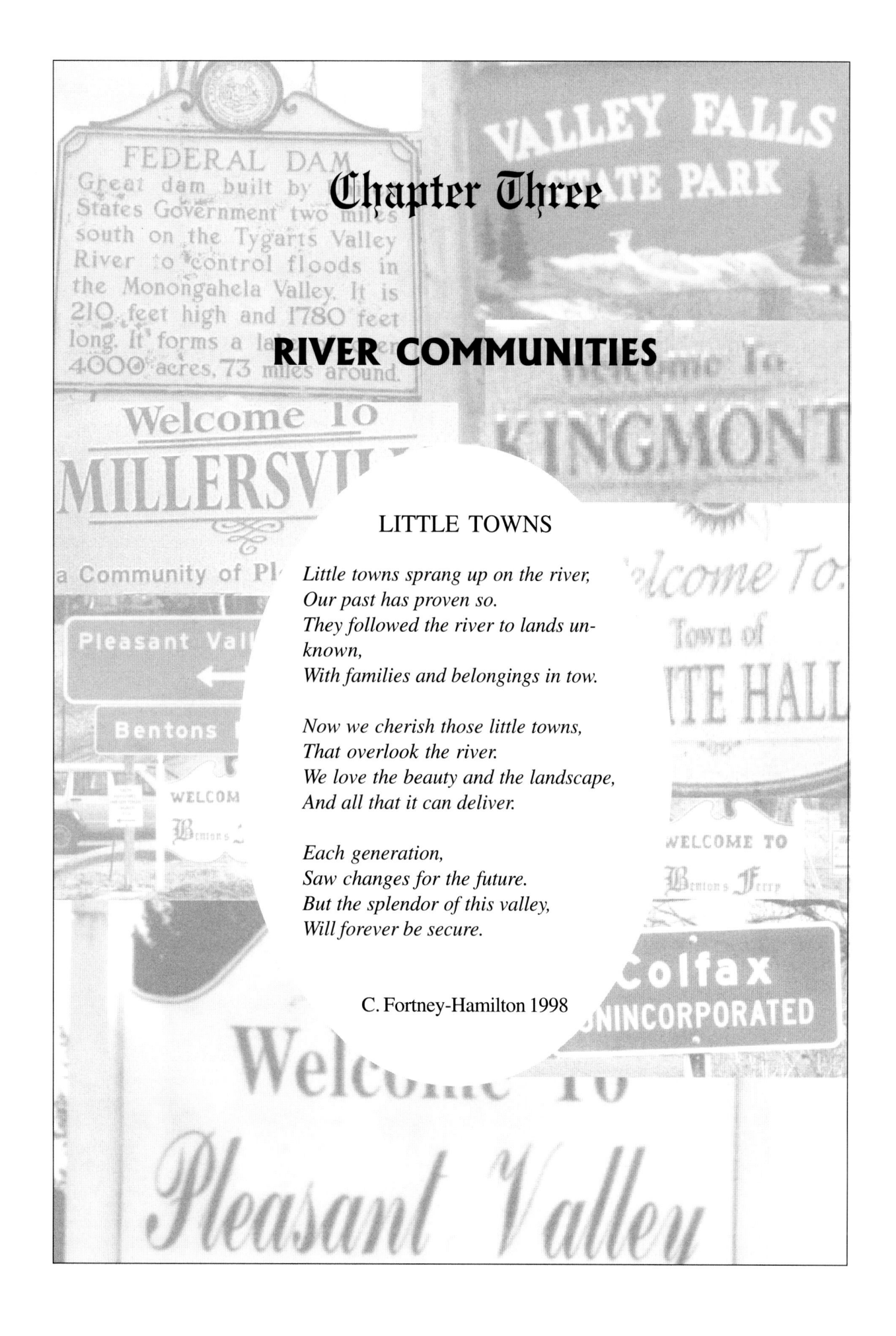

RIVER COMMUNITIES

LITTLE TOWNS

Little towns sprang up on the river,
Our past has proven so.
They followed the river to lands unknown,
With families and belongings in tow.

Now we cherish those little towns,
That overlook the river.
We love the beauty and the landscape,
And all that it can deliver.

Each generation,
Saw changes for the future.
But the splendor of this valley,
Will forever be secure.

C. Fortney-Hamilton 1998

West Virginia's Lower Tygart Valley River

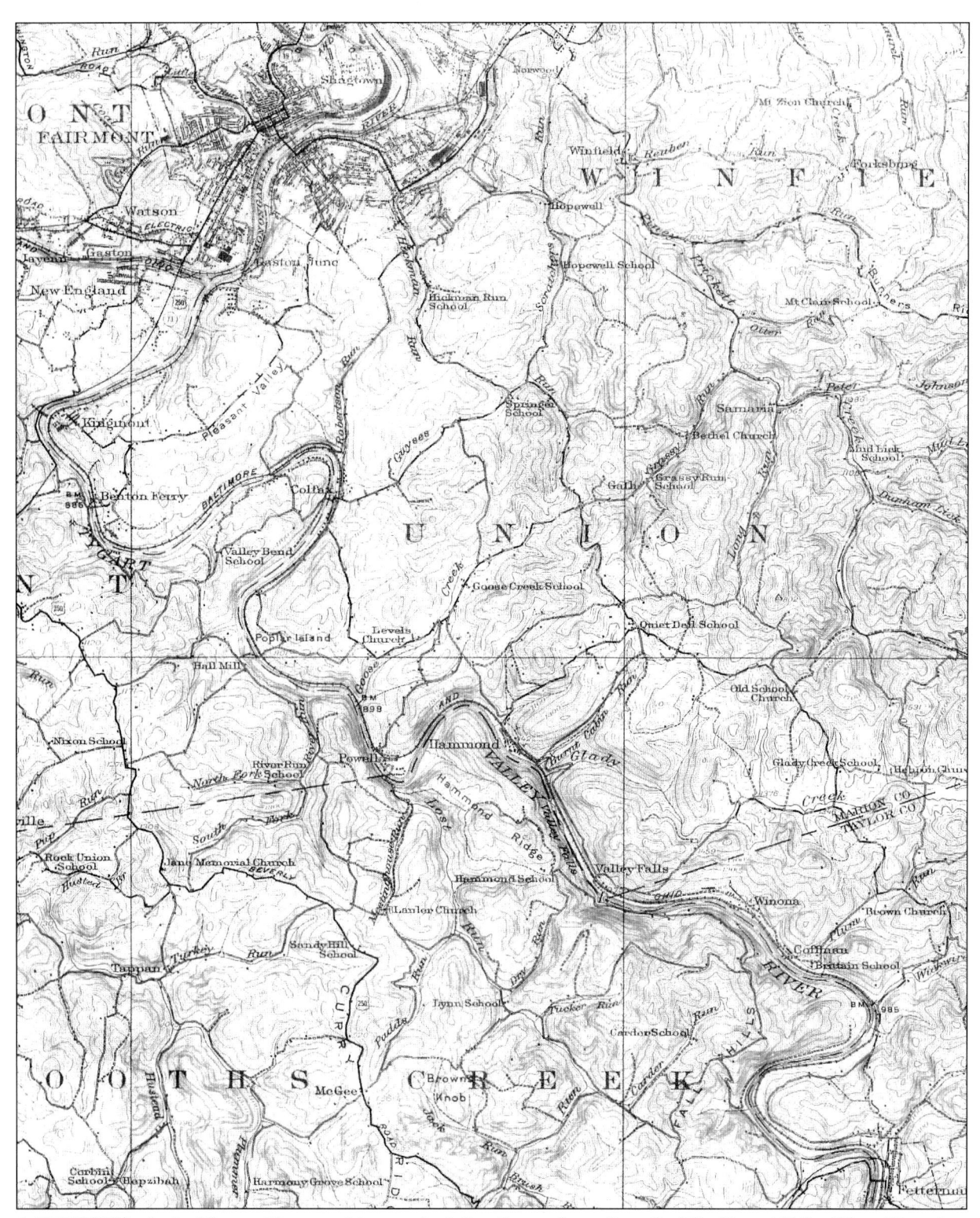

A 1923 WV Geological Survey Topographic map depicting the north-south path of the Tygart Valley River. Note the communities and the location of the early nearby schools.

People and Places

THE WILDERNESS OF VIRGINIA

In 1634, our valley belonged to the vast territory of Orange County, Virginia (named for the Prince of Orange). It remained so until 1738, when this area, which was considered the wilderness west of the Blue Ridge Mountains, became known as Augusta County, Virginia (later known as West Augusta). Today what was Augusta County included 48 counties of West Virginia, all of the states of Kentucky, Ohio, Illinois, Indiana, Michigan, Wisconsin east of the Mississippi River and three counties in western Pennsylvania.

Governor Alexander Spottswood of Virginia and his party made the first attempt to penetrate the mountain wilderness in 1714. He didn't make it beyond what is now Harpers Ferry but for this feat, King George made him a knight and presented him with a golden horseshoe. The next effort was made in 1740 when traders and adventurers began working their way into the interior trading with the Indians.

In 1730, the craving for more land for settlements increased, so Virginia at first began offering 1,000 acres of land to anyone who was willing to stake a claim providing each family was from outside of the state. This resulted in several different nationalities, like the Scotch-Irish, German, Dutch, English and French migrating to the wilderness. Their unique combined personalities were the beginning of our Appalachian culture.

Prickett's Fort on the Monongahela River was built in 1774. Two years later (1776) West Augusta County was divided into three counties—Ohio, Youghiogheny and Monongalia. The name Monongalia was a misspelling of the name for the Monongahela River. In 1784, another new county, Harrison, was formed from Monongalia County. It was named after Benjamin Harrison, who was then Governor of Virginia. His son, William Henry Harrison, later became the ninth President of the United States. Clarksburg became its county seat. The formation of this county brought Harrison county borders to the banks of the Tygart Valley River where there were several isolated homesteads.

For 58 years, Harrison County was situated on the west bank of the Tygart Valley River in what is now Marion and Taylor counties. Marion County was formed in 1842 by taking land from both Harrison and Monongalia counties, and was named after the Revolutionary War hero General Francis Marion (the Swamp Fox). This meant that both sides of the lower Tygart Valley River fell under Marion's jurisdiction. When it was formed, the towns within its territory were: Middletown (now Fairmont); Palatine (now part of Fairmont); Barnsville (now part of Fairmont); Worthington; Willeytown (now Farmington); Rivesville; Boothsville; Nuzum's Mill (later Hammond) and Hoult Town. The second deed recorded in the new county of Marion was on April 9, 1842. It was a land transfer from Richard Nuzum to Enos Nuzum at Nuzum's Mill for $400. The first is unknown.

In 1844, Taylor County was formed from Marion, Harrison and Monongalia counties. On the day the bill was passed for the new county, it read: "A new county was created in the northern section of the state on the Tygart Valley River. It was given the name of Taylor in honor of Senator John Taylor, of Caroline County, one of Virginia's most distinguished statesmen."

MILLERSVILLE

In the 1770's, William, a surveyor, and John Pettyjohn were ambitious brothers who established and operated a trading post and a ferry at the forks of the Tygart and West Fork rivers. On the east side of the river they set up a log cabin where hunters, settlers, and traders came to buy or trade for ammunition, food and ale. It was called Pettyjohn. The brothers operated a ferry service at the forks of the Tygart Valley and West Fork rivers. Later they expanded their operation upstream at what is now called Kingmont, Benton's Ferry, Mundell's Ferry and even farther upriver near Poplar Island. It is thought that a postal route was initiated from upstream to the settlement of Pettyjohn. Ninety years later, the settlement was known as Johntown.

In 1781, the Pettyjohns owned 200 acres of land each on the east side of the Tygart. Eventually, the brothers owned 2,800 acres of land scattered along the river. They both had fought in the Revolutionary War, and claimed title to some of the land by grants. Later, their sons, John, Jr. and William, Jr., also owned considerable amounts of land on the Tygart. William (1716-1799) and William, Jr. (1751–1796) are buried upriver in the Linn Cemetery on upper Glady Creek.

In 1783 the Governor of Virginia gave land in western Virginia to anyone who would cross the mountains and establish a homestead. One of those sturdy pioneers was Rymer Miller who decided to settle at the top of the hill overlooking the Tygart Valley River, close to where the Pettyjohn brothers had a trading post at the confluence of the West Fork and Tygart.

Aerial view of Millersville. 1999

Millersville was named after that family. Rymer Millers' descendant, Joseph Miller (d.1853) married Sarah Barnes who lived on the farm next door. Their son, John Bunyon Miller, 1830-1897, was a carpenter. He bought the old Jacob Barnes farm at the head of what is now Pleasant Valley. John married Emaline Beaty and they had nine children. They spent their entire life on this farm.

John Bunyon Miller, Jr. (1862-1921) married Alice Harr and raised their 10 children on his grandfather's farm. They operated a general store at the head of the valley. Being devoted Methodists, in 1901 the Miller family donated a lot for the purpose of building a Methodist church (see Churches). The family also had a school built on their property to serve the large, nearby families. Date of the school is unknown. Over time this area become known as Millersville. Descendants of this pioneer family still reside on a section of the Miller estate that was part of the original Miller property. Portions of this estate were eventually sold and was divided when I-79 came through in 1968. The top of Millersville hill offers a birds-eye view of the City of Fairmont. Many homes were built on the hillside for just this reason. Interstate 79 sliced through the middle of the community cutting off the only road leading to it. However, the state built a new access road.

William Barnes, Sr. was a millwright who grew up at George's Creek, Maryland. He built and operated a mill on what is now Pump Station Road. Before 1782 and sometime after the Revolutionary War, William brought his wife to the Tygart Valley River. William and Mary had nine sons and one daughter. For a homestead he chose a five-acre site on the east bank where there was a small stream boasting a gradual 40-ft. waterfall suitable for a mill. It would eventually be called Mill Run. William built a mill to grind corn for the settlers. History tells us he was known for miles around.

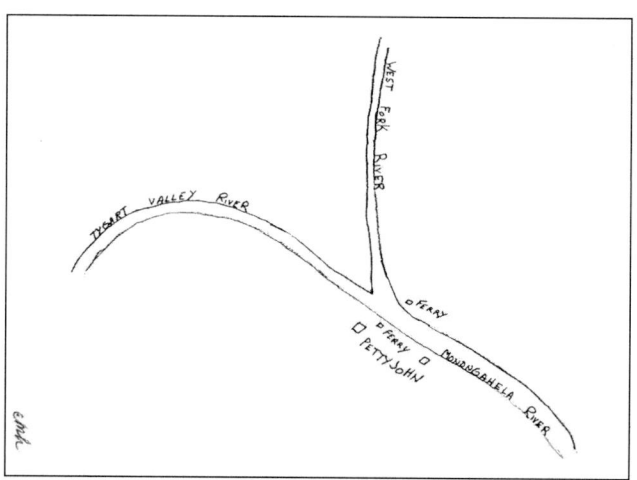

Map showing the location of where the Pettyjohn trading post and the ferry once existed at Millersville.
Illustration by C. Hamilton 2000.

FAIRMONT PUMP STATION / RESERVOIR

Charles Straight, Plant Supervisor, submitted the following information:

The Fairmont water system was first installed in 1903, and water was pumped from the Monongahela River. The intake was located on the east side of the river across from Fifth & Sixth Streets. Steam-driven pumps were used but there was no treatment of water.

In 1911, a new pump station was constructed about a quarter of a mile from the mouth of the Tygart Valley River at Millersville. Water is pulled into the intake structure by pumps. The water passes through a double set of screens to keep out the larger debris. These screens must be pulled up by a hoist and cleaned as the debris builds up.

Front view of the pumping station.

A slow sand filter was built at the reservoir on top of the hill and thus began the treatment of the water. Sometime between 1911 and 1924, chlorine was added to the water at the pump station.

In 1924 the treatment plant, designed by George Warren Fuller, was put into service. The plant was considered one of the most modern plants of its time. Water demand at that time was a million gallons a day (MGD) and the plant could produce six MGD.

Several times during the history of the plant an acid condition in the river water caused the water to become very hard. This occurred in 1935 from coal mine drainage in the West Fork River, which backed up into the Tygart to the pumping station. This back up was also caused by the Government Lock No. 15 at Hoult. Another serious case of hard water occurred during the drought of 1930.

In 1942, the steam pumps were taken out of service and electric pumps put in. Three 250 horsepower (HP) motors drove the pumps with a pumping capacity of seven and one half MGD. In 1952 two additional filters were added to the plant, making the capacity nine MGD. At the same time, an additional pump was added to the pump station.

In 1963 two more filters were added to the treatment plant. In 1972 one of the 250 HP pumps was replaced by a 500 HP, which increased the capacity to 12 million MGD. In 1984, new chemical handling methods were adopted at the treatment plant and new intakes were added at the reservoir. All of the plant control valves were replaced with other improvements.

While this work was underway another 250 HP pump was replaced by a 500 HP pump. That gave a pumping capacity of 14 MGD. In 2000, the plant had a total capacity of 12 million MGD. In 2002, it produced 6.2 MGD of safe drinking water and serves 12,000 households, industries, businesses and nine Public Service Districts. The water is in compliance with the Federal government's Safe Drinking Water Act standards. In 1997, our water was considered one of the nation's safest. The plant produces drinking water to all of Fairmont and all the surrounding communities including communities as far away as Valley Falls.

For the Valley Falls Public Service District two water-holding tanks were installed on top of Morgan's Hill at Crossroads. Water is pumped from the filtration

River view of Fairmont's city pumping station. Water is pumped from the Tygart Valley River to the reservoir at Morris Park.

plant uphill to the tanks then to customers in the Grassy Run, Levels, Quiet Dell, Glady Creek and Rock Lake areas.

A $10 million ultra filtration facility replaced the aged filtration plant directly beside the old one on the highest point in Fairmont. This was part of the city's $30 million water improvement project which also replaced some of the waterlines laid in 1903. The city could not meet current Federal water standards without the new system which was accompanied by a 60% rate hike. Progress always comes back to our pocketbook but good, clean drinking water is a necessity.

The new filtration plant has the capacity of 10 million gallons of clean drinking water per day. The technology used for the modern plant was a first for West Virginia and is one of a few in the nation.

PLEASANT VALLEY

It's hard to imagine today's town of Pleasant Valley as mostly farmland with a few scattered homes dotting it, but that's how it was even after World War II. Looking out over the valley from Dodd Cemetery at 1,335 ft. altitude is an awesome experience. This valley was named with this view in mind. According to Walter Balderson's book *Fort Prickett Frontier and Marion County*, it has beeen known as Pleasant Valley for more than a 100 years.

As late as 1983, the beginning of Pleasant Valley began at Morris Park, extending two miles southwest towards Benton's Ferry. About one mile from Fairmont, it is a fast-growing community and a favorite residential area. Over the hill on both sides of the Pleasant Valley Road is the Tygart Valley River. Today the city limits of Pleasant Valley extends to Pleasant Street on Pleasant Valley Road next to Fairmont.

There never was a post office in this valley, but when rural free delivery of mail began in 1920 mail carriers delivered from Fairmont to mailboxes put up along the road. Some of the mail carriers have been J. D. Herron, Burley Tennant, Ralph Watkins, Tony LeDonne, Tim Mallonee and Ed Dicken.

Kingmont, Benton's Ferry, Millersville and Pleasant Valley joined forces to become an incorporated city, although each community kept its own identity.

EARLY SETTLERS

According to Monongalia County Unpatented Land Records for 1775, **John Johnson** owned 400 acres on the southern end of the valley. Legend has it that he owned a large plantation worked by several slaves. When the Morgantown-Bridgeport Pike was established, his home was used as an overnight inn for the passengers on the stagecoach. One of John Johnson's daughters married Alza Dodd. As a part of her dowry, she was given a portion of Johnson land and a slave to go with it. This portion was later sold to the Work family and became known as the Atkins Work farm in Kingmont. Another daughter married Samuel P. Nixon of Grant District and was also given a slave woman as a gift.

In one of his historical *Times/West Virginian* newspaper articles, Rev. I. A. Barnes told the following story:

Jacob Barnes lived on what was known as the John B. Miller place near the pump station road where Mrs. Barnes did weaving for the neighbors. One autumn she had woven some linen for the Johnsons and one of their slaves was sent to pick it up. Now along the road not far from the Robinson Mine, there was a dense grapevine thicket which people thought was haunted. Most youngsters were afraid to pass by this area after dark. The by-road leading to the home of Abraham Barnes down on the river intersected the public road near the thicket. On the evening that the Johnson slave was returning home by moonlight with his roll of linen on his shoulder, one of the Barnes boys happened to be out on the road. Being in the vicinity of the haunted thicket, each took the other to be a ghost.

You need to understand that the Barnes family held a number of old German superstitions inherited from their grandmother. One was that if you spoke to a ghost, asked its name and what it wanted and it would answer you. Young Barnes decided to try out the old German formula for ghosts. He called out in frightened tones, "Who are you and what do you want?" Relief sank in when the ghost replied, "I'se Massa Johnson's man and I wanna go home!"

TOLL RATES

Forevery score of Sheep or Hogs.	6 cents
Forevery score of Cattle.	12 cents
Forevery Horse and Rider.	4 cents
Forevery led or driven Horse, Mule or Ass.	3 cents
Forevery Sleigh or Sled drawn by one horse or pair of Oxen.	3 cents
Forevery Horse or pair of Oxen in Addition.	3 cents
Forevery Dearborn, Sulky, Chair or Chaise with one horse.	6 cents
Forevery Horse in Addition.	3 cents
Forevery Chariot, Coach, Cochee, Stage, Phaeton or Chaise with two Horses and four wheels.	12 cents
Forevery Carriage of pleasure by whatever be it called the same according to the number of wheels and horses drawing the same.	
Forevery Cart or Wagon whose wheels do not exceed three inches in breadth, drawn by horse or pair of Oxen.	4 cents
Forevery Cart or Wagon whose wheels exceed three inches and does not exceed four inches in breadth for every horse or pair of oxen drawing the same.	4 cents
Wheels exceeding four and not exceeding six inches.	3 cents
Wheels exceeding six and not exceeding eight inches.	2 cents
All Carts or Wagons whose wheels exceed eight inches in breadth.	Free.

DAVID T. SHRIVER, Supt.

Sign on the National Road Toll Gate House at LaVale, Md. A fine example of what the toll rates would have been when the tollgate was in operation on the Morgantown-Bridgeport Pike in 1839. The National Road was under construction for fourteen years and cost seventeen hundred thousand dollars. Cost of the Morgantown-Bridgeport Pike could not be found.

Jordan Hall came to the valley sometime after the Revolutionary War with a party of prospectors and became impressed with the beauty of the land. He had grown up in Dover, Delaware and was the second son of Thomas and Rebecca Hall. After his father's death, he returned to the valley that he remembered so well to start a new life. He brought his widowed mother, brothers and sisters with him. His brothers were Asa, Ryner, Nathan, and Allen Hall.

Jordan Hall married Nancy O'Neal from Little Falls on the Monongahela where her family had immigrated to Monongalia County. By 1783, they owned a large portion of the northern end of Pleasant Valley. They lived in a log house near what is now Morris Park. The Halls were devoted Presbyterians and attended the First Presbyterian Church in Middletown after it was established in 1815.

Abraham Barnes, 1784-1872 was the eighth son of William Barnes, who was a millwright and who built one of the first mills on the Tygart Valley River. After William's death Abraham continued to live on the homestead and operate the mill. He married Mary Ann Hall, daughter of Jordan Hall, who had also settled in the valley. The couple had seven sons and four daughters. Their home was situated well above flood level, and their garden sloped down towards the river. In 1850, Abraham sold a small portion of land to the B&O railroad, dividing his garden into two parts.

With the coming of the railroad, two new mills were built—one upstream (Hayhurst Mill) and one downstream at Middletown (Fairmont). They were both large and prospered well, so after a short time, the smaller Barnes mill was shut down. Abraham died in 1872 and is buried in Maple Grove Cemetery in Fairmont.

Mary Ann Barnes, ninth child of Abraham, married **Christopher Robinson,** 1819-1896, of Yorkshire, England. He came to America in 1853. Mr. Robinson was a coalmine worker who was familiar with outcropping signs of coal seams. He and Mary's brother, Peter T. Barnes, opened a coalmine on Abraham's old home place. It became known as the Robinson Mine. Coal from the Abraham Barnes' property supplied the surrounding communities for 50 years. The Barnes family was one of the coal pioneers of Marion County.

The mine was later sold to the Watson family. Christopher and Mary Ann moved to Pruntytown where they operated a hotel for a while then purchased a large vein of fine coal. He opened a mine and operated it until his died in 1896. His sons continued operation of the mine until the State of West Virginia purchased the land to create additional acreage for the State Institution for Boys. Today, it is a minimum-security facility for people who are convicted of non-felony offences.

George W. Wiley married Asenath Barnes, 11th child of Abraham Barnes. He was one of the gatekeepers on the Morgantown/Bridgeport Pike. It was a toll road and the gate was located up hill from the present Valley Chapel United Methodist Church, and was not raised until the toll was paid. The income contributed to the maintenance of the road. The toll varied depending on the load. Folks going to schools, funerals, elections, militia training, public worship or going from one farm to another were exempt from the charge. Today nearly 150 years later, toll roads are still popular with governments.

In 1812, **James W. Thomas** owned over 300 acres of land atop the hill on the old Mundell Ferry Road extending down to the river. Before he sold this particular parcel of land to the Hughes family, he reserved a lot for the use of a cemetery. Thirteen members of the Thomas family are buried there. James T. Dodd, for whom the cemetery is named, owned this parcel sometime later (see Cemeteries).

Pleasant Valley School opened on February 28, 1929. Note the original structure in the middle. 1999.

PLEASANT VALLEY SCHOOL

The early families who lived in Pleasant Valley had large land holdings and large families as well. As portions of land were either given away to family members or sold, there was a need for another school to accommodate the population growth. School No. 1 was already in operation at Benton's Ferry.

In 1851, 12 years before the State of West Virginia was formed, Sarah and Isaac Courtney deeded a lot for a school to Trustees James Cochran, William H. Barnes, Dennis Miller and Isaac Courtney. The men of the community built a one-room structure "…for the benefit of neighbors so long as they shall see proper to occupy the same and by keeping a good school house." It sat on the original Morgantown-Bridgeport Pike, which led to Mundell's Ferry.

In 1870, five years after the Civil War ended, the Board of Education (BOE) bought the school for $500. It was called Union District School No. 2. That same year the BOE purchased a lot from Richard Thomas, an adjacent landowner, for additional land to be used as a playground. Walter Balderson and Mary Linn were among the last teachers at this school.

Classes were held in the one-room building for 76 years until 1928 when overcrowding again became a major issue. It was divided into two rooms, which helped for a while, but the community still outgrew the school. In 1928, the building was sold to William and Stella Barker, who converted it into a residence. The home is still in the family—the Barker's daughter, Thelma LeMasters, now resides in it.

The old Pleasant Valley School built in 1851 closed in 1928 and is now the private residence of Thelma LeMasters.

People and Places

In 1928, the board of education purchased two acres of land in Millersville for a new larger school. The school consolidated the Millersville School and School No. 2 in Pleasant Valley. L. D. Schmidt of Fairmont designed a six-room school, the most modern in the county at that time. It was designed so that a second story could be added when the need arose. The R. Nichols Lumber Company of Colfax held the contract for all of the work on the building. It cost the county $27,000.

Approximately 125 students and four teachers made up the February 28, 1929 opening day. Walter Balderson was the principal and Estel Balderson, Mary Linn and Avis Martin were the teachers for grades one through eight. This school became known as the Pleasant Valley School.

Over the years the original six-room school has had several additions including that second story. More recently, in 1992, a much needed, multi-purpose room was added at a cost of $447,000. Approximately 250 students attend grades one through six. Grades seven and eight attend East Fairmont Junior High in Fairmont.

Teachers who have taught here are Patricia Adams, Betty Bennett, Linda Bond, Mary DeBalski, Therese Laratta, Brenda Morgan, Joan Morgan, Janet Mundell, Betty Phillips, Debra Sabo, Carol Schoolcraft, Paul Sedera, Linda Stalnaker, Karen Stanley, Beverly Stewart and Cathy Tobrey. Other teachers who have taught here includes: Ann Lightner, Alma Donald, Wilma Ford, Gene Pence, Louise Arnett, Teresa Slamick, Barbara DeMayo, Carol Booth, Mabel Stanley, Eleanor Wilt, Ms. Carder and Ms. Phillips. Iva Cervo and Willa Morgan are past principals. Karen D. Richman is the present principal.

MORRIS PARK

On January 6, 1903 the City of Fairmont purchased 31 acres of hilltop land known to the old timers in the area as Log Cabin Hill. This site, 462 feet above the Tygart Valley River, was selected because it was one of the highest points in the vicinity. The altitude is 1,260 feet above sea level.

One mile from Fairmont's city limits, the land originally was bought for a waterworks purification plant and emergency reserve water supply that would protect the city should the city pumping plant fail. Fairmont purchased an additional 6.02 acres on March 10, 1905. After realizing that the purification plant needed a caretaker, a fine brick house was built on

Entrance to Morris Park. 1999.

it. Then on July 1, 1922, another 8.8 acres of land was purchased as a general improvement to expand the reservoir property.

During the summer of 1927, a coal mine was in operation on a tract of land adjoining the reservoir property. Core drillings were being driven toward the location of the 21,000,000-gallon storage tanks. Fearing serious damage to the tanks, the city felt it necessary to purchase an additional 25.18 acres as a protection measure. The property was wild, rough and was left neglected.

In 1932, J. Claude Morris was the city water director. It was his idea to utilize the property for a city park. He had the assistance of several work relief agencies which provided men and materials. A splendid park was developed under his supervision. Director Morris died in office on February 24, 1939. As a memorial to his name, the city board passed a resolution officially naming the site Morris Park.

Today there are 145 acres, about 50 of which are still heavily wooded. Many evergreens and species of trees have been planted and labeled. The one-mile long road around the park is paved. Picnic tables, rustic fireplaces, drinking fountains, a tennis court, playground and pavilions have been added over the years. It is a wonderful place for a day's outing. Many of us remember being in the little kiddie pool on a hot, summer's day.

Today the maintenance of the park is under the supervision of Marion County Parks and Recreation (MCPAR) and is owned by Fairmont's Municipal Water System. In 2000, the filtration plant at Morris Park was annexed by the city of Fairmont.

VALLEY VOLUNTEER FIRE DEPARTMENT

Home of the Pleasant Valley Fire Department and Heritage Room on Pleasant Valley Road. 1999

The Valley Volunteer Fire Department was first organized in November 1957. However, due to the lack of funding, a firehouse was not constructed until August 1964. The large block building was built on the main road for easy access to Pleasant Valley, Millersville, Benton's Ferry and Kingmont. It has served as a community building for several years until it was remodeled into what is now the Heritage Room. It is rented out for banquets, dinners and parties. The income helps support the fire department. A women's auxiliary also was formed to help support the fire department and it coordinates the use of the Heritage Room.

Thirty-two trained volunteers are on call day or night. The VVFD boundary extends to the Taylor County line on U. S. Route 250 South, to the intersection on State Route 73 South; White Hall, Deerfield, and up to Fairmont City Limits.

The purchase of a heart defibrillator in 1998 added to the current concept of first response. The state-of-the-art machine was purchased for about $3,000 through fundraisers and by the Women's Auxiliary. The town of White Hall donated a vehicle to be used as a first response emergency vehicle so the department can arrive before other rescue personnel for cardiac-arrest situations.

Until 2001 the King-Mill Valley Public Service District (PSD) was located in the basement of the fire department. The PSD serves Kingmont, Millersville, Benton's Ferry and Pleasant Valley. The sewage system was added in 1984. Sewage goes to a collection station and then on to the treatment plant in Fairmont.

PLEASANT VALLEY COMMUNITY EDUCATIONAL OUTREACH
(Former Homemakers Club)

The Pleasant Valley Homemakers Club was organized June 4, 1940 with the help of Miss Margaret Rexroad, Home Demonstration Agent from West Virginia University. There were 19 members in the original group. The club was incorporated on April 28, 1952. Its main purpose was the promotion and the advancement of the education of the residents of Pleasant Valley, Millersville and surrounding communities as well as building a better community.

The Homemaker's Club did Red Cross work during World War II; the women took home nursing courses; first aid; and purchased war bonds. They bought a pressure cooker and electric mixer for Pleasant Valley School so they could can food for the school's hot-lunch program.

Today the club has 26 members on its roll and continues to educate the community and work towards making Pleasant Valley a nice place to live.

People and Places

PLEASANT VALLEY COMMUNITY BUILDING

The Homemaker's Club charter members worked toward building a community center. After careful investigation of several prospects, on May 23, 1952 the club purchased Mr. and Mrs. Glenn Shaffer's historic blacksmith shop. The lot size was 100x172 ft. The cinder block building, 24x50 ft., needed a good deal of work. The men of the community poured a cement floor, installed a new ceiling with fluorescent lighting and a ceiling-type furnace was installed. Someone even donated a sink and stove before the first club meeting took place on October 5, 1952.

In the spring of 1955, a kitchen and restrooms were added to the building. Over the years a small parking lot was graded out. Community men worked hard for many hours to make the building program a success. But as time went by the community kept growing and outgrew the community building. In 1965, the building was in need of major repairs and became inadequate for their needs. It was decided to take the invitation of the Valley Volunteer Fire Department and start using its building as a community building. The old building was sold.

TOWN COUNCIL

In 1995, the City of Fairmont's administration thought of annexing Pleasant Valley, Benton's Ferry, Millersville, and Kingmont. The people of these communities did not like the idea. At a special meeting, the idea of forming a separate town council was discussed. As a result a special election was held on October 18, 1995 by the residents to incorporate all four communities. The vote passed the issue and Pleasant Valley was incorporated by the state in November of the same year. A mayor and a representative from each community (two representives from Pleasant Valley representing each side of the Pleasant Valley Road) were elected. Elections are held every two years on the first Tuesday. Jack Bish serves as the first Mayor.

The 1995 population of the communities was 2,540. The 2001 population increased to 3,124.

The City of Pleasant Valley Municipal building. First meeting in the new chambers was held November 14, 2001.

In September 2000, representatives from the Marion County Board of Education presented the deed and keys of the former Kingmont kindergarten school to Pleasant Valley town council. The previous schoolhouse became known as the Pleasant Valley Municipal Building. Over a period of five months the building was completely renovated to house the council chamber, offices for the city and the King-Mill Valley Public Service District.

EAST FAIRMONT HIGH SCHOOL
1993 Airport Road

In May 1989, Marion County voters approved a $12.3 million bond issue for a new East Fairmont High School. The old school, which was built on the east side of Fairmont in 1921, had been overcrowded for at least 40 years.

In December 1985, representatives appointed by Parent Teachers Organizations and administrators from Central, Colfax, East Dale, East Park, Pleasant Valley, Quiet Dell, State Street and East Fairmont High Schools formed a task force to evaluate facilities, curriculum, enrollment and other aspects relevant to the overcrowding issue. At a special meeting in July 1986, 280 persons attended, and a plan for a new school was presented to the Marion County Board of Education (BOE). Petitions with nearly 800 signatures and letters of support from over 140 businesses were presented to the board, and it voted to support the construction of the new facility.

After voters passed the bond issue, 102 acres of land were purchased on a hilltop between Kingmont and Pleasant Valley overlooking the river. The architectural firm of Gandee & Partners, Inc. designed the building. It

West Virginia's Lower Tygart Valley River

Main entrance of East Fairmont High School completed in 1993.

has specialized labs for science; art and design; a 900-seat auditorium; gymnasium; "common area" for lunches; interior courtyards, and a child-care center, modeled after a pilot program at Capitol High School in Charleston, WV, which was the first day care center in the state. East Fairmont's is the second. The primary purpose of the center is to keep teenage parents in school.

After several setbacks, which held up the project for about 18 months, construction finally began. As the school neared completion on the inside, nothing was being done to the grounds. Due to the tight budget, the allocations for landscaping had been cut in half. Board member Dr. George "Doc" Boyles designed a plan to use volunteer labor for the project. A successful plan was initiated to sell trees and shrubs for the grounds. Over time, some 50-60 volunteers planted trees and shrubbery, removed rocks, and prepared the soil for grass planting. This endeavor saved the BOE nearly $100,000.

Five months before the opening of the school, Sunday afternoon tours were given through the new building. At first Dr. Boyles began the tours with only a few people. But the effort soon escalated into a major endeavor. Tour guides officially escorted over 5,342 people through the facility and grounds.

The new two-story facility was dedicated on August 14, 1993 with a ribbon-cutting ceremony. Kent Gandee, the architect, presented the keys to the building to High School Principal George Dragich and Marion County School Superintendent Jane Reynolds so the fall 1993 term could begin. Assistant Principal David Nuzum presented Dr. Boyles with a plaque from the faculty, staff and students. The new school marked the beginning of a new era of Education.

The former East Fairmont High School in Fairmont is now the home of East Fairmont Junior High.

EAST FAIRMONT HIGH SCHOOL
1993 Airport Road
Fairmont, WV

August 14, 1993
2 p.m.

Ribbon-Cutting Ceremonies and Dedication

Program

Musical Selections..........................Busy Bee Band
Earl E. McConnell, Jr., Director
National Anthem..............................Busy Bee Band
Mistress of Ceremonies..............Tamara Stevens
President - Student Body
Invocation...Amber Kinney
President - Senior Class
Pledge of Allegiance.....................John Mainella
President - Junior Class
Welcome...Thomas Dragich
Principal
Remarks & Introductions........Jane M. Reynolds
Superintendent of Schools

Remarks
Ronald D. Allan, Sr., President
Dr. George J. Boyles
James "Rat" Saunders
Shirley Stanton
Dixie Yann

Presentation of Keys
Mr. Kent Gandee, Architect
Gandee & Partners, Inc.

Program at the ribbon-cutting ceremonies and dedication.

People and Places

FAIRMONT MUNICIPAL AIRPORT

Airport Road at the Kingmont Exit off I-79 leads to the Fairmont Municipal Airport. In 1939, before the original airfield was built, this was a recreation spot known locally as the "Sandy Eagle Ball Field" and was home to Kingmont's coal company ball team. Many exciting ballgames were played here with opponents from other coal towns. Nick Julian was the coach for Kingmont's main recreation before World War II loomed upon us. After the war the airfield was built on the old ball field.

Fairmont Municipal Airport at the I-79 Kingmont exchange.

In 1966, it had to be relocated because Interstate I-79 was coming through. Moving over towards the river, the new airport was completed by 1969. This time the runway was paved and lengthened to 2800 feet to accommodate medium size twin-engine airplanes. Owned by the City of Fairmont and governed by a Board of Directors, the airport is called Frankman Field in honor of the distinguished local flyer, the late Samuel J. (Sam) Frankman. Frankman's flying days were all accident free and spanned a half-century of aviation that included the sport of "barnstorming" in an open-pit biplane. After World War II he owned and operated the Fairmont Seaplane Base on the Monongahela River and gave flying lessons. It was the only flight facility of its type in WV. He served for several years on the airport board.

T-Hangars at the Fairmont Municipal Airport.

The 50-acre airport is designed for small business and private aircraft. Marvin Franks owns and operates Frank's Aviation Flight School and Banner Towing Service. Mark Scritchfield of Fairmont is one of the instructors. New airplanes can be purchased here. Steve Weaver of Fairmont is in charge of aircraft sales. A contractor, Weaver provides services including fueling and maintenance for incoming airplanes. He also provides charters, flight planning, snow removal, grass cutting, and general runway maintenance.

There are 14 T-hangars available for rent and three private hangars and two large hangars belonging to the City of Fairmont. In 1998, 12 additional hangars were added. In 1999, an additional 600 feet of runway was built to make the runway 3,400 feet in length. Private flying by residents in and around Fairmont has become a popular mode of travel in recent years as well as a very popular sport.

KINGMONT

Before 1800, the area now known as Kingmont was forest situated above the banks of the Tygart Valley River. There were no roads but there was an oversize path that led to the local farms. In 1813, Thomas Durn King owned 190 acres along the river. Several generations of Kings lived here.

Sometime after 1820, the King family started a ferry operation across the river. The Kings first had a ferry operation above Robertson Island upriver from Colfax, but moved operations downriver to where the present site of Kingmont is today. The name Kings Ferry followed them. In 1849, Baltimore and Ohio Railroad engineers completed their surveys for a new railroad along the river. Landowners eagerly sold land for this endeavor without really knowing the full extent of its impact on their lives.

William Worth had 1000 acres of timberland here, which he timbered out into rafts and took them downriver to market.

Aerial view of Kingmont, taken in November 1999.

KING STATION

The railroad arrived in 1852, and changed the name of this community from King's Ferry to King Station, 3.5 miles from Fairmont by rail. A small railroad platform was installed so patrons could board the train. Exactly when is not known but there were still members of the King family in residence.

Directly across the river in Grant District, the Hayhurst family built a mill. Their farm was on the hillside. Orlando Hayhurst and his wife, Dorcas, raised their family of eight children on his father's homestead in a log cabin. The cabin was located close to what would later be known as the old Hite mine entrance. The Hayhursts sold a plot of land to the board of education in 1886 for School No.1 in Grant District.

A disastrous flood destroyed the mill in 1888. With no hope of rebuilding, the Hayhursts sold eight acres of their land to the Virginia & Pittsburgh Coal Company in 1892. Others who sold land to the coal company were John Hall (1892), M. Murphy (1895) and A. Work (1909-10)

Ben King, an ancestor of the original King family, lived at Kingmont and worked at the Hite Mine in 1914. It was his ancestors for which the community was named.

BLACK GOLD

Our early settlers gave no attention to the black rocks lying on the hillsides and banks. Considered worthless, they were left alone. Then someone discovered that they would burn and give out heat lasting twice as long as wood. Landowners began looking for the "black rock" on their farms. In 1850, "coal" was discovered on Abraham Barnes' property. He lived about a mile downriver from King's Ferry. Using only a pick and shovel, a tunnel was dug in the hillside on his farm and he hired someone to dig the coal. It was hauled out with an ox team and two horses. The coal was then sold for domestic purposes at a local market. Neighboring farmers, who did not have a coal vein on their properties, sometimes were permitted to dig it for a penny a bushel. Who among them would have believed that those little black rocks would turn into black gold?

Not long after the arrival of the railroad in 1852 shipments of coal to Baltimore opened the coal market for the industry in this county. This gave birth to the local coal barons.

440 ft. long pit-car bridge across the Tygart Valley River. The steel structure carried small coal cars from the mine tunnels in the hillside on the west side of the river to the coal tipple on the east side of the river. Kingmont can be seen in the background. Picture taken in the early 1900's by S.H. Rudy. *Courtesy of FSC Folk Life Collection, Donated by Buddy Myers.*

VIRGINIA & PITTSBURGH COAL & COKE COMPANY

In 1889 Peter Yost Hite came to Marion County from Pennsylvania where he owned a coal mine. He purchased property on the banks of the Tygart Valley River at King's Station (Kingmont) where there was a rich coal vein. The corporate title of his company was the Virginia & Pittsburgh Coal & Coke Company and its holdings consisted of 1,108 acres of coal and 55 acres of surface coal. In the beginning, the main office was at Benton's Ferry where there was a post office, train station, general store and hotel.

Operations began in 1891 and were slow in the beginning. There were neither enough equipment nor workers. All the coal was dug by hand and brought out of the mine with mules. Coal was brought over to the east side of the river in buckets hauled over by a cable. The coal then was loaded to waiting railroad hopper cars at a tipple. The first shipments of coal began in 1892.

The coal company built hillside houses on 50x150' lots on the east side of the river to rent to the miners and their families. The workers crossed the river to the mine entrance on the ferry.

Kingmont coal tipple. *Courtesy of Carl & Wilma (Curry) Johnson*

The ferry landing at Kingmont, WV in 1900. Note the Fairmont and Beverly Turnpike on the left (now US Rt. 250). It was paved for the first time in 1932. *Courtesy of FSC Folk Life Collection, Donated by Buddy Myers. Photo by S.H. Rudy.*

Peter Yost Hite in association with sons Rolfe, Samuel and John organized and owned the business. According to the *West Virginia Gazetteer* in 1898, P. G. Hite was president, William J. Wright was secretary-treasurer, and Samuel R. Hite was assistant treasurer. At that time, the company had capital of $200,000. Rolfe M. Hite was the General Manager.

In 1900, coal production still was low so an all-out effort was made to recruit more men to work in the mine. The effort went as far as the hills of Italy. Mining interests advertised in Italian towns for people willing to move to a new world for a job. Many of the Italian employees came from the province of Abruzzi in the central mountains of Italy. Speaking only their native tongue, they arrived in boxcars at King Station. Families followed later, also arriving in boxcars. All the possessions they could carry were placed in bed sheets for the journey. Other ethnic groups, such as the Poles, also left their homeland to work at the mine. Most of them adapted well in their new country.

More housing was quickly thrown together in rows on the hillside. The houses had four rooms with bare floors. There were reports that, in some cases, moonlight could be seen through the boards in the ceiling. There was no such thing as wallpaper for these folks and the heat came from a coal stove used for cooking. The toilet was outside of the house and was known as the "outhouse." All of the 150 houses looked alike. Rent was $5.75 per family, due at the first of the month.

Mine structures included a coal tipple, coke ovens, fan, supply houses, company store, blacksmith shop, corncribs and a stable for the mules. Later, the stable gave way to motor barns and oil houses. A pit-car bridge was built across the Tygart Valley River to ferry coal across. It was a 440-foot long steel structure that carried mine cars from a tunnel on the west side of the river to the tipple on the east side.

By 1918-19, Kingmont had a population of 550. The mail arrived daily by train. There were two sand companies in operation on the riverbank downriver, and construction of the Fairmont Brick Company was underway. The coal company employed a doctor to care for its miners and their families. On his regular schedule of visits two or three times a week, Dr. Henry D. Causey found his schedule full. Dr. Henry Criss was also on call at times. Two barbers were kept busy, and there was a movie theater and a poolroom for entertainment.

In the 1920's, Kingmont was a booming town but the mine owners suppressed all efforts of the unions to organize. Friction between pro-unionists and the mine operators caused many fights. Safety in the mines was so bad that the company had to bring in the county police with their rifles to patrol the only road into town to keep anyone from leaving. But in 1930 conditions for the miners began to improve, and in 1931 the union was organized.

Kingmont grew into a typical coal-mining town. Everything depended upon coal. An average of 330 men labored to fill up 15-20 hopper cars a day for Owens-Illinois and the power plants in Philadelphia and New Jersey. Coal for shipment also was being loaded into barges on the west bank of the river.

WEST VIRGINIA GAZETTEER

KINGMONT: Population 550. Or the B & O R R, in Marion County, 3 miles east of Fairmont, the county seat and banking point. M P church Telephone connection.' Express, Wells Fargo. Mail daily. R R Hunsacker postmaster.
Belcastro & Manfreidi Co, general store and meats.
Causey Henry D, physician.
Fairmont Brick Co, S A Shuttlesworth mngr.
Morgan Loyd, barber.
New England Sand Co, C C Durret' mngr.
Powell Joseph, barber.
Valley River Sand Co.
Virginia & Pittsburgn Coal Co.

1918-19 *West Virginia Gazetteer and Business Directory.*

People and Places

The ferry across the Tygart Valley River closed in the 1930's. Its landing was on the west side of the river on U.S. Route 250 straight across from Kingmont. Today the wide pullover where the ferry docked is sometimes used by various vendors selling a wide variety of produce and flea market items.

The supply of coal finally was worked out and the mine was closed and sold. It was reopened for a short time but closed for good in 1957. After 68 years of mining coal, it never produced again.

The houses were bought by many of the workers, many of whom continue to live in Kingmont and adjusted to life without the mine.

Then in 1973, the tipple—a landmark along Route 250 South—was removed from the railroad, and the bridge across the river was torn down. Two huge, square-cut, sandstone piers are all that remains from one of Marion County's earliest coalmines. They stand on the riverbanks today as a monument to Kingmont's coal era.

THE COMPANY STORE

The company store was the center of life in the community selling everything from groceries and dry goods to furniture, cook stoves, cradles and coffins. Townspeople of all ages gathered on the porch to await the mail, gossip or to just loaf around. The company store recycled a large part of the coal miners' payroll back into the company coffers. So, as was typical in all bustling mining towns, the workers kept getting deeper in debt at the company store. Mine employees were paid wages in company coinage, termed "scrip," which was redeemable only at the company store.

In June of 1952, the company store was closed and torn down soon afterwards.

POST OFFICE

In 1905 King Station again had a name change. Its population had increased and was on its way to becoming a thriving community. The mine officials successfully petitioned the government for a local post office. On March 13, 1905, Andy Poling became the first postmaster and the Federal government changed the town's name to Kingmont.

The first post office was located in the company store where a company employee handled the mail. It remained there for many years. In the early 1950's, the post office was moved to a vacant company house near the company store and stayed there until the new community building was built in 1968. The new post office was added onto the side of the building.

There were several acting postmasters for the community of Kingmont. Here is the official list of the permanent postmasters. This list was provided by *The National Archives*:

March 13, 1905	Andy Poling
October 16, 1908	Nellie L Gerkins
November 23, 1909	Nellie L. Boyce
1912	A. C. Poling
March 2, 1915	Robert Hunsaker
August 5, 1927	Frank O. Hinebaugh
April 18, 1929	William Jarrett
March 6, 1931	Lester H. Harman
November 30, 1964	Guy J. Cattafesta
1988	Pat Piercy
June 4, 2001	John Cervo

Pat Lindsay Piercy was a 30-year employee of the postal service when she retired June 1, 2001. She was Postmaster of Kingmont for 13 years. She and her husband Charles S. Piercy, Jr., who was a Monongahela Power Company employee, are from Randolph County. They moved to Kingmont in Marion County in 1962 and raised their three children there.

Pat began her postal career as a postal clerk under Guy Cattafesta. She is a past-president of the North Central Postmasters Association

John Cervo, postmaster of Kingmont post office and Pat Piercy, former postmaster.

The late Guy J. Cattafesta, former Kingmont postmaster. *Courtesy of the Kingmont Improvement Association.*

for Marion, Harrison and Monongalia counties and was active in NAPUS, a national organization for postal workers. She and her husband are members of the Kingmont United Methodist Church and are active in the community. After 30 years Pat retired as postmaster on June 1, 2001. John Cervo, who was postmaster at Metz, WV was already a resident of Pleasant Valley and chose to apply for the position in Kingmont to be closer to his home. He began his duties on June 4, 2001.

The zip code for Kingmont is 26578. The Kingmont Post Office has advanced from a fourth class station to a second-class station with mail being delivered from Fairmont daily.

SCHOOLS

In 1864, the first free school (School No. 1.) in Union District opened. It stood where the BP service station is now located on the Pleasant Valley Road. Miss Emma Griffith was the first teacher. All children of school age in the valley, including King Station, attended this school. In 1902 a new brick school was built across the road from the original school.

By early 1910, Kingmont was growing so rapidly the mine owners decided to build an additional school. It was built where the present community building now stands. In time, even that structure became too small. Overcrowding worsened, and classes were held in the mine recreation room and the post office building. In 1928, to alleviate crowding, the Marion County Board of Education built a one-room schoolhouse on the hill on land purchased from Albert Fortney. Some of the teachers who taught here were: Earl O'Donnell, Lillian Stanley, Charles Jarrett, Grace Michael, Beulah Winter, Martha Davis, Olive Virginia Linn, and others with the last name of Feather and Miller.

In 1950, the board of education came to the rescue. The one-room school was torn down and a three-room brick structure was built. Grades K - four attended the new Kingmont School; grades five - eight attended Pleasant Valley School. Some of the teachers were: Arlie Toothman, Nick Fantasia, Sr., Carol Chapman, Mary Lou Louman and Irene Robey.

After the mines closed in 1957, school enrollment dropped as a natural consequence and the board of education decided to close the school in 1976-77. After the closing, however, the board reconsidered its use and decided in 1978 to continue using the school for two kindergarten classes and a pre-school special education class. Kindergarten teachers in 1999 were Joan Morgan and Brenda Morgan. Linda Bond and Debra Sabo taught the special education class. At the beginning of the school term in the fall of 2000, the Board of Education moved those classes to the Pleasant Valley School where an addition was added.

Kingmont School 1900-1950. The building is now used as a community building and post office. *Courtesy of the Kingmont Improvement Association.*

Students from kindergarten to grade six from Kingmont now attend Pleasant Valley School; grades six-eight go to East Fairmont Junior High and grades nine - 12 go to East Fairmont High School.

ROADS

In 1922, US Rt. 250 was constructed across the river from Kingmont. Since the ferry landing was there, a narrow wagon road already led to "Monkey Wrench Hollow" (now Holbert Road) and to Marion County's Poor House, where the indigent homeless were sheltered, clothed and fed. It sat on the hill across the road from where Muriale's Restaurant is today. Ten years later in 1932, that old wagon road (Rt. 250) was paved.

Kingmont Community Building remodeled in 1973. *Courtesy of Kingmont Improvement Association.*

In the early days the road down into Kingmont was always difficult to travel. It was full of large ruts until it was paved for the first time in 1928. Local laborers received $35.00 for two weeks of work on the 14 foot-wide road. Armstrong Construction was the contractor.

I-79 from East Grafton Road to Rt. 250 South was opened on June 4, 1968. The only interstate exchange for Benton's Ferry and Kingmont was at Pleasant Valley, which was to serve all three communities. After 16 years, the state added another exchange to accommodate the growth of Kingmont and Benton's Ferry. It was opened December 7, 1984.

Progress in Marion County significantly improved with the advent of I-79. Four years after the Kingmont exit was opened, the narrow Benton's Ferry Bridge was deemed unsafe and was closed. All traffic was routed over the Tygart Valley River via I-79.

Acting under a May 1997 ordinance, the Marion County Commission and the U.S. Postal Service began the task of renaming streets and roads. The project was completed by the year 2002, converts long-standing rural mail routes to street addresses with house numbers. This is a big change for our once slow-moving small towns set in a fast moving modern world; not necessarily the better.

KINGMONT COMMUNITY BUILDING

In 1950, when the Marion County Board of Education built a new school for Kingmont, the old school was converted into a community building. In 1963, the old building and the half-acre of land around it were purchased by the Kingmont Improvement Association. It became the site for a new community building. By October 1967, a decision was made to proceed with the project.

Once the Kingmont Elementary school, it later became the Pleasant Valley kindergarten school. When the kindergarten was closed the building was sold to the City of Pleasant Valley by the Marion County Board of Education in 2000.

The old building was razed; excavation for the new one began in December. Its goal was to improve community life by offering educational, fitness and senior programs. They moved into the new building in 1969.

The community building is 44x80. The first floor is at ground level and has three rooms. One of which is rented to the Kingmont Post Office and the other is the kitchen. A long hallway between the two rooms leads into the main assembly room where a stage is the focal point. Restrooms are located in the back of the building.

There is a full basement with a recreation room for the youth. To secure funds to complete the basement, a decision was made to sell the Kingmont TV Cable Company to Fairmont's Teleprompter service.

Much of the credit for planning and overseeing the work goes to the board of directors of the association at that time: Joe Carunchia, Mike Onderko, Benny Simmons and William Police. These men contributed greatly in developing a community cable television and street light projects. Construction of the building was managed by Steve Onderko, local builder and resident. His brothers, George and Mike, and Dave Jarrett helped him do the masonry and carpenter work.

Selected Short Subjects

- In the early days Kingmont's "red neck" coal miners lived in a section of Kingmont called Scab Town.
- The Hite Mine mined coal under Cook & Hart hill across the river from Kingmont and towards what is now Middletown Mall.
- East Fairmont High School was built on top of a hill known as "Hungry Man Hill." As the legend goes, during the Depression a man lived lived up there on the hill and was always hungry.
- Pine Lake housing development is on the old Atkins Work farm (1870). The Work family cemetery was on the edge of this housing development.
- Before World War II, Nick Julian, a Kingmont resident, coached the mine's ball team. The team's playing field was where the airport is today.
- Holbert Road off Rt. 250 near Wood's Boathouse is still referred by some as *"Monkey Wrench Hollow."* Legend has it that a man who worked at the Kingmont mine lived on this road. One day after payday, he was hit on top of the head with a monkey wrench and was robbed. The road has been called Monkey Wrench Hollow ever since until recently when a formal name change took place.
- In 1951, the Monongah Municipal Water Works put a filtration plant on Holbert Road on the Tygart Valley River in Grant District. The pump station pumps 600,000 gallons of water a day up to the plant. The treated water is then pumped to the two holding tanks on top of the hill. From there it goes to the following communities: Monongah, Koon's Run, Carolina, Four States, Idamay, Farmington and South Farmington.
- In 1977, a pump station was installed for the Shinnston Water Treatment Plant on the Tygart. It pumps 1.5 million gallons of water per day (MGD) to the filtration plant on Manley Chapel Road. From there it is pumped to two holding tanks and there the water is distributed to Shinnston and its surrounding communities.

Pump station for the City of Shinnston and Monongah's Water Works Department located on U.S. Route 250 south near Wood's Boat House.

BENTON'S FERRY

The village of Benton's Ferry was established on the Morgantown-Bridgeport Pike where the road met the ferry on the Tygart Valley River. Today, however, Benton's Ferry boundaries extend to the Kingmont exchange of I-79 and across the river to the camp road on the west bank.

The town is named for the ferry which once operated across the river here. With the arrival of the B&O Railroad in 1852, the ferry became a major form of passage to and from the railroad, which was located 4.6 miles by rail from Fairmont.

In 1911, Emma F. and B. F. Thomas sold lots in what they called Tygart City. One hundred lots were sold and the deeds are recorded in the courthouse as in Tygart City but the name never became official. Benton's Ferry did. According to court records, families who bought lots between 1912-1920 were Hillberry, Gaskins, Carpenter, Durrett, Brannon, Stanley, King and McDougal.

Benton's Ferry always has been a popular spot for water recreation and summer camps on the river. Before the Grafton Dam was built in 1939, the normal water level was much lower than it is today. There were several sandy beaches along the shoreline. A person could wade across the river in some places. On hot summer days, people would flock to the local sandy beaches to escape the heat.

In 1995, Benton's Ferry united with Kingmont, Millersville and Pleasant Valley to form a Town Council and together became an incorporated town in Marion County. Today the community's population is 594. It is mostly residential.

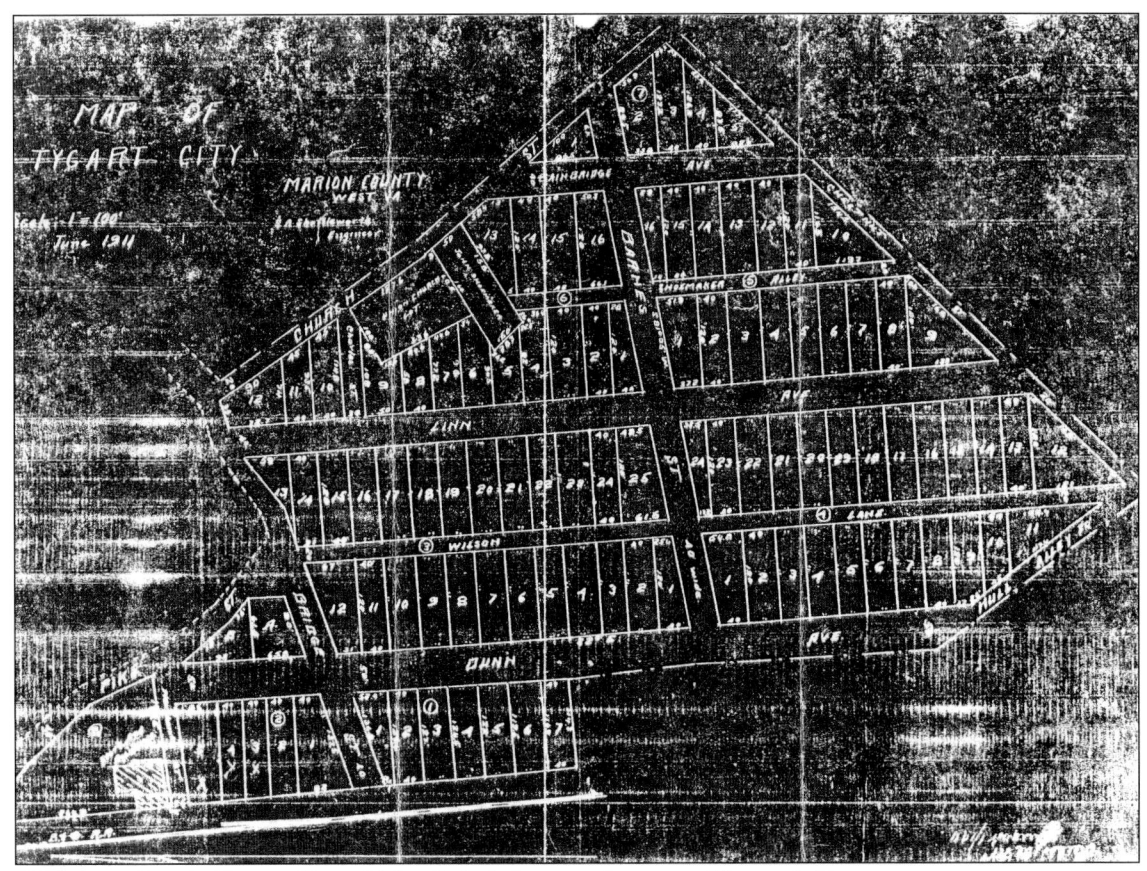

1911 map of lots in Tygart City, which officially became the town of Benton's Ferry.
Courtesy of Barbara Metcalfe.

THE FERRY

For the most part, ferrymen were landowners on at least one side of the river. They were farmers who provided this service only when there was a need. Sundown usually stopped river traffic because after dark, travel was not safe. Ferrymen gave officers of the law, doctors and ministers preference over all others who might be waiting to cross. Of course, officers of the law always rode for free.

Local history books say the ferry was established by Asa Bee and was put into operation in 1796. At that time the road was only a trail leading to the river's edge. A short time later Asa Bee moved to Doddridge County. History says at some point the Pettyjohns took over the operation. They owned land downriver near the West Fork River and eventually had other ferries further upriver.

In 1807, the Commonwealth of Virginia passed an act giving the courts power to establish ferries and to regulate their rates. Anyone who wanted to establish a ferry service had to go through the county court to do so. The court fixed the rates of passage and could raise the rates after two notices were posted on the courthouse door. Passage rates for a man were the same as they were for a horse; the same held true for every wheel of a carriage and each head of cattle. Each hog, sheep or goat cost one-fifth part of the rate for a horse.

Quick for the honest penny, ferryman John Mellett provided a log raft that had long poles that prodded the river's bottom to take travelers across the Tygart. After Mallett gave up the job his father-in-law, Thomas Veach, became the next ferry operator. Strong arms and backs were the only prerequisite, it took hard work and skill to cross. Many times the ferrymen could not withstand the trials presented by Mother Nature as the river's current increased and the water level rose.

Benton Lane at Benton's Ferry. Namesake of the elusive Bentons from which the town got its name.

Local historians claim a Mr. Benton was in charge of the ferry at one time but no information could be found about him including his first name. However, there was a James T. and a Mordecai Benton who were from western Virginia who fought for the Union during the Civil War. According to the Unclaimed Civil War Medal list for West Virginia, they never received their Civil War medals. Our Mr. Benton, the potential ferryman, disappeared at the beginning of the war. Possibly he was one of these gentlemen who left never to return.

My theory on the Benton name comes from a stagecoach line co-owned by Senator Thomas Hart Benton (1782-1858), a Senator from Missouri for 30 years. He had large interests in the stagecoach line that ran on the Morgantown-Bridgeport Pike and crossed the river at Mundell's Ferry. Ferries at that time were privately owned. When the new road on the pike was put in from the tollgate to the river at what is now Benton's Ferry, Senator Benton's stagecoach line would have needed a new crossing on the river. Thomas Hart Benton was elected Senator from Missouri in 1815 and traveled quite a bit to and from Washington DC. He supported all legislation that aided settlers and western exploration. If Sen. Benton financed the building of the new ferry, as he did on the upper Monongahela River, the ferry could have easily have been named after him. Whatever the facts, a new ferry was established with a new wider wagon road leading towards the river. Benton Lane in Benton's Ferry was a part of this road.

Ferryman John W. Hull

In 1859, John Wesley Hull married Samuel Linn's daughter, Sarah Ann. Hull was born in Pennsylvania in 1837 and moved with his parents to Newport (Catawba) and then to Glady Creek with his parents. He was the son of Rev. John and Jane Hull, who were Methodists. After his marriage to Sarah, the couple resided on the river at Benton's Ferry for a while then moved to Parkersburg, WV. After a short time, they moved back to Benton's Ferry where the Hulls entered into a partnership with Hugh W. Linn, Sarah's brother, operating a general store and the ferry across the river.

Mr. Hull would ferry customers free of charge across the river to and from his store where they bought their supplies. After a number of years, J.W. Hull sold his interest in the business to Hugh Linn and moved back to Parkersburg but later returned to Benton's Ferry and then to Grafton, where he finished raising his family. Everywhere the Hulls lived they operated a retail store.

Ferryman Will Bishop

To overcome the inconvenience of moderately high water, ropes and later cables were stretched across the river and fastened to trees on either shore. This gave the ferryman a sure handhold to haul the ferry back and forth across the river, even in heavy fog. The ferry's course was at an angle towards the far shore. The Westside landing is still visible; nothing remains of the landing on the east side.

From "History of the Family of William Linn," May 11, 1881:
"Samuel Gideon Linn, son of John and Rachel (Powell) Linn, was born March 4, 1863. The Linn family owned a large farm in what is now White Hall. He was crossing the Tygart Valley River with his sister, Mollie, and little brother, Charlie. The ferryman, Will Bishop, was not using the oars as he usually did with the small skiff but instead was pulling by the rope used for the heavy-wagon boat. Gideon Linn got up to help the ferryman pull at the rope and in doing so, upset the boat— throwing them all in the water. Mollie climbed up on the upturned rowboat and helped her brother Charlie on it. The ferryman held the rope. These three were rescued, but Samuel Gideon, not being able to swim, drifted into the deep water and drowned. Although his body was quickly recovered, he could not be resuscitated. His death cast a great gloom over the entire community."

Ferryman B. F. Thomas

In 1900, B. F. Thomas operated Benton's Ferry across the Tygart. When a passenger was ready to cross the river, the passenger would ring a bell. On the return trip, the ferryman would ring another bell on the other side for the return trip. The late Ted Boyles, whose parents lived close to where the ferry was, related to me that one of the ferry bells is in the steeple of the Benton's Ferry United Methodist Church.

According to the 1807 Ferry Act, a penalty was imposed upon the ferryman if he did not reply to the bell in a reasonable amount of time; he had to forfeit the fare. This is the reason the ferrymen had to live on the landing. If for some reason, other than ice, high water or fog, the ferryman refused someone passage and the person filed a formal complaint, the ferryman had to pay the county $2.00 for that refusal. That meant keeping the ferry in excellent condition and accepting passage from anyone at all times. In those days, $2.00 was a huge fine one that few could afford.

The development of automobiles meant the building of better roads, and that brought the need for bridges. The building of the Benton's Ferry Bridge brought the demise of the ferry in 1918. The Super 8 Motel complex at the top of the hill off I-79 at Exit 133 has been appropriately named "The Landing." The sign reminds the community of the history of the airport and the ferry landings and gives visitors a hint of the historical background of the area.

GROWTH OF THE COMMUNITY

The following information came from the WV State Gazetteer *collection at the WV State Archives, in Charleston, WV. It depicts the growth of Benton's Ferry in the early days.*

With the arrival of the post office in 1853, an express agent was also established. The mail arrived by express cars attached to passenger trains. It was dispatched in the same manner. The express agent's job was to make sure the packages and freight got on and off the express cars safely and that it was delivered to the postmaster. Mail arrived daily. In 1918, Wells Fargo merged with six other companies to form the American Railway Express Company.

1882-83

In 1882, Benton's Ferry, with its population of 25, located four and one-half miles by rail from Fairmont. It was referred to as an unimportant town on the Baltimore & Ohio Railroad. There was a general store owned by Hugh R. Linn, who was also postmaster and railroad express agent. Postmasters' pay at this time was the money they made from selling stamps. Orlando Hayhurst owned a gristmill. Both were near the river and railroad.

```
BENTON'S FERRY.
Population, 500. On the B. & O.
R. R. and Tygart Valley river, in
Union township, Marion county, 4½
miles southwest of Fairmont, the judi-
cial seat and banking point. Tele-
phone connection. Exp., U. S. C. J.
Thomas, postmaster.
Blakemore John, barber.
Crow C D, sand.
Dunn Owen, shoemaker.
Ellifritt Mrs M L, boarding house.
Kenduck Frank, news agt.
Koch Mrs Elizabeth, laundry.
Lilley George, sand.
Malone Fred, news agt.
Rowland Wm, ice cream.
Thomas B F, ferryman and carpenter.
Thomas C J, Express and Railroad
    Agent.
Thomas C L, physician.
Thomas Chester, bicycles.
Thomas E C, genl store.
Vincent Josiah, carpenter.
Virginia & Pittsburgh Coal and Coke
    Co.
Watkins A E, carpenter.
```

← 1902-03

Rev. Isaac A. Barnes

1914-15

Benton's Ferry's population remained 500 for eleven years. The post office was closed. Mail came Rural Free Delivery (RFD) from Kingmont. The Railroad Express, post office and the general store had closed. The Baptist Church and Methodist Church, as well as Wells Fargo, Phillips Coal Company, Elizabeth Koch's laundry, and George Lilly's sand business were still in operation.

EARLY RESIDENTS OF BENTON'S FERRY

Samuel Linn was born in 1789 and lived on Glady Creek near Valley Falls, with his parents, William and Isabella Linn. He met and married Anzy Reese there. In 1822, they decided to move to down the Tygart Valley River to what is now called Benton's Ferry, where they raised their nine children in the log cabin Sam built. He died in 1852, the same year the B&O Railroad arrived in town. He is buried on the family farm. Anzy continued to live in the log home until her death in 1893 (see Cemeteries).

Today the well-preserved 167-year-old log home is used as a rental property. It is one of Marion County's historic treasures—a landmark in Benton's Ferry. It looks very much like it did in the 1800's.

Hugh R. Linn, son of Samuel and Anzy Linn, was born in 1840. Maria E. Thomas became his wife in 1862. She was the daughter of Richard and Hannah Thomas who owned property in the valley. The Linns had seven children and were members of the M.E. Church.

Near the railroad tracks and the train depot, Hugh and Maria opened a general store. Hugh Linn became the postmaster of Benton's Ferry in 1877 and remained so for 19 years.

Samuel Linn's log cabin built in 1836.

Aerial view of Benton's Ferry. November 1999

In 1889, Hugh Linn, who was a Republican, was elected Sheriff of Marion County while in office as postmaster. Four years later, he gave up the office in order to run for a second term as sheriff. He was re-elected. The Linns lived on the corner of Fairmont Avenue & Fifth Street in Fairmont when Hugh died in 1899. He is buried in the Sam Linn Cemetery at Benton's Ferry.

Rev. Isaac A. Barnes, fourth generation, was born in 1857. He was the grandson of Abraham Barnes. He married Margaret Linn, daughter of Robert and Rachel Linn of Benton's Ferry. A prominent Methodist Protestant minister, he helped establish the Benton's Ferry Methodist Church, as well as many others within Marion County. He was Superintendent of Schools for Union District, and he authored several books. He lived on Benton's Ferry road not far from the Benton's Ferry brick school, where he once taught. He died in 1944 and is buried in the Linn Cemetery.

Sanford B. Hall and his wife Jane settled on the Tygart Valley River not far from the ferry. He was a Justice of the Peace in 1851, and became the first postmaster of Benton's Ferry in 1853.

In 1861, Mr. Hall gave one-half acre of land for a "meeting house." A school and church combination was built and deeded to trustees Alexander McAllister, H. C. Morris and Robert Linn. The church became known as the Union Church (see Churches).

Alexander McAllister was the son of John and Jane (Work) McAllister. He was born in 1818 in Pennsylvania. He and his parents settled here in Grant District in 1839. They owned a large farm across the river from Benton's Ferry. At that time, their land was all timberland and had to be cleared. They made rafts of handhewn logs that were sent downriver to be sold for a princely price.

During the Civil War, the McAllisters hid their horses from raiding horse thieves in the hollow on Kettle Run. Everyday, someone of the family would go and feed them and sneak back home without being detected. The raiders never did find the horses. Alexander married Nancy Linn. They had 11 children. He was a Justice of the Peace from 1861 for two terms and was the first school commissioner in Grant District under the free school system. Alexander McAllister died in 1907 and is buried in the Linn Cemetery.

Other notable residents of Benton's Ferry were Robert Linn, a farmer and a sheriff of Marion County in 1888. Harold McDougal, a local missionary who, along with his wife, took his mission to other countries, and George R. Jefferson, a teaching school principal.

By the railroad tracks near the ferry stood a large brick building. It stood where Raleigh Mine and Industrial Supply is today. Here the post office, the train depot, apartments and a boarding house once stood. The locals simply called it "The Brick." After the opening of the Benton's Ferry Bridge in 1918 and the post office closure in 1920, activity and business began to decline. Today, only memory of this building remains.

Across the river on the camp road at the bottom of Vinegar Hill at the river's edge stands a beautiful log cabin known as *"The Log."* It can be traced through eleven different owners since the Civil War. Made of hand-hewned chestnut and ash, the cabin has walls 18 inches thick — built to last many years and sturdy enough to withstand the flood of 1888. During this flood the water got as high as its second floor. A nail on the wall marks the high water level and serves as a reminder just how forceful the river can be (see Log Cabins).

"The Log" located on the west bank of the river at Benton's Ferry which legend says was a station for the underground railroad. *Courtesy of Bob and Janene Hurst.*

BENTON'S FERRY BRIDGES

Old Benton's Ferry Bridge, built in 1918 and closed in 1989. It was torn down in 2001.

In 1918, 16 years after the construction of the Colfax Bridge, the residents of Benton's Ferry made getting across the river a priority. Crossing the river by ferry had become outdated although one could ford the river when the water depth was right. After convincing the State of the need, a new bridge was built. Contracted out, the two piers and two abutments were made from hand-cut local stone. Built by the Meredith Construction Company the narrow steel structure was designed only for wagons and light automobiles. The bridge was given a wooden floor (unaware that the future would bring large heavy trucks and incredibly increased traffic). In 1928, the Helmick Foundry in Fairmont and the B&O Railroad raised the bridge to create more clearance for locomotives under the bridge, which was 540 feet long. Located on the old Morgantown-Bridgeport Pike from Fairmont, it connected with US Route 250 in Grant District.

When I-79 was being constructed in 1965, twin bridges were built across the river. This project took several years to complete. The interstate highway from Middletown Mall at White Hall to East Grafton Road on the east side of Fairmont was opened to the public on June 4, 1968. At a special ceremony on November 2, 2002 the bridges were dedicated in honor of Paul Prunty (northbound bridge), a 22-year veteran of the House of

People and Places

Interstate 79 twin bridges across the Tygart Valley River was completed in 1968. Both were repaired in 1995. In March 2002, the West Virginia Legislature adopted the bill to name the bridges in honor of Delegate Paul Prunty and his brother, the late William Lee Prunty.

Representatives for Marion County, and his brother, the late William Lee Prunty (southbound bridge), a music instructor at Fairmont State College.

After a lot of persistence by Delegate Nick Fantasia of Kingmont, a new Kingmont-Benton's Ferry exchange was built by the state and opened December 4, 1989. The new exit off the Interstate made local business and homeowners more accessible. Four years after the opening of this exchange, the state declared the old Benton's Ferry Bridge unsafe. It was closed to all traffic, including pedestrians on March 16, 1989, effectively cutting off a portion of the community from fire and emergency service during high-water periods. Once again, the citizens of Benton's Ferry were in need of a bridge across the Tygart. Delegate Fantasia petitioned the West Virginia State Legislature for a new bridge. In March of 2000, the state highway department opened bids for the project. Upon This Rock Construction Company of Mercer, Pennsylvania submitted the low bid of $2,741,002. Brush-clearing operations began in June 2000. The bridge has a 520-foot long span made of pre-stressed concrete girders. It was completed and opened for traffic on Tuesday evening, December 11, 2001. The new bridge once again reunited the community and eased traffic on the I-79 Kingmont interchange. With the opening of the bridge, future development was expected to increase in the area.

A plaque installed on the bridge reads: "The Benton's Ferry Bridge In Honor of Nick Fantasia, 2001."

Left: The Benton's Ferry Bridge completed in 2001. Above Right: Construction of the new Benton's Ferry Bridge. June 2001

POST OFFICE

Benton's Ferry post office was established in 1853, one year after the coming of the railroad. The post office was one of Union District's earliest. Stamps cost one cent. They honored Benjamin Franklin on the stamp because he was our nation's first Postmaster General.

Postmasters

July 14, 1853	Sanford B. Hall
July 2, 1861	Post office discontinued
July 20, 1861	George M. Bishop
January 8, 1877	Hugh R. Linn
February 13, 1896	William M. Thomas
March 12, 1903	Columbus Thomas (also RR Express Agent)
August 4, 1904	Emma C. Thomas
August 5, 1908	James McClelland
February 9, 1911	Lillian B. Snyder

(In 1912 the Post Office was discontinued. Mail was received via Rural Free Delivery from Kingmont.) It was re-established:

September 10, 1917	Wade H. Curry
1919	I. L. Rider (also RR Express Agent)
February 14, 1920	Discontinued

After the post office closed, all mail was picked up at the Kingmont post office or delivered by rural route. In the 67 years that there were post offices in Benton's Ferry, the cost of postage stamps only increased one cent.

BENTON'S FERRY SCHOOLS

Before the Civil War in 1861, a "meeting house" was built on land donated by Sanford B. Hall. He said specifically that the land was to be used for a school and a church. The establishment of the free public school system was developed in 1864 and its new school system allowed for the establishment of a school fund, school commissioners and county superintendents in each of the districts.

In this same year, a one-room school was built on the southern end of the valley. This was School No. 1. It was located at the intersection of today's I-79 Kingmont exchange. Emma Griffith was the first teacher for the three-month term.

In 1902, the Board of Education bought a half-acre of land for $60 from Jacob and Elizabeth Work's large farm. The school was made of local brick and was built on the hillside overlooking the road that led to the ferry.

Designed for grades 1-8, it had two floors with two rooms on each and had beautiful hardwood floors. There was a playground in the back. Walter Balderson and Mary Linn Janes were two of the teachers who taught there.

After 57 years serving the community, the school was closed in 1960. Today elementary grades 1 through 6 attend Pleasant Valley

Benton's Ferry School as it looked in 2000. Opened in 1902 and closed in 1960.

Benton's Ferry School class of 1936.
Front row: Bennie Huffman, Charles Roderick, Kenneth Osburn, Junior Shaffer, Joseph Ashcraft, Bill Huffman and Benny Linn. Second row: Howard Linn, Elma May Watkins, Lee Linn, Eugene Osburn, Ralph Carpenter, Ramer Dale Watkins, Emmel Clelland, Herman Curtis, Helen Osburn and Joan Moore. Third row: Eloise Roderick, Evelena Osburn, Howard Tharp, Arthur Watkins, Don Clelland, Vanda Boyles, Janet Clelland, Paul Watkins, Joe Boyles, Allen Barnes and Lloyd Linn. *Courtesy of Missy Esultante.*

Elementary. The higher grades attend schools in Fairmont. Today the old abandoned school still stands on Schoolhouse Lane overlooking the traffic below, harboring many memories of days gone by. In the 1970's Joe Kovach of Kingmont purchased the property.

Vinegar Hill Road

The name "Vinegar Hill" has been around since the Civil War has been host to folk tales and legends for many years. Some of them still survive today. The road begins at the top of the hill on the west bank of the Tygart where it intersects with today's Coal Bank Road. It was used for local traffic and to transport apple cider vinegar in barrels for shipment. Several farmers in the area had apple orchards and made their living by them. The largest orchard around was the orchard at what is now called Apple Valley in White Hall where the golf course is today.

The slow natural process of converting apple juice into vinegar took one to two years. It was stored in wooden barrels with air holes at the top. When the vinegar was in the final stage horse and wagon took it to the Tygart River where it was ferried to markets downriver. It was also taken over to the Benton's Ferry train station where it was shipped by rail to area merchants.

On one such occasion, a couple of brothers, who made their living by making and selling cider vinegar, were transporting some of the vinegar down the hill towards the river. A barrel fell off the wagon and rolled down the hill leaving a trail of vinegar in its wake. The odor lingered in the air for quite some time. Neighbors began calling the hill Vinegar Hill and still do today.

In those days Vinegar Hill did not follow quite the exact same route as it does today. There was no sharp turn around the deep ravine. Instead the road went at an angle straight down towards the river. It would have been a very steep grade for a team of horses. Little wonder barrels of vinegar came rolling off wagons. The road today is no longer as it used to be. It now goes around the ravine and ends at "The Log."

West Virginia's Lower Tygart Valley River

WHITE HALL

The first settler who came to this area was John Tucker, Jr., who received a 400-acre land grant in 1771 and purchased an adjoining 1000 acres. Five years later his father, John Tucker, Sr., received a grant of 1000-acres which extended from the river to what is now Sapps Run next to Eldora.

In 1843, Samuel Nixon came and eventually owned 600 acres at the intersection of what is now State Route 73 and U.S. Route 250, mere wagon roads then. At that time, White Hall was solely farmland and had no name. In the mid 1800's, the closest communities were Boothsville, Watson or Benton's Ferry. The few residents who lived in the area which was to become White Hall got their mail at Benton's Ferry.

SCHOOLS

John Nixon, son of Samuel P., owned several hundred acres of land at the big intersection of what is now White Hall. The number of school age children in the area had increased greatly so he gave a plot of land for the purpose of a one-room subscription school. It was small and stood back among the oak trees across from where Middletown Mall is on Rt. 250. Very little is known about this school.

The first free school in the White Hall area was the Nixon School at Apple Valley. In 1867, two years after the Civil War, the school was built on land donated by Rev. Jesse F. Nixon (1816-1906), son of early pioneer Jonathon Nixon. It was the second school built in Grant District. Sarrietta School was the first and Boothsville School was the third. James T. Davis and sons, George and Marshall of Boothsville, built the Nixon School.

Rev. Jesse Nixon had nine children. His brother, John G. Nixon, had seven children and his cousin, Robert P. Nixon, had twelve. The school was composed mostly of Nixons. **Robert P. Nixon**, who was 65 years old at the time, was the first teacher. The second teacher was **Harmon Nixon**, son of Robert P. He later became a Baptist minister. **Charles B. Davis**, who helped build the school, was the third teacher. The fourth teacher was **Elias Nixon**, son of John G. Nixon who was a cattle dealer and shipped cattle to the eastern markets. The fifth teacher was **J. W. Faust**, a veteran of the Civil War and was a graduate of the state university. He was probably the best educated teacher the school had until later years. Other teachers of this school were: **Belle Hartley Burgreen, Miss Daddisman, Robert Smith, A. P. Harr, John Currens, John A. Russell and Miss Lillian Welt,** who was the last teacher at its closing in 1934. Students then attended the White Hall School.

In June 1886, John and Mary Tucker, Jr. sold three-quarters of an acre at the entrance of what is now Pine Lane on US Rt. 250 to the Board of Education (Deed Book 39/Page 512) for $41.00 for a new school. The one-room wooden building was known as School No. 8 in Grant District. Ben F. Mundell, Eliza Martin and T. J. Little were trustees. It served grades 1 through 8. On a 1923 topographical map, the well-established school was referred to as White Hall.

As the community grew, so did the school. It was divided into two rooms and had a hallway down the middle of the building. There was no water in this school so the students took turns carrying it from Scott Day's house next door. A potbelly stove in the middle of the room provided heat. The community of White Hall got its name from the white halls in this school.

In 1939, the school was closed because of the lack of students, who were being bused to Fleming School in Fairmont. Community growth during the ensuing twelve years increased the number of students to a point where White Hall itself merited a new elementary school.

In 1952, the BOE purchased one acre of land from T. M. and Florence Carpenter for the purpose of building a new community school. Construction began during that summer and the new building was completed in time for the beginning of the 1953 term. Originally the red brick school had four rooms which would accommodate six grades— three classrooms and a lunchroom. Each classroom had two classes in it. For the 2000-2001 school year, the Marion County Board of Education provided a new multi-purpose room, kitchen, and two new restrooms. Renovations enlarged the media center, created a special education classroom, and provided more space for the school offices.

Less than a mile from the river, White Hall is located in Grant District on U.S. Route 250 south. Its boundaries extend from the Taylor County line to Wood's Boat House.

People and Places

White Hall School Class of 1942. First row: Baxter Lakey, Gene Knight, Harriet Huffman, Patti Nixon, Frances Rutherford and brother Franklin. Front row: Christine Anderson, Joann Luzadder, Wanda Kuhn, Lucille Morgan, Marguerite Rutherford, Eugene Luzadder. Second row: Helen Huffman, Raeanna Anderson, Doris Reese, Meryle Collins, Dean Travelute, Davy Reese and Donnie Carpenter. Third row: Donnie Morris and Buddy Reese. Back: Lonnie Huffman. *Courtesy of Harriet (Huffman) Toothman*

    In the early 1930's, White Hall consisted of a store, a school, a Pentecostal church and not long after that, a coal tipple. The population was about six families.

    The Virginia and Pittsburgh Coal and Coke Company already had a coal mine at Kingmont. One of their mineshafts was in front of Curry's store on what is now Greenwood Drive off of Rt. 250. Many miners entered the mine at this point. This particular mineshaft was sold to Harry Huffman who operated it for awhile. Though now sealed off and boarded up, the mineshaft entrance still can be seen today.

    Mr. Huffman formed the H. B. Huffman Coal Company. He built a coal tipple on the old Rt. 250 not far from the mineshaft. It was located beside the fabric shop. His brothers, Blake and Bill worked for him, as did their sons, Junior, David, Lonnie and Eugene. Coal was also hauled in from other places to the tipple where several other men were employed.

    The Huffman mine was a slope mine in the hill behind their house and tipple. There's a cemetery on that same hill (see Cemeteries). According to Harriet Toothman, her siblings would go up there and have a look around. The land in that area had been badly undermined, leaving huge cracks in the ground. Occasionally, they could see the corner of a casket and when they did, they would all run home. A fright for anyone!

    In 1940, Huffman and his wife, Fern lived next door to the coal tipple where they owned a gas station and restaurant combined. It was called The Blue Ridge Lunch. Another roadside lunch stand was just next-door on the site of a filled-in pit, which had been created by removing the soil for the upgrading of Rt. 250 in 1939. Later the lunch stand was remodeled into a restaurant. It was called, "The Hi-Way Shoppe." Sally (Peterson) Hamilton lived nearby. She recalls how she worked as a carhop for $2.00 a night plus tips in 1962. The Fabric and Foam store now occupies this spot.

Class of 1938-39 at the old White Hall School. Teacher Viola Linn. Back row left to right. Doris Hudson, Evelyn Corbin, Eloise Reese, Robert Corbin, Jimmy Connor, Bill Nixon, Jimmy Tucker and Elmo Kemble. Middle row. Bobby Connor, Dorothy Little, Jack Nixon, Barbara Reese, Paul Connor, June Swekler, Faye June Lakey, Vivian Rutherford, and Glen Dunaway. Front row. Pauline Connor, Twila Rutherford, Doloris Smedley, Carl Lakey, Billy Reese, Joan Nixon, Dorothy Connor, Joe Courtney Anderson and Leroy Kemble. *Courtesy of Pat (Nixon) Connor.*

In the 1960's, the Hi-Way Shoppe was a restaurant owned and operated by Bernadine and Charles Swisher. *Courtesy of Sally (Peterson) Hamilton.*

Rare picture of the 1940's lunch stand at White Hall. Later it became the site of the Hi-Way Shoppes on U.S. 250. Very little information could be found about this early lunch stand. *Courtesy of Harriet (Huffman) Toothman.*

The Blue Ridge Lunch on Route 250 in 1940. It was owned and operated by the Huffman family who lived upstairs. *Courtesy of Harriet (Huffman) Toothman.*

CURRY'S STORE

In the early 1930's, Alfred "Alf" Curry owned and operated "Curry's General Store," located on the old Route 250, which is now Greenwood Drive. Alfred Curry was married to Elenora ("Nora") Nuzum; they had seven children; Lena, Wiley, Maude, Ellis, Charles Garland, Walter and Harold Dale. In his younger days, Alf was a blacksmith but he gave it up when cars replaced the carriages. Running the store was his primary occupation; he also raised white turkeys, which were in demand, particularly for Thanksgiving. The Curry home was just up the road from the store.

Harriet Toothman can remember going to the store during World War II when ration stamps were required to buy sugar, flour, and other items. Alf sold a little bit of everything including penny candy and bubble gum, stored in large glass jars. A potbelly stove stood in the center of the room. Loafers would come in everyday and sit on boxes around a table and play checkers.

Alf died at age 82 on March 18, 1953. His youngest child, Harold Dale, operated the store until he, too, died in 1973 when the store closed. About this same time, Ralph Steel opened Farmer Brown's Market at the intersection of Rt. 250 and Rt. 73. Later the name was changed to Gateway Market.

Curry's General Store in 1938. Owned and operated by Alf Curry. *Courtesy of Carl and Wilma (Curry) Johnson.*

Left: Mine shaft in front of Alf Curry's General Store, 1938. The children are unidentified. Right: Mine cars and track were used to carry coal from out of the Kingmont mine. *Photos courtesy of Carl and Wilma (Curry) Johnson*

FIVE-MILE HOUSE

A hot dog stand owned and operated by Ronald and Mary Nixon in 1922. Ronald was a descendant of one of White Hall's first settlers. *Courtesy of Pat (Nixon) Connor.*

John and Minerva Nixon owned several hundred acres next to the junction of Route 73 and Route 250. Their son, Ronald, and his wife Mary Nixon picked a site on the family farm to build a roadhouse in 1922. Nixon contracted Ben Ammons and his son to move an abandoned school building to the intersection of Rt. 73 and Rt. 250. The Nixon's began repairs and remodeled it on this site. They opened it as a hot dog stand in 1922 when business soon picked up. The kitchen was enlarged and a dining room and dance floor was added. As far as we know the Five Mile House was the first roadhouse in WV. Taking its name from the distance from Fairmont it became a well-known landmark. The Nixons added a dining room where they served hot meals. There was a dance floor for square dancing. Every Saturday night, Ronald Nixon played at the piano and Pete Rutherford played his fiddle for the dances, which were attended by people from all over. On weeknights patrons danced to the jukebox.

Sunday was a favorite day for folks to go out and eat. The roadhouse's Sunday special was Spring Chicken, Mashed Potatoes and Gravy, Homegrown Green Beans, Combination Salad, Homemade Bread, Coffee or Tea for just 50 cents. Homemade pie was extra.

The Five-Mile House received a set back in 1939 when underground mining cut off the natural well water supply. City water was not yet available so the Nixon's were forced to close. They reopened in 1947. Vandalism had all but destroyed the building so it had to be remodeled again. In 1949, the Nixons closed and left the business for good. Others reopened it but none of them was successful. In 1961, the building was sold to a wholesale glass outlet called "The Glass Barn."

The property was sold to the Crown American Corporation in 1969 to make way for Middletown Mall. At that time, the old place was carefully burned down, marking the end of an era at that intersection.

Pictured in front of the Five Mile House are William Nixon and Ronald Nixon, Jr., children of Ronald and Mary Nixon. *Courtesy of Pat (Nixon) Connor*

The Five-Mile House, one of the first roadhouses in WV, stood where Hardee's is today in Middletown Mall at the intersection of Rt. 250 and 73. Picture taken in the 1950's. *Courtesy of Eugene Sapp*

ROADS

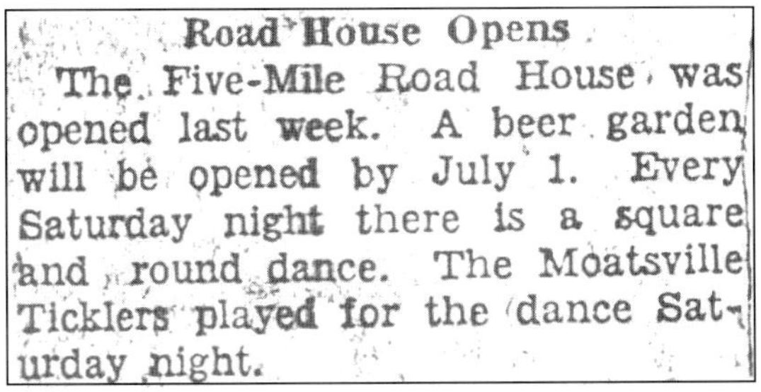

> **Road House Opens**
> The Five-Mile Road House was opened last week. A beer garden will be opened by July 1. Every Saturday night there is a square and round dance. The Moatsville Ticklers played for the dance Saturday night.

Above: *(Times West Virginian* **newspaper article) Exact year unknown. Below: 1939 Grand opening of the new improved Rt. 250 at White Hall. Note the pit where the fabric shop is today.** *Courtesy of Harriet (Huffman) Toothman*

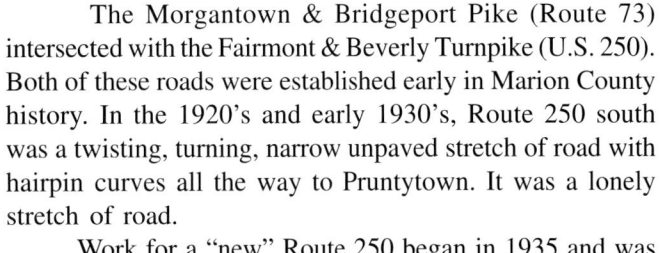

The Morgantown & Bridgeport Pike (Route 73) intersected with the Fairmont & Beverly Turnpike (U.S. 250). Both of these roads were established early in Marion County history. In the 1920's and early 1930's, Route 250 south was a twisting, turning, narrow unpaved stretch of road with hairpin curves all the way to Pruntytown. It was a lonely stretch of road.

Work for a "new" Route 250 began in 1935 and was finished in 1938. Under WPA supervision, curves were straightened and the road widened. It was paved with concrete seven inches thick. Upon its completion in 1938, many motorists attended its grand opening. Remnants of this road can still be seen in places today.

In the early 1960's the states of West Virginia and Pennsylvania agreed to build a new super highway. It became known as Interstate 79 (I-79). In 1962 the work finally began in Grant District taking portions of the Nixon farm.

After several years of work, the first section of I-79 in Marion County was officially opened on December 21, 1967. The section from where the Five Mile House once stood to McAlpin in Harrison County was finally ready for traffic. Six months after that, on June 4, 1968, another section from East Grafton Road joined it, and on October 15 of 1970, the section from East Grafton Road to Uffington in Monongalia County opened. Governor Arch Moore, Jr., was present at the ceremony marking the opening of this road, which was important to WV's growth and economy. The David Morgan Bridge crossing the Monongahela River in Fairmont was still under construction.

Rt. 250 in 1939 at White Hall. *Courtesy of Harriet (Huffman) Toothman*

MIDDLETOWN MALL

With I-79 in the development stages in 1969, the Crown American Corporation purchased 52 acres from Joe Morgan and Charles Curry in White Hall for a multi million dollar shopping mall complex. The name Middletown Mall was chosen in honor of the original name of Fairmont from early Marion County history.

In May 1969, a groundbreaking ceremony marked the beginning of construction. The huge shopping complex was projected to eventually house 25 stores and provide parking space for 1,865 cars. Within 16 months, the landscape was altered forever.

On August 19, 1970, the first store, W. T. Grant, opened. Congressman Robert H. Mollahan presided over the ribbon-cutting ceremony. Middletown was the first mall in the Morgantown-Clarksburg areas that was air-conditioned. It led the way with its new concept in retail shopping. Official opening of the mall was March 11, 1971. Soon afterward, the Tygart Valley Mall (Murphy's Mart and Foodland) across the road opened to make White Hall the major shopping district for the Tri-County area. It was to be only a matter of time till the other counties caught on.

Middletown Mall presently is owned by Middletown Investment, LLC, which is overseen by Steve Fansler, Jay Morgan and Richard Toothman. Future plans for the mall include expansion of the outside, which will give more space for indoor businesses, and more restaurants. The many additions to the mall has revitalized county shopping.

On December 8, 1992 the residents of White Hall voted at a special election to incorporate and form their own town. Some 85 per cent of the eligible voters showed up to cast their vote. The new town included Wal-Mart, Sam's Club and Mountain Gate as well as Middletown Mall.

The special election came about because White Hall feared annexation by the City of Fairmont. Several years before, C.W. Stickley, George Pigott, Andrew Hauge and Kenneth Brand had spearheaded a movement to incorporate. They had numerous meetings where possible incorporation was discussed. Businesses and residents alike agreed the effort would be challenging but they decided they would be better off if they formed their own town.

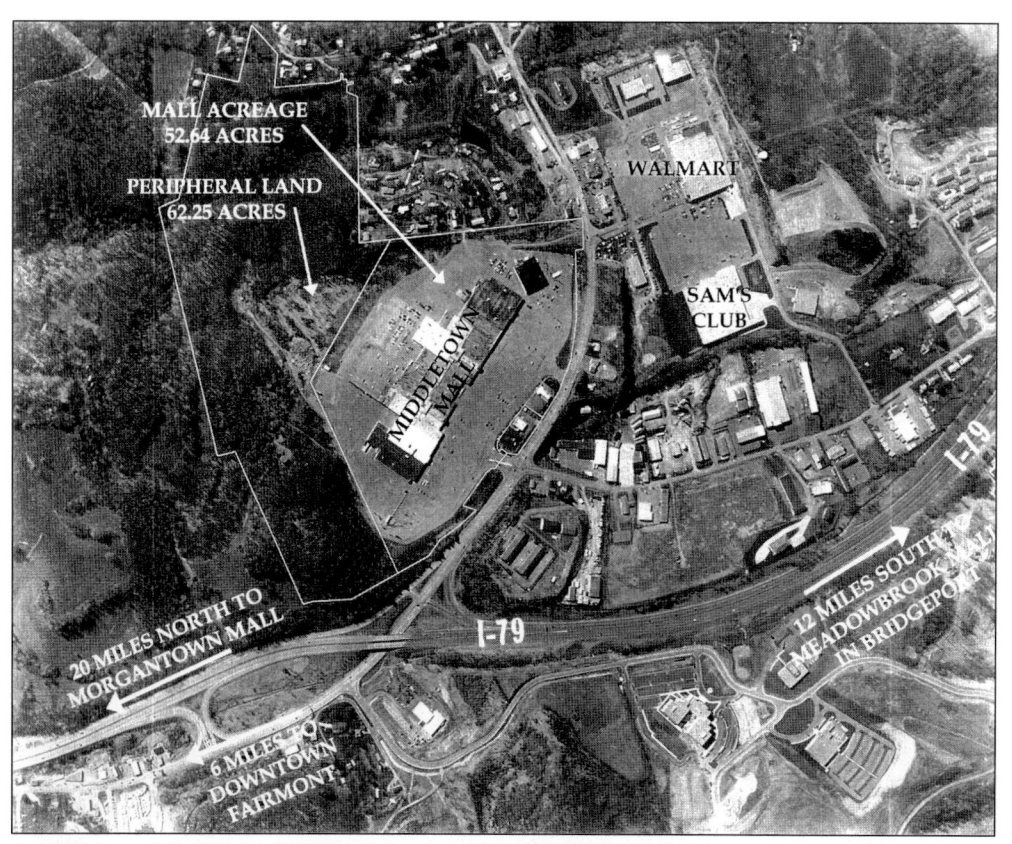

Residents elected William McIntire as the first mayor of White Hall. Sadly, he died three months later. His secretary, Sandra Early, completed McIntire's two-year term. His wife Norma later became a member of the White Hall Town Council. Jesse Corley currently is in his third term as Mayor. In 2002 population within the White Hall city limits was 595. Elections are held every two years on the second Tuesday in June.

Aerial view of the White Hall business district in 1995 before additions were added to Middletown Mall. *Courtesy of the Middletown Mall.*

COLFAX

The wilderness of Virginia was composed of hundreds of thousands of acres of virgin land and timber. When the white man arrived he had no thoughts for the Indians who owned all the land, nor did he care. He carried a "long stick" that, when aimed and fired, killed both man and beast. To him they were savages and an obstacle.

Indians are reported to have had many camps along the Tygart Valley River. They considered it to be their valley. Various types of artifacts have been found in gardens when plowed and along the banks of the river. Of all the Indian tribes our ancestors came into contact with, the Shawnees were the most bloodthirsty and terrible. They did not bother other tribes and wanted the other tribes to leave them alone. The wilderness beyond the Blue Ridge Mountains gave the red man a decent and humble way of life. Nothing changed until the white man arrived and began to settle the land. The British encouraged the Indians to attack the settlers, which helped to bring on the Revolutionary War.

Hostile Shawnees and Delawares traveled the north and south length of the Tygart Valley River. The path they followed along the river became known as the Great Catawba Indian Warpath Trail. It eventually led to the Mason-Dixon Line survey. In 1759, Captain Jacob Prickett owned a trading post called Prickett's Post. The Indians eventually drove him out. Eight years after that, Jacob settled there and organized a company of rangers. Prickett's Fort was built in 1774.

Highway road sign on Rt. 62 (Colfax Road).

In 1763, it was recorded that a fur trader named Richard Falls traded with the local Indians. Being a pioneer trapper-trader, he likely never lived here but he is believed to have been one of the first white men in what is now Colfax. A short distance upriver on what is known as Burnt Cabin Run, the Indians murdered Richard Falls.

According to Monongalia County Survey Book No. 3, in 1769 Frederick Ice acquired 400 acres of land in the valley where Colfax is now situated but he never lived on the property nor did he make any improvements. He was living on Booths Creek when the Indians killed him. One year later in 1770, the property was assigned to Joseph Davis. The Shawnees also killed him.

In 1776, Captain James Booth was killed on nearby Booths Creek and Nathaniel Cochran was taken captive but later escaped. Times were hard but the white man kept coming.

Downriver, below the Colfax Bridge, are two sets of riffles. In the second set there is a natural ford that crosses the river. The Indians, as well as the settlers, used it. According to Glenn Lough's book *Now & Long Ago*, 1969) late in the Fall of 1778, David Edwards had traveled to a trading post on the South Branch of the Potomac in Hampshire County. He traded his furs for salt and necessities to survive in the wilderness. On his return trip, he encountered Indians at the crossing. He was tomahawked and scalped to death.

Several months later on January 31, 1779 Stephen Morgan, youngest son of David, was traveling the same route. He made a note in his journal that he had found and buried Edward's body. He noted that by then the body had been half eaten by wolves.

The Edwards family, who had a patent to 400 acres of land in the Booths Creek area in Taylor County, built a small fort for protection after that incident. It became known as Fort Edwards and was a lookout post for Indians in the Lost Run area.

The settlers were determined to occupy the land in western Virginia despite the Indians. Between 1764-1774, "Tomahawk Rights," where settlers marked their claims by cutting their mark on trees for their boundaries were made. All of this was, however, with the observance of the Indians who felt this was their land. Frontiersmen and Indians alike respected "Tomahawk Rights." Those "rights" were later merged into land grants in 1779.

*JOHN SPRINGER

In 1798, John Springer and his family were the first to have a permanent settlement in the area now known as Colfax. The land was all forest but it offered good rich soil for growing crops and plenty of timber for fuel. John's sons, Job and Dennis, helped to clear the land and grow the crops.

The Springer family ancestry is important in the history of Colfax. Their lineage is found among the earliest of families who settled here and dates back to 1592 to Christopher Springer (1592-1669) of Lamstedt, Hanover,

Germany. He married Lady Beatia Hendrickson of Sweden. The children, then, were of royal blood. Of the five sons, three came to America: Lorentz, Charles Christopher and Jacob. Jacob settled in Fayette County, Pennsylvania. It is Jacob's line that we shall follow.

Jacob married Phoebe whose maiden name is unknown.

First Generation American born: Children of **Jacob Springer** were:

Benjamin (born 1706);
John (born 1708) and
Humphrey (born 1709).
Dennis, born 1712 in Wilmington, Delaware. Married Ann Prickett, Jacob Prickett's sister. They settled on Prickett's Creek near Prickett's Trading Post.
Phoebe (born 1714).
Dorothy (1715- 1785) was born in Wilmington, Delaware, married Jacob Prickett, also from Wilmington. In 1745, Jacob's father (John Prickett) had to post a bond of $500 for the marriage of his son to Dorothy because she was of royal lineage. They moved to Monongalia County about 1766.
Amos (born 1718).

Second Generation: Children of Dennis Springer were:

Josiah (born 1737).
Hannah (born 1739).
Zadoc (born 1742) who became a Captain in the Revolutionary War and was named commander at Prickett's Fort.
Levi (born 1744) built the "Levi Springer Homestead" located on US Route 40 near Uniontown, Pennsylvania. The home is on the National Register of Historic Places.
Druscilla (born 1745). In 1765, she married widower Zackwell Morgan, who was the founder of Morgantown, West Virginia and became sheriff of Monongalia County in 1783.
Dennis, Jr. (born 1748).
Jacob (born 1750) built a mill on Prickett's Creek about 1800.
Nathan (born 1752) married Hannah McDaniel.
Uriah (born 1754).
*__John (born 1756) married Bathsheba Merrifield in 1792,__ and
Job (born 1758).

John Springer was the tenth child, eighth son, and second-to-the-youngest, born to Dennis Springer and his wife Ann Prickett, who was a Quaker. John was born April 15, 1756 in Frederick County, Virginia where they were well established and lived not far from Morgan Morgan in Berkeley County. His father, Dennis, died when John was only four years old. His older brothers Zadock (18) and Levi (16) helped their mother Ann care for the younger siblings. His mother never remarried.

In the middle of the 1760's, the older Springer children, by then adults, staked claims to land in several western Pennsylvania counties, as well as part of western Virginia. When John came of age he came south to the Monongalia Valley to be on his own. He chose to be near his older sister, Drusilla, who had married Zackwell Morgan who, with his brother, David, surveyed a site for a town to be called Pleasantville, now Rivesville, in Marion County.

The earliest land record for John Springer in the Monongahela Valley is in 1773, when he was patented 400 acres in Monongalia County "in right of residence to include his improvement made on Salt Lick Creek, a branch of the Little Kennaway." John's brother, Jacob, also received land in the same area.

During the Revolutionary War, John volunteered as an infantryman. His brothers Nathan, Uriah and Jacob also volunteered in order to keep their land. John probably returned periodically to his settlement to make the required improvements, as others did during the war years.

By an act passed in 1777, the General Assembly provided "that all persons who or before June 24, 1778 has settled on the western waters should be allowed 400 acres for each family." The law also stipulated that through the payment of a consideration in money, the settler would be entitled to the pre-emption of additional land adjoining his tract not to exceed 1000 acres.

The land-entry book for Monongalia County shows that in 1778, John Springer (still single) received 400 acres on Little Creek and White Day Creek. He received an additional 1000 acres, again on Salt Lick Creek. John's brother, Dennis, also staked a claim in Monongalia County.

The Homestead Act of 1779 was amended to require a settler to live one full year on his claim or to raise a crop of corn. Undoubtedly, settlers still were looking over their shoulders for Indians even after peace was made at the close of Lord Dunmore's War in 1774. Even then life in the wilderness still was not safe from the Indians. It was 1791 before the settlers saw an end to the raids and killing of the whites in what is now Marion County.

SPRINGER'S BEND

By 1792, John Springer, 36 years old, owned several large tracts of land. He married 18-year-old Bathsheba (Bashy) Merrifield, who was eighteen years his junior. She was the daughter of Richard Merrifield and Phoebe Tucker. According to 1797 courthouse records, John owned land on Prickett's Creek adjoining land belonging to Samuel Merrifield, Bathsheba's uncle. That same year John sold 100 acres of land, on the west bank of the Monongahela River adjoining Joseph Batten's acreage, to Uriah Morgan. This was part of a larger tract that was patented in 1789. In 1798, after selling several parcels of land, John and Bathsheba bought 100 acres of land on the east side of the Tygart Valley River for $100. They brought their young family to the valley that, much later, became known as Colfax. Eventually, they would own almost the entire valley and land up Guyes Run.

John and Bathsheba had 11 children—the youngest being a year old at the time of John's death.

Third Generation children of John and Bathsheba Springer:

Job (1793-1874) was in the War of 1812. He married (1) Phoebe Nuzum in 1817 and (2) Rebecca (Johnson) Bartlett;
Nancy Ann (1795-1877) married Joseph L. Bunner;
Phoebe (1797-1859) married Richard (Black Dick) Nuzum;
Elizabeth (1800-1852) married Richard (White Dick) Nuzum;
 Both sisters married a Richard Nuzum and both sisters died on the same day, March 8, but different years).
Dennis (1802-1884) married Jane Harris;
Hannah (born 1804) married David Staats;
Drusilla (born 1807) married Henry Irons;
Bathsheba (1809-1841) married John Bunner;
Alpheus (1812-1894) married Mary Griffith;
Roanna (born 1815) married Oliver P. Morgan.

Fourth Generation:
The children of **Job** and **Phoebe** (Nuzum) Springer; First wife.

Paulina (born 1818) died in infancy.
Lucinda (born 1819) died in infancy.
Malinda (born 1821) married John Norris.

Children of **Job** and second wife **Rebecca** (Johnson) Barlett Springer: Second wife.

Ruhama (1823-1899) married Zadoc Nuzum;
John J. (1825-1855) married (1) Ruth Nuzum, (2) Rebecca Dodd and (3) Margaret Johnson;
Jane (1828-1902) married James Nuzum;
Swedon (1831-1876) married Lucinda Thomas;
Hannah (born 1833) married Manassah McGee and
Reason T. (1838-1869) married Sarah Thomas. They are buried in the Colfax Cemetery.

Fourth Generation:
Children of **Dennis** and **Jane** Springer:

Zadock (born 1828) died in infancy.
Levi Cornelius (born 1830).
Sylvanus H. (1832-1907) married (1) Lucinda Ross and (2) Mrs. Anna Christen. Sylvanus was elected county commissioner for Marion County in 1882.
Hannah (b. 1835) married (1) Edward Vincent and (2) John Sanders;
Bashaba (1837-1844);
John (1839-1923);
Zacheus (1842-1915) married Christina McKenny. He was a Civil War veteran and is buried in the Colfax Cemetery.
Richard (1845-1913) married Jemima Garlow. They are buried in the Colfax Cemetery.
James (born 1847) married Elizabeth Barker;
Edith (born 1849) married John Harr (she was his second wife).
Eliza (born 1853-1913) married Luther Haymond McKinney.

All of those surnamed Springer settled in the area where each contributed to the growth of the communities along the river. Brothers Job and Dennis appear on many older deeds throughout the Colfax community.

Due to the lay of the river, the area that the Springer family called home became known as Springer's Bend. It was an unofficial name but remained that way until it was officially called Texas. Today the curve in the river is still referred to by the old timers as "Springer's Bend."

John Springer died on December 24, 1816 one year after the birth of his youngest child. He died at the age of 60, which was considered old in those times. His will was written the day before his death. Recorded in the Monongalia County courthouse, Will Book 1, Page 265, it reads exactly as it was written:

"In the name of God, Amen, I, John Springer of the County of Monongalia and the state of Virginia and being weak of body but sound of mind and perfect of memory and mind blessed be the almighty God for the same do make and publish this my last will and testament in manner and form following. To witness: First I bequeath to my son Job a piece of land which I purchased of John Bonner (Bunner) containing 100 acres bounded as follows: Adjoining my own old tract on Youghiogheny River on (the) Youghiogheny's north side adjoining lands of William Rice Senior on (the) Youghiogheny's east side also adjoining land of the widow Vincent on (the) Youghiogheny's east side adjoining land of Casper Bonner (Bunner) on Youghiogheny side of said river also another piece of my own tract being at my own corner of s'd River adjoining the said hundred acres and running on a straight line unto the northwest corner of my large meadow then along Youghiogheny meadow fence two rods within Youghiogheny's same to the great road thence along said road easterly to a large white oak called Youghiogheny two mile tree thence a southeast line to bring parallel to Vandergrift's corner thence to said corner a straight line and along the same to Henry Barns line less the said two pieces of land I allow Job to have. I also request that my old farm be cultivated to support the children in common until my youngest son Alpheus becomes of age then that remaining part of my farm be divided agreeable according to quantity and quality the one part for my son Dennis, the other part for my son Alpheus the both agreeing among themselves mutually or to cast lots for choice. Also that Job, Dennis and Alpheus agree amonst themselves to pay each of their sisters, then living, the sum of fifty dollars in common, good trade, at the time of their marriage or as soon as practicable, after I also request that my beloved wife, Basheba, for her support in victuals and decent clothes from my three sons during her natural life time. I also request that Gardner F. Leonard and my son, Job, be executors of this last will and testament."

Signed December 23, 1816 Witness-Horatio Morgan, Willis Lawler and Phillip Patterson.
Presented January 1817.

Basheba Merrifield Springer outlived her husband by 40 years, dying on June 4, 1859. She lived to see the railroad completed and her village named Texas. She was buried next to her husband, John, on their property beside the river. John's grave marked the beginning of the Springer graveyard (except for some Indians who are reported to have been buried there), which is known today as the Colfax Cemetery. According to family history their graves are marked with fieldstones in the back with no identification.

TEXAS

No one knows for sure when Springer's Bend was officially named Texas. No official records could be found. It was called Texas during the Civil War. There are two theories as to how the community got the name. One of them is this:

Springer's Bend was underdeveloped. Growth was slow and neighbors were still few and far between. The various branches of the Springer family, which was quite large, had settled in other communities and states. They kept in touch and would visit from time to time.

When the Mexican War was fought, in what is now the state of Texas, to win independence from Mexico, several members of the Springer family volunteered for service. Thomas Jonathon (Stonewall) Jackson from Harrison County also served in this war. After the war was won and Texas became a state, the Springer family may have thought it fitting to name their unnamed community for it since the family had personal knowledge of its struggle.

The second theory is believed by some to have been brought about when a mistake was made printing tickets for passage on the B&O Railroad. For some reason, tickets for a place called Texas were used for our stop on the Tygart Valley River. Since there was no objection from the small village (where there was only one store and one post office), the name stuck. Whichever theory is right, the railroad was finished in 1852 and the little station was built much, much later. In view of the fact that Texas was already named by the time the railroad arrived, the second theory is eliminated.

In the 1850 census of Marion County, Bathsheba Springer can be found living with her eldest son, Job, and his family in Union District. To make way for the railroad, Job Springer's house had to be torn down. The B&O gave him the money to build a new house. Job built it from homemade bricks from a clay deposit found on his property. Today that land encompasses the whole valley of Colfax. A large pine tree grew at the site of the house on the present day Genevieve Barnes' property for many years before it was cut down. The family's fresh-water well was filled in when city water arrived in the community in 1956.

Job and Dennis Springer remained in the area all their natural lives. As their families grew, the land began to change hands but not necessarily out of the family at the time.

Land along the river was being developed and that meant new neighbors. Some of the other families who lived nearby were the Nuzums at Nuzum's Mill; Elzy Dodd; Richard Thomas; P. S. Gallahue, who lived up on the hill from Mundell's Ferry and William Powell at the Levels. Thomas Little Sr. and Mathew Fleming lived on the west side of the river, and Charles Irons and Jacob Shriver lived upriver.

COLFAX

In 1875, the postal authorities in Washington informed the postmaster, Abraham A. Howell, that the State of West Virginia had two communities named Texas, which had created predictable confusion in sorting the mail. A mandatory name change came when the post office of Texas (Colfax) reopened. Marion County voter registration in that year indicates the village of Texas was largely Democratic. It is curious that when it came time to rename the village it was named after a Republican.

Schuyler Colfax was the first Vice President of the United States under Ulysses S. Grant (1869-1873). Colfax was born in 1823 in New York State but during his boyhood, his family moved to Indiana. As a young man, he became a journalist. He later edited a newspaper. Schuyler was a Whig who helped to form the Indiana Republican Party. In 1855-69, he served in the House of Representatives as Speaker of the House. In 1869, he became the first journalist to become a Vice President of the United States.

During his term, Schuyler Colfax was involved in the "Credit Mobilier Scandal." An investigation revealed that many government officials accepted bribes from the Union-Pacific Railroad in exchange for favors. Colfax was accused of accepting 20 shares of stock plus a substantial sum in dividends. Fortunately, he had many powerful friends in Congress and he escaped censure and impeachment in view of the fact that his alleged misconduct occurred before his election to the vice presidency. Congress allowed him to retire quietly; however, it marked the end of his public and political career. He died in Mankato, Minnesota on January 13, 1885.

The community's name is one of ten Colfaxes scattered across the United States. It is an unusual name but it is dear to the hearts of us residents.

References from *West Virginia Gazetteer*

1882-83

COLFAX, also known as Texas Station, on the Baltimore & Ohio Railroad. 84 miles from Wheeling, W.Va. in the southeastern part of Marion County, is 7.7 miles southeast of Fairmont. It contains one Baptist Church, one public school, and a steam sawmill. Grain, lumber, railroad ties, bark are shipped. Population, 60. Daily mail. Charles Madeira, Postmaster, also runs the general store. John Harris is Justice of the Peace. S. Myers, railroad and express agent.

1891-92

COLFAX. Also known as Texas Station. 7.7 miles southeast of Fairmont, WV. the county seat. Population 50. William F. Springer, Postmaster. Ezra Cordray, saw mill; Ed Fleming, saw mill; William Hawkins, shoemaker; William Hawkins & Bro., general store; W. R. Jasper, general store; Robert Knight, blacksmith; and Z. Nuzum & Son, general store.

1904-05

COLFAX. Population, 80. Known as Texas Station on the B&O RR 4 miles southeast of Fairmont. William H. Hawkins, Postmaster; Colfax Brick Company; Colfax Red Brick Works, T. B. Williams, Proprietor; Harry Faber, mechanical engineer; John Fleming, sawmill owner; E. L. Hawkins Dairy; William H. Hawkins, general store; Joseph Irons, blacksmith; Willis Irons, teacher; Martin A. Keener & Bros., general store owners; Rev. J. J. Phillips, Methodist Protestant Church; Hattie Satterfield, dressmaker; Joshua Shaw, Justice of the Peace.

1914-15

Population 120. Has two churches, Methodist Episcopal & Methodist Protestant. One school. Railroad telephone connection (L.E. Fortney), W.H. Hawkins, Postmaster. Daily mail. Colfax Brick Company. W. H. Hawkins, general store; W. R. & R. H. Satterfield Dairy; Charles L. Shorter, telegraph agent; George Thomas, feed; Ida Clinton, dressmaker; Hattie Satterfield, dressmaker; Harry Faber, mechanical engineer; John Fleming, sawmill; William H. Hawkins, general store owner; G. A. Johnson, general store; E. L. Hawkins Dairy; C. L. Shorter, telegraph agent; Rev. J. J. Phillips, Methodist Protestant Church; Robert Knight, blacksmith, and Joshua Shaw, Justice of the Peace.

LOGGING

Mother Nature blessed our state with a wealth of beautiful trees. With the arrival of our pioneers, standing timber was a resource that meant survival. Logging up and down this valley began when landowners started clear-cutting the forests, making way for cornfields and pasture. Our resourceful forefathers utilized the assets at hand. With the river at their back door, it was easy to transport the one commodity that was abundant, *timber*. After a log cabin, a split rail fence and a barn, logs were cut for a profit in order to make a living. If the settlement was only partly cleared, the winter months were spent felling trees.

Hauling the timber to the river required an excellent team of horses. Thomas Little, Sr. An experienced driver with a six-horse team could make a decent living. Some even used oxen. After the logs were cut, they were dragged to the river. Here they were tied together into rafts and floated to market on high water from spring rains. Sawmills were located all along the river. It did not take long for the owners to realize that there were too many logs for the mills.

Unidentified man on logs backed-up behind a log boom on the Tygart Valley River. Date unknown. *Courtesy of JoAnn Lough*

A logging saw mill on the Tygart Valley River near Nuzum's Mill during the late 1800's. *Courtesy of FSC Folk Life Collection, Donated by Buddy Myers.*

Rafts were made for a one-way trip only. Their size and length were determined by knowledge of the river depth and the bends in the river. Usually a raft was 15 logs or more wide and 50 or more feet long. When they were sold upon reaching their destination they were then dismantled.

The virgin timber was in abundance and most of it was of superior quality. In 1870, Job and Dennis Springer had a sawmill on the river in what is now Colfax. The sawmill was called Timberland, where railroad ties were made for the railroad. The river landing to put the logs in the river was in a low area behind the old feed mill, which was located near the river beside the railroad tracks.

Behind the mill, just above the riffles, a log boom was stretched across the river from shore to shore to hold back the logs. During low-water level, the logs were gathered to await the hazardous job of being made into rafts. They could not be safely transported downstream during low water because of the large rocks in the riffles. By 1900 there were three sawmills operating in Colfax.

A rudder was built onto the back of the raft to help guide it around rocks and bends. When high water arrived, the rafts were let loose and manned with at least two men. Rafters had to be very skilled because it was a dangerous job. The rafts were sent downriver to be sold in developing towns and at sawmills along the Monongahela River. Some went as far as Pittsburgh, Pennsylvania where the price for timber was much higher than it was locally.

After the log rafts were sold, the raft operators would then walk or obtain a horse for the return trip home. They were paid $25.00 per raft if they were delivered safely. After the arrival of the railroad in 1852, the shipping of logs was much easier. Rafting soon died out but logging continued. Tan bark from a local tannery; coffin oak, cross ties for the railroad and locally made furniture were among some of the by-products of the timber that was shipped by rail.

By the 1860's, steam-powered sawmills were in operation along the Tygart and there were quite a few sawmills in the area. Growing towns created a demand for more and more lumber. Forest management was non-existent; therefore, by 1889 the virgin forests of hardwoods and pines had diminished. The log industry had exhausted itself on the river.

MUNDELL'S FERRY
(Colfax)

The Pettijohn brothers, William and John, are believed to have had the first ferry in the bend of the river in the early 1800's. In 1844, according to courthouse records (Deed Book 1/ Page 447), William J. Gallahue, because of debts, sold his ferry business here to John Gallahue. Exactly when or if the business was ever sold to Bailey Mundell is not known. It is possible he may have only leased the business.

William Bailey Mundell (1823-1899) is known to have operated the ferry across the river near Springer's Bend for many years. He was the last such operator there. Used daily, it was a regular link for the stagecoach line on the original Morgantown/Bridgeport Pike before the road was rerouted toward Benton's Ferry. The pike went under the railroad tracks and through a trestle to a sandbar on the river's edge. The ferry crossed the river at an angle, using a cable from shore to shore. On dry days, the shallow river could be forded. Rain would make it rise very quickly.

In Colfax (Texas), when high water prevented fording the river, folks took the small road (Antioch Road) to Mundell's Ferry to cross to the other side. It was either a flat raft-type ferry and/or a boat. The narrow road, was only wide enough for one wagon, lead to Antioch railroad platform. It is believed to have been an old Indian trail that hugged the bank in the curve above where the railroad is. It was still in use in the 1930's although the Colfax bridge was built in 1901. It was frequently traveled before the Colfax bridge was completed in 1902 and afterwards especially if one wanted to go to the Pleasant Valley. Later, a landslide on the Antioch road stopped all traffic, the road was abandoned. The new property owner, Mike Heston, repaired the old wagon road but it's for private use only. It leaves many of us with a good feeling that a bit of local history has been renewed.

Ferryman William Bailey Mundell was born in 1823. He married Joanna Vincent. They had one child, Benjamin, who later became a teacher in Grant District. The Mundells lived on the west side of the river where Bailey made his living as a cabinetmaker and ferryman.

The Little Family History provides a story about how Bailey Mundell delivered a table to Amos and Juliann Little, who lived near the pond on what later would become the Edd Barnes' property on route 250. The usual custom in those days was for the manufacturer to leave table legs quite long. The customer was expected to cut them off to the length that suited them.

On this particular day after having set her new table with food, Juliann called the family in for the evening meal. Having a sense of humor, she said, "Come to supper, boys, if you think you can chin Bailey."

They were surprised to find they had to eat standing up at the long-legged table, which came up to their chins. After the meal, the legs were cut down to the proper length.

Bailey Mundell died in 1899, three years before the bridge was built across the river at Colfax. He lived to see Springer's Bend develop into a community named *Texas* and still later to *Colfax*. He and his wife are buried in the Vincent Cemetery on Vinegar Hill. All that is left of the ferry days are the narrow roads which lead to it on both sides of the river and the old original ferry lantern which continues to overlook the river on the west bank.

In 1995, the year the postal authorities asked local residents to name unnamed roads or lanes for rural route purposes, west bank residents asked that the old ferry landing road, which went to the Colfax road, be officially named Mundell's Ferry Road. Considering the history of the area, this one is rightly named.

COLFAX BRIDGE

During the 1800's, the people who lived in Colfax were stranded during high water. There was no way to cross the river unless they went to Mundell's Ferry by way of the Antioch Road which followed an old Indian path down river to the ferry. There was a ford in the second set of riffles in the bend of the river. It could be very dangerous since there is a notorious whirlpool just below this set of riffles. During the logging era, horse teams hauling logs could not get them to the railroad for shipment. The only other mode of crossing was by boat. Most people living along the river had one.

He was William Ezra Cordray (1846-1913), a timber man who once had interests in the local logging operations during the 1870's. He became a county commissioner and a Justice of the Peace for Marion County and had first-hand knowledge about the community's need for a bridge across the river. When contacted by his two friends about a bridge, he used his influence with the right people to begin negotiations.

After the bridge was approved, the state purchased land from Edgar Fleming who owned property from Mundell's Ferry Road to the river. A road was cut on the side of a cliff for a new approach to the bridge. It was treacherous work. The bridge was completed before the road was finished.

The county court awarded William B. Ice, a local well-known stonemason, the contract to construct the two abutments and two piers. The hand cut stone was quarried up the hill from the bridge in Grant District near today's Jungle wood housing development. Italians and a few local men were hired to transport the huge hand-cut stones down the hill by horse and wagon.

Construction of the bridge began in 1901. The contract was awarded to the Canton Bridge Builders Company from Canton, Ohio. The steel frame bridge was 15 feet wide and 375 feet long. The triple-span structure

Unidentified Colfax residents dedicate the town's new bridge, built by the Canton Bridge Company, Canton, Ohio in 1902.
Courtesy of Mark Thorne; reproduced by Warner Studio.

Colfax Bridge after it was completed in 1902. Colfax M.P. Church and the first school are circled in the background. *Courtesy of the Hamilton Collection.*

consisted of one pony truss 75 feet in length and two pratt trusses 150 feet long each. The total length of the finished bridge was 450 feet. The floor was made of wooden planks that had to be replaced quite regularly. It was the first bridge to cross the Tygart Valley River in Marion County.

Edgar Fleming died November 11, 1900. Valentine Nichols died June 9, 1901, thirteen months before it was opened to the public. Neither man lived to see the bridge open but their perseverance gave Colfax a jump-start into the new century.

During the winter of 1918, the abutments for the bridge had their first real test. Freezing weather created an ice jam before the outdoor temperature rose and it began to rain. The jam broke apart and came thundering downriver over the banks into people's yards. The ice stayed there until late spring. On the riverbanks, ice was piled up 48 feet high in some places.

In 1900, two local men decided it was time for Colfax to progress with the times. Edgar Fleming (1837-1900) and Valentine Nichols (1826-1901) lived on the west side of the river. Their church was on the east side. Both men saw the need for a bridge across the Tygart. They had a mutual, influential friend from Colfax who was in the county government.

Wood planks were still used in the 1950's. Many can still remember the big wide gaps in the floor, which provided a view of the river below. In the late 1960's, the floor was replaced with wooden 2x4's laid side by side to create a thicker, more lasting floor and the abutment on the eastern shore was reinforced with steel beams.

In the bridge's last few years, overhead clearance bars were added to restrict tall vehicles from crossing. There was a weight limit of three tons maximum, and a speed limit of 30 miles per hour. The bridge closed September 28, 1993 at 5:00 p.m. John Hayhurst, a Colfax resident, drove the last vehicle across before barriers were put up. The bridge was built to last and so it did. For 91 years.

THE BACKBONE OF OUR TOWN

In 1902 our old bridge was built,
By men seeking a bright tomorrow.
For many years it served us well,
Humans, horses, and cargo.

As the years passed by we took her for granted,
Our beautiful Tygart and structure.
But time has a way of turning new into old,
Overlooking all of the fractures.

Now a legend etched in the past,
It's history is in our keep.
We shall never forget her,
As into a new century we leap.

Now we think of those years gone by,
For now a new bridge has taken its place.
No more worry of sagging from the weight,
91 years of growing old with grace.

I'll never forget the first old bridge,
As the piers came tumbling down.
That she was a landmark,
The backbone of our town.

C. Fortney-Hamilton 1993

People and Places

THE 'NEW' COLFAX BRIDGE

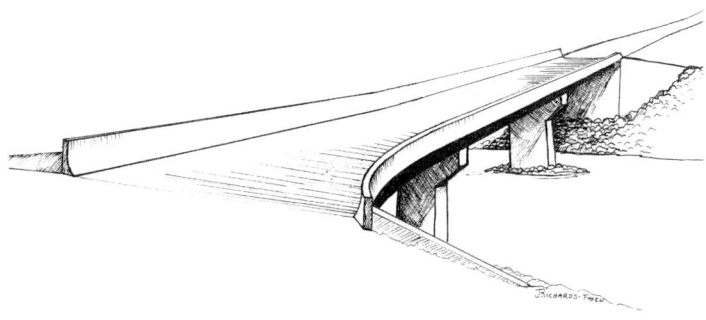

**Right: Illustration of the old bridge by James Fleming. 1993
Below: Illustration of the new bridge by Jackie Richards. 1993**

On May 7, 1985 a public meeting was held at the Colfax Elementary School especially for community residents. Thirty-three people attended to hear a representative from the West Virginia Department of Transportation present four plans for a new bridge. The residents were to make a first and second choice for the bridge site. Although it was never clear how this meeting came about, it was thought Martinka Mine, then in full operation, might have played a major role in it. It was in the company's best interest that the bridge in Colfax be replaced.

Seven years and five months later, a site had been selected and property purchased so construction could begin October 26, 1992. The bridge contract had been awarded to Orders Construction Company of St. Albans, WV. Soon the friendly workers arrived with equipment necessary to remove trees. The men adopted "Rose Bud," a dog belonging to resident Jerry Kinty, as their mascot. Rose Bud was always welcomed amid the activity.

Traffic on the existing bridge was maintained during the construction of the newer one. On November 2, 1992 earth-moving equipment arrived. By the end of that month the foundation for the first abutment on the west side of the river had begun. A land bridge for equipment was created halfway across the river.

A small building was brought in and put beside Thorne's old store building. It had a water tank inside and a heater that was used to test samples of cement for hardness and stability.

On December 9, demolition of the old mill, which had belonged to Ila Fortney, began. David Nuzum from Levels razed the building in exchange for the lumber. Due to the inclement weather, deer season and the Christmas holidays, all bridge-building activity halted until the beginning of 1993.

During this slow period on December 21 the telephone company came to cut down a telephone pole behind the old mill. Rose Bud was wandering around as usual and got in the way of the falling pole. Her death saddened everyone.

During the early months of 1993, construction continued when weather and high water allowed. When the weather finally broke serious work got underway.

The new Colfax Bridge, downstream from the old one, was opened to traffic on Tuesday, September 28, 1993 at 5:00 P.M. It is 450 ft. long, 30 feet wide and has a slight curve on the west bank.

The bridge is designed to withstand flooding conditions, as the waterway opening is greater than it was for the old bridge. Rex Dotts, a Colfax resident, was the first person to drive across the new bridge.

Local residents commended the Orders Construction Company crew for their fine manners and workmanship while in the community. Those workers were: Superintendent John Robinson, Foreman Rick Nickols, and laborers Windal, Rob and Douglas Stalnaker, Mike Thomas, Jessy (Chuck) Blankenship, John Long, Fred Belkeep, Jim Vance, Paul Legg, Lane Bowyer, James Mouse) Lusher, Allen Smith, Dave Mitchell, Bill Wallas and crane operator James C. Dalton.

Large equipment moved in for the construction of the Colfax Bridge. November 1992.
Courtesy of Orders Construction Company.

Federal funding for the new bridge was $1,375,968 while state funding was $344,242. Right-of-way costs came to $89,000. Total cost was $1,479,000. Once again Colfax celebrated a new bridge.

The Colfax Community Association sponsored a Bridge Dedication Day on Saturday, December 18, 1993 at 2 p.m. Charles Reese, a local resident and President of Fairmont's Chamber of Commerce, was the Master of Ceremonies. Harry Carr, District Engineer for the WV Department of Highways, gave the dedication address. Colfax Elementary School students presented a short musical program under the direction of teachers Chris Lavorata, Joetta Fisher and Lois Branson.

Above: A crane in the middle of the river placing the heavy steel beams. June 1993. *Courtesy of Orders Construction Company.* **Left: Colfax's old mill, demolished in December of 1992 to make way for the new bridge.**
Courtesy of Ila Fortney.

People and Places

Construction continued when weather allowed. March 1993. *Courtesy of Orders Construction Company.*

Man-made land bridge was constructed in the river allowing heavy machinery to access pier construction. March 1993. *Courtesy of Orders Construction Company, St. Albans, WV.*

Construction and Dedication December 18, 1993

Above: Old and new bridges. July 1993. Shortly after this picture was taken the old bridge was razed. *Courtesy of Orders Construction Company* **Left: December 18, 1993 ribbon cutting ceremony at Bridge Dedication Day.** Left to right: **Delegates Nick Fantasia and Roman Prezioso, Sen. Joe Manchin, Del. Cody Starcher, Marion County Commissioners Jack May and James Sago, WVDOH Harry Carr, Robert Orders, and Colfax resident Charles Reese, Master of Ceremonies.**

Right: Students from Colfax Elementary School performing at the December 18th bridge dedication under the direction of teacher Chris Lavoreta, 1993.

COLFAX POST OFFICE

In 1804, the very first place that mail was left for an individual was at the Pettyjohn Trading Post on the east side of the Tygart Valley River where it meets the West Fork. The postage rate was 25 cents per letter. The mail arrived by boat coming up the Monongahela River. Unlike today's system where the writer pays the postage, at that time the receiver (if they could find him), had to pay for the letter before it was handed over. It was not in an envelope nor did it have a stamp. That rate was an extravagant price for that era, but mail was handled many times and took months before it got to its destination. The volume of mail in those days was miniscule because very few people could read or write. Mail was usually for the upper classes.

As early as 1820, there was a post office at Polsley's Mill in Palatine (East Fairmont). Jacob Polsley was the postmaster. When the Morgantown-Bridgeport Pike was completed in 1837, by way of Mundell's Ferry, Colonel J. J. Johnson ran a tri-weekly stagecoach through Palatine. A horse and rider would meet the stagecoach at the ferry and bring the mail back to Springer's Bend. The rider would also meet the stage on the return trip. Letters were simply folded and stuck together with sealing wax and marked with current rates of "three cents." Stamps did not come into use until 1847 and when they did, the income from them was the postmaster's sole pay.

According to Earl Core's *Monongalia Story I*, by 1822 six post offices existed in Monongalia County. They were in Morgantown, White Day, Knottsville (a swamp settlement), Polsley's Mill (East Fairmont), Barnes Mill (now Bellview) and Kings Ferry (which was upriver from Colfax at that time). The postmaster of Kings Ferry was Job Springer. David Barker later replaced him.

With no television, newspapers, radios or telephones, mail was the main connection to the outside world. Each day news from town and the outside world was passed on by word of mouth with the arrival of the mail.

With the completion of the Baltimore & Ohio Railroad in 1852, community life, as everyone knew it then, was changed forever. However, mail was not delivered by rail until 1862. Train delivery was a major improvement in speed and reliability—a revolutionary change for the postal system. The village of Colfax was born from this change.

On April 29, 1863, during the Civil War, the B&O railroad bridge crossing the Monongahela River in Fairmont was destroyed in the Jones Raid (see Civil War Stories). Of course, train delivery of the mail came to a stop and did not resume until the bridge was rebuilt within two years.

With the arrival of faster engines and more modern techniques of distribution, postmasters along the railroad were required to hang the mailbag on a special hanger by the tracks, where it would be suspended in the air until the mail train came along to pick it up. Devices called *catching arms* were attached to the mail car. The train could then pick-up mail sacks from small towns as the train went speeding by, thereby saving precious time. The mail clerks on board the mail car would have a mail sack ready for each town as it passed through and tossed it onto the railway platform from the moving train, which was always on time. In 1954, arrival time for the northbound mail train at Colfax was 6:20 a.m. six days a week. You could set your watch by it.

This saying is engraved on the General Post Office building in New York City, "There is no mortal thing faster than these messengers…Neither snow, nor rain, nor heat, nor gloom of night stays these couriers from the swift completion of their appointed rounds."

POSTMASTERS

The names and appointment dates of the following postmasters were taken from microfilm kept in The National Archives in Washington D.C. The information about each postmaster was carefully researched from several resources.

Seventeen years after the arrival of the railroad, a post office officially opened in the Village of Texas. The mail came in by train. On January 9, 1869 **Jacob Jolliff** was appointed the first postmaster. He was 27 years old and was one of nine children of a family of lumbermen. He was a grand nephew of John and Drusilla Springer. The location of the post office, according to official papers, was 75 yards from the train station, located at what is today known as the Fortney/Kinty railroad crossing. The Jolliff home was near the railroad tracks. The post office was closed after only six months for some unknown reason. Patrons then got their mail at the Palatine post office.

- Exactly six years later on August 11, 1875 the post office was re-established with **Abraham A. Howell** as postmaster. The only thing we know about him is that he served for four years. Records show that the post office served 50 inhabitants of the community. Upon the request of the U.S. Post Office Department, the community had been renamed Colfax before the re-opening of the post office but the B&O Railroad station was still known as Texas Station.

- **William R. Jasper** was appointed postmaster on November 4, 1879. He and his wife, Nancy, lived upstairs over the feedmill near where the bridge was later to be built. They had a store/post office combination and a saloon on one side of the building, which was demolished to make way for the 1993 bridge. The mill ground corn and it had a steam-driven engine that pulled logs in from the river, having been gathered in a log boom. Then they were moved to the sawmill next door. It was owned by Dennis Springer. Mr. Jasper grew up in Boothsville where his father had been a miller. He was postmaster for two years and one month before he died in office in 1881. He was buried in the "Springer Graveyard" which is now known as Colfax Cemetery.

The millstone from the feedmill beside the Colfax post office.

- **Charles R. Madeira** was a clerk in the store at the time of Mr. Jasper's death and he assumed the duties of postmaster. He was officially appointed on December 28, 1881. Charles was born in 1852, the son of George and Margaret (Pierpont) Madeira. He married Leah Swearingen and they had one child, Bessie. The post office was in the mill building, which was still owned by the widow, Nancy Jasper.

- Mrs. **Sarah Nuzum**, widow of Ulysses Nuzum who died in 1882, became the first female postmaster on January 19, 1885. The post office remained in the mill/general store. Mrs. Nuzum lived in a small house beside the mill. That house disappeared long ago. After 15 months, Mrs. Nuzum resigned because of illness and died five months later.

- When **Mark W. Little** became postmaster on April 8, 1887, the post office was moved to his cousin William Little's mill-general store on Guyses Run. Later it became known as the "Web" Fleming place. Mark was the son of Thomas Allen and Eliza (Harr) Little from Sarrietta. He married Tillie Garlow; they had two sons. Mark

Mill/post office by the B&O railroad tracks in Colfax, WV in 1899. Note the brick kilns of the Colfax Red Brick Company. *Courtesy of the Hamilton Collection.*

West Virginia's Lower Tygart Valley River

Mill/Store/Post Office (far right) where Mark W. Little was postmaster. Much later it became the home of Web Fleming. The building has since been torn down. *Courtesy of the Hamilton Collection.*

Little was postmaster for a year and two months. When Wm. Little sold the store in 1888, before the great flood, he gave up the office of postmaster.

- **William H. Hawkins** was appointed postmaster on June 15, 1888. The son of Isaac and Margaret (Irons) Hawkins, his family lived in a house located between the river and the railroad tracks where the Fortney/Kinty railroad crossing is today. He and his wife Susan (Downey) had three children, Fred, Pearl and Emma. Mr. Hawkins operated a general store with a post office in part of his home. The railroad station and telegraph office were just across the railroad tracks. Only 10 months later, having lost a leg to a moving locomotive, Mr. Hawkins gave up his post as postmaster. 1888 was the year of the great flood in Colfax. The Hawkins' place, which once housed the post office and general store, came loose from its foundation and floated down to the bend in the river where it was snagged by a tree. With permission from the B&O railroad, the rails were greased and the building was slid back onto its foundation.

- **Charles R. Madeira**, a good friend to Mr. Hawkins, took over as postmaster on April 1, 1889. He was already familiar with the duties since he had held the job in 1881. Madeira owned and operated the mill on Guyses Run so the post office was moved back there. When he sold the mill building in 1891, he again gave up the office. They moved to Monongalia County.

William H. Hawkins, twice postmaster of Colfax. *Courtesy of Joan Thorne.*

- **William Firman Springer** was the son of Swedon and Lucinda Springer. He bought the mill and general store from Charles Madeira (later it became known as the Web Fleming place) and accepted the job of postmaster on March 12, 1891. Married to Viola Swearingen, they had five children. He sold the mill/store building and gave up the position of postmaster within nine months. The Springers moved to the bottom of Michael's Hill near the East Grafton Road, where he pursued the farming life. Springer School was later built on this property. William Firman Springer was also a farrier and got seriously kicked in 1893. He died at age 36 from complications of that accident. His youngest child was only nine days old at the time of his death.

People and Places

W. H. Hawkins General Store/Post Office. The train depot building on the right. 1910.
Courtesy of Mark Thorne and Warner Studio.

• On December 14, 1891 **Miles Frankenberry** (1858-1920), son of William Frankenberry (who was a trackman for the B&O), asked for and received the job as postmaster. Mr. Frankenberry and his wife, Luvada, lived across the railroad from the train station in a remodeled B&O storage building. Their home was where the Kinty home place is today on Pinchgut Hollow Road. His parents lived across the railroad tracks. That home burned down in 1967. Mr. Frankenberry gave up his post and started working for the B&O railroad.

• On April 17, 1893, **Staats M. Nuzum** (1858-1904) became postmaster. He was a brother-in-law to former postmaster Sarah Nuzum. He and his wife Cora had a store located approximately where the community building is today. They lived on a small farm beside the railroad tracks, which my husband and I now own. They had no children. Mr. Nuzum ran the post office in that store for 13 months before giving up the post. He died at the age of 47 in 1904, and lies buried in the Colfax Cemetery (Nuzum No. 2). *1893 was the first year commemorative stamps were sold by the postal system.*

• **Marion L. Herron** (1860-1936) was the next postmaster. He took office on June 5, 1894 and moved the post office back over to the widow Jasper's feed mill. She also operated a boarding house in the building. Mr. Herron and his wife, Helen, rented rooms there. After three years and eleven months, he resigned his post and became a co-owner in the first brick company in Colfax. In 1901, he sold his interest in the brick factory and moved to Hammond. Later, he bought a large dairy farm on Goose Creek and settled into farming. He died in 1936 at the age of 76 and is buried in the Nuzum No. 1 Cemetery next to the Church of the Brethren at Goose Creek.

• **Icie Dora (Fleming) Vincent Irons** (born 1856) was appointed postmaster on May 12, 1898. Dora was the mother of Virgil (Punk) Vincent. She later became the second wife of Joe Irons and they had a son named Orville. It is unclear where the post office was during her tenure. Dora was postmaster for one year and nine months. She died of typhoid fever in 1925 at the age of 69. *Special Delivery was instigated in the postal system in 1898, and free home delivery of the mail was initiated in the city of Fairmont. There were four carriers.*

Dora (Fleming) Vincent Irons and son Orville.

117

- On March 6, 1900, **William H. Hawkins** (1850-1937) again became the postmaster. Still living in the store by the railroad tracks, Mr. Hawkins brought the post office back there. Now adjusted to the loss of his leg, Mr. Hawkins had devised a way to walk without crutches by making himself a pegleg. For the remainder of his life, he was known by the nickname of "Peg." Mr. Hawkins was postmaster throughout World War I. He retired after 28 years when he was 76 years old. He died in 1937 at the age of 84. Charlie Oiler ran the store and disbursed the mail for Mr. Hawkins in later years but was never an official postmaster. *In 1903 free local rural delivery began in Marion County. The carriers received $600/yearly salary, which included money for the hiring of a horse. In 1913 the post office department introduced parcel post, insured mail and C.O.D. (Collect On Delivery) service. This same year saw the beginning of mail delivery only 6 days a week.*

Fannie Jacobs appointed postmaster in 1928.
Courtesy of Helen (Nichols) Carpenter.

- Mrs. **Fannie (Bennett) Jacobs** (1869-1947) was appointed postmaster on November 30, 1928 upon the retirement of William Hawkins. Fannie was a former schoolteacher and, according to Walter Balderson's book *Fort Prickett Frontier and Marion County,* was one of Hammond's earliest teachers. According to the strict rules laid down by the boards of education of those times, married women were not allowed to teach.

- Sometime after her marriage, she and her husband, Luther, came to Colfax to live. They had three daughters; Pearl (who married Russell Nichols), Dana, and Sara. In 1915, Russell Nichols built a new store building beside his mother's home in the center of Colfax. When Fannie was appointed postmaster, Nichols partitioned off a small room on the side of the store for a post office. It remained at this site for the next 42 years. Postmaster for 11 years, Fannie gave up her job in 1937. She died in 1947 and is buried in the cemetary in Triune, her hometown, on the Halleck Road in Monongalia County.

- Mrs. **Agnes (Robertson) Irons** (1903-1994), a former school teacher, assumed charge of the post office on July 20, 1937. She never was confirmed as postmaster, but she worked in that position for eight months until someone permanent could be found. She and her husband, Orville, lived in a small house beside the Methodist Church. During our 1994 interview, she recalled having to bring her three-year-old son, Charles Joe, to work with her because she had no one to watch him. Agnes continued working as a substitute for Effie Vincent, who became the official postmaster. Mrs. Irons died in 1994 and is buried in the Colfax Cemetery (Nuzum No. 2).

- In March of 1938, **Effie (McCord) Vincent** (1885-1964) officially became the next postmaster. The post office was still in the Hawkins store building. She and her husband, Virgil, known as "Punk," lived up the tracks on Sandy Beach Road. They had four children: James, Bernice, Beatrice, and Arthur. Effie walked the half-mile to work every day in all kinds of weather. She worked through World War II and remained in office for 15 years and five months until she retired in July 1953. She died in 1964 and is buried in the Vincent Cemetery on Coal Bank Road.

Effie (McCord) Vincent.
Courtesy of Delbert Smith

- *In 1939 daily airmail service began in West Virginia. Airmail drop off and pick up for Fairmont was only two miles away from Colfax as the crow flies. This location was in a clearing above Fairmont's children's shelter on State Street extension. This hill was cut through for I-79.*

- Foreseeing the retirement of Mrs. Vincent, **Ila M. (Dubay) Fortney** was among three applicants who took a Civil Service test and applied for the position of postmaster. Being the widow of a World War II veteran and in need of a job to support my brother and me, my mother was overjoyed when she was chosen for the position. She became the

Ila M. (Dubay) Fortney, postmaster for 46 years.

17th postmaster of Colfax, continuing in the job for the next 46 years. She was confirmed on October 20, 1953. The post office still was located in the Hawkins store building.

Mother was born in 1917 in Saginaw, Michigan where she met my Dad, Charles D. Fortney, a West Virginian who was working for General Motors there. In 1938, they married and settled down in his hometown of Colfax. Three years later, World War II broke out. It took Dad to the Pacific. Shortly after returning home from his tour of duty, he became ill and died from a brain tumor in 1947.

Soon after my mother started her job, the mail train stopped to deliver the mail instead of "grabbing & throwing," as had been the usual custom. Dale Hunter, who was the B&O track foreman on the line from Fairmont, lived in Colfax. He was ordered to stop the train each morning so he could send in his work orders. My mother, who is only four feet nine inches tall, liked the idea because it was hard for her to reach the bag hook. She used a small wooden box to stand on so she could reach the mailboxes when she was putting up the mail inside the post office.

The old brickyard office building was converted into the Colfax post office. Dedication was on Saturday, July 24, 1971. *Courtesy of Ila Fortney.*

Starting in 1955, the daily mail was delivered to the post office by a rural mail carrier instead of by train. Burley Tennant (1919-2001) of Fairmont delivered mail to the surrounding communities for several years before the Colfax post office was added to his route. Mr. Tennant was always faithful in his rounds and was a friend to all. By 1969, all mail in and out of Fairmont was carried by trucks. Other mail carriers were Ralph Watkins, Tony LaDonne, Maryln Roades and Ed Dicken, who currently carries the mail.

In 1963, the postal service introduced postal codes under the Zoning Improvement Plan (ZIP Codes). This was devised to make the delivery of mail faster. The ZIP Code is a five-digit number, which directs a piece of mail to an individual town. Colfax's zip code is 26566.

In September 1970, the post office was moved to a tiny, red brick building that the Colfax Brick Company had built for an office. It is all that is left of the brickyard. It was on the property when she purchased it from Bill and Betty Blosser as a part of Nichols Addition. She later built a home behind it. The post office was small but larger than the room in the store building where it had been for 42 years. Besides increasing workspace, it allowed customers to pick up their mail from the lock boxes after hours.

In 1999, a bathroom and additional room were added allowing more space for handling the mail. After 45 years of faithful service, Ila Fortney retired as postmaster of Colfax on Oct. 1, 1999 at the age of 82. Genevieve Barnes, a long-time resident of Colfax and Ila's loyal leave replacement for 41 years retired at the same time.

Many changes in the postal system had taken place during Ila's tenure. Regular postage was only three cents when she first took office in 1953. For those who have complained over the years of the soaring prices of postage stamps, here is a table showing that stamp prices have remained a bargain.

Year	Price	Year	Price
1885-1917	2 cents	May 1978	15 cents
1917-1919	3 cents	March 1981	18 cents
1919	2 cents	November 1981	20 cents
July 1932	3 cents	February 1985	22 cents
August 1958	4 cents	April 1988	25 cents
January 1963	5 cents	February 1991	29 cents
January 1968	6 cents	January 1995	32 cents
May 1971	8 cents	January 1999	33 cents
March 1974	10 cents	January 2001	34 cents
December 1975	13 cents	June 2002	37 cents

Not many companies, corporations, businesses, or organizations raised the price of their product or service by only 35 cents in 119 years. *During the administration of President Richard M. Nixon (1969-1974), the postal system was redesigned so that their employees could have unions. In 1995, bar codes were required on every piece of mail, including letters, flats, and parcels in the larger post offices. They were sorted on a bar code sorter which required two operators. It sorted 30,000 pieces of mail per hour.*

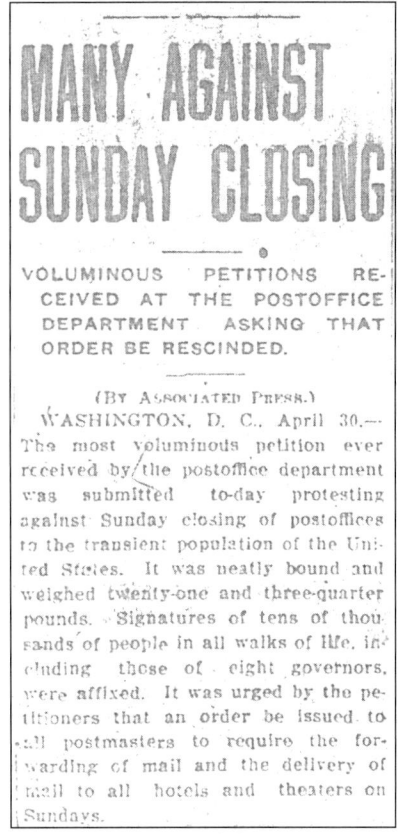

1913 newspaper article about Sunday closing of all post offices. *Fairmont Free Press.*

At the time of Ila's retirement, **Mark Taylor,** 40, was a mail clerk at the Clarksburg, WV plant when he applied for the postmaster's position in Colfax. He had held various postal jobs within the system since 1986. He was accepted and was officially sworn in at a special ceremony at the Colfax Community Building on August 8, 2000. Mark was born in Preston County but grew up in Harrison County. He attended Fairmont State College where he received a Bachelor of Science degree in Business Administration. In May 2000, he was elected President of the North Central Postmasters' Association. Being an avid hunter, he enjoys hunting on his days off.

As in the beginning, the post office is still the center of activity in the community. The community building is across the street and is a stop for two school buses. After 124 years, friends and neighbors still exchange the latest news as they eagerly wait for the mail just as our ancestors did.

Ila Fortney and Mark Taylor, on the day of his induction as Postmaster of Colfax, WV on August 8, 2000.

COLFAX BRICK COMPANY

The history of the brickyard began when Job Springer (third generation of John Springer) built a brick house using clay from a deposit found on his property. This discovery was made when, in 1850, the B&O railroad bought a strip of land from him for the new railroad. His home was on that strip. The railroad company agreed to build the Springer family a new home. Job himself made the bricks in hand molds. Unfortunately the brick was lacking in quality, so the house lasted only about 50 years.

After the railroad was in place, Job Springer built a mill only 15 feet from the railroad tracks near the river. It was constructed of the fine-quality, rough-cut local timber—the only kind being sawn at the time. In 1870, Job sold the mill and 107 acres, including the natural clay deposit, to Ulysses and Zadoc Nuzum for $3,000. Zadoc Nuzum was Job Springer's son-in-law, having married Ruhama Springer, Job's daughter. Ulysses was Job's grandson. According to the deed, Job reserved for himself the mansion and the garden for the rest of his natural life. He died in 1874.

After the untimely death of Ulysses in 1882 his older brother, Staats, acquired a share of the property. Then when his father, Zadoc, died in 1893, Staats and his wife, Cordelia, inherited another tract which included the clay deposits. The Nuzum family never made bricks commercially. They did have a general store/post office combined on the lot where the Community Building sits now. Staats was the postmaster.

In 1898, four acres of the clay deposit property

Business card for the Colfax Brick Company. 1926.

was sold to Martin A. Keener and Marion Herron, an ex-postmaster. Together, they started a brick factory. The bricks were fired in an open kiln but it did not produce an even color or hard brick. Due to their lack of knowledge in brick making their endeavor did not last long. Late in 1898, the property was sold to T. B. Williams, whose family was experienced in making high-quality bricks. Mr. Williams had the Grafton-Fairmont Gas Company bring in a gas line and then built a large closed-in kiln. He hired a skilled brick burner who produced much better quality bricks.

Unfortunately, Williams lacked the funds to expand as he wanted, so he decided to sell a one-third interest in the company to J. P. Conn and another one-third to John C. Fulton, both of Uniontown, PA., at $1,600 each. This was the beginning of the company known as the Colfax Brick Company. Conn and Fulton were silent owners who left the operations to Williams. John L. Johnson, of Crofton, PA, was secretary, treasurer and general manager.

The company purchased additional property from Staats Nuzum to expand the growing operations. Two more large kilns were built. In 1903, new machinery was installed and red shale shipped in from Thornton, WV. It was mixed with the local river clay creating dark red bricks of excellent quality. They were shipped throughout the United States and were in high demand during the early 1900's.

In 1902, John Fulton died. Lawrence Lietzell from Scottsdale, Pa. bought his share of the company for $3,200. The company became incorporated with Joseph Irons, from Colfax, as President.

Many fine homes in the surrounding area are made from Colfax brick. Brick homes on Fairmont Avenue and the Fairmont Hotel in Fairmont as well as a whole city block in New York City were made from its brick. Three homes in Colfax, the Morgan home at Crossroads, Powell School, Levels School, Colfax School, Grassy Run School and Hickman Run School were are all made from Colfax brick.

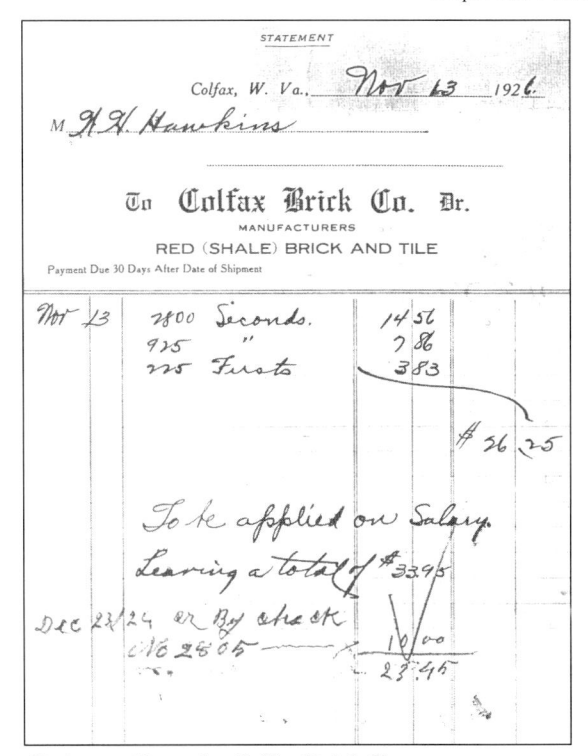

Statement from the Colfax Brick Company.

Colfax Brick Company in 1916. Production at the time was 16,000 bricks per day.
Courtesy of the Hamilton Collection.

The last remains of the Colfax Brick Company as it looked in 1943. *Courtesy of Delbert Smith.*

In 1913, the brickyard employed 20 men. Production totaled 16,000 bricks per day. Tests had proven that the bricks were well adapted for building purposes. Gerald Griffith, 15, of Colfax, pushed a wheelbarrow from the clay pit many times during a day's work at the yard and Willie Boice of Colfax worked there before he got a job on the railroad.

In later years, Mamie French became the company's bookkeeper and Emma Long was the office manager. The Colfax post office building was once a part of the brickyard. Today that building is all that is left of the once-thriving company. It is a fine example of Colfax brick.

Only a few people can remember how the brickyard work whistle blew at starting time in the morning, at lunchtime and at quitting time. It became a familiar sound in the valley where thick black smoke drifted from the smokestacks.

During World War I (1917-18), the Colfax Brick Company made a spiral, hollow cylinder of red brick. They were called acid rings and were used by the military to store mustard gas. This was a top-secret project for the Federal government. It wasn't till after the Korean War in 1955 that the public learned what they were used for. By this time, the brickyard had been closed for many years.

In 1927, the brickyard closed due to lack of funds. The company was disadvantaged by their open pit method of mining the clay. Bricks could not be produced during the winter because of the rainy, cold weather. When concrete came into use, there was less demand for brick. These two factors plus mismanagement of the company brought about its closure. The company was bankrupt.

A lawsuit between Samuel Johnson, et al (plaintiffs) and the Colfax Brick Company, et .al (defendants) sprang out of this closing over $30,071 in unpaid bills. The Brick Company was sold to the highest bidder on the courthouse steps. Joseph Irons bought it for $6,000. Two years later the stock market crashed and Joe's son, Willis Irons, sold the brick company to the R. Nichols Lumber Company.

The R. Nichols Lumber Company was an operation located on the river beside the cemetery. Russell Nichols, Harry Nichols and W. Fred Hawkins were all partners in the lumber trade. They bought the brick

Colfax Brick Company workers. Center is John L. Johnson, General Manager.

People and Places

company with the high hopes of getting it started again. The new owners could not call the brick company by its former name so they renamed it the Tygart Valley Brick and Tile Company. When reorganization failed, they decided to lease the brickyard to M. Williams and David Ritchie of the Sarrietta community.

Mr. Williams and Mr. Ritchie agreed to renew and repair all the roofs where necessary within 30 days and repair all the kilns, machinery and keep them in good operating condition. The R. Nichols Lumber Company was to supply the bricks for necessary repairs to the four remaining kilns. The fifth kiln was partly taken down. The lease also allowed them to have use of the railroad switch which had been purchased for a private railroad siding for shipments. Allowing time to make the repairs, the lease was to start April 1, 1931 but never happened because of the Depression and the brickyard never produced again.

Coal tipple as it looked before it was torn down in 1966.
Courtesy of Delbert Smith.

In later years, the neighborhood kids dammed up the clay pit in the winter for ice-skating. The word got out and soon people from other places came to Colfax to join the fun. The neighborhood lads also made a ballfield on the upper end of the brickyard property. Many fine ball games were played there against other communities for about 30 years.

After the closing of the brickyard, most of the buildings had begun to deteriorate; only one of the smokestacks still stood after 15 years. The R. Nichols Lumber Co. still owned the property.

In the summer of 1945, the company decided to lease the property to Lester Kaufman for a coal tipple. The location was ideal because the second siding track could be used for coal shipment. Cecil Kinty was hired to build a tipple. Before Mr. Kaufman could begin operations a portion of the brickyard had to be cleared away. But even after operations began, they still needed more space, so the last remnants of the brickyard were burned down in June 1947. The fire accidentally spread towards the ball diamond but it was put out by community volunteers.

Legal notice that appeared in the *Times West Virginian* on February 26, 1927.

Cecil Kinty, a Colfax resident, owned and operated his own truck. He hauled coal for the Railing Brothers from many places including Coal Bank Road and at a strip job at White Hall. All the coal trucks had to stop to be weighed at the weigh station before dumping the coal into the coal cars. John J. Cook and a Mr. Morgan were the scale operators. "Doc" Knight, Jim Lantz and Dale Fluharty were among several local men who worked on the tipple.

Coal was a dirty business, so all the workers were covered with coal dust most of the time. It was also a dangerous business. On September 28, 1945 Vincenzo Gardi, a 66-year-old Italian who worked at the tipple, lost his life when he was closing the door on the bottom of a coal car. Gardi did not hear his fellow workman calling out to warn him of the approaching train. He was crushed between the railroad ties and the bottom of the coal car. In 1947, an unidentified black man was working on the tipple when he fell to his death. He was buried in the Colfax Cemetery in an unmarked grave.

The coal tipple closed down in 1952. It stood inactive for several years before it finally was torn down in 1966. Russell Nichols bought out the other shares and developed the property as a site for a housing development. He called it Nichols Addition. In 1967, the property was

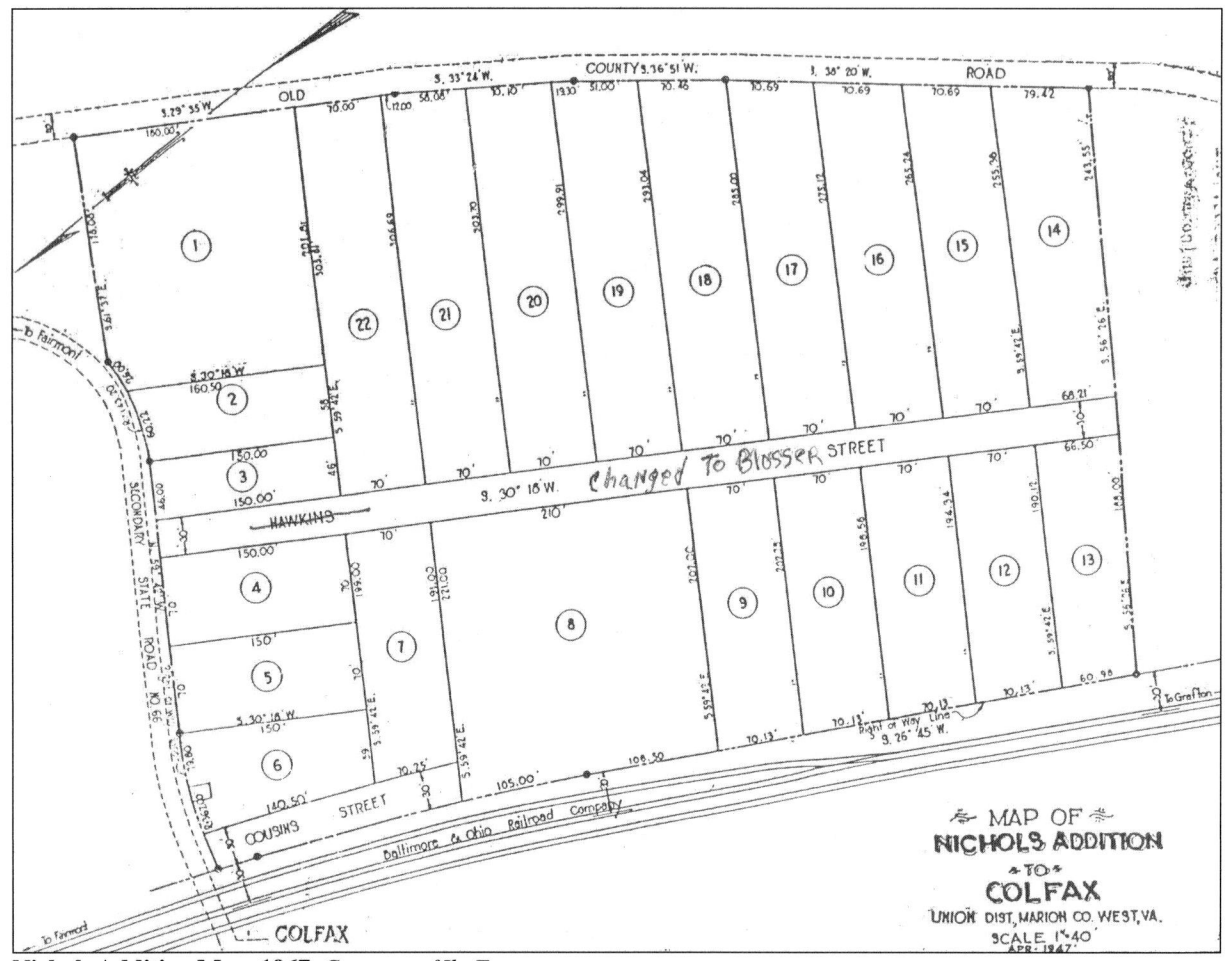

Nichols Addition Map. 1967. *Courtesy of Ila Forney.*

surveyed into 22 lots with two streets—Blosser Street, which became the main entrance, and Cousins Street, which was to have run along the railroad tracks was never developed. Russell died in 1974 never having seen the residential area as it is today. The project transformed the community of Colfax. Today the brickyard and coal tipple are only recollections of days gone by.

COLFAX SCHOOL

Before the Civil War, the first school for the village children was held in a little one-room building that stood on what was then the Isaac Holman property. This school was located near the present Winfield Fire Department station on the Colfax Road. It was a subscription school, in session only four months in the winter and perhaps two months after planting time. Parents would have paid a tuition fee of maybe 50 cents a month for a child under twelve and perhaps a dollar for children twelve and older.

After the Civil War ended in 1865, the new State of West Virginia, born in 1863, established a public school system. It provided for a Board of Education (BOE) for each of the districts so they would have the power to establish schools and appoint teachers. The newly organized BOE for Union Township bought the subscription school building from Isaac Holman on December 17, 1869 (Deed book 26, page 355). It became known as School No. 5. It was one of the first free public schools built in Marion County under the new system. Church services for the Calvary Baptist Church also were held in this building until the congregation built a place of worship across the road in 1870.

Isaac Holman built the gristmill at Valley Falls. Shortly thereafter he purchased property on Guyses Run where he built a mansion for his wife, Mary. Their home still stands beside the Winfield Volunteer Fire Department on the Colfax Road. Isaac was sheriff of Marion County from 1861 to 1889 during the Civil War. He was a delegate to the Wheeling Convention, which led to secession from Virginia and independent statehood.

People and Places

In 1858, Zadoc Nuzum bought 17 acres of land from the Holmans. He built his home on this property and in 1870, he built a Baptist Church. By 1885, as the surrounding area continued to grow in population so did the attendance at the one-room school. Due to the increasing number of students, additional space became necessary. The school had started to deteriorate and there was no funding available for repairs. The Baptist Church and Zadoc Nuzum gave use of the church building as a temporary school until Springer and Colfax schools were built in 1895-6.

The church was used until the Union District Board of Education could increase funding to support an extra school. When funding became available, two plots of land were purchased within six months of one another—one at the intersection of East Grafton Road and one in Colfax.

Guyses Run—Home of Isaac Holman, who was sheriff of Marion County, 1861-89.

The Springer School was built on land belonging to Firman and Viola (Swearingen) Springer. It was sometimes called the Swearingen School because the land had for so many years been in the Swearingen family. The one-room school was built in 1896 (Deed Book 74/ Page 78) and continued to educate children until it consolidated with Colfax in 1935. Molly Morris and Frank Morgan (Naomi Morgan's mother and father) were among its early teachers.

The Colfax School was built on a small plot of land the BOE purchased from Emory Hawkins in September of 1895 (Deed Book 74/ Page 79). Located on Colfax Road, it later became the home of Gerald and Nondice Griffith. School was taught here for 31 years before a new brick school was built. Some of the teachers who taught in the old school were: Alice Springer Zinn, Nellie Raikes Springer, Dorothy Giles, Lucie Holbert Shackleford, Earle Michael, Mabel Stanley, Grace Kinsey Straight, Mary Stanley Lewis, Mary Ellen Staggers, Blanche Williams and Estyl Balderson Hunsaker.

THE NEW BRICK SCHOOL

In 1925, during his term as president of Union District's Board of Education, Russell Nichols executed the purchase of property for a new school from Eddie and Emma McDonald for $1,200. It was located below the then existing Colfax School. After 30 years in the one-room school on the hill, it was time to move on.

The new two-room school (Deed Book 274/Page 526) was constructed of red brick purchased from the Colfax Brick Company. Colfax and Hickman Run schools were built from the same plans. Each room had its own entrance under the bell tower. In the early days, the school bell rang each morning. The students appreciated the cupola since it allowed them to get in out of the rainy weather.

Gaslights hung from the ceilings and a coal furnace heated the building. At first there were indoor chemical toilets but they proved to be unsanitary and were taken out. Later the WPA built two outside toilets with cement floors behind the back of the building. Students were used to outhouses because they were similar to ones at home. Toilet paper usually met with disaster so the teachers kept it inside until it was needed.

The wooden desks, with their ornate wrought-iron sides, were designed in such a way that the front of each desk was the seat for the desk in the front of it. Desks were arranged so that the larger students sat in the back of the room. Desks at the front of the class were smaller. Each desk had an ink well in it and parents purchased all school books.

Colfax School had no running water so students took turns going to a spring up on the hill from the school. After a couple of months trekking up the hill, they began going next door to Charles Hoffmaster's well, which had been hand-dug and had excellent tasting drinking water. In later years, water for the school was piped from the spring on the Nuzum property. It was a natural spring which also supplied several of the neighbors.

Above: Marshall University's Northern Autism Training Center. Opened in 1996 after the Colfax Elementary School was closed in 1995. Right Inset: Colfax Elementary School soon after it opened in 1926.

The first teachers at the new school were my Aunt Elizabeth Fortney (Bice), and Agnes Robertson (Irons). During the Depression, they went to the Marion County Courthouse to get the school on a Works Project Administration (WPA) list to have the road leading to the school graded. They succeeded.

The school term was eight months. The Board of Education still did not allow female teachers to marry so Agnes Robertson quit teaching to get married. Elizabeth eventually married Fred Bice but not until after BOE adopted a resolution allowing married females to continue teaching. She remained at Colfax for 12 years before taking another teaching position but after 36 years, she finished her career here where she had started.

Colfax Elementary School Trivia

- In the early days, a folding door separated the two classrooms. It was opened up only for box socials, Christmas plays, square dances, etc.
- Softball was the favorite recess recreation before the playground was built.
- In November 1938, a new piano was purchased for $10.00. It served both rooms.
- The Hot Lunch Program started Monday, January 9, 1944. Meals were 10 cents.
- Over the years, cooks included: Ethel Henderson, Nondise Griffith (26 years), Beulah Hewitt and Janice Griffith (Nondise's daughter-in-law). The school closed in 1995.
- Cook's helpers were: Gladys Satterfield, Margaret Wilson, Phyllis Hunter-Vincent, Parris Williams, Gerry Satterfield and Joan Thorne.
- During the summer vacation of 1952, another schoolroom and a kitchen were added onto the building. Franklin Cain was the teacher.
- Inside restrooms were installed during the summer of 1956.
- In 1960 new oak floors and modern desks replaced the old out-dated ones.
- In July 1965, the BOE approved the request of the PTA to transfer the seventh and eighth grades to Fairmont. Hanning Canfield was president of the Colfax PTA.

Colfax School in 1926. Teachers were Elizabeth Fortney (Bice) and Agnes Robertson (Irons). Students are unidentified. *Courtesy of the Ila Fortney.*

1936 Colfax School students. Teacher and Principal was William T. Lawson, who later became a medical doctor. Back row (left to right) are: Raymond Hoskins, Bud Hoffmaster, Arthur Vincent, Robert French, Sarah Tatterson, Betty Davis, Paul Lee Michael, Jack Whitlock, Rex Stutler, Kenneth Swearinger and Charles "Doc" Knight. Middle row are unknown visitor, Martha Coffman, Joann Nuzum, Mildred Stutler, Peggy Plasman, Mary Martha Bunner, Betty French, Virginia Barnes, Beatrice Vincent, Alma Rose Koon, Lucille Lance, and Helen Tatterson. Front row: Harold LeMasters, Wilbur Tatterson, Don Nichols, Tommy Graves, Dale Hayhurst, "Tink" Satterfield, Johnny French, Bailey Barnes, George Stackhouse, Teddy Mowrey and Abe Hoffmaster.
Courtesy of Lucille (Lance) Carroll.

West Virginia's Lower Tygart Valley River

Class of 1945-46. Left to right: Tommy Hayhurst, Bill Storms, unidentified, Warren Compton, unidentified, Donnie Troy, Tommy Mowrey, Dave Miller, Janet Henderson, Mary Jane French and Judy Satterfield.
Courtesy of Jackie (Keener) Richards

After 69 years, Colfax Elementary School closed at the end of the 1995 school term. Parents protested the closing but because there were only 39 students, the BOE held fast. The school was the heart of the community. When it closed, the town lost a portion of its identity.

After some remodeling, the BOE leased the school to Marshall University to be used as an Autistic Training Center for the northern part of the state, but the community misses the sight of children and the sound of their laughter.

Teachers who taught at Colfax Elementary School were:

1926-34—Elizabeth Bice	Carl Martray	Christine Palmer
1926-29—Agnes Irons	Mary Davis	Lois Beckner Branson
1929—Beatrice Stanley Wilt	Pam Vincent	Mary Jean Hewitt
1937—Martha Davis	Ila Shea	Elizabeth (Fortney) Bice
1937—Francis Rudy Swisher	James J. Carpenter	Joetta Fisher Blake
1934—W.T. Lawson	Nancy Securro	Debby Harrington
1953-57—George Jefferson	Margaret Bailey Phillips	Lorena Mustacchin
Naomi Morgan	James Shaw	
Carolynn Janes Sipe	Patty Resetar Fletcher	
Gwendolyn Haas	Cris Lavorata	
Jemima Hayhurst Goode	Don Stoops	
Stella Moran	Vicki Utt	
Grace Current	Karen Donner Richman	
Edythe Baker Rogers	Masel Rogers	
Franklin Cain	Patty Connor	
Christine Gainer Ridenour	Minnie English	

People and Places

ATHA POULTRY FARM

Atha Poultry Farm on Colfax Road 1950.
Courtesy of Wesley and Mildred Berry.

Probably everyone who lived in Colfax and the surrounding area in the 1950's remembers the Atha Chicken Farm. It was located on the same property that Southern Ohio Coal Company later purchased for its ponds on the Colfax Road. Inherited from his father, P. C. "Bud" Atha, Jr. owned the farm that raised white leghorns for meat and eggs. Bud invested a lot of money on the farm; small A-frame chicken coops dotted the fields on both sides of the road. One of them can still be seen on the hillside. Every spring, the neighborhood kids looked forward to watching the baby chicks running around following their mothers. After a three story-brooding house burned down, Mr. Atha built a huge, five-storey hen house of cinder blocks. A hand-operated elevator was installed so workers could easily get to each level. Watch dogs prowled at night to protect the chickens. A new concept in the design of incubators was installed as were conveyor belts which separated the small, medium and large eggs. Every day, each egg was dated before it was taken to market. Mr. Atha installed special lighting, which allowed checking for blood spots on the eggs. Spotty eggs never made it to market.

Ethel and "Rome" Law, living not far from the farm, fed the chickens twice a day from the huge amount of feed that was purchased. Chicken feed came in 50 lb. cloth sacks, which were popular with housewives because they had several designs printed onto the very strong, durable fabric. Clothing like aprons, dresses and children's clothes, as well as sheets, dishtowels, quilts and tablecloths were made from these sacks. During the Depression, by using the sacks families not only saved money, but many would have had nothing new without them.

Feeding, gathering and sorting eggs for market were a priority among the many chores to be done. Cleaning out the hen house, however, didn't always get daily attention. That resulted in disaster for the poultry farm. In the late 1950's, the five-story building collapsed under its weight during a windstorm one night. Then it caught fire. The stench of dead chickens and manure drifted in the air for weeks.

This unfortunate event created financial problems for the Athas and resulted in foreclosure. That spelled the end of the Atha chicken farm.

The Atha Farm chicken house after the collapse. *Courtesy of Wesley and Mildred Berry.*

COMMUNITY BUILDING

In 1955, the community of Colfax began another growth period. New families and more children moved into the area. All community activities were held at the school until the board of education issued a ruling saying such activities had to be school related. The logical solution was for the community to have its own meeting place.

A public meeting was held at the Methodist Church on March 22, 1957 to discuss the formation of a community association and the possibility of acquiring a community building. The idea was popular and the Colfax Community Association was born. Charles "Bailey" Barnes was elected president; Dale Hunter, Vice President, and Ila Fortney, Secretary. Russell "Junie" Satterfield was Treasurer. In 1958, it was decided that the association would purchase the vacant Barnes Store building, which was centrally located and easy to get to. It was within walking distance of most homes.

The association bought the building from Hubert "Hez" Barnes for $3,500 on a three-year payment plan. In June 1961, the final payment was made. The Colfax Community Association became incorporated in 1961. Improvements to the building began in 1965 when wood siding and new windows were installed.

The Community Association, The Homemaker's Club and the Methodist Church used the building regularly and made gradual improvements over the years. It remains a meeting place for the community and is rented out to help support the building. In 1997 the Marion County Commission gave a grant of $5,000 for major improvements. They included a new entrance for the handicapped; ramp; new ceiling and upstairs bathroom off the main room.

Bailey Barnes (left) and Gene Smith (right) standing on a rig where the Colfax Community building is today. February 1943. *Courtesy of Gene Smith*

In 1965, wood siding and new windows were added to the Colfax Community Association building. *Courtesy of Ila Fortney*

Left: Colfax Community Center as it looked in 1960. Formerly the Barnes Store. *Courtesy of Delbert Smith*

COLFAX GROCERY STORES

There has been a store in Colfax as long as there has been a post office, and in the early days, the two were combined. Sometimes there were two stores operating at the same time. Past store owners in the community were C. A. Madaria; Scott and Brady Springer owned a furniture store; Peter T. Barnes, Staats Nuzum, Martin A. Keener, William H. "Peg" Hawkins and Charles Oiler were also store owners. The G.K. Little Store and George "Granddaddy" Johnson had a store at what later became the ball diamond. Other store owners were: Sybil and Pete Keener, (Keener and Stevens Store), Fred Hawkins, Willis Irons (who had the first gas pumps for automobiles); C. L. Shorter, Mildred and Henry Stevens; Gordon C. Martin, Hubert "Hez" and Charles "Bailey" Barnes; Orville Mowery; Wayne and Sylvia Batton; Elbert Keener; Ruth Nichols; Joan Thorne, "Buck" Vangilder, and Ron Maze, whose store closed in 2002.

Barnes Store opened Saturday, June 15, 1946 and closed in 1957. Thorne's Grocery closed on May 21, 1971.

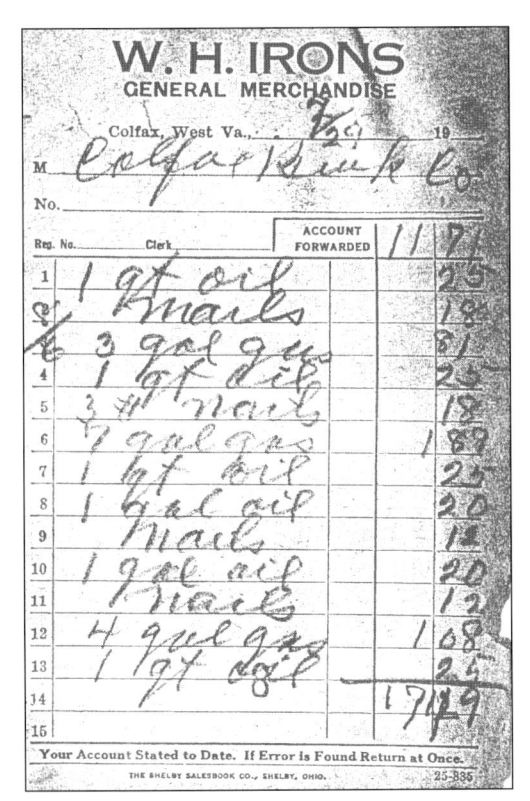

Nichols Grocery and Colfax Post Office 1965. Store was operated by Ruth Nichols. *Courtesy of Delbert Smith.*

James Vincent, Nick Hando and Helen Summers in front of Nichols Grocery.

1929 Sales receipt from the Willis Irons Store.

Martin's Store, located in the old mill by the railroad tracks in the early 1930's. *Courtesy of Ila Fortney*

ROADS

In the early days, going to town meant an all-day journey over dirt roads with wagon ruts deep enough to lose a wheel. "Town" to the people in Sarietta, Valley Bend and Colfax in the 1800's, meant Boothsville. After the railroad was built in 1852, train travel to Fairmont became the lifeline for the communities on the river. Later, roads were developed and improved enough to make possible more frequent visits to Fairmont.

At one time, the main road going to Fairmont's east side from Colfax was the Sandy Beach Road which once was connected to the Sand Bank Road. It went up through our farm to Barker's Road and led out the Colfax road to East Grafton Road. Many old deeds refer to it and its "two-mile tree" marker up at the church. It indicated that the distance was two miles from the East Grafton Road to Colfax.

When the bridge was built in 1902, new approaches were built on both sides of the river. The Colfax Road from the bridge to State Rt. 310 was paved for the first time on June 27, 1928. The road was closed during the paving. The limestone cement that was used was seven inches thick. The road was built to last, which it did until it was repaved again and widened in the 1960's.

The road going up the hill on the west side of the river to US Route 250 was paved for the first time in 1939 by the Works Projects Administration (WPA).

The road (Main Street) between the cemetery and railroad tracks was built in 1928. When excavating for the railroad in 1850, workers filled in a gully in front of the cemetery and smoothed it out. It stayed that way for many years until Staats Nuzum gave the ground in 1928 for a road that would connect Sandy Beach Road to the Colfax bridge. The B&O Railroad Company granted permission to build a crossing. Paving from the bridge to the crossing took place August 27. Traffic began flowing for the first time on Friday, October 19, 1928.

Pinchgut Hollow

Before the white man came, roaming Indians from the South formed a path along the Tygart Valley River. It was called the Catawba War Path Trail. It left the river and went up Robinson Run to the top of the hill and beyond. The very narrow path meandered in and out of the creek. As time went on, our pioneers also used it. When the water was running low, a horse and rider could barely squeeze around the rocks that jutted out. Legend has it that a horse had to "pinch his gut in" to get through. Another hypothesis as to how Pinchgut got its name is from the wild geranium and periwinkle plants that grow in abundance here. They were used as a treatment for diarrhea by pioneers who probably adopted its use from the Indians. The plants were said to "pinch the gut" in order to stop the ailment. In those days diarrhea had a reputation for being the cause of many deaths. Pioneers used the Solomon's Seal plant to help close wounds and Black Cohosh (papoose root) to hasten childbirth. Many medicinal plants grow in the hollow but some had other uses such as the sap from the root of the Bloodroot plant. It was used for Indian war paint and dye for clothing.

Newspaper article from the *Fairmont Times* dated June 19, 1928 concerning road contracts.

The name of Pinchgut Hollow signifies a time in our history when words were simple, down to earth and had meaning. Many of the West Virginia pioneers used archaic words like "gut" to name streams and roads. Those words linger in our hills today. In the dictionary, "gut" means a channel or run of water in a narrow passage, which perfectly describes this hollow. Pinchgut Hollow has been the unofficial name of this place for over a century. Everyone for miles around knows where Pinchgut Hollow is. On August 15, 2000, Marion County's Advisory Committee For the Conversion of Rural Routes to City Type Addresses took into consideration the desire of the majority of the residents who lived on the road to officially name it Pinchgut Hollow Road. The request also had the approval of the County Commission but the City Council of Fairmont, who had annexed the upper portion of the road close to Stoney Road, feared the name was not dignified enough and wanted it changed. After months of consideration even the council agreed the name should stay.

During the 1888 flood on the Tygart, the mile-long canyon beside Robinson Run was flooded from the backwaters of the Tygart. The water backed up through the railroad trestle and got high enough to flood two homes on the lower end of Colfax. After the water receded, huge boulders appeared throughout the hollow.

Waterfall from a small run draining into Robinson's Run in Pinchgut Hollow.

In the 1940's, the Stemple family, who lived on the upper end of Pinchgut, built a small wooden bridge across the creek. Every time a gully-washer came along, it would wash out the bridge. Mr. Stemple kept his car parked a half-mile away by the railroad tracks and walked home every day. The road was in the creek and had never been graded or ditched, so there were several fords.

In 1948, the WV Department of Highways dredged the creek bed of rocks and piled them to the side thus allowing the creek to flow better. A road was cut beside the creek. Large drain tiles were used to create a bridge. On the upper end of the road, for the first time a large wooden bridge was built allowing traffic to get through the hollow to Stoney Road, but the road still washed out in the winter and usually stayed that way until Ssring.

In 1973, the road was again widened, ditched and tar-graveled for the first time. In 1996-97, a new permanent concrete bridge was built to replace the old wooden one. That same year, the bridge across Guyses Run was replaced. Today, Pinchgut Hollow Road is still single lane; the sharp curves remain and still gets washed out on occasion in hard rains. Nonetheless, it's the shortest route to Fairmont.

For seven-tenths of a mile near the railroad trestle, the hollow goes through a canyon with steep cliff walls on both sides. Pinchgut Hollow is famous for the flora in the springtime, summer and fall. The canyon is situated in such a way that the sun creates an abundance of flourishing wild flowers, some of which are very rare. Over 200 varieties have been found there. Many people have visited this extraordinary place to simply observe the wild flowers. The temperature is at least ten degrees cooler in the canyon on any given day due to the shade and elevation. On a hot summer day, it offers relief from the heat as well as taking you back in time to when the Indians came through in their travels.

The Gypsies

My grandmother Fortney told me that in the early 1900's Gypsies used to make camp by the train trestle at the mouth of Pinchgut Hollow. The small glen across the creek would hold about six horse-pulled wagons. Gypsies loved the location because it was private and close to the river. Flickering campfires could be seen there quite often.

Gypsies traveled in caravans, making a living any way they could—some less desirable than others. They came as fast as they went—usually in the early morning hours. They were rumored to steal anything that was loose, including children, whom they held for ransom. So every time the Gypsies came to town, an alert was made throughout the community. Mothers did not allow their children out to play while they were here.

One time a fortuneteller came to my Grandmother's house and detained her at the front door by telling her fortune. At the same time another Gypsy went into the house through the back door and stole the chicken that was cooking on the stove for supper—pot and all.

The last time the Gypsies camped in Pinchgut Hollow was in 1914. The local Ku-Klux-Klan scared them off by burning a cross on the hill where they were camped. Neighborhood folks said it must have put the fear of God in them because they never returned to this community again.

COLFAX TV CABLE SYSTEM

In 1950, if anyone had asked me if a picture could be sent through the air and into a box in my living room, I would not have known what they were talking about. My eight years did not allow me to fathom what was about to silently descend on our quiet valley. It was a wonder of electronics and would change home life forever. To the old timers it was called the "picture box" but the world knew it as "television."

Russell Knotts (1912-1998) who ran a small, part-time business called the Knott's Radio Repair in his basement, bought the first television set in Colfax in 1950. It was a Garod table model and had a round screen. It had an enchanting feature that allowed the picture to go from full round to rectangular at the push of a button. At first, the only TV station available to him was WDTV, Channel 3 out of Pittsburgh. It was owned and operated by Allen B. DuMont, who began operations in 1949. In 1955, DuMont sold the station to Westinghouse, which owned KDKA Radio station, also in Pittsburgh. The FCC then required the station to change its call letters to KDKA and to switch from channel 3 to channel 2, where it remains today. KDKA then began transmitting signals by cruising over Pittsburgh at 25,000 feet in a B-29 airplane allowing very rural areas, such as Colfax, to receive reception.

Mr. Knotts experimented at his home on how to get the best reception with the use of an antenna. First he put one on his house. That did not work well because of it being in the valley. Then he made three other attempts using the antennae and amplifiers at other locations up the closest and steepest hill which was through Faye Nuzum's field. Knotts finally achieved his goal at 1,300 feet at the top of the hill on Ralph Dollison's Farm. After his connection by antenna was perfected, others in the valley began buying TV sets. By 1952, when my family bought their first television set they were considered a "cool" status symbol. *The Lone Ranger* and *Captain Video and his Video Rangers* became our daily companions.

Russell Knotts was an electrical equipment design engineer at the Westinghouse plant in Fairmont. He pioneered a cable system for Colfax that was a very early forerunner of those on the market today. The system was available to those who owned TV sets in the Colfax valley; it was called the Colfax TV Cable System. Each subscriber paid fifty cents a month for upkeep. Commercial equipment was not available to sustain the system, so through the radio shop in his home, Knotts designed and built whatever was needed to do the job, from amplifiers to channel converters. The word got around about his expertise and he was called upon to create TV Cable Systems in several other communities in the county.

Other early TV set owners in the community were Delbert Smith, Fred Bice, Pete Keener and the Fortneys. When a storm came along and blew branches on the cable wires, reception was destroyed. Every member of the

Russell Knotts, owner of the Knott's Radio & TV.
Courtesy of Delbert Smith.

People and Places

cable system was expected to help clear away debris but that didn't always happen. Mr. Knotts made many repair trips alone in the dark of night.

The cable system was incorporated in 1960, when a board of directors was formed that included Russell Knotts, Delbert Smith, Ben Keener, David Nuzum and Ila Fortney. The cable system expanded to the point where hired help was necessary. Mr. Knotts could not keep up with repairs alone due to his full-time job so Henry Richards of East Grafton Road was hired to handle the repairs. In time, the system grew even too big for Mr. Richards to handle so James E. Eddy was added to the payroll.

Built in 2001 at Colfax, Adelphia calls this building a "Hub." A fiber-optic facility that serves all of Marion County.

In 1974, Mr. Eddy agreed to maintain, operate, improve and extend the non-profit cable system for a regular subscriber fee of $4.00 per month. That permitted the upkeep of the system. The lease was for a ten-year period.

On November 4, 1982, Eddy bought the Colfax TV Cable System. He also purchased the Pleasant Valley-Millersville system, Tom Lakes' system at White Hall, Henry Richards' system on East Grafton Road, Levels and Grassy Run systems which eventually became the E&E Cable System. Ron Elliott was Eddy's assistant. At that time, there were 12 available channels. Mr. Eddy made many improvements including changing the cable lines from 408 corrugated-copper lines to three-quarter inch aluminum cable. He installed three satellites near the original antenna on top of the hill, which allowed additional channels. After eight years (on February 15, 1990), Mr. Eddy sold the system to Century Cable in Morgantown. The company's main office was in New Canaan, Connecticut. Once more, the system was improved by the addition of more channels and switching to microwave signals. In 1998, fiber optics came into use, creating yet a greater number of channel choices.

In October 1999, Century Cable sold to Adelphia, based in Coudersport, Pennsylvania. It is another of the nation's earliest cable systems, that was also created in the 1950's. Utilizing fiber-optics technology, the whole system will eventually switch to digital, which will include digital cable and music service, long distance telephone, and high-speed Internet access. The whole system currently is being upgraded to provide additional channels. In 2001, Adelphia built a hub facility in Colfax. All Marion County services come from it. With this upgrade, Adelphia once again uses the satellite up on the hill where it all began so many years ago. It had not been used since 1992 when the satellite on State Rt. 119 between Morgantown and Grafton, 12 miles away, was used at a much higher altitude of 2,400 feet.

Today, television with its changing technology remains a marvel. It has been proven a television set will still keep kids closer to home just as it did early on. Who would have thought that most everyone in the valley would own a television set by 1975? Television has become almost a necessity for most households but sadly, what it's broadcasting on the air waves has become a controversial issue.

COLFAX PUBLIC SERVICE DISTRICT

The first public hearing concerning a sewage system for the Colfax community took place in November 1971. The Marion County Commission approved the creation of the Colfax Public Service District (PSD) that year, but it was not until 1978 that grants were sought to procure funding for the project.

The consulting engineers were Parrott, Ely & Hurt from Lexington, Kentucky. They worked on the project in a joint venture with Environmental Energy Engineers of Morgantown. The sewage collection system was built by General Paving Contractors of Morgantown. The treatment plant was built by Mineral Contracting Corporation of Fairmont. Officially, the Colfax PSD went into operation in 1981.

Landowners donated most of the rights of way. Charles and Nancie Fortney, Junie and Gerry Satterfield, and James and Dot Keener all donated land for the pumping stations. Charles and Nancie Fortney donated the sewage plant property. The plant houses an office and onsite laboratory for making the required environmental tests. Considered an extended Aeration Water Treatment Plant Class II, it is equipped with an auxiliary power

Colfax PSD sewage treatment plant built in 1981.

system in case of power outages and is elevated well above the high-water level on the Tygart Valley River. The sewage collection system serving the community consists of approximately 18,000 ft. of main trunk line, nearly 100 manholes, one submersible pumping station and two grinder-pumping stations. It has the capacity to serve 500 families.

Going on line in 1981 it was a first for an unincorporated community in Marion County. Colfax resident and PSD Board Chairman Bailey Barnes spent many hours planning and supervising the project before his death in 1987. Senator Robert C. Byrd, Congressman Alan B. Mollahan and Engineer James Carpenter were successful in obtaining grants totaling $1,123,526 for the PSD, which was one-hundred percent grant funded.

The paid three-member PSD Board is appointed by the Marion County Commission. It consists of a plant operator, secretary, and a billing clerk-bookkeeper. Genevieve Barnes has been secretary since 1981.

THE FARM WOMEN'S CLUB

The following history was written by Ila M. Fortney.

For several years, it had been hoped that a Farm Women's Club could be organized in Colfax. Ruth Hunter made an attempt to start one but no definite plans could be decided upon.

Around 1948, Naomi Morgan, representing the Victory Farm Women's Club at Crossroads, asked several women of the Colfax community to join their club. The following women joined: Ruth Hunter, Mrs. Franklin Cain, Mamie French, Dorothy Knotts, Ethel Henderson, Agnes Irons, Elizabeth Bice, and Ila Fortney.

After two years of friendly get-togethers, transportation difficulties developed. Club members decided a club in Colfax would be more practical.

Ila Fortney contacted Margaret Rexroad, Home Demonstration Agent for Marion County, about the possibility. In January 1950, she sent Miss Rexroad a list of 35 names of people who wanted to join. Then on February 16, 1950, 18 women met to form the Colfax Homemakers Club. Dorothy Knotts, Janice Mowery, Ollie Taylor, Ruth Hunter, Pearl Tillett, Sylvia Kinty, Betty Mowery, Sylvia Batton, Dale Barnes, Hilda Mowery, Nondise Griffith, Hazel Ruston, Ada Pearl Shorter, Agnes Irons, Etta Satterfield, Elizabeth Bice, Ila Fortney, and Genevieve Barnes.

Later the club members saw a need for a meeting place for community groups, especially the local 4-H Club, Scouts and themselves. In 1958, the club made a down payment of $355 towards the purchase of the Barnes Store building for a Community Center. The Farm Women's Club became the WV University Homemakers Club. They helped make payments for the Community Building.

At the close of 1964, the club was discontinued due of lack if interest; it was reorganized again in February 1969 when Ila Fortney again contacted the County Extension Service. Geraldine Belmear was then Marion County Agent. Several community women, as well as some of the past members, attended a meeting and regular monthly meetings have continued ever since.

In 1999, the Extension (or Homemakers) Clubs within the state of WV all underwent a name change, becoming Community Educational Outreach Service Clubs. Deborah Shriver is the current County Extension Agent, having taken the job in 1980.

People and Places

SELECTED SHORT SUBJECTS

- In 1971, Kathleen Hawkins-Wilt donated land for a new sub-station on the Colfax Road to the Winfield Volunteer Fire Department.
- In the late 1930's hand-cut stonewalls were built on the Colfax road at the sharp curve near East Grafton Road, near Country Estates, at the old Faye Nuzum farm and the wall at the church. The mortar was mixed on the spot for each project by the WPA.
- East Grafton Road was paved for the first time in 1920. Starting at Fairmont, it was paved only to Garlow Hill. Two years later, it was paved on to Luke's Store, and finally on to Morgan's Crossroads. All of it was resurfaced in 1948.
- In 1917, the Monongahela Valley Traction Company decided to build a central power station to supply electricity throughout the county. The site selected was on the Monongahela River north of Fairmont. Thus, the Rivesville Power station was born. Thirteen years later (on December 11, 1930), Austin Satterfield and several others in Colfax received electric for the first time at 4 pm. J. R. and Susie Knight, among those first to get electricity, put a light bulb in a bedroom ceiling-light fixture and the bulb was still working when their son, "Doc," died in 1991. How's that for durability? They don't make'em like they used to!
- Howard Hayhurst had a dairy farm at the top of the hill from the Colfax Bridge. He delivered milk in Colfax by horse and sleigh during the big snow in 1950.
- In March 1947, the old mill became the Gordon Martin Store. Three other families who once lived there were Guy and OllieTaylor (Ollie, a beautician, operated Taylor's Beauty Parlor), the Troy family and Hazel Mowery.
- Daylight Saving Time went into effect throughout the U. S. for the first time in 1918.
- Widening of the big curve at the intersection of East Grafton Road to Colfax was completed in November of 1987.
- City water arrived in Colfax in 1956. Barnes Construction Co. and Edwin Nuzum Construction Co. installed the main line and service lines from Morris Park through Pinchgut Hollow to Colfax.
- The first person to own an automobile in Colfax was Joe Irons. The car was a 1922 Stanley Steamer built in Pittsburgh. It arrived by train at the Colfax depot. The salesman came with the car and stayed until Mr. Irons knew how to drive it.
- In 1938, a restaurant called "The Homestead Inn" was built on the Colfax road. It was built of logs that had been cut down behind the dam before it was flooded. The restaurant was owned and operated by Fay and Oda Nuzum. Their son, Edwin, married the cook, Doris Barnes, and lived on the family farm.
- Guy "Pappy" Martin was a bus driver for the Yellow Cab Company in Fairmont. He made three roundtrips to Colfax and Hammond everyday during the late 1940's and early 50's. (Some folks still remember some of those wild rides from town after he'd a nip or two). "Pappy" died in 1958. Then Loftis Willis made the daily rounds up until the time that the bus route was discontinued.
- Sometime in the 1800's, the men of the community came together to build a wooden bridge across Guyses Run. It was used until the state replaced it in the 1920's. The wooden floor lasted through the '50's. In March 1997, the Department of Highways replaced the structure with a steel foundation and cement sides.
- In 1938 Chester Berry built a log home on the Colfax road. It is currently the residence of his late son Wesley and wife Mildred Berry. The logs were from trees cut down behind the Grafton Dam before the area was flooded.
- In the early 1900's a Hawkins family mistakenly built an oil rig on the Satterfield property. After settling the issue and not striking oil, they gave up and tore the rig down.

Colfax station for the WVFD on the Colfax Road was built in 1972.

West Virginia's Lower Tygart Valley River

Looking down on Howard Hayhurst's dairy farm as it looked in the 1950's. Photo enlarged from original. *Courtesy of Delbert Smith*

An oil rig built by the Hawkins family in the early 1900's. It was accidentally built on the neighbors' property and never did bring in any oil. *Courtesy of Mark Thorne. Photo reproduced by Warner Studio.*

Aerial view of Colfax in 1997.

- The Irons family were early pioneers on the Tygart Valley River. Born in 1888, the legendary Vallie Irons Phillips (daughter of Joe Irons) was a school teacher in her younger days, teaching at several local schools. Being a good Christian lady, she faithfully walked to church every Sunday for about 70 years. She lived alone at her old home place on Sandy Beach Road and made a daily trek down the railroad tracks to Colfax to the store and post office. She died in 1981 and is buried in the Shriver Cemetery.
- Vallie's nephew, James Dale Irons (1905-1989), owned several acres of land once part of the original homestead across the road from Vallie on Sandy Beach Road. Starting in the early 1950's, Mr. Irons allowed thousands and thousands of used tires to be dumped on his property. The practice continued over a period of 30 years. A brush fire, burning 300 acres, swept the Sandy Beach March 20, 1969. The tires on Dale Iron's property escaped the fire as did James Vincent's home although it had to be watered down by Winfield Fire Department and its 30 volunteers. Dale Irons died at the age of 83. He is buried at Maple Grove Cemetery in Fairmont. In November 1999, after the property was sold, politicians announced plans for the clean up of the tire dump that was now considered illegal. Fearing in July 2000 a potential encephalitis health hazard, state officials promised to help with funding for removal of the tires. Removal actually began two years later on July 8 and was completed in October 2003.
- The heaviest snowstorm in the lower Tygart Valley history began on Friday, November 24, 1950. The morning after Thanksgiving Day, huge snowflakes began to fall and didn't stop snowing for a week. There was 42 inches of snow on the ground in Colfax and record setting depths all over the entire state, which was paralyzed. Schools were closed for weeks. Railroad crews were continually clearing the tracks to keep the trains moving. Milk for the community was delivered by horse & sleigh from the local dairies.

West Virginia's Lower Tygart Valley River

COLFAX MEMORY ALBUM

Vallie (Irons) Phillips

Dale Irons

Boyd and Locia Stemple

Joyce, Jill and Charles Joe Irons

Glenn Parrish

Betty (Nichols) Blosser

Gerald and Nondise Griffith

Russell and Pearl Nichols

Anna Davis

Pictures for the memory album were courtesy of Delbert Smith, 1960, except where specified.

People and Places

Albert (Abe) Hoffmaster

Darl Storms

Lester "Bud" and Etta Lee "Ted" Satterfield

Marquita, Bill, Allison, Darlana and Christen Storms

Dale, Eileen, Eric and Phyllis Hunter

Cassie Fortney and Elizabeth (Fortney) Bice

Effie Vandergrift

Tim Vandergrift, D.D.S.

141

West Virginia's Lower Tygart Valley River

Ila, Carolynn and Charles (Larry) Fortney and "Candy"

Elbert and Marsilete Keener Kenner

Gladys and Tom Nunnally

Bill and Mary Lou Hammond, *Courtesy of Dot Keener.*

Elizabeth and Fred Bice

Irene and 'Pop' Lance

Ed Thorne, *Courtesy of Dot Keener.*

Alice Storms Eddy, *Courtesy of Dot Keener.*

People and Places

Mary, Lorretta Jean, Connie (Cookie), Roy, Edith, Raymond, Wanda, Donna (Susie) Fancher and Phillis Fancher Hunt holding Debbie and Wesley Hunt in front

Vance, Ruth and Patty Hunter

Sylvia Kinty *Photo by C. Hamilton*

Icie (Nichols) Hawkins

Charles 'Doc' and Suzie Knight

Greg, Clifford, Crystal and Margie Hill

Sheila, Sharon and Jim Prahl

143

West Virginia's Lower Tygart Valley River

Randy, Avolene (Abby), Paul, Diana, Debby, Matthew and Danny Moran

Russell and Dorothy Knotts

Dale (Winnie) and Clarence Barnes

David, Genevieve and Bailey Barnes

Ruth and Levi Hayhurst

Willie and Lillian Boice. 1968. *Courtesy of Shirley Sanford.*

Mrs. Annie (Boice) Wilson

People and Places

Janet, Karen, "Kookie", Sylvia and Wayne Batton

Gerry and Junie Satterfield

Delbert and Iretta Smith, *Courtesy of Dot Keener*

Harry and Lizbeth Huster, *Courtesy of Dot Keener*

Mildred and Wesley Berry, *Photo by C. Hamilton*

Kathy, Bob, Bill, Sylvia and Mitchell Smith

Doris, Linda Faye and Edwin Nuzum

145

West Virginia's Lower Tygart Valley River

Margarete and Gus Wilson

Charlie and Wilbur Fleming

Judy and Junior Smith, *Courtesy of Dot Keener.*

Jimmy, James, Dot, Lillian, Tiny and Chucky Keener

Oda and Faye Nuzum

Barbara Nichols, Sybil and Pete Keener

Guy and Ollie Taylor, *Courtesy of Dot Keener.*

146

People and Places

Arthur and Mabel Miller

Orville and Agnes Irons

Albert and Hazel Rushton *Courtesy of Dot Keener.*

Ronnie, Willa, Glenn and Gary Irons

Linn, Annalore and George Barnes

Genevieve Barnes

147

West Virginia's Lower Tygart Valley River

VALLEY BEND

This area was strictly farmland and encompassed the families who lived in the bend of the river and on the plateau along Mundell Ferry Road. About a half mile from the river on the main road near the Robert Hunt property, sat Valley Bend School. Many new farming families had moved to the area by 1895, which necessitated building a public school. Some of those families were: Malone, Fleming, Mundell, Shaver, McDonald, Fortney, Hunt, Smith and Mason.

Valley Bend was located in Grant District on the main road (now known as Colfax Road) between Sarrietta and Colfax. I say "was" because it is no longer referred to that way. The road was paved by the WPA for the first time in 1939. Up to 1929, it was still a dirt wagon track, which had several roadside watering troughs along the way. One of them can still be seen going up the hill from Colfax. In even earlier days, before the bridge was built, this road led to Mundell's Ferry.

Mundell Ferry Road is still on the original road down to the ferry

VALLEY BEND SCHOOL

In August 1896, Nancy (Shaver) Prunty sold one acre of land from the farm she had inherited from her father, John Shaver, to the Board of Education for the establishment of a school (Deed Book 79/Page 416). The deed says that the $40.00 purchase price was to be paid by the Sheriff of Marion County out of the levy of 1896. Further, it said that those at the school had the privilege of going to Nancy Prunty's spring for drinking water.

This was about the same time that the property for the Colfax and Springer schools was purchased.

The one-room Valley Bend School housed grades one through eight. Charles Hayhurst was the first teacher. There were about 50 students. Some of the other teachers who taught there over time were: Carrie Rust, Josephine (Merrifield) Little, Pearl (Smith) Kyre, Marceline Little and Lillian Wilt.

The following is from an Interview with Mary (Smith) Fleming, former student. In 1974 the Union Mission in Fairmont named a lodge at the Mission Farms on Glady Creek after Mary for her faith and her dedication towards the camp.

"I started at Valley Bend School when I was five years old. Mrs. Rust was the teacher. She used to hold me in her lap and teach. The one-room school was schooling for all eight grades in all subjects. In those days, students had to pass a state examination in the eighth grade before they could go on to high school. In Grant District the only high school was in Monongah.

"Valley Bend was heated in the wintertime by a coal stove located in the middle of the room. Buckets carried from the spring at the Eldon Smith farm made drinking water available. Recess was always enjoyed for games and trips to the out building. Fifteen minutes in the morning and fifteen minutes in the afternoon. School hours were from 9-12 and 1-4 five days a week. We had one hour for lunch. Many of us went home while others brought them. Box suppers were always the highlight of the year and holidays were always observed."

Top: Front view of Valley Bend School built in 1897. Bottom: Side view of Valley Bend School. It closed in 1931.

The school was closed in 1931; it was sold in 1936 to Mrs. Eldon (Clara) Smith for $340.00. Layman Welk and Ray McDonald later dismantled the abandoned school for the lumber to build a chicken coop and barn.

The steps into the school building were two very large flagstones given to Raymond McDonald for his place at the top of Vinegar Hill, where they are today. After the closing of the school, the children attended Sarrietta School near Poplar Island.

Pupils in the 1922 class of Valley Bend School were Martha, Juanita and John McDonald; Beatrice and Goldie Rutherford; Anna Kelly, Mary and Darrell Smith; Nellie and Howard Shaver; Glenn and Hubert Irons; Julia and Floyd Oiler; Glen and Junior Watkins; Jack Coffey; and Hugh Fortney. Miss Josephine Merrifield was the teacher. Over the years, other students included the Malones, Hunts, Russell, Clarence and Harry Nichols; Ruby Wilt; Elba Fortney; Glenn, Orville and Hubert Irons.

The following is a true event experienced and written by Miss Josephine Merrifield when teaching at Valley Bend.

Miss Josephine (Merrifield) Little, teacher at Valley Bend School 1926-27.

"Last year was my first year teaching. I stayed near the schoolhouse until the latter part of March; then I decided it would be fun to stay at home and ride horseback to school. That weekend when I went home, I consulted my grandfather, as I was making my home with him, as to whether or not it would be all right for me to stay at home and ride horseback. I told grandfather that my uncle had promised me a good horse to ride.

"Grandfather said, 'It is alright for you to stay at home, but you could just walk across the hill to school; it will only be two miles through the field. You do not know enough about riding, to ride that horse.'

"This didn't please me at all, because I had planned to do this and I thought I could ride well enough to ride that horse. On Sunday evening I went back to the place where I stayed with the determination to go home the following Wednesday and ride horseback to the school. But for some reason I didn't go home until Thursday.

"Friday morning I got up early and called my uncle and told him to have the horse ready, that I would be down in a little while. When I went down I found that the horse was ready to go.

"I got on the horse, not the least afraid. I hadn't gone very far until I came to a car in front of a house. The horse turned around and went into the field. Finally, I got her turned around, out of the field and past the car. Still I wasn't afraid. Just a little farther up the road she turned around and started toward home. I succeeded in turning her around again. When I reached the schoolhouse the children were out on the porch to see me on the horse. One of the larger boys took my horse to the barn and tied her and went after her in the evening for me.

"That evening I felt my horseback riding was a success. I had to go around by Boothsville, a little country village, to see a certain lady. After I talked to her awhile, I started on home. As I was going down the hill, the horse started to run. I tried to stop her but all was in vain. My hat went off, but that didn't worry me, because I was thinking of myself. My strength became exhausted and with hasty conclusions, I decided it would be better to fall off than for her to throw me off. As I had heard my grandfather say to never put your feet through the stirrups, I took mine out and let go of the bridle, to fall on the frozen ground.

"I never felt such a feeling before or since, as I did when I let go to fall. I supposed the next place I would be, would be the hospital.

"I fell on the frozen ground and after struggling a few seconds, found to my surprise that I could walk. I managed to walk to a house close by and ask to sit down. I must have been a pretty sight, blood and mud on my face and a bump bigger than an egg on my forehead. I was getting very sick, so I told the man of the house to call home and tell them to come after me as soon as they could.

"They sent a neighbor man after me. When they came I tried to walk, but couldn't. They carried me to the car. It seemed to me that the car wouldn't go fast enough, because I wanted to be home.

"When I got home, the doctor came and examined me. He said that I was fortunate to get off with only a cracked rib, black eye, black nose, and a bump on my forehead. The doctor bandaged me up and told me to remain in bed a few days. I suffered from my fall and also from having to stay in the house.

"I often thought afterwards that it would have paid me to listen to advice given by older people and people of experience."

SARRIETTA SCHOOL

Sanford B. Hall, a businessman who purchased several acres along the river in the 1860's, gave a small portion of the property to the Board of Education in 1871 for a community school. He had plans to develop a little town, which he called Sarrietta. He platted it with streets running east and west; north and south. He combined the names of his two daughters, Sarah and Etta, to come up with the name for his proposed town. Hall's plans to fill up the gullies and sell lots failed because he could not find enough men with money to help him build the town, although he did sell several lots. The railroad on the other side of the river was the final death blow to his little town. Mr. Hall also purchased the Thomas Hughes' mill by the river between Poplar Island and Scout Island. During the Civil War, the Jasper family, who later operated the mill at Colfax, operated this same mill.

Sarrietta is one and one-half miles from US Rt. 250 South on Poplar Island Road in Grant District. The only public building that was ever built for the would-be town was the red brick schoolhouse. It was one of Marion County's oldest free public schools. Built in the middle of a meadow in 1871, it was constructed of rough, red bricks from an abandoned brick kiln on the west side of the river across from Nuzum's Mills (Hammond). The bricks were hand-made, cleaned, then loaded on an old ferry and sent downriver to the mill. From there they were loaded onto wagons and hauled up to the building site. David J. Little and Orlando Griffith were the main builders. Legend has it that the bricks are held in place with horsehair in the mortar. The meadow surrounding the school provided one of the largest playgrounds in the county.

School No. 1, as it was called in Grant District, had a large potbelly Burnside stove in the center of the room and four rows of desks varying in size. In the early days, Vallie Irons taught school here and rode her horse, Buck, to school. She lived on the east side of the river between the two Islands and forded the river to school. On days when the river was too high, she came across the bridge at Colfax. She left her horse tied outside the school to graze until it was time to go home. However, Vallie saved her money, and in 1926 she bought a new tan, two-door Chevy coupe, paying cash for it. Fearing our WV hills, she always drove it in second gear.

At Sarrietta School, the children learned the three R's plus grammar and spelling using McGuffey Readers. By 1951, though, teacher Mary Conturo had only 23 students due to the population decline. The Board of Education decided it was time to close the school and did so at the end of the May. Area children began being bussed to the brand new school at White Hall in the fall of 1952.

Many Sarrietta people were sorry to see their own school—the oldest standing one-room school in the district at that time—close. It had a long history of education and service to the community although its largest enrollment never got beyond 88 children nor below 13. The last teacher was Mary Conturo who had two grown sons of her own. She lived on Marion Street in Fairmont. Each morning she rode the school bus on US Rt. 250 to the Colfax Road, and then walked a mile and a half to the school in all kinds of weather, carrying her lunch just as the students did.

Four years before the closing, Mrs. Conturo was instrumental in organizing Sarrietta Parent-Teacher Association (PTA). One of the most notable improvements was the replacement of the historic pot-bellied stove for a modern coal burner. The naked light bulbs were replaced with fluorescent lighting.

Some of the early families whose children attended Sarrietta School were the Malones and Nixons from Valley Bend; the Griffiths, Keeners and Wilsons from River Run; the Flemings from near

Sarrietta School the year of its closing in 1951. Teacher was Mary Conturo.

Colfax, and the Crisses from Vinegar Hill. Families from Sarrietta represented at the school were Little, Hartley, Vincent, Shaver, Wilt, Linn and the Smallwoods.

Among the early teachers at Sarrietta School were: David Barker, (first teacher); Belle Stanley, Thomas Thickson, Willa Berry, Mr. Johnson, Cora Miller, Nan Howe, Susie Hall, Joshua Nixon, Alice Love, Granville McAllister, Ben Mundell, Willie Martin, Delphia Shaver, Lily Arnett, Hyson Christie, Rosa Hobert, Ada Valentine, Dick Mason, Mamie Vincent, Watson Carpenter, Vallie Irons, James Kendall, Mr. Allender, Rosa Smith, Lenora Hale, Frank Smith, Joe Chaney, Elsie Little Cather, Clark Reed, Willa McClure, Lillian Wilt, Pearl Chevrount, Agnes Robertson and Viola Linn.

In November 1953, Thurmond Vincent bought the 110-year-old building and grounds at public auction on the Marion County Court House steps for $100. Then he deeded it over to the trustees of the Sarrietta Community Church. Today that little brick schoolhouse is closed but is still standing and is the entryway of the Sarrietta Church (see Churches).

RIVER RUN SCHOOL

In Grant District, River Run begins about one mile from the Tygart Valley River in two valleys that hug a ridge at 1,200 feet. It has two forks: The North Fork of River Run, which is in Marion County, and the South Fork, which is in Taylor County. The two forks merge near River Run Road and then drain into the Tygart Valley River.

Poplar Island Road merges with the River Run Road after it passes Poplar Island. It follows the river and fords the run before it makes a turn and goes uphill, where it closely borders Taylor County. The dirt road changes to pavement before it winds a mile and a half to US Rt. 250 South. In the early days the Hall Mill was situated just above Poplar Island. It served Valley Bend, Sarrietta, River Run, the White Hall area and the northeastern portion of Taylor County.

River Run had a school about a half a mile from the river on the North Fork. The one-room wooden building opened in 1889 on land donated by Joseph L. Smith and Elza Wilson. The school term at that time was only four months a year. Over the years, 30 teachers taught there.

The little school was closed in the early 1950's when consolidation became common. Area children then attended White Hall School while the old school sat vacant for a couple of years before it was sold at the courthouse to Larney Radford in 1956. Shortly afterwards, the community developed a church in the abandoned school. (see Churches).

LEVELS

Across the river from Sarrietta in Union District is the community of Levels, named for the flat, level bottomland in the bend of the river. In 1773 a man by the name of John Forshey started a settlement on the East Side of the Tygart Valley River on a level plateau. This rustic and rugged area was referred to as *Forshey's Levels*. Many early land grants used Forshey's Levels as a landmark. For example: "Will Roberson assee to Philip Shiveley is entitled to four hundred acres of land in Monongalia County on the North side of the Tigar Valley adjoining or near a place call'd **Forshey's Level** lying opposite the mouth of Lost Run to include his settlement made in the year 1773."

Sanders Grocery was owned and operated by Jessie (Nuzum) Sanders of the Levels community. It opened in 1943 and closed in 1956. Sitting on the porch is Howard "Pete" Jarvis.
Courtesy of Nola (Sanders) Jarvis.

West Virginia's Lower Tygart Valley River

A sketch of the Levels stockade built around 1773.

John Forshey and a few settlers built a crude stockade for protection against the Indians, who were hostile most of the time. The area was unsafe and so Jacob Prickett escorted him and the others back across the mountains to safety.

Records show that John Forshey lived in Hampshire County nine years later. He is listed in the 1782 Census of Hampshire County where he had resettled with his family. There were eight whites and three blacks (slaves) living in the household. I found it interesting that Hampshire County also has a community named Levels. It makes one wonder if John Forshey had a place in its history as well.

Today the community of Levels is mainly a beautiful residential area with farms stretching out along the countryside. Many of these farms have belonged to the same families for several generations. There are no community signs and it cannot be located on a state map. Those who live there like it that way.

LEVELS SCHOOL

Before, during and after the Civil War, a little log cabin built by the Shriver family served this community as a subscription school and a Methodist church called the Gilboa Church. It was located on the original Levels road not far from the present-day Sand Bank Road entrance. This structure burned down the result of a brush fire from sparks from a railroad engine. It swept the area.

Then in 1869, after the formation of the Board of Education, Jacob and Anna Shriver sold it a small plot of land in Union Township for $25.00 (Deed Book 26/Page 358). It was one of the early schools in Marion County.

The first one-room school was built from local rough-cut lumber. It was located close to where the red brick school was later built. After the closing of the old school in 1907, the building was bought by Tobe and Nettie (Shriver) Simmons. It was later moved down the hill where it served as a dwelling.

In 1907 the board of education completed a red brick, one-room school not far from the old one. The red brick for the "new" school came from the Colfax Brick Company. Orlie Cheuvront Knight was its first schoolteacher. This building also served the Powell community until it became over crowded. Eight years later, in 1915, a school was built in Powell.

The Levels School taught grades one through eight. Everyone walked to school

Above: Levels brick one-room school was built in 1907 and closed in 1958. It is still standing and now belongs to David Nuzum.

Right: The first Levels School built in 1870.
Courtesy of Frank Spevock.

Levels School Class of 1953-54.
Row 1: Joe Shorter, Floyd Vandergrift, Shirley Goodwin, Linda Canfield, Bonnie Morgan, Merle Shorter, Roger Cunningham, Shirley Shorter. Row 2: Larry Morgan, Sue Vandergrift, Regina Vangilder, Dwayne Boyce, Bonnie Collins, Diana Rose, Melvin Shorter, Linda Vandergrift. Row 3: Richard Knight, Carl Rose, Sue Knight, Frank Shorter, Elizabeth Bice, teacher; David Wadsworth, Carol Cunningham, Kenneth Vandergrift and Janice Kline.
Courtesy of Blanche and Albert "Slicky" Collins.

in all kinds of weather; there was no such thing as "snow days." In those days, the BOE hired teachers who lived close by because they too, in some cases, had to walk. The traditional potbelly stove heated the large room. The school never had running water but there was a hand-dug well with a pump in front of the building.

Outdoor bathrooms were common and were at the side of the building. The entrance to the school had a large cloakroom with at least two dozen hooks for coats. Those who attended this school say they will always remember the box socials, parties and school gatherings.

Before the road to Levels was improved, students attending the high school in Fairmont had to walk to Colfax to catch the school bus. The late Isaac Knight recalled how in the 1930's, he and others made the long walk down the hill to Grandma (Anna Belle) Nichols' house. She opened her home every morning to Levels and Colfax students so they could come in out of the cold to wait for the bus. The only requirement was that they had to take off their boots, so each morning an assortment of boots were all lined up at her door.

The BOE closed Levels school in 1958. Elizabeth (Fortney) Bice had taught there for several years and was the last teacher. The following school term, the students were consolidated with Colfax School. Students were transported by bus. Powell School remained open. After the closing of the Levels School, it became a community building. A kitchen was added but the effort to maintain the building lacked support, so it sat idle for several years. In 1999 the building was sold to neighbor Albert and Blanche Collins.

Other teachers who taught at Levels were Orvilla Duckworth, Elsworth Morgan, Basil Herron, Fay Curtis, Alma Kelly, Gertrude Dietz, Ethel Balderson, Jemima Goode, A. P. Harr, Vallie Irons Phillips, Beatrice Stanley Wilt, Opal Tatterson, Walter Balderson, Florence Hall, Mary Vangilder Herron, Beryl Herron, Goldie Harbert, Patricia Osburne and Mildred Rudy Niehaus.

Anna Belle "Grandma" Nichols, who welcomed school bus students into her home each morning.
Courtesy of Barbara Nichols.

WILSON'S IRON WORKS

Valley Furnace in Barbour County, Col. Wilson's Iron Works could have looked similar to this.

Old timers from my grandmother's day told a story of an iron furnace located on the river in the early 1800's, before the B&O Railroad arrived. Lawrence Sanders of Goose Creek, told that, as a boy, his father remembered the furnace. In my research, I could find nothing in the local history books about this, but in the WV Archives in Charleston an old survey map of Monongalia County drawn up by John Wood in 1821, I found Col. Benjamin Wilson's Iron Works. The iron furnace was located on the east bank of the river across from the mouth of Lost Run.

Benjamin Wilson was born in the Shenandoah Valley of Virginia in 1784. When he was a boy, his family moved to what is now Hardy County here in West Virginia. When Wilson was a 27-year-old lieutenant, Virginia's last royal governor, Lord John Murray Dunmore chose him to be a member of the marauding expedition in the west—the one that resulted in what came to be known as Dunmore's War in 1747. Wilson was with Dunmore when they negotiated a peace treaty with Chief Cornstalk. On his way home from Ohio, Wilson saw the Tygart Valley River for the first time. He was so impressed with its beauty that he bought out two Tomahawk Rights from settlers at the river's headwaters near Beverly. He soon moved his wife and children to the valley and built a fort on his land. It became known as Fort Wilson.

During the Revolutionary War Wilson was made Colonel; anytime an Indian raid occurred in the Tygart Valley, he and his volunteers were in pursuit. In 1784, he was appointed clerk of Harrison County. Living in Randolph County, he had to move to Harrison where he bought 400 acres on Simpson Creek. After 30 years' service as clerk, he resigned in 1814. His son John succeeded him in that office.

Sometime after his retirement from that office, Wilson bought land below Levels in what was later called Powell Bottom, where he built an iron furnace. He owned a flour mill, sawmill and woolen mill—all near his home on Simpson Creek. He was successful in several other business ventures, as well as the iron furnace on the Tygart Valley River.

Several men would have been needed to operate the furnace. Acres of trees would have been cut to create the heat required, thus clearing the forest. Considering the location of the furnace, it is quite probable coal was used to burn wood into charcoal to creat more heat. It had to have been located near a limestone outcropping and near a vein of iron ore on the earth's surface. Raw pig iron was developed from these three ingredients: limestone (for flux), charcoal (for fuel), and iron ore.

Pig iron bars were the raw material for pioneer blacksmiths, who could make needed farm tools, household items, nails and even cannonballs from it. Some of the cannonballs for the War of 1812 could possibly have been made here. Neighboring landowners Joseph Irons and John Shriver were blacksmiths.

The pig iron was probably shipped by raft. During high water, the smelted iron could be taken to larger markets downriver. The stone for the furnace could have easily been quarried nearby or Wilson could have used rocks from the riverbed. When the railroad came through, men had to blast through solid rock to lay the track in this area, which became known as Benny's Cut to the railroad workers.

Time has a way of erasing historic objects such as the iron furnace, leaving nothing physical as evidence. When the railroad came through in 1852, all remnants of the iron furnace on the riverbank were erased. Thanks to a small map and a 1913 report from the WV Geological Survey, it was documented as a fact that the iron furnace was operating on the river in 1821.

Wilson died in 1827 two days after his 80th birthday. He was a very accomplished man in his lifetime and achieved much more than mentioned here, especially in Harrison County, which at that time was just across the river on the west bank. Wilson was the father of 12 children by his first wife, and with his second wife he had 17 more children, the last of which was born when Wilson was 73 years old.

People and Places

(1821 John Wood map) showing Col. Benjamin Wilson's Iron works.

155

THE SAND BANKS

Down by the river, opposite Poplar Island, was a natural deposit of sand in the hillside. Three huge veins of sand stood in dunes that looked out of place in West Virginia. The Shriver heirs owned these dunes that all the neighborhood kids loved to play in. In 1909, 157 acres were sold to the East Side Utility Company, reserving the Shriver Cemetery and right of way up to it. Brent Swearingen was the proprietor. This company had a siding track long enough to accommodate 12 hopper cars which came in from the main line of the B&O railroad so they could load the sand. Sand was shipped out to a glass factory in Morgantown and other parts of the eastern seaboard. Henry Shaffer of Levels was a boss here before he went to work at the Liberty Mine. When the stock market collapsed in 1929, so did the East Side Utility Company. It suffered many losses and closed down. The railroad siding was removed sometime in the early '30's.

The original road leading from Colfax to Levels was later called the Sand Bank Road, obviously because of the sand dunes. In the beginning, this road was an Indian trail, probably a part of the Great Catawba Indian Warpath Trail which followed the Tygart Valley River.

In 1969, The West Virginia Sportsmen and Firearms Association bought 25 acres of the old utility's property. It developed a rifle, skeet and trap shooting range. In 1980, after the opening of Martinka Mines, they were forced to trade its 25 acres for land upriver on the Hammond road. After the mines acquired all the surrounding land, the Sand Bank Road leading to Colfax was cut off, ending over a century of travels.

LEVELS ROAD

The original Levels road to Colfax was by Sand Bank Road. It ended up where the present Sandy Beach Road meets the present Levels Road near the railroad crossing at Colfax. The narrow, dirt road had a fork that led to the ford that crossed the river just above Poplar Island. It was originally an Indian path.

In 1929, the George Barnes family lived in Levels. Barnes owned a construction company that had a grader. He instigated a movement for the State to build a new road to Colfax, offering help with his grader. After the property was purchased by the State, the existing road to Colfax was built. The road was rough and full of potholes most of time but was an easier way of getting from one place to another. When school busing began, the Board of Education refused to send the school bus down this road. Students from Levels and Powell had to walk to Colfax when they boarded the school bus to the high school.

During the tenure of Russell Nichols as Sheriff of Marion County, the Levels Road was paved to Goose Creek for the first time (October 1944). After the paving, the school bus pick-up for high school students began. The bus went through Colfax, then Levels to Goose Creek, where the paving stopped. The bus turned around and went back to Fairmont the way it came because the road was too bad beyond Goose Creek. Levels Road connected with East Grafton Road where there are now water storage tanks up on the hill next to the Rudy place. Two years later, the road was paved all the way to the Frank Morgan place. He gave up some ground to allow the road to connect at Morgan's Crossroads. In 1974 the road was widened and resurfaced.

GOOSE CREEK

Goose Creek originates at the bottom of a 1,400 ft. plateau next to the Vangilder property, about one mile from Morgan's Crossroads. It meanders beside the county road to Levels and Powell, where it empties into the Tygart Valley River. Originally this area was referred to as Hampton Valley after a family who lived there and because of the many geese that once populated the unnamed creek, it acquired its present name. Geese, renowned for being good watchdogs, freely roamed the valley. Some were quite aggressive; therefore walkers had to carry a stick to keep them away.

In the early 1900's, before the road was paved, farmers regularly used a lane that went over the hill to the Colfax Road, located today beside the Winfield Volunteer Fire Department substation. It was known as Town Hill Road and was the quickest way to town for folks who lived at Goose Creek. In 1903, Sylvester Vandergrift owned and operated a grocery store for the community, and an undertaker's business where the Beckner farm is today. The fertile Goose Creek valley still has beautiful farms on both sides of the road—some of which have been in families for several generations. The creek now runs dry most of the time due to undermining in the area.

GOOSE CREEK SCHOOL

In 1883, Richard and Josinah Knight sold a half-acre of land to the BOE for $15.00 for a one-room school. It was a 30x23 ft. wood frame building known as the Hampton Valley appointment. The only door was in the front and there were three windows on each side. Twenty-two years later in 1905 it was replaced with a new school on the same site. The old school was sold and moved across the road for use as a Free Methodist Church called Nain. (see Churches). The school was discontinued in 1934 when Marion County replaced the old district schools. (In 1933 by virtue of an act of the legislature, all district and independent boards of educations were abolished and were replaced by county boards.) Students were then sent to the Powell and Levels schools. Goose Creek School (Hampton Valley) was dismantled shortly afterwards.

The first Goose Creek School built in 1883. It is now the garage of Dale and Anna Fisher.

Teachers who taught at the Goose Creek School were Watson Carpenter, Frank Morgan, Mollie Morris Morgan, Naomi Morgan, Ellsworth Morgan, Mattie Morgan Hall, Cecil Parrick, Allison Parrick, Alice Springer Zinn, Belle Wimer, Sweden Satterfield, Myrtle Hill Meredith, David Satterfield, Edith Baker, Hattie Davis, Earl Michael, and Wesley Vangilder.

POWELL

Powell Road branches off the Levels Road. The original road went past Powell school, down the hill towards the railroad tracks and river. Here there were about 14 homes in what used to be referred to as "Powell Bottom."

Powell was located 10 miles south of Fairmont in Union District, Marion County by rail. It was situated directly across the river from Lost Run where it flows into the Tygart Valley River from Taylor County. Powell was named after John Powell who was the first Powell to settle on the river. He received a land grant that extended downriver about a mile towards the Shriver property and upriver as far as the Nuzum property.

In 1847, John owned and operated a ferry, which became known as Powell Ferry, not far from the ford crossing over to Taylor County. Our pioneers had blazed a road that forded the river near this point from Morgan's Fort to Bridgeport. After the railroad was constructed, Mr. Powell sold the riverside property to Richard Kirk, who continued the operation of the ferry. It was then known as Kirk's Ferry. Kirk built a new ferryboat that was propelled by a system of ropes and pulleys instead of oars. After the death of Richard Kirk, Ebenezer Vandergrift bought the land and the ferry, which was discontinued.

John Powell died in 1852—the year the railroad arrived. John, his brother Joseph, and a nephew, William B. Powell, who was a Civil War veteran, are buried in the cemetery on the hill at the Church of the Brethren.

West Virginia's Lower Tygart Valley River

POWELL SCHOOL

Powell School built in 1915, was converted into a dwelling in 1961. It was later bought by Martinka Mines for use as an office building but it is now abandoned. *Courtesy of Frank Spevock*

With the influx of new residents to the community, the population had grown to the point that they could support two schools close together. Student enrollment at Levels School had doubled. In 1915, D. J. and Minnie Crouser sold half an acre of land to the Board of Education (Deed Book 207, Page 389) for $100. The Powell School was built at the top of hill from Powell bottom. The one-room building was made of Colfax red brick and was slightly larger than the Levels School.

Three years after the Levels School closed, consolidation affected Powell School and in 1961, it, too, closed. All elementary students were bused to Colfax thereafter.

Empty, the red brick school building was sold and converted into a dwelling until Martinka Mines opened up in 1973. They purchased the property and the old school became the company's first office. Today It remains mine property, standing vacant and in need of care.

Some of the teachers who taught at Powell were: Mattie Curry, Mr. Robertson, Curtis Boyce, Annie Curry, Nerva Shuman, Virginia Neptune, Martha Satterfield, Ruby Tatterson, Jasper Elder, Edith Lewis, Madeline Motter Pendergast, Bernice Snyder, Rita Wilson, Elizabeth Gillespie, Beryl Herron, Elizabeth Fortney Bice, Carolyn Janes Sipe, Martha Davis, and Olive Davis Canfield. Ethel Long was the last teacher in 1961.

LIBERTY MINE

At the onset of World War I, the Liberty Coal & Coke Company was founded. It was in full operation in 1920 and employed 50 people at the peak of its production. In the early days when the Shriver family owned the property, coal was found in the side of the hill. The coal bank supplied fuel for them and their neighbors for many years before it was ever thought it could be sold commercially. Little did they know that they had hit upon one of the richest bituminous coal veins in the United States— the Lower Kittanning coal seam.

Little by little the Shriver property, including the coal bank, was sold. The late Isaac Knight, a Levels resident, remembered when he was a boy, how the mine used the smallest of ponies to bring the coal out of the mine. The stable for the ponies was near his home place. The Shetland pony, which stood no more than 36 inches from the ground, was the only breed they could use because of the shallow, narrow tunnels. William Goodwin, of Levels, was the caretaker of the ponies and stable.

Liberty Coal was located near the Shriver Cemetery, close to the site where Martinka Mine began operations in 1974. At that time, the miners who worked for Martinka built several homes in the Levels area. Some of the local men who worked there were Henry Shaffer, mine superintendent; Lawrence Sanders, Lawrence Sanders, Jr.; Fred Sanders, Dorrie Martin, George Haddix, Guy Able, Ralph Keener and John Collins. The men wore cloth hats with a carbide lamp on top for light in the slope mine. The mine closed in 1928-29, at the beginning of the Depression years.

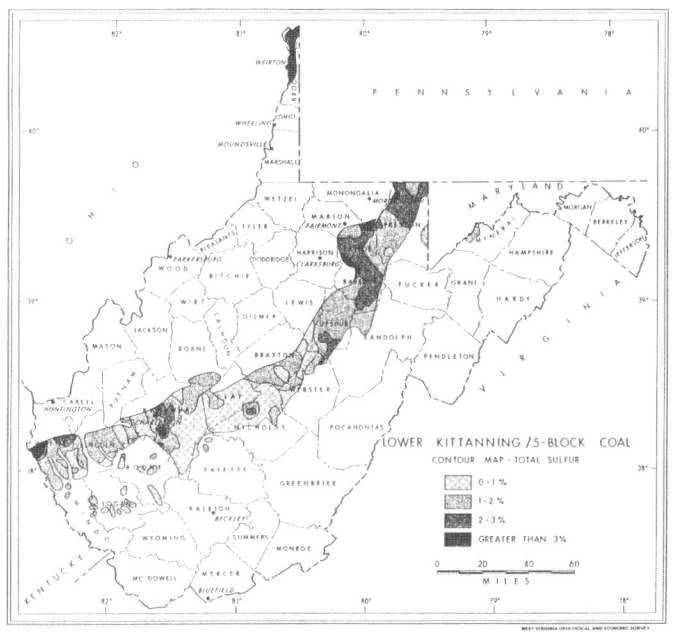

Courtesy of WV Geological and Economic Survey

POWELL COAL & COKE COMPANY

According to the 1870 US census, George M. Hite, age 51, lived at Powell with his wife Hulda. They had five children. George worked at the clay brick factory at Nuzum's Mill.

In 1885, George bought land from the Hendersons, Joshua Shaw, Davis, Nuzum, Vandergrift and the McMahon family. He built beehive coke ovens near the railroad tracks and fed them with coal shoveled out of the hillside only six feet above the river. He named his business the Powell Coal & Coke Company.

Coke is a high temperature fuel. It is made by baking coal at a controlled temperature for a given period of time. All of the fuel was washed in the river in what they called a coal washer. (This was at a time before pollution regulations were instrumented.) The formation of coal into coke required baking that usually took 48, 72, 96 or 120 hours to remove the impurities. This was all done in those beehive ovens located down by the railroad tracks. The coke was then shipped by rail to steel mills.

Liberty Mine or the Powell Coal & Coke Company owned by George M. Hite as it looked in 1900. This picture is the only known picture in existence of the mine. The glass negative was cracked but Fairmont State College was able to reproduce it. *Courtesy of FSC Folk Life Collection, Donated by Buddy Myers.*

Employing men to support this operation created growth in the community to such an extent that the B&O Railroad built a platform so passenger trains could stop regularly. Mr. Hite built a hotel and a company store and his wife operated them. They petitioned through the railroad company for a post office for the community. On August 10, 1888 George M. Hite was confirmed as the first postmaster of Powell. The following are the others who served as postmaster of Powell (according to The National Archives): July 23, 1903; Jerome (Pete) C. Motter appointed July 23, 1903; John E. Hamilton appointed October 21, 1904, and Frank Smith appointed April 25, 1905.

On September 30, 1905 the post office was discontinued. Mail for patrons was sent to neighboring Hammond. Population in Powell at this time was 75. Mr. Hite died in 1907 and his wife died in 1903. Both of them and two of their sons are buried in the Nuzum No. 1 Cemetery on the hill at the Church of the Brethren.

By 1913 the boom days of the community were over. The company store and post office had closed and the train platform was taken up. The exact closing date of the Powell Coal & Coke Company is not known, but many people remember the abandoned beehive ovens along the railroad tracks. The small sloped mine had been abandoned and fallen shut. The ovens were excavated when Martinka came to town in 1974. Their large office complex was built at Powell Bottom. The mine made a new private entrance to the complex by cutting off forever the road down the hill to the Powell community, as everyone knew it. Today Powell encompasses only the homes on Powell Road.

TYGART RIVER MINE
(Martinka)

Some of the richest coalfields in the world are along railroad lines in West Virginia. The B&O Railroad was no exception. Coalfields opened to make some men into "coal barons." On the Tygart Valley River in Marion County, two huge coal mines as well as the railroad became two of the county's largest economic assets. Those mines were the Virginia & Pittsburgh Coal & Coke Co. in Kingmont and the Martinka Coal Company at Powell. The mine closings in 1955 and 1994 respectively brought economic decline to the county.

In 1973, when the news that there was a possibility that a new coal mine might open hit the small communities of Colfax, Levels and Powell, everyone was caught by surprise. The neighbors who lived in Powell had mixed emotions because the mine had chosen Powell as its main site. Property in and around the community began selling for a healthy price—giving some an opportunity to start over somewhere else. It was a deal hard to refuse. But others whose farms had been in the family for generations saw them being ripped apart.

The Martinka Mine officially opened on March 15, 1974 and at its peak employed 600 men. The area grew in homes, population and traffic. The mine was expected to produce coal for at least 20 years and it did. The Southern Ohio Coal Company owned Martinka, and it was very generous to the surrounding communities and their organizational groups.

As with most coal mine operations, there came the undermining of homes in the area. One by one Martinka had to repair foundations to the satisfaction of the owners. In Powell, a huge gob pile (waste coal) became evidence of the volume of coal that was being mined. Two other such piles would come to dominate the Levels community. On November 16, 1991, Martinka Mines experienced its first major cutback (135 miners) since its opening in 1974. Then on March 6, 1992 Martinka laid off another 167 employees. This affected many local families. Most of them knew their jobs were lost forever and that they would have to endure some hard times until another job could be found. Some had to move away; others went back to school to be trained in another field of employment.

On July 1, 1992 Peabody Coal Company purchased Martinka Mine. They changed the name to Tygart River Mine (although everyone still referred to it as Martinka). It operated with less than half of the employees the mine once had. On December 18, 1995, after 21 years of mining bituminous coal in one of America's richest coal veins, the mine closed. There were 359 employees put out of work at its final closing.

Sign at the entrance of Tygart River Mine at Levels.

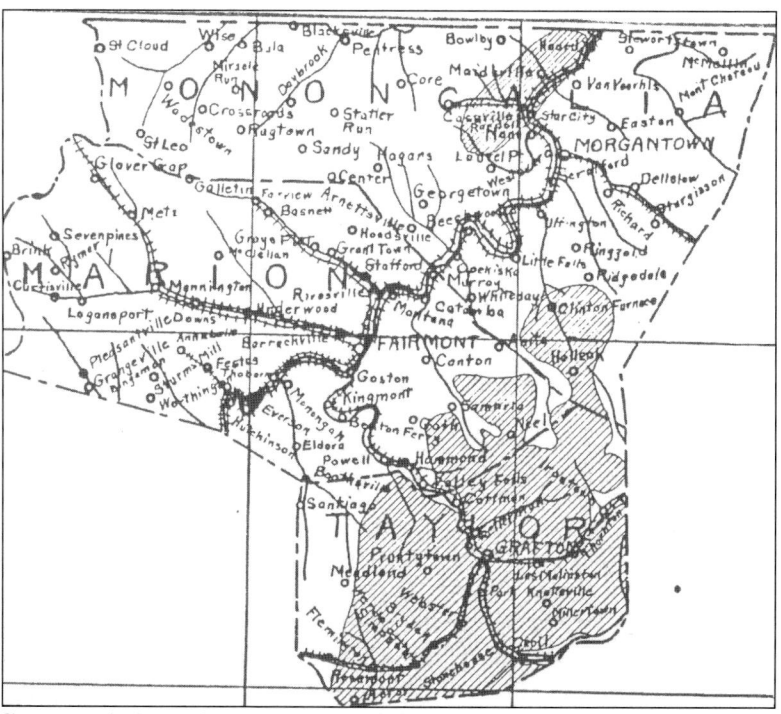

Gray area is the region of the Lower Kittanning coal seam in Marion and Taylor counties. *Courtesy of WV Geological Survey and Economic Survey.*

Coal tipple at Martinka Mine in 1980. It is no longer in operation. *Courtesy of Terry Arbogast, photo by American Electric Power.*

MINE'S WATER TREATMENT PLANT

The water treatment plant and settling ponds were built on Guyses Run, which flowed through Colfax and emptied into the Tygart Valley River. The plant was built over the objections of the Colfax community when the mine opened in 1974.

Although residents feared acid mine drainage, the water treatment plant did its job with no major problems over the 21 years that the mine was in operation. However, within two weeks after the closing of the mine in 1995, Colfax residents started to notice a deposit in the creek bed. In January of 1996, it was reported to the Department of Environmental Protection (DEP), which determined that Martinka illegally stained the creek from the water that came from the water treatment plant. The company was fined more than once and had several extensions but the staining of the creek continued.

As a result, concerned citizens from Colfax formed a group called F.R.O.G. (Friends For the Restoration of Guyses) to fight for the clean-up of Guyses Run. David and Joanne Nuzum II, Tom and Patricia DeVito, David and Helen Nuzum, L. D. and Misty Skarzinski and Mike and Misty Cristy lived downstream from the treatment plant and monitored the stream for discharge. Over time, the little creek went from running clear to orange to red, then to a thick orange slush created by the chemical treatments.

The Tygart River Mine built a new treatment pond during the summer of 1997. This was to provide additional retention time for the water in an attempt to reduce deposits in the creek. The staining of Guyses Run continued.

By the summer of 1998, the creek had a solid layer of tan-colored sediment that completely covered the stream bed. The experimental chemicals used at the treatment plant created a cement-like material in the creek, killing all vegetation and life, which began producing an odor. The sediment was later identified as calcium carbonate that had built up on the rocks.

Aerial view of Tygart River Mine's new water treatment complex and gob piles at Levels.

On August 5, 1998 the Tygart River Mine announced plans to build a new on-site treatment plant at Levels, which meant that the mine would stop discharging into Guyses Run. Meanwhile the staining continued.

One day later, on August 6, the Tygart River Mine was fined $87,000 by state environmental regulators for polluting the Tygart Valley River. This problem was not for Guyses Run. The agency cited the mine for discharging untreated "black" water from the old nearby Liberty Mine that was closed down. The Tygart Valley River had a black plume of water emptying into it from Goose Creek. Pollution of the Tygart Valley River then became everyone's concern.

In January of 1999, after countless meetings, the Tygart River Mine management announced that it would build a new state-of-the-art, computerized water treatment plant at the Levels mine site. Project completion date was targeted for September of 1999 at a cost of $4.4 million. After a few setbacks, the new plant was finally working properly by January 2000. The water treatment system is capable of treating underground mine water (containing alkaline) and refuse-area runoff (acidic, heavy in metals and contaminants) at the same time. The water PH levels are from 6.7 - 6.9 as it feeds into the Tygart Valley River. In February 2001, the State Department of Environmental Protection (DEP) presented a Reclamation Award to the Tygart River Mine officials for the water treatment plant, which was the answer to Guyses Run problems.

During the summer of 2001 the former Tygart River Mine, which was sold to Eastern Associated Coal Corp., loaned the ponds, holding tanks and grounds to West Virginia University's Aquaculture researchers to explore the viability of aquaculture, the raising of fish for food and sport. After three months of testing, charting and purifying the water

Tygart River Mine's old acid mine drainage holding tanks— now a fish hatchery.

People and Places

the study was a success. There are plans to continue in the future, hoping to boost the state's economy— by selling the fish to recreational facilities offering fee fishing. Who would ever have thought that an acid-mine drainage plant could make such a complete turn around? Today Guyses Run no longer has a connection to the mine as far as water flow is concerned. The ponds and tanks now contain rainwater and runoff.

In June of 2003 a "catch and release" fishing derby was held for children of the area and another one in September for Senior Citizens. It was sponsored by WVU, Martinka and Marion County Parks and Recreation.

THE GHOST TOWN OF HAMMOND
(Nuzum's Mills)

The history of Hammond begins in 1800. Richard Nuzum was the only son of Thomas and Elizabeth Nuzum from Wexford County, Ireland. They immigrated to this country and settled in Nether, Providence (near Philadelphia) Pennsylvania. When Thomas died in 1791, Richard inherited his father's extensive lands. He had married Hannah Worrall, a Quaker, in 1760. Since Richard was not a Quaker, Hannah was shunned by her Society of Quakers for marrying an outsider. Seventeen years later Richard converted and rose to the equivalent of a deacon, which was a position of high importance in the church.

Eleven years after his father's death and with his own family grown, Richard had become increasingly concerned about the decline of timber, caused by increasing population in their region. He convinced his family that they should relocate and sent several of his sons to the wilderness of western Virginia to look for a sizable tract of land blessed with large stands of virgin timber on it—timbers that could be used for both building and fuel.

The sons selected a site on the Tygart Valley River—one that had several runs flowing through it just below a two-mile long gorge giving rise to a beautiful set of falls. The land was all in virgin timber, and the threat of Indians was at an end.

Richard obtained a grant for 1000 acres. In 1802, Richard sold his father's land in Pennsylvania for $1,498 and moved the whole family to this western Virginia wilderness where they cleared the land, built log cabins, and developed a settlement that became known as Nuzums.

The children of Richard and Hannah Nuzum:

John (1761-1844) a millwright. He and his brother William built the first mill on the Tygart Valley River. John remodeled the mill several times before he died. He and his wife Jane had eight children.

Elizabeth (1763-1843) married Joseph Dickinson and settled finally in Ohio. She married again late in life to Samuel Gregg.

Thomas (1765-1843) After a year in the valley, he and his wife Margaret and family moved back to Delaware County, Pennsylvania to a 50-acre tract he had inherited from his grandfather. They had eight children.

James (1767-1841) was dismissed from the Quakers for marrying out of the Society. He and his wife Sarah had six children. They moved near to what later became Fetterman.

William (1772-1845) After he helped his brother John build the mill, he built an overshot sawmill on Burnt Cabin Run. It was operated by a waterwheel. Later he became a distiller of several kinds of liquor (moonshine) and was also disowned by the Quakers. He and his wife Martha had twelve children.

George (1774-1867) and his wife Ruth (Martin) were Quakers and obeyed the strict rules of their Society. They spent the rest of their lives at the Nuzum settlement, but their sons came under many influences. They participated in the Civil War, which was one of the factors that brought about the end of the local Quaker society. George and Ruth had nine children. The couple is buried in the Nuzum No. 1 Cemetery.

Sarah (1777-1851) and her husband Gardner Leonard lived at the settlement all their lives. They died on the same day and are buried in the cemetery up on top of the hill.

Phoebe (1779-1802) died soon after the family arrived in the valley. Her gravesite is on the hillside with only a flagstone as a marker.

Richard Nuzum lived to see his family flourish, the clearing of the land with the building of his son John's invaluable mill, a sawmill upriver, and a Quaker Society, which met regularly. This settlement became known to everyone around as Nuzum's. Richard Nuzum died at the age of 88 in 1822 and is buried at the Colfax Cemetery (originally called the Springer Graveyard), even though Richard had conveyed several acres of land from his original land grant for a cemetery on the hill by the Quaker church.

NUZUM'S MILL

> NUZUMS.
> On the Tygart Valley river and the B. & O. R. R., in Marion county, 12½ miles southeast of Fairmount, the county seat and banking point. A. H. Springer, postmaster.
> Bradshaw John, railroad and exp agent.
> GLADE FIRE BRICK CO, Fire Clay and Paving Brick.
> Linn S R, coal miner.
> Mason R F, teacher.
> Rudy John, jeweler and gunsmith.
> SPRINGER A H, Mnfr of Soft Brick.
> Steel James, flour mill.
> Steel Mrs J, hotel.
> Vincent A J, live stock.
>
> WV Gazetteer 1898-99

John Nuzum, age 41, oldest son of Richard, was a millwright. With the help of his brother William, 30, they built the first mill on the Tygart Valley River not long after their families arrived in 1802. John rebuilt and remodeled the mill several times during his lifetime. The original millstones from that mill rest in the Nuzum No. 1 Cemetery beside the Church of the Brethren.

Many years later in 1850, John's son, Richard (Black Dick) and his son, Joel, sold land near the river to the B&O Railroad. This sale was made with the stipulation that the B&O build and maintain a station and a sidetrack to receive and send shipments of goods for the mill at the settlement. The railroad was in operation in 1852, and a station and sidetrack was indeed put in. It became known as Nuzum's Station, 12.6 miles from Fairmont.

Richard (Black Dick) Nuzum (1795-1887) was the first to create bricks that were handmade from the natural clay deposits in the hillside by the river. He was also an experienced blacksmith.

Joel was a millwright and had been operating the mill when property was sold to the railroad. Five years later, Joel sold his 100 acres of land from his inheritance to his father Richard. Joel and his family then moved to Morgantown, where he and associates built the town's first iron foundry.

That left "Black Dick" Nuzum owner of most of the original land grant. He continued operating the mill and produced handmade bricks that were sold only locally. By the end of the Civil War, Richard was 70 and had begun to slow down due to age. The place called Nuzum's became known as Nuzum's Mill.

THE BEGINNING OF COAL PRODUCTION ON THE TYGART

Three years after the arrival of the B&O Railroad, James O. Watson, at the age of 41, came to Nuzum's Mill to investigate rumors of coal near the headwaters of Prickett's Creek. Among all his other interests, Mr. Watson became the first postmaster of Nuzum's Mill in 1856. He held that position in name only for 17 years but never actually dispersed the mail himself. He traveled by train from Fairmont when he was at Nuzum's Mill. Later he moved on to other ventures, becoming known as the Father of the West Virginia coal industry.

In 1859, the Marion Cannel Coal Co., with which Mr. Watson was associated, was part owner in a cannel coal mine at the headwaters of Prickett's Creek that employed several men. Cannel coal is formed from the spores of giant tree ferns that lived billions of years ago. In Glenn Lough's *Now & Long Ago,* Lough says, "The coal was shipped to Philadelphia where it was distilled into coal oil." The coal oil or kerosene was used in Baltimore, Maryland street lamps.

The coal vein was five feet thick. A bushel of its coal produced two gallons of oil worth 60 cents a gallon in 1859. The coal produced gas, oil and paraffin for candles. Judge Harry Shaw said to E. E. Meredith for his *Do You Remember* newspaper column in the *Fairmont Times* (7-27-36) that he did not recall having seen cannel coal used for lamps, but he did recall how bright it burned in a grate. It threw out plenty of light for a room, he said.

A tram railroad was tunneled through the hill to transport the coal to the railroad for shipment at Nuzum's Mill. Some of the coal was used at the brickyard. The tram railroad had wooden cars that were drawn by mules or horses and could carry passengers, including women and children on the return trip back to the mine. After the mine closed down, the tunnel through the hill also was closed when East Grafton Road was improved. To this day, the road leading down to Prickett's Creek is still called Tunnel Hollow.

After the Civil War ended, in 1865, Richard (Black Dick) Nuzum sold 370 acres of his grandfather's original land grant to James O. Watson. The sale included the land, the mill, all coal rights and the clay deposits in the hillside. Black Dick lived to be 92 years old and saw the brickyard progress. He observed the beginning of the coal industry in the valley. He died April 4, 1887 and is buried in the Nuzum No. 1 Cemetery.

Watson's interests included taking over the operation of the mill and adding to the brick making business. Coal was abundant in and around the Village of Nuzum's Mill as were natural clay deposits suitable for making bricks. Watson formed a brick factory which continued to be profitable until 1872 when the coal was exhausted on upper Prickett's Creek and Tunnel Hollow. Then, at age 57, Watson decided to move elsewhere with his other investment ventures in coal.

THE BRICK COMPANIES

Courtesy of WV *Gazetteer 1900.*

HAMMOND FIRE BRICK CO.
HIGH GRADE FIRE CLAY PRODUCTS
FOR
FURNACES, COKE OVENS, PAVING AND BUILDING
OFFICE, 414 JACOBS BUILDING
BELL PHONE 161
CONSOLIDATED PHONE 221
FAIRMONT, W. VA.

When Nuzum sold his property, he probably never imagined it would become one of the most famous brickyards in northern West Virginia. It was slow in the beginning but when coal ran out in Tunnel Hollow, brick making became the only interest at Nuzum's Mill. Mr. Watson, whose main interest was coal, sold the property to Smith & Porter Company in 1872. Buckner and Lewis Smith and Jasper M., John, James, and James M. Porter purchased the property to produce building bricks. Up until then there was only one kiln. Smith & Porter Co. built another kiln but still only produced one grade of brick. They owned the brickyard for 15 years and made only a few improvements.

In 1887, Smith & Porter Company sold the brick factory to the Glade Fire Brick Company. One year later, as the result of torrential rains, the Tygart Valley River flooded the whole valley. The flood destroyed the mill, store and post office and severely damaged the brickyard. Although the community quickly recovered by building a new store and post office, the mill was lost forever. The brick company took several years to regain what it had lost; it sold brick only to supply local demands.

In 1899, the Hammond Fire Brick Company purchased the ailing Glade Fire Brick Company. Brothers James B. Hammond, President, and E. R. Hammond, Vice President, operated the company as a branch of the Reese-Hammond Fire Brick Company of Bolivar, Pennsylvania. The men owned several brick companies in Ohio, West Virginia, Kentucky and their home state, Pennsylvania. The property included 410 acres of land with three different kinds of fire-clay seams that were two feet thick and of excellent quality. The clay was located 100 feet below the coal-level seam. There was abundant coal to feed the coke ovens. The B&O built a sidetrack for shipments.

The Hammond family house at the corner of McKinley and Sixth Street, Bolivar, PA. The house still stands. *Courtesy of Westmoreland County, PA Historical Society.*

Hammond Brick Yard Workers in 1926.
Those identified are: Fred Klepful, Fred Motter, "Keg" Charley Haney, Gaither "Tuck" Dailey, Herman Boyce, "Lige" Currey, John Smith, Fred Martin, Brooks Goodwin, Johnny Hammer, Aubrey Cheuvront, Will Goodwin, George Haddix, Robert McKenny, Lawrence Sanders, John Phillips, "Buck" Vandergrift, Tom Lawler, Raleigh Cheuvront, Jhonny Keener, Bud Morgan, Lloyd Morgan, Gerald Griffith, Claude Biddle, James Kelly, Homer Henderson, Phillip Vangilder, Tom Motter, Aaron Sanders, old Mr. Maze, Henry Fast, Ernie Griffin, Charles Nuzum, Walter Goodwin and Hiram Boyce. *Courtesy of the late Gerald Griffith.*

HAMMOND FIRE BRICK COMPANY

James Brett Hammond was born in 1867 in Bolivar, Pennsylvania, the youngest child of James S. and Elizabeth (Brett) Hammond, who were from Ireland. His father had started in the brick-making business by mining clay in Bolivar. Later he started his own successful brick making business. James Brett, after teaching school for ten years, became his father's treasurer and general manager at the Reese & Hammond Fire Brick Company.

Company letterhead dated 1900. *Courtesy of WVU Archives.*

James Brett had an older sister named Margaret. Her daughter Sarah married Albert Nuzum, a cousin to Richard ("Black Dick") Nuzum. By this time the Nuzum family had spread out over different directions and the mill was gone. When the Hammonds bought the brick factory in 1899, the name of Nuzum's Mill was changed to Hammond, bringing the end of an era for the village of Nuzum's Mill.

In 1903, the Hammond Fire Brick Company hired W. J. Snowden and Son, of Hancock County, to build new round kilns. W. J. Snowden was 70 years old at the time and claimed he and his workers laid 3,800 bricks in one day getting the job done in record time.

Tom Britt and an unidentified man in Hammond Brickyard. *Courtesy of FSC Folk Life Collection, Donated by Buddy Myers.*

Several dwellings were built for the brickyard workers. The company hired over a hundred men in the early days. A large home for the general manager, Thomas I. Brett, was built high above flood level across the railroad tracks from the plant. Other houses were built for the mine bosses in a section the miners called Jersey Town.

The brick plant was expanded and modernized. New machinery with experienced men operated them. In 1905, the company was producing firebricks for coke ovens. These bricks were always in demand. Every year the plant made improvements and by 1910, production reached 50,000 bricks per working day. By 1945, the output was 100,000 bricks per day.

Shipments of brick went cities on the eastern coast and were sold locally as well. The workmanship and quality of the bricks created a high demand by construction firms wanting the very best. Large orders like the ones for the Hoult Locks & Dam, the Hartley Building in Fairmont (1929), West Fairmont High School, Quiet Dell and Millersville schools and the Veterans Hospital in Clarksburg were among the hundreds of homes and buildings, streets and highways made of Hammond brick. After the stock market crash in 1929, the large order for bricks for the Empire State building in New York City kept the men working and the company afloat. It is believed the Hammond bricks also were used for the Ford Motor Company in Detroit, Michigan.

Samples of Hammond brick were taken to the Chicago World's Fair, where judges declared them the best fire clay in the U.S. A. In 1945, the Hammond Fire Brick Company purchased the Thornton Fire Brick company in Taylor County.

Ovens at Hammond brickyard. *Courtesy of Carl & Wilma (Curry) Johnson.*

Hammond Fire Brick Company. Note the Tygart Valley River in the background and the small tramway towards the clay pits. The tramway led up the hill to a place called Heiferville where several workers lived. *Courtesy of Tom Koon.*

Hammond bricks were a buff or gray color. They were colorful bricks and were engraved with names like TYGART, HAMMOND, FAIRMONT W.VA, BESSMER, TEMPLE and RESIST among many others. In 1940, there were 25 families living in Hammond. Except for at the very beginning, no red bricks were produced until 1944-45, when economic problems developed along with strong competition. Then, in 1952, a major fire broke out and destroyed the brickyard. Many men lost their livelihood and had to move away. In less than five years, the once-thriving little community became a ghost town. In 1965, only eight families remained in Hammond.

When Southern Ohio Coal Company bought the land in 1972, all that was left of its former glory were piles of broken bricks. The kilns, smokestacks and all of the buildings were razed in September 1972. Souvenir seekers carried away many of the bricks that were left on the ground. One of the most prized bricks in my flower garden is a very rare brick marked TYGART.

Hammond brickyard in 1912. *Courtesy of Robert Collins*

Thornton Plant Sold to Hammond

Purchase of the old Thornton Fire Brick Company plant near Grafton, which has been operating with only a few men on the payroll, has been announced by Ralph Ervin and his associates of Morgantown.

Ervin said the Taylor county plant, erected in 1903, would be modernized and expanded and will be operated jointly with the Hammond Fire Brick Company installation at Hammond, which was acquired last January.

Main offices for the two operations will be maintained in Morgantown.

Ervin, who reported that each of the two plants had a capacity of 12,000,000 bricks per year said that orders on hand insured full-scale production at both places through 1946 and part of the following year.

Brick for most of the new buildings on West Virginia university campus came from Thornton, Ervin said.

Oct. 22, 1945

Newspaper article from the *Fairmont Times* dated October 22, 1945.

Hammond store/post office in 1905.
Courtesy of FSC Folk Life Collection, Donated by Buddy Myers.

NUZUM'S MILL POSTMASTERS

Less than two months after the opening of the Valley Falls Post Office, Nuzum's Mill Post Office opened in 1856. Situated 12 miles southwest of Fairmont, it remained open during the Civil War. Valley Falls Post Office closed in 1861 but re-opened six days after statehood—1863.

The following names and appointment dates for Nuzum's Mill-Hammond post office are from microfilm from The National Archives in Washington D.C.

POSTMASTERS

July 3, 1856,	James O. Watson (1815-1902)
July 25, 1867,	James O. Watson (reappointed)
April 18, 1873,	Daniel L. Morrow
April 5, 1878,	George M. Hite (1817-1907)
April 6, 1888,	Daniel L. Morrow, and
November 12, 1895,	Andrew Springer.

In 1899, the name Nuzum's Mill was changed to Hammond. Those postmasters were:

October 28, 1899,	Daniel L. Morrow
November 24, 1900,	Thomas I. Brett
December 13, 1913,	Phillip Vangilder
November 25, 1925,	Margaret Mae Sines (1878-1963)
October 27, 1927,	Maxmillian A. Zollinger (1893-1961)
July 15, 1958,	Marguerite Vincent.
Closed in 1959.	

Some of the names of families who received mail at Nuzum's Mill in 1860 were: Heck, Hirons, Vincent, Satterfield, West, Ferrell, Sigler, Kirk, Rice, Hartley, Mundell, Nuzum, Swearingen, Hall, Shaw, Hawkins, Vandergrift, Springer, Griffith, Ferguson, Thompson, Shriver, Spicer, Smith and Kenney.

Thomas Hawkins carried the mail from Fairmont to Bunner Ridge Post Office and then traveled on to Hammond three times a week. Henry Rudy was also a mail carrier; he delivered the mail on horseback when it was Rural Route 1. Brady Linn from Glady Creek was the last mail carrier for the Hammond and Valley Falls area.

The post office at Hammond was discontinued on November 30, 1959. The last two years the post office was in the S&S Grocery on East Grafton Road. The village of Hammond at this time had very few homes left.

West Virginia's Lower Tygart Valley River

Hammond in 1910. *Courtesy of FSC Folk Life Collection, Donated by Buddy Myers*

Freight receiving agents for Nuzum's Mill were: 1884, James Steel; 1895, Andrew Springer; 1898, John Bradshaw; 1908, J. R. Wilson, and 1914, I. A. Brett.

1893 WEST VIRGINIA GAZETTEER LISTING OF HAMMOND

The population of the Village of Hammond in 1893 was 50. The following businesses were listed:

Glade Fire Brick Company, Linn & Vincent Flour Mill, General Store, D. L. Morrow (store and post office together); Jeweler and Gunsmith, John Rudy; Justice of the Peace, Joshua Shaw; RR Express Agent, Andrew Springer; Flour Mill, John Steel; Hotel, Mrs. John Steel; Livestock, A. J. Vincent; Veterinarian, E. L. Vincent; Lawyer, G. A. Vincent; and Blacksmith, Henry Vincent.

HAMMOND. Population 100. On the B & O R R, in Marion County, 12 miles southeast of Fairmont, the county seat, 10 from Grafton, the banking point, and 90 from Wheeling. Expres, Wells Fargo. Telephone connection. Mail daily. Philip Van Gilder, postmaster.
Brett T I, R R and exp agt.
Hammand Fire Brick Co.
VAN GILDER PHILIP, General Store.

WV Gazetteer 1918-19

170

Hammond School in 1931. Teacher Opal Tatterson. Front (left to righ)t. Edith Nyrne, Ruby McCabe, Maxine Boyce, Frank Byrne, Betty McCabe, Marjorie Phillips, Geraldine Boyce, Wilma Sinclair, Susan Klepfel, Jackie Shaffer and George Sanders. Back (left to right). Lewis Vangilder, Margaret Mae Vandergrift, Theodore Henderson, Freda Phillips McKenny, Hie Boyce and Johnny Boyce. *Courtesy of Blanche Collins*

HAMMOND SCHOOL
(Marion County)

Before the War Between the States, Hammond had a subscription school, which continued to operate until the first free school in Union District was established under the new system. It was first held in a dwelling house and was taught by Phyllis Sertees. Later, a genuine schoolhouse was built on Hammond Road, two miles from East Grafton Road at the bottom of the hill. It was a one-room brick building made of hand-made bricks and it closely resembled the Levels brick school building. A potbelly stove was used to provide heat and there were kerosene lamps for lighting.

John Nelson "Net" Nuzum was a pioneer teacher for Hammond. Other teachers were: Ada Saunders Thompson, V. P. Atha, Vallie Irons, Lynn Herron, Basil Herron, Elsie Little Cathers, Lizzie Robinson, Hattie Davis Armstrong, Martha Davis, Rufus Davis, Olive Mason Motter, Glen Vincent, Andy Henderson, Max Zollinger, Ruby Tatterson, Opal Tatterson Hawkins, A. Cheuvront, Angelina Julian and Gwendoyln Haas.

After the brickyard fire disaster in 1952, the school was closed. Very few families remained in the community. Their children attended Quiet Dell School, three miles away.

The following poem was written by Rufus A. West (1867-1950). It was submitted by Terry Arbogast who found it in an old issue of the Fairmont Times.

"NUZUM'S MILLS"

One day in early summer, Bill
I walked across the hills
And visited my former home,
Not far from Nuzum's Mills:
The town is known as Hammond, now
With much smoke and noise,
But I prefer the name we used
When you and I were boys.

I stood upon the old mill site
With mingled joy and pain,
To see that of the former mill
But fragments now remain,
With scattered stones about the spot,
And here and there a trace
Of what in bygone happy days
We always called the "the race."

I closed my eyes and saw again.
The farmers waiting round
With wagons loads of golden grain
Their corn to have it ground:
Though many years have passed away
I call again to mind
The eager interest they showed
To see the mill stones grind.

I heard them talk about their crops
As in the long ago
And tell how the crop of grain was short
For lack of winter snow
Or floods because the rain
Was heavy in the fall.
It made me weep to know these men
Had vanished, one and all.

I saw again old Jasper stand
Beside the whirring stones,
And heard him tell his awful tales
In sad and mournful tones,
Or play upon his violin
The tunes that pleased our ears
Poor Jasper has been sleeping now
For nearly fifty years.

I visited again the place
Where on a winter night
I romped and played at the store
With George and Odie Hite.
The old storeroom has tumbled down
The place is bare and chill,
And George and Odie long have slept
Upon the Dunkard Hill.

The Valley Falls are just the same
As in the days gone by,
In summer with a gentle flow:
In winter wild and high
I listened to the pleasant sound
And wished that I could stay
Where I could hear the tuneful song
Till life had passed away.

And when my time shall come, Bill
To bid the world goodbye,
I hope they take me there to sleep
Where friends and neighbors lie.
Above the Tygart Valley stream,
Beside the oak tree on the hill,
Where childhood's happy days were passed
Not far from Nuzum's Mills.

By: Rufus A. West (Date Unknown).

Rufus A. West (1867-1950) was born and raised near Hammond. He taught mechanical drawing for 41 years at West Virginia University. In 1939, Mr. West was a Trustee of the Nuzum No. 1 Cemetery but did not get his wish to be buried up on Dunkard Hill (known today as the Nuzum No. 1 Cemetery at the Church of the Brethren). He was buried in the East Oak Grove Mausoleum in Morgantown. He and his wife, Mattie, had no children.

People and Places

HAMMOND RIDGE
(Taylor County)

The history of Hammond and the brickyard would not be complete without pointing out Hammond Ridge on the Taylor County side of the river. Just above the mouth of Lost Run and across the river from Nuzum's Mill was Owen McGee's land grant. He sold his grant to a group of men from Morgantown who built kilns for the purpose of making firebrick from the clay deposits on the hillside. A small village by the name of Spriggville emerged. In that village, Owen McGee built a large boarding house. At his death, a family by the name of Chalfant moved from Morgantown and took over the business. During their residence, the Chaldant's oldest daughter married Joel ("Dode") Nuzum. After a few years, these families moved to Morgantown and sold the place to John Mason. He married Owen McGee's oldest daughter and moved into the boarding house, which soon went out of business. The big plans to make brick never materialized. The little village of Spriggville disappeared.

The kilns, which were made of red brick, were torn down in 1871. The bricks were then cleaned and sent downriver on an abandoned ferry to Sarrietta, where they were used to build a new school.

Hammond Ridge School was located just across the river from Valley Falls about a half-mile up the hill. It was a traditional wooden structure with three windows on each side and a Burnside stove for heat inside. The school was built in 1894 by William Tucker, Dolice Tucker and Jonah Curry, and served the brickyard families living on the ridges above Hammond and Valley Falls in Taylor County. The workers who lived on the west side of the river crossed the river by boat everyday, regardless of the weather. Mortimer Lawler was the first school teacher.

Some of the other teachers were: Joseph Reed, Jr., Jennie Chidester, Brooks Martin, Samuel Dadisman, Truman Lawler, Vernon Morrow, Alcinda Cochran, William Richardson, Jean Barlett, Mary Giles Curry, Fanny Reese, Curtis Boice, Lloyd Shriver, Ned Shriver, Vallie Irons, Gail Irons, Nola Johnson, Kenneth Little, Mason Tucker, Ray Michaels, Helen Mason, William Hustead, Asby Curry, Betty Grimes Flesher and James Brown.

The Hammond Ridge School closed sometime during the early 1930's. After the school closed, the children went to Linn School (today known as Linn Chapel). John H. Klepfel bought the building after the school closing. He and his wife Anna had boarded the teachers of Hammond Ridge School because it was so remote during the school term.

The old Hammond School in Taylor County as it looks today. It closed in the early 1930's.

1914 School souvenir with Miss Vallie Irons as teacher.

HAMMOND
PUBLIC SCHOOL
Booths Creek Dist. No. 11
Valley Valls Twp., Taylor Co., W. Va.
VALLIE IRONS, Teacher
PUPILS
Boys
Hugh Mason — Willie Mason
George Helsley — George Boice
Herman Klepfel — Paul Klepfel
Odie Motter — Russel Boice
Clarence Hill — Conny Shriver
Ralph Helsley
Girls
Flossie Wiseman — Minnie Boice
Hazel Klepfel — Rosa Helsley
Olive Wiseman — Pearl Mason
Mary Shriver — Bertha Shriver
Helon Wiseman — Clara Boice
Merle Boice — Amanda Wiseman
Claudie Motter — Lela Motter
Roxie Helsley — Mildred Mason
School Officers
C. Lee Reynolds, Pres.
A. C. Morris, Sec'y.
Dellet Newlon, Co. Supt.
Trustees
Had Lambert — John Klepfel
Lonnie Wiseman

QUIET DELL SCHOOL

Growth in the area where the Hammond Road intersected with East Grafton Road was increasing rapidly. Children either attended Hammond School or the Hull school closer to Glady Creek. This area was known as Williams Crossroads. In 1837, Gath Post Office was located here but was later moved beyond Crossroads on East Grafton Road. W. E. Morgan was the postmaster.

Unidentified Quiet Dell School students in 1906. Picture taken by S. H. Rudy, a resident of Quiet Dell. *Courtesy of FSC Folk Life Collection. Donated by Buddy Myers.*

The first school was located where the present-day Quiet Dell Baptist Church is today. The Board of Education bought land from Enos L. Nuzum, Jr. (Deed Book 90/Page 165) for $25.00. The wooden frame one-room school was built in 1899. The first teacher was Miss Grace Michael. Some of her students were "Rem" Rudy, Lucy Linn, Walter, Clint and Han Williams. Teachers back then were qualified to teach without going to college if they passed a test prepared by the Board. The school trustees then hired them.

Molly Morris Morgan was the wife of Frank Morgan, who owned and operated a store at Morgan's Crossroads on the East Grafton Road (as it was now called) to Fairmont. She taught at the school soon after its opening in 1902. After several other appointments she returned in 1920, but still there was no official name for the school, so she named the area and school Quiet Dell. She felt the community was quiet and a nice place to live. It has been called that ever since.

In 1922, a new cloakroom was added to the school. Indoor chemical restrooms were also added, but they proved to be unsanitary and were taken out. With the increase of population in the community, attendance grew to nearly 60 pupils. Overcrowding by 1927 resulted in expanding the school. This was accomplished by converting the cloakroom and restroom space into another classroom. A partition was built through the center of the building to create two rooms.

In 1928, the school began a hot lunch program. Students' parents provided home canned food, which was heated by putting them in a large container of water on a hot plate.

Teachers at this school were: Goldie Price, Fay Lake, Mollie Morris Morgan, Dave Satterfield, Grace Boone, Edith Rogers, Cecil Parrick, Minnie Davis Strum, Mary Poe Rudy, Lem Stansberry, Henry Orr, Willis Wilson, Cora Clayton, Hoyt Harper, Omer Jones, Andrew Henderson, Hattie Davis Armstrong, Andrew Henderson, John Lake, Lawrence Miller, Meryl Berry Holsberry, Myra Hoover, Naomi Morgan, Avis Martin and Ruby Tatterson.

Quiet Dell school students in 1948-49. Those identified are left to right in first row: Luella McRobie, Alyce Smith, Marcella Jenkins, Bonnie Kirk, Carolyn Armstrong, Phyllis Shahan, Russell Canfield, David Hamrick & Danny Williams. Second row: Myron Vincent, Jean King, David Armstrong, Lawrence Moore, Karol Moran Wamsley & Beverly Williams. Third row: Steve Miller, John King, Jerry Williams, Vickie Smith, Shirley Perkins, Karen Corbin, Alberta Faulkner & Beverly Shoemaker, Nancy Williams, Bernice Carpenter, teacher.
Courtesy of Francis Swisher.

THE "NEW" QUIET DELL SCHOOL

On account of overcrowding, the Board of Education quickly responded to the need for a new school in 1933. Basil and Mary Rudy gave up one acre of land from their farm for the new two-room school. It was constructed from bricks from the Hammond Brick Company. Students moved into their new school in the spring of 1934. In May, there was a dedication ceremony. Marion County School Superintendent J. J. Straight gave the address.

After World War II in early fall of 1946, the school began serving a hot lunch with food that was prepared in a room in the basement equipped for cooking. This upgraded the school to then-modern standards.

Consolidation of schools in the area began in 1947 with the closing of Glady Creek School. Those students were bused to Quiet Dell along with Hammond students after their school shut down. Again, in 1952, overcrowding caused a need for a fourth classroom built in the back of the building. The new room was dedicated in 1953, again by Mr. Straight. The PTA sponsored a dinner for the occasion.

In 1955 indoor restrooms were added. The PTA helped with this, as it had with many other fund raising projects for improvements such as equipping the kitchen with needed utensils and developing a playground.

The Board of Education decided to close Quiet Dell School at the end of the 1988 term. June 8, 1988 was the last day that classes were held. In March 1989, the BOE sold the school to the Marion County Commission

Quiet Dell School opened in 1934 and closed in 1988. It now houses the Quiet Dell Community Association and the Valley Falls Public Service District.

for public use. The community bought the building from the commission for $10.00 and formed a Community Association to oversee it. Currently the Valley Falls Public Service District occupies one of the classrooms using it for office space. The building is rented to the public for various meetings, parties, etc. To bring in income to support of the building.

Teachers at this school (when it was two classrooms) were:
1933-34, Mabel Stanley, Principal, and Martha Davis;
1934-36, Faye C. Berry, Principal, and Martha Davis;
1936-39, Walter Balderson, Principal, and Martha Davis;
1939-42, Walter Balderson and Mary V. Herron;
1942-43, Walter Balderson and Mrs. Lester Holt;
1943-45, Walter Balderson and Bernice Carpenter;
1945-46, (Substitute Teacher/ Principal) and Bernice Carpenter, and
1946-47, Charles Herron, Principal and Bernice Carpenter.

Three classrooms:
1947-51, Charles Herron, Principal; Bernice Carpenter and Berl Herron;
1951-52, Vanden King, Principal; Bernice Carpenter and Martha Davis.

Four classrooms:
1952-55, Vanden King, Principal; Pauline Springer, Elinor McCullough and Bernice Carpenter;
1955-56, Vanden King, Principal; Gwendlyln Newton, E.M. McCullough and Bernice Carpenter;
1956-57, Vanden King, Principal; Mildred Satterfield, Madge Mathey and Bernice Carpenter, and
1957-58, Lawrence Linn, Principal; Mildred Satterfield, Madge Mathey and Bernice Carpenter.

Three classroom: (School had cut back to three classrooms).
1958-59, Lawrence Linn, Principal; Mattie Hall and Bernice Carpenter;
1959-61, Walter Balderson, Principal; Mattie Hall and Bernice Carpenter;
1961-66, James Carpenter, Principal; Mattie Hall and Bernice Carpenter;
 (Bernice Carpenter retired in 1966 after 23 years)
1966-68, James Carpenter, Principal; Mattie Hall and Flora Nuzum;
1968-70, A. G. Toothman, Principal; Flora Nuzum and Marie Scott;
1970-73, Masel Rogers, Principal; Flora Nuzum and Marie Scott;
1973-74, Masel Rogers, Principal; Irene Bunner and Joan Kirby;
1974-76, Masel Rogers, Principal; Martha Cordray and Joan Kirby;
1976-77, Masel Rogers, Principal; Cecilia Miller and Joan Kirby;
1977-78, Masel Rogers, Principal; Martha Cordray and Joan Kirby;
1978-79, Masel Rogers, Principal; Deborah Harrington and Donna Hoyland;
1979-85, Dwillia Wallman, Karen Carpenter and Joetta Fisher, and
1985-88, Dwillia Wallman, Karen Carpenter, Joetta Fisher and Steve Rodriquez.

Right: Old Hull School located on East Grafton Road. It was open from 1869-1907. *Courtesy of Francis Swisher.*

Left: Hull School in the winter. Built in 1869 and closed in 1907. The dirt road in front is now the East Grafton Road (Rt. 310). Picture taken in 1905 by S.H. Rudy. *Courtesy of FSC Folk Life Collection, Donated by Buddy Myers.*

HULL SCHOOL
1869-1907

Six years after the new State of West Virginia was formed and developed its free public school system, the Glady Creek area petitioned for a school to serve the families in the still-growing area. The closest school was at Nuzum's Mill (School No. 8), two miles away. On December 23, 1869 Samuel ("White Sam") and Betsy (Rudy) Linn deeded over a small plot of land to Union District Board of Education for the purpose of a school (Deed 26/Page 356). The school commissioners were William Gray, William Linn and Nelson Hull when the school was built. It became School No. 9 in the district. Ella Myers was the first teacher.

The one-room school was referred to by the community as the "Hull School" because it was very close to the home of the Rev. John Hull and his wife Jane, who lived near the tunnel. Rev. Hull was a Methodist Protestant minister and held Sunday sermons in the school in its early days.

The school was located on the Fairmont-Grafton Pike, where there was a regular stagecoach run. It was also near the tunnel where coal was transported from upper Prickett's Creek area to Nuzum's Mill. Today the tunnel is gone and the tramway road is known as Tunnel Hollow.

At the end of the school term in 1907, the school closed. A new school was being built on Upper Glady Creek. It opened that same year for the fall term. The Hull School was sold to the McKinney family; it was used as a meetinghouse for the Primitive Baptist Church ("Hard Shell" Baptist). The minister was Elder James Linn. After the Chester Moore family bought the property, the old school (church) building was torn down in 1955.

Teachers who taught at this school were:

1869	Nancy Gaskins	1886	Charles Barnes
1870	R. E. Harr	1887	Elsworth Morgan
1871	Samuel L. Linn	1890	Morgan Travis
1872	Ella Myers	1891	Frederick Vangilder
1873	Florence Swearingen	1893	George A. Vincent
1874	Ella Myers	1897	S. C. Boyce
1875	Matty Reese	1898	John L. Lake
1876	John L. Lake	1899	M. Earl Morgan
1877	Frank Wilson	1900	James L. Clelland
1878	Kate Mason	1902	David E. Satterfield
1879	John L. Lake	1903	Zoe Vincent
1880	Miner Nuzum	1904	Mary McDaniel
1883	W.W. Carpenter	1906	Arthur N. Allender
1885	Harry Harr		

Quiet Dell Grocery Stores

One of the earliest grocery stores in the Quiet Dell community was started by Archie and Lillian VanMeter in 1941. They lived in the house beside the now-closed S&D Grocery on East Grafton Road. He had a store in the basement of their house. In 1946 they sold the property to Edna (Davis) and Abe Springer. They built another building on the property for a store. It became known as the S&D Grocery. The S standing for Springer and the D standing for Edna's former name, Davis. They were the friendly hometown grocers who gave credit to the surrounding community. Legend has it that grocery bills were sometimes paid with guns as collateral from the local moonshiners. No questions asked. This store was sold to Marcellus (Ed) and Annie Lough in 1965. Another grocery store just down the road towards Fairmont was the Hill Top Grocery, owned and operated by Charles H. and Olive Faulkner. At Williams Crossroads Hans Williams owned and operated a grocery store. It closed down in the early seventies. Today in this quiet community—with fast cars, good roads and supermarkets—there is only one grocery store and that is Q Dell's Grocery. It opened in 1995 and is the modern version of a convenience store.

ROCK LAKE

Rock Lake community is located .08 of mile from East Grafton Road on the road to Valley Falls State Park. A ride through the beautiful countryside takes you past a log cabin barn that once belonged to the Sam Linn family. It has been mended over the years and is still used as an animal shelter (see picture in Chapter Six). Most of the farms along the road have been in families for several generations. Rock Lake is less than a half-mile from the river, as the crow flies.

In the 1800's, this area was all farmland. Those who lived on the lower portion of Glady Creek considered themselves a part of the Valley Falls community, where there was a store, a gristmill, post office, saloon. A person could even catch a train to Grafton or Fairmont there. This was the way it was until the forestland was timbered out and Valley

Entrance to Rock Lake Club incorporated in 1932.

Falls became devastated by fire and flooding. After the post office and mill closed down in 1906, farmers in the area had to do business further downriver at Hammond. I find it interesting that folks in this area either shop in Grafton or Fairmont, since it is halfway between the two towns. In the 1800's, before the automobile, train travel was just over the hill from here.

In 1929, owners of the Realty Development Company purchased ten acres of land from David and Tabatha Hayhurst and 33 acres from the Kingery K. Lake heirs on lower Glady Creek. They wanted to develop portions of the land into a camping area with a manmade lake covering 32 of the 44 acres they envisioned. This same company had also built Lake Floyd and Maple Lake on U.S. Rt. 50 prior to buying Rock Lake. The natural decline in elevation of Glady Creek and numerous springs feeding into the property proved to make it an excellent location for the project. On lower Glady Creek, there was a waterfall 27 feet high hidden on the steep hillside that emptied into the Tygart Valley River.

After the excavation was completed for the lake, a cement dam was built on the lower end with a traffic bridge leading to lots on the other side. The plans included a culvert under the bridge and two spillways for excess water. In the early spring, the excess of the winter's collection of water had backed up behind the dam. The excess was released into Glady Creek. Although the company started selling lots, the sales were very slow because of the Depression. Like so many others during that time, the developer could not pay the mortgage and went bankrupt. The property was sold on the courthouse steps to three businessmen who represented the Glady Realty Company. Each of the three reserved a lot for himself and gave the rest of the lots to the previous buyer, the Realty Development Company, to form the Rock Lake Club. The owners of the Glady Realty Company purchased additional land from Thomas Shrieve and Thomas B. Nixon, who lived nearby.

Top: Rock Lake with the swimming area in the background. Bottom: Rock Lake in the early developing stages in 1929.
Courtesy of Madelene Burke.

Lower dam on Glady Creek at Rock Lake. 1999

The Rock Lake Club was incorporated in August 1932. Over a period of several years, all the lots were sold—some for summer homes and some for more permanent ones. Each owner pays dues to support the care of the grounds. A board of directors, comprised of 12 lot owners, was formed to oversee the business and policies of the club which has an election every year.

FISH CULTURIST AT ROCK LAKE

State Worker Inspects Pond; Makes Suggestions to Aid Owners

APRIL 29, 1933

T. C. Fearnow, state fish culturist, of Charleston, was here yesterday and was in conference with members of the Rock Lake Club with reference to the fish problems at Rock Lake. Mr. Pearnow accompanied by E. L. Lively, L. L. Crawford, James J. Coughlin, Hiram Linn and Frank Frisch visited the lake.

Mr. Fearnow said that the lake has great possibilities and is one of the finest artificial lakes that he has ever seen. He advised the members of the club to obtain additional plant food and that the lagoon should be stocked with golden shiners for bass food. That the construction of breeding ponds is not necessary for the lake is sufficient to take care of that. He said that this body of water will supply all of the fish needed by the club members. He told the members that it would yield from 2,500 to 3,000 pounds of fish annually.

Club members were much encouraged by Mr. Fearnow's visit. Through his advice they will not have to incur any expenditure for breeding purposes. The club had contemplated the construction of a breeding pond.

Fairmont Times West Virginian.

A caretaker was hired to oversee the grounds and lake. A small house was built for his use shortly after the club became incorporated. More rooms were added in 1952 after caretaker Orval Mowery retired. In the early 1960's, a clubhouse was built and a complete kitchen was added in 1984. Fenced-in tennis courts are beside the community building. A large swimming area and playground are other popular features.

Rock Lake is approximately 20 feet deep in the deepest section and is stocked with trout, crappie, perch, bluegill and catfish. A grate was installed on the upper end of the lake to prevent the fish from swimming up Glady Creek, and at the same time a grate was put in at the dam to keep them from escaping downstream. The dam is inspected yearly for certification. In 1956 the U.S. Geological Surveys recorded Rock Lake at 1,341 ft. above sea level making the lake considerably lower than the surrounding hills at 1,800 to 2,00 feet.

ROAD TROUBLE
Hammond, W. Va.,
March 27, 1933.

Editor The Fairmont Times:

We are wondering why thousands of dollars are being spent on the Rock Lake road which leads merely to an amusement center of the community and the Upper Glady Creek road which intersects with the Grafton road at the same place is left unimproved. The latter road leads to the local schoolhouse and church and to two of the largest cemeteries in this part of the county. During the past week a funeral party started from Fairmont to the Linn Cemetery on Upper Glady Creek. It was necessary to transfer the corpse to a truck at the hard road and said truck and the few automobiles which attempted to get to the cemetery had to be pulled by a team of horses. Some months ago a petition signed by more than a hundred local citizens was presented to the County Court asking some improvement on this road, but as yet not a single mud hole has been touched.

A GLADY CREEKER.

Letter to the editor in the *Times/West Virginia*, 1933.

In 1989, the lake was drained and dredged along the sides to remove the silt and fill which had collected there. After the lake filled up again with water, the lake came back better than ever. From the road the hardy water lilies on the lake's edge can be seen basking in the sun sometimes in little more than a quiet, warm pool. Their blossoms are a sight to see.

On the night of July 10, 2001 more than three inches of rain fell in the area in just a couple of hours. The waters from upper Glady Creek and the surrounding watershed came surging downstream into Rock Lake. Fearing the earthen dam would break, volunteers stretched heavy plastic tarps over the dam for protection but the cover failed when the floodwaters kept rising. A large chunk of the 17-foot dam was swept away leaving a portion of the two-foot thick concrete wall exposed on the dry side of the dam. The "over-the-top" flood also destroyed a small block building that housed the valve for the dam.

Since the Rock Lake Club was a private entity, it did not qualify for emergency State or Federal funding for repairs. Delegate Paul Prunty, a Rock Lake Club member and a member of the WV House of Delegates, got the attention of WV's Governor Bob Wise and Public Safety Secretary Joe Martin for private funding to help with repairs. One month later, the 71-year old dam was restored with even better protection.

Owens-Illinois Glass Works in Fairmont used to hold its annual picnics on its private property very close to the lake. When Owens shut down, that property was sold to Ray Clayton, who later sold the property off in several portions.

The Winfield Volunteer Fire Department built a sub-station at the lake and placed it into operation on December 23, 1982. It operates out of Winfield Volunteer Fire Department, which houses Engine No. 138. Three volunteers in the immediate area are on call 24 hours a day.

VALLEY FALLS
Beauty spot six miles north on the boundary of Taylor and Marion counties where Tygarts Valley River dashes through a mile-long gorge in series of lovely falls and rapids. Included in 1000-acre grant to Thomas Parkeson in 1773.

WV highway marker at the U.S. Rt. 250 and Rt. 310 intersection at Grafton.

Left: Millrace for the saw and gristmills at Valley Falls. Right: William Haney, an English stonecutter, cut through solid rock by using black powder explosives for the millrace in 1837.

VALLEY FALLS

Long before finally getting to the bottom of the hill and getting a first glimpse of the huge sandstone boulders, the roar of Valley Falls greets you. Lying in wait at the top of the falls it has quiet, serene water that masks impending danger. The river takes a sudden plunge over room-size boulders in a series of four falls that have given the place its name. The upper falls stretch 300 feet across the river and are 18 feet high. Approximately 100 feet downriver is the second or lower falls which are 12 feet high. Two other smaller falls are farther downriver in the gorge within two miles from the main set of falls making the gorge very treacherous.

Long before the white man arrived in this valley, Indians were the first to discover and observe the beauty of the falls. According to local historians, in their travels downriver various Indian tribes visited the falls just to see and appreciate the waters that dashed over the rocks and into the pools below. Fur traders and trappers made their way to the falls area to exchange goods with the Indians. Their reports of the falls made the area sound like an explorer's dream. Indian artifacts were found in abundance in the early days up and down the river and taken away as souvenirs.

Jacob Horn and John Hardman explored northern Virginia and the Tygart Valley, ("Cherokee Valley" as it was referred to), in June 1750. Horn made many diary notes of the area, which were passed down for several generations in his family, before they were finally published in 1945, as the *Horn Papers*. Anyone traveling either up or downriver obviously experienced difficulty getting around the gorge and falls. They became known to the white man as "the hard around falls." To the Indian they were known as "Evil Sprit Falls" because of the treacherous waters in the gorge.

The Indians made camp at the falls and had a path along the east side of the river that went downstream to where Nuzum's Mill was later built. The path was used to get around the falls while carrying a canoe. It could very easily have been a part of the legendary Catawba Indian War Path Trail that followed the Tygart Valley River. In the 1800's, this same path was made wider for wagons and eventually became a road on which a stagecoach carried mail and passengers from Valley Falls/Nuzum's Mill to Middletown. It became known as part of the Middletown-Wheeling Turnpike.

In 1773, Thomas Parkeson, a gunsmith, was entitled to 1000 acres of land by the right of pre-emption that included his improvements in Monongalia County. This tract of land included the great falls on the "Tygers River." Mr. Parkeson lived in Williamsport, Pennsylvania and is believed to have never actually lived on the property.

Other land owners in the vicinity at that time were Jonathon Boyers (1774) at Forshey's Levels, William Pettijohn (1774) at what is now Rock Lake, William Tucker (1775) on the west side of the river and Absolum Little (1776) on both sides of Glady Creek. In 1801, William Pettijohn owned property on Glady Creek but later sold his property to William Linn.

Governor Patrick Henry of Virginia granted land, described as a tract "on both sides of the Tygers Valley River including the great falls of said river" to David Gray and Samuel Hanway (who was a surveyor for Monongalia County). The tract was patented on October 3, 1781. Two years later, the Harrison County Court ordered a bridle road built from Clarksburg to Wickwire's Ford, upriver from Valley Falls.

The next owners of the falls were John Reed and Standish Ford in 1796. They were partners in a trading business in Philadelphia and bought an additional 1,385 acres in the falls area. Ford died in 1805, leaving a son by the same name among his heirs. In 1835, Reed and Ford's heirs sold the 2,385 acres to Sam Frew, who was a lawyer and recognized the

Captain William Fetterman, nephew of Washington Wilfred Fetterman, led 80 cavalry troopers to a disastrous defeat near Ft. Kearny, WY on December 21, 1866. *Courtesy of Peggy Ross-Fortney.*

potential waterpower that the falls could generate. He decided to build a whip sawmill. First he set out to cut through the solid rock for a millrace but after several tries and failures, Frew got discouraged and abandoned the idea. In 1837, he sold the property to a friend, Washington W. Fetterman, who had seen the property while on a survey of the canyon for a canal around the falls. Fetterman was a prominent Pittsburgh attorney, who held large interests in a Pittsburgh navigation company.

Earlier in that same year, the Virginia Legislature voted for a survey to see if a canal could be built around the "Big and Little Falls" of the Tygart Valley River. The canal was supposed to provide navigation from Pittsburgh to near Elkins, WV, and also would allow fish to swim upstream. Needless to say, the survey found the area too remote and rugged to fulfill these aspirations. The project was dropped but Fetterman could visualize a healthy investment return in the tall virgin forest in the valley.

Based on his 1837 visit to the valley, Fetterman decided to purchase the property from Sam Frew. He went to work on Frew's idea of building a whip-sawmill even before the actual paperwork for the transfer of property was finalized. Fetterman hired William Haney, an experienced English stonecutter, who claimed he could cut through the solid rock for a millrace, which would power the mill. However, cutting the rock proved to be extremely difficult. It was accomplished only by using black-powder explosives. It was the first time explosives were used in the area and very expensive. A wooden dam was constructed across one portion of the falls to divert the water to the millrace, which was 150 yards long, 20 feet wide and four feet deep. The millrace still bears the drill marks from where the explosives were placed. They can be easily detected.

Flour Mill and Saw Mill at Valley Falls in 1888. *Courtesy of Ron Fawcett. Photo by Steven Shaluta, Jr.*

Born in 1802, Washington W. Fetterman, of German ancestry, was the oldest of three sons of George and Hannah (Plummer) Fetterman from Pittsburgh, Pennsylvania. The Fetterman's were very experienced in owning and operating saw mills in other areas. Washington married Sarah

Constantine de Bulan, granddaughter of Baron de Bulan, then Austrian Ambassador to the United States who was involved in the iron business in Pittsburgh. Their children were Gilbert L. B., George W., Gertrude, Wilfried B. and Frances. Their cousin, Captain William Judd Fetterman, (Washington W.'s nephew) was killed in 1866 by Chief Red Cloud and the Sioux Indian nation in Wyoming. He and 80 cavalry troopers were massacred near Fort Kearny, which was later renamed Fort Fetterman in his honor.

Fetterman engaged J. A. and William Work to build and operate the completed sawmill, which was 80 feet long and 30 feet wide. It had two sets of saws and one butting saw that had all the necessary fixtures for sawing steamboat timber. Operations began July 15, 1837 cutting large stands of timber that were in the immediate neighborhood. A planing mill was built so that furniture and spindles could be marketed. A coffin factory opened up using the finest of white oak. To avoid the treacherous gorge, the logs were put in the river where they drifted to the far shore to a tramway on the west bank above the falls. The logs were loaded on tramcars and taken downstream to a clearing. Today that tramway still can be detected leading downriver. The logs were loaded on keelboats and drifted downriver to the Monongahela and onto Pittsburgh markets, where logs were in high demand.

OLD CATHOLIC CEMETERY
About 500 graves of early Grafton settlers, dating 1857-1917, are in old cemetery located on land given by Sarah Fetterman to St. Augustine Catholic Church. Headstones include names of Irish and German emigrants. Buried here is Thomas McGraw, B&O Railroad construction supervisor, local merchant and father of John T. - lawyer, banker, politician, and coal, railroad and lumber developer.

Located on U. S. Route 50, Grafton.

The mill was the beginning of a small community made up of mill men, log haulers, logging men, trappers and traders. Eventually, it would supply all of the lumber used in the building of the Valley Falls community, which included around 100 structures scattered on both sides of the river.

Upon completion of the sawmill in 1837, Mr. Fetterman had a summer home built overlooking the natural beauty of the falls. The Fetterman house was a two-storey, L-shaped building with nine rooms and double porches on the front and the back. It had hand-cut sandstone fireplaces on both ends of the house. The fireplace mantles, according to a family member, were said to be stone slabs eight feet long quarried there at the falls. The exterior of the house was covered in half-inch yellow-poplar clapboard siding. Each piece was six inches wide.

It was in this house that the Fettermans invited a Colonel Spalding, who was a writer for a New York newspaper, to visit their summer retreat to write about the progress of the B&O Railroad. The Fettermans were hoping to attract land developers to the valley. Spalding met and fell in love with Frances Fetterman and married the bright, sparkling brunette. Col. Spalding was killed in the Civil War while leading his Confederate command. Frances later remarried and eventually lived and died in Europe. A street in Grafton was named after her.

The only problem traveling to this beautiful site was getting there because it was so remote. W. W. Fetterman had a road built from Pruntytown (then called Cross Roads and after that Williamsport) down to the falls on the west side of the river. That same country road still leads down to the river and falls from Linn Chapel and is still in use. Once the road reached the bottom of the hill at the falls, horse-drawn wagons had to cross the river at the top of the falls to get to the other side, provided the river was low enough. Despite the swift water current, a solid rock base provided sound passage. A ferry was used upriver during high-water stage.

Washington W. Fetterman unexpectedly died on December 12, 1838 in Philadelphia, Pennsylvania, leaving his holdings to his wife, Sarah. In May 1841, she placed a For Sale advertisement for the property on the front page of the *American Manufacturer* magazine. Published in Pittsburgh, the ad failed to attract a wealthy investor so Sarah and the children continued to develop the property.

Lands for a new railroad were being purchased in 1847-50. Foreseeing the opportunity to make a huge profit, the Fetterman family purchased nearly 6000 acres of land from twelve miles above the falls to one and a half miles below the falls. About 35 acres of this estate was purchased exclusively for a steamboat yard situated some twelve miles down river. Owning all the land around Valley Bridge, the family sold a tract of land to the B&O for their railroad shops. One of the conditions of the sale was for the B&O to establish a first class passenger and freight station and change the name of Valley Bridge to Fetterman.

The Fettermans had their land surveyed and plotted into town lots. Lawyer and merchant, Col. James K. Smith, who lived in Pruntytown, moved to Fetterman in 1850. He built the first house and opened the first store.

He was the town's first railroad agent and postmaster and held these jobs for more than 40 years. At first, the lots were so highpriced that most families could not afford them. The railroad needed more land for their shops and objected to the high prices the Fettermans were asking. The Fettermans had overpriced their land and for this reason, the B&O put their shops further upstream which later, became the Grafton railroad yards.

The town of Fetterman was incorporated in 1854. It had been called Valley Bridge because of the covered bridge that crossed the river at this point. The bridge was completed in 1836 and was swept away by the 1888 flood. For several years Fetterman was a shipping center for cattle, lumber and farm products. In 1903, the town was incorporated into the City of Grafton.

Being dedicated Roman Catholics, the Fettermans donated land on Fifth Avenue in their hometown of Pittsburgh for the site for St. Paul's Cathedral Church in downtown. They were also very generous to the local Catholic community in Grafton.

With certain knowledge that the railroad was on the way, the Fettermans hired Isaac Holman, a millwright from Pennsylvania, to build a grain mill at the falls (Isaac Holman was the grandfather of Judge Harry Shaw of the local circuit court). The millrace had to be extended, it was built very close to the sawmill. It was completed on June 5, 1850. Corn was ground for the first time in August. The mill was an important part in the lives in the people of the valley. The miller also acted as the ferryman who brought farmers across the river to grind their grain. The gristmill was the place where farmers and friends met, transacted their business and exchanged news while their grain was being ground. Eleven years after the mill was built Isaac Holman became sheriff of Marion County during the formation of the Restored Government of Virginia in 1861.

In 1847, John Bradshaw, a stonemason, arrived at Valley Falls to supervise the construction of the new B&O Railroad. He was destined to become one of the pioneer developers of the area. His name became connected with Valley Falls for over half a century. He was the first to utilize the ice in the serene waters above the falls. In the wintertime he cut large chunks of ice from the river and stored it in sawdust. It was stored in an icehouse underground. Ice also was retrieved from the river for the B&O passenger trains. John was born in Lisburn, County Down, Ireland about the 1820. He came with his parents, who were Scotch-Irish, to this country when he was a small. They settled near Baltimore, Maryland, where the B&O began building a railroad. He was hired by the railroad as a water boy and remained under their employ for the remainder of his life. He rose to high accountable positions with the company. He was responsible for superintending the arching of the Clarksburg tunnel, as well as others in West Virginia. John and his wife, Rebecca, came to live at Valley Falls during the construction period of the railroad. Four of their nine children grew to adulthood at the falls.

In June 1852, the railroad was completed. Soon after that, day sightseers began to appear to see the falls, and of course, lumbermen kept coming seeking work. The railroad became the best transportation in and out of town. It meant more business for the mills and made shipping much easier.

Valley Falls is located 14.1 miles from Fairmont and 7.2 miles from Fetterman. The trains coming and going created a need for a train platform. Later a hotel was built to accommodate visitors for overnight lodging. The Valley Falls Hotel was a two-story building with 18 sleeping rooms. It had a great hall that was used for a subscription school and had dances there every Saturday night with old-time fiddle music. The same hall was used the next morning for Sunday church services. In 1856, John and Rebecca Bradshaw helped organize the First Presbyterian Church of Fetterman, where he became an elder. It was Fetterman's first church.

Moonshine stills dotted the entire valley. They became a renowned and legendary part of our early Appalachian culture. The local Scotch-Irish perfected the homemade concoction. Soon even some of the area farmers began "farmin' in the woods" to make ends meet. Despite local temperance meetings, a saloon and gambling hall were favorite hangouts in the frontier town of Valley Falls. Local lore has it that even a saloon, floating on a raft, was built to escape prying eyes. It was anchored above the falls near the Taylor County line. In the later years, bootlegging was a subject nobody talked about but the trade continued till the early 1940's.

In 1861, at the beginning of the Great Rebellion, word arrived at Valley Falls that Rebels were encamped at Fetterman. The Fettermans were Yankees and expected difficulty with the Confederates, so they quickly decided to go back north. It wasn't long before the railroad on the river became busy with soldiers from both the North and the South. The sawmill at Valley Falls began making gunstocks.

After the Fettermans left, they leased the falls property to John Bradshaw, who decided to quit working for the railroad and operate the mill fulltime. John and Rebecca moved into the Fetterman's summer home. Soon after he quit the railroad a train from Wheeling stopped at the falls. Colonel Wilson, the B&O roadmaster, stepped down from the train and asked for John Bradshaw. He was told to go to the mill. The train waited while Wilson went to the mill, where he insisted that Bradshaw again enter the employment of the railroad service to build one

Early 1900's "Moonshine still" located in the Valley Falls area. *Courtesy of West Virginia Archives, Elizabeth Windsor Collection.*

of two train bridges across the Ohio River. He was to take his pick between the Benwood and Parkersburg bridges. Wilson was successful. Bradshaw oversaw the building of the Benwood Bridge, which he did for four million dollars less than was first estimated. The cut stone used for the piers and arch on the Ohio side was quarried at Valley Falls. John was responsible for the arching of many railroad tunnels in West Virginia.

Another tale about John Bradshaw involved John Work Garrett, who was President of the B&O Railroad at that time. Garrett and Bradshaw were very good friends and John stood in high favor of Mr. Garrett. Garrett's nephew was in charge of the railroad between Baltimore and Philadelphia. One day Bradshaw and the nephew had a few words over some construction and Bradshaw again quit the railroad.

When Garrett returned from a trip abroad he went to Deer Park, Maryland and sent for Bradshaw. It is believed that Garrett always reserved a room at one of the famous hotels there for the man from Valley Falls. When he arrived they finally talked. "John," said Mr. Garrett, "I was in Switzerland and bought three watches. One is for me; the other is for my son and the third is for you." As a result, Bradshaw returned to the B&O as General Roadmaster and served for many years afterwards.

Bradshaw took on two new partners to help him with the mills. They were Gilbert L. B. Fetterman and George M. Whitescarver. Gilbert L. B. Fetterman was born in 1824, the son of W. W. and Sarah Fetterman. His Godfather was a family friend, the Marquis de Lafayette, French general and statesman. Lafayette stood sponsor at his baptism and gave him his name, Gilbert de Lafayette de Belan Fetterman. Gilbert followed the family tradition and became a Pittsburgh attorney. Sarah Fetterman died in July 1862 and left the property to her children. She is buried in the Fetterman lot in the St. Mary's Cemetery in downtown Pittsburgh, Pennsylvania.

Whitescarver, a good friend of the Fettermans, was a surveyor and land agent for the B&O. Later he became general manager of the railroad from Grafton to Philippi. Bradshaw and Whitescarver set out to improve the gristmill. It was enlarged with steam power and remodeled to produce 70 barrels of roller-processed flour a day. This was the beginning of the cereal grain products and flour brand, "Pride of the Valley." Grain was being shipped in from the West to be ground at the mill, which was earning $500 a month, very good money in those days.

West Virginia's Lower Tygart Valley River

Valley Falls flour mill in the background. Date unknown. Left to right. Myrtle Motter, Pansy Stiles, Edith and Ethel Motter. Picture taken in 1906. *Courtesy of Ron Fawcett.*

    In 1883, Bradshaw purchased the gristmill from Gilbert L. B. Fetterman and George Whitescarver. Whitescarver and his wife, Henrietta (St. Clair) moved to Randolph County where he purchased a large tract of land for timbering. He later founded the town of Pickens, WV where he built his own sawmill. He stayed in the employ of the railroad company as real-estate agent and oversaw the construction of 30 miles of new rail line from Pickens, WV in Randolph County to Addison, WV (Webster Springs). That railroad opened up a vast territory of natural resources. By 1900, he had retired in Grafton, where he and Bradshaw were members of the board for the First National Bank. In 1909, he built the men's dormitory, known as Whitescarver Hall, at Alderson-Broaddus College in Philippi. Whitescarver died in his home on Wilford Street in Grafton, on November 15, 1914. He is buried in the Bluemont Cemetery. His brother John T. owned a large farm at Pruntytown.

VALLEY FALLS.

Population, 75. A station on the B. & O. R. R., in Marion county, 14 miles by rail and 7 by pike southeast of Fairmont, the seat of justice, and 7 from Grafton, the nearest banking point. Exp., U. S. Tel., W. U. Sarah Canning, postmaster.

Canning Sarah, express agent.
Mason C N, general store.
Stiles Harry, telegraph agent.

WV Gazetteer 1902-03

DEATH OF JOHN BRADSHAW.

A Prominent Citizen, After a Long And Useful Career, Passes Away.

John Bradshaw, one of the oldest citizens of this county, died at his Valley Falls residence about 5 o'clock last Monday morning, after a short illness from a stroke of paralysis with which he was recently prostrated. His funeral took place last Wednesday, the interment being made at the Keener graveyard, a half mile west of Fetterman about 12 o'clock, noon, the remains, accompanied by a large party of friends, having been brought up from the Falls on the 11:40 a. m. train, and from the Fetterman depot proceeded at once to the graveyard. The funeral party that came up on the train was here joined by a large number of friends and members of the Masonic fraternity, the latter of whom took the casket in charge and escorted the remains to the cemetery where they were interred with Masonic honors. The deceased had long been a member of Grafton Lodge, No. 15, of this city. The funeral services were held at the residence at the Falls previous to leaving for the cemetery. The services were conducted by Rev. J. H. Flanagan, D. D., pastor of the Presbyterian church of this city, of which Mr Bradshaw had long been a member.

John Bradshaw was born in the north of Ireland, about the year 1820. He came with his parents, who were Scotch-Irish, to this country when he was a small boy. They located at or near Baltimore. Mr. Bradshaw began work for the B. & O. when the viaduct was built at Relay Station, as a water boy. He continued in the employ of that company nearly all the remainder of his life, and rose to a high and responsible position with the company. He stood in high favor with John W. Garrett, so many years the President of the B. & O., and under the administration of John L. Wilson, Master of Roads, held the position of Assistant Master of Roads. Mr. Bradshaw superintended the arching of the Clarksburg tunnel in 1860. He built the stone piers of the Bellaire bridge which was constructed some years later. He was also at one time Superintendent of the Hempfield road, and later was President of the G. & B. railroad. Mr. Bradshaw moved to Fetterman from the east about 1852, near where he has lived ever since, owning besides the Valley Falls property a fine farm about two miles north of Fetterman, on which he lived for many years. He was a stockholder in the First National Bank of this city and has been one of its Board of Directors nearly ever since it was organized. Mr. Bradshaw leaves quite a valuable estate. His wife died about a year ago. He leaves one son, Jas. W., and two daughters, Mrs. Robt. Johnson and Mrs. James Canning, and two grandsons, Loyd and James Canning.—Grafton Sentinel.

Obituary of John Brandshaw, who died June 10, 1901, *Fairmont Free Press*.

This cut-stone column is all that remains of the old mill.

The Valley Falls sawmill continued to operate. A log boom was placed above the falls. Cables were stretched from shore to shore to hold the logs back. Periodically, they were taken out of the boom to be cut or to be shipped to markets down river. A coffinmaker took up residence in this little town and used the fine quality oak from the sawmill.

In 1886 a dreadful fire, of unknown origin, swept through the little town destroying several buildings. Only a few were ever rebuilt. Several families were without shelter and moved away. The gristmill escaped the fire but times were very hard after that.

Two years later, during five days of abnormal rain, an unusual amount of water came pouring down the slopes of the Tygart Valley watershed causing the river to suddenly rise. The week of June 10, 1888 was disastrous for all the little communities along the river. At Valley Falls, the log boom snapped under the tremendous amount of pressure. Some 3000 logs ready for shipment went crashing over the falls that day, destroying everything in their path. Layers after layers of logs took houses, barns, mills, livestock and whatever else was in the way, and even reshaped the riverbanks in some places. The hotel survived because it was on higher ground, but the Valley Falls community was never to be the same again. The gristmill was badly damaged. One of the millstones was found a mile and a half downriver. Today, it is on exhibit on the Valley Falls park grounds.

The flood created a great need for another local mill. All the other mills downriver were destroyed. John Bradshaw, who was by now getting on in years, had the Valley Falls gristmill repaired in 1889. Two years later, his wife, Rebecca, died in the cholera epidemic of 1900. John died one year later at the age of 80 on June 10, 1901. Both are buried in the old John Keener Cemetery near the river and railroad they loved so much. It is located one-fourth mile from Fetterman on the original U S Route 50.

Sightseers awaiting the train at Valley Falls. 1918—*Courtesy of Ron Fawcett.*

VALLEY FALLS POSTMASTERS

The following list of names and appointment dates for the postmasters of Valley Falls is from microfilm in the National Archives in Washington DC. The post office was located eight miles from Fairmont and seven miles from Grafton.

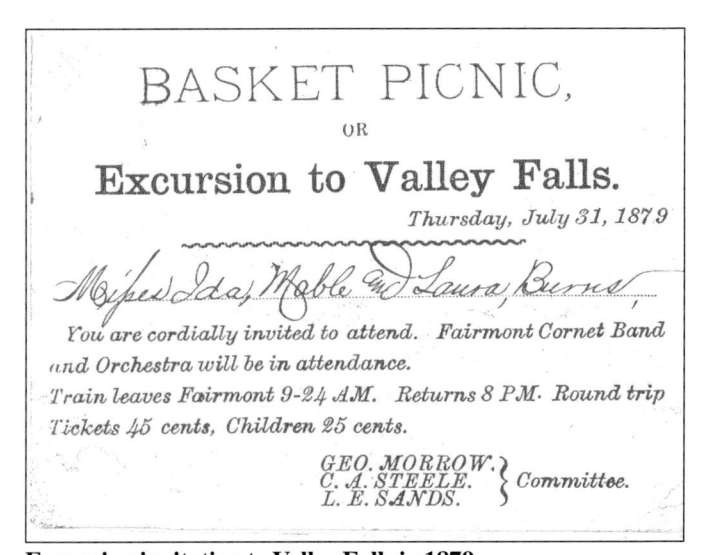

Excursion invitation to Valley Falls in 1879.
Courtesy of Ila Fortney.

April 15, 1856: Wilfied B. Fetterman (1822-1910) was the first official postmaster of Valley Falls. He was the third son of W. W. and Sarah Fetterman. It is theorized this appointment was in name only for it is believed by Walter Balderson that Isaac Holman dispersed the mail at the mill. At the onset of the Civil War on **June 8, 1861** the post office was closed. At his death in 1910 Wilfied was a well-known Philadelphia attorney.

June 26, 1863: The post office was re-established six days after the new state of West Virginia was born by the proclamation of President Abraham Lincoln. The postmaster was **John M. Rogers,** who was employed at the gristmill.

People and Places

February 16, 1869: John Bradshaw (1820-1901) was appointed postmaster. Bradshaw was also an employee of the B&O Railroad. He remained postmaster for the next 13 years. The post office was at the mill. He and his wife Rebecca had three children to survive to adulthood; James W., Agnes (Johnson) and Sarah (Canning).

1882: Charlotte Westerman was appointed postmaster for one year. Her husband A. P. Westerman was employed at the mill. There were 75 people living at Valley Falls.

October 12, 1883: Sarah (Bradshaw) Canning (1845-1905) was appointed postmaster. She was the daughter of John and Rebecca Bradshaw and was married to John Canning, who had been born in Ireland. They had three children, James B., store/mill clerk; Lloyd, a lumberman and daughter Minta. The Cannings operated a well-stocked store and boarding house. The post office was in the store, which supplied most of the little town's needs. The hotel was located where one of the pavilions is today. Sarah remained postmaster until her death in 1905. Her position as postmaster was never refilled. On **March 16, 1906** the post office was discontinued. Valley Falls' population had dropped to 50. Mail for the village was sent to Hammond Post Office for pick-up. Later the mail was delivered by RFD (Rural Free Delivery).

The old hotel which later became "Camp Victoria" at Valley Falls as it looked in 1963. Picture was reproduced from an old 35 mm movie reel by Charles L. Fortney. *Permission to reproduce by Charles L. Fortney.*

Note the population decline between 1884 and 1906. By 1903, the logging business had decreased dramatically because most of the timber had been cut. The lumbermen had moved on. The train depot and platform continued in use as sightseers came from the city but even they dwindled down to a very few. Soon the railroad found it no longer feasible to stop. The platform was removed.

In 1916, all that was left in operation at Valley Falls was the general store in the mill operated by Clem N. Mason. He also operated the ferryboat across the river above the falls. The last owner of the mill was Harvey Shane of Fairmont. When he died in 1934 the mill was torn down. The Canning Hotel was later sold to Dave Victor, a coal operator, who named it "Camp Victoria." The hotel was one of two buildings still standing in 1963. For many years the hotel stood as a symbol of the good old days.

The other house at that time was the legendary "Ghost House" which still had a dark stain on the floor which was supposed to have been blood. A good indication something horrible happened in this house. All of the buildings are gone today. A short tour of the grounds of Valley Falls State Park still reveal many reminders of what once existed here. Foundations still exist from some of the buildings; the millrace, and the old Wheeling Turnpike leading downriver towards Hammond is now a trail in the park system. The brick walkway leading up to the hotel can still be seen from the railroad tracks. Today a pavilion is in its place. Even the sound of the whistle of the train has changed over the years but still using the original line as it was in 1852.

VALLEY FALLS SCHOOL

The first official school for the children of the Valley Falls area was taught in a building on the Sam Moore farm on the Valley Falls Road. Lawrence Miller was the teacher.

In 1916, school was held in a log cabin near the site of the dam at Rock Lake. Minta Shaffer was the teacher. It wasn't long before the volume of children attending this school grew to the point that more room was needed.

In 1923 the board of education purchased one acre of land from Hiram Linn (Deed 265/Page 91) for $50.00. A one-room school was built at the top of Valley Falls hill (between the first school and the log cabin school). There was no electric so kerosene lamps were used. There was no water except what was carried from the closest neighbor, George Washington Kirk. Last names of some of the children who attended this school were Linn, Vangilder, Kirk, Bell and Johnson.

In the spring of 1937 the school was closed. The children were transferred to Quiet Dell School. In 1940, G. W. Kirk bought the vacated property and converted the school into a dwelling.

The teachers who taught grades 1 through 8 at the Valley Falls school were: Lawrence Miller, Minta Shaffer, Edyth Rogers, Elsie Dale Little Cather, Roxie McKinney Sayers, Margie McKinney Henderson, Walter Balderson, Daisey McVicker, Pauline Satterfield Clayton, Edna Brown Boyles, Agnes McKinney Nuzum and Stella Moran.

LINN SCHOOL

Directly across from the falls is the country road leading up to the spot to the Linn school building that is now Linn Chapel. Located on Lost Run, it was one of Taylor County's earliest schools dating back to 1869. William Linn and Marshall Wiseman donated the land for it. It was called Linn School because William Linn gave most of the ground. Located about a mile from Valley Falls, it was a small wooden structure built by Lemuel Tucker, John Riley and James Brown, all of whom had children attending the school. It was also used as a meetinghouse. The structure was built on a triangular piece of ground. The two roads beside it branch off. One leads to Lawler Church; one to Valley Falls; one to Rt. 250 and one to U S Rt. 50 by way of Tucker Run.

Inside, the desks were attached to the walls under the windows. The children sat on benches facing the walls like in some of the Quaker schools. This school continued in use till the end of the school term in May 1938. That fall, the children were transferred to Pruntytown Grade School.

Mortimer Lawler was the first teacher. Other known teachers were Samuel Dadisman, Truman Lawler, Orval Clevender, Alcinda Cochran, William Richardson, Jean Bartlett, Mary Giles Curry, Joseph Reed, Sr., Curtis Boice, Lloyd Shriver, Farrel Yates, Mattie Curry Goodwin, Ada DeMoss Wilson, Bessie Loughridge, Edgar Poe, Richard Reed, Jr., Charles Ross, Louis Steward, Minnie Cole Stillwell, Kenneth Little, Louise Lambert Robinson, Mabel Groves Ashby, Myrtle Auvil and Clara Boice Knotts.

After its closing, the little one-room school was kept in repair by The Linn, Carder, and Hammond Reunion Organization, which was governed by three trustees. Today the building is known as Linn Chapel, an interdenominational church, although at one time it was a Methodist church. Since the original school was very small, a large addition was built onto the back in 1992. Services are every Sunday; Dwayne Keener is the pastor. Some of the early families connected with this church are: Able, Lovejoy, Brown, Holt, Klepfel and Hawkins.

Valley Falls School 1925. Walter Balderson was the teacher. Front row, left to right: Blanche Shreve, Elsie West and Clarence Moore. Back: Bessie Shreve, Dessie Moore, Daisy Moore and Nancy Shreve, a visitor. *Courtesy of Blanche (Shreve) Collins.*

Linn School. Known today as the Linn Chapel.

VALLEY FALLS STATE PARK

When Rock Lake was first being developed in 1930, a newer road was put in from East Grafton Road to the falls. The road was paved for the first time in 1933 and a more permanent highway trestle bridge was built over the railroad tracks at the same time. It replaced a wooden bridge and that had been replaced many times for wagons to cross over the railroad tracks to get to the mills in the early days. Today the trestle bridge is closed to the general public but is still regularly inspected by the Department of Highways.

The area that once was a thriving community was left to deteriorate after the railroad took out the train platform. Despite that, visitors still made their way to the falls. The general store remained open until 1917. Crowds still kept coming to relax and picnic. Unsupervised swimmers sometimes found themselves in peril. A young man named Gilbert was one of them. He dived off the turtle head-shaped rock in middle of the lower falls and never came up. Since then, the local senior citizens called the rock "Gilbert Rock." The falls became a favorite hangout with the young people from Grafton and Fairmont. Because of the unruliness and litter, citizens and officials began to take action to ask the State to create a state park there. The beauty of the falls propelled many to work toward preserving the area.

Entrance to Valley Falls State Park.

The first purchase of land for the park was made in 1964 from Ross Bradshaw Johnson, grandson and heir of John Bradshaw. In his younger years he lived with his mother, who was sister to Sarah Bradshaw Canning, at Valley Falls. He had attended Hammond School for one year in 1906. Johnson was a historian and was President of the WV Historical Society, which played a large part in obtaining the historical highway markers throughout the state.

Left: Millstone from the gristmill on display today near the millrace at Valley Falls State Park. Right: The old Middletown-Wheeling Turnpike, the old stagecoach route, leading downstream towards Hammond from the parking area of Valley Falls State Park.

Harvey Havlichek, local businessman from Colfax on a weekend outing at the park, in his one-man "duckie," a kayak. *Courtesy of Debby Havlichek. August 1993.*

The WV Legislature provided funding for the purchase of the land, but the property costs rose when the mineral rights were included in the sale. Therefore, additional funding was added in the next year's legislative session. The state purchased property from Ross Johnson, 450 acres; Nathan Goff Estate, 200; Don Potter, 72; Alphonse Carrrone, 100; John Roy Alcorn and Ingle Biddle, 34; Hallie Able, 19; Samuel Reese heirs, 46; Charles Greippe, 15; C. H. Whitescarver, 31; Thomas J. Gates, 95; Ronald, Pearl and Carl Mason, 5; Wanda Hayes, 22; Glenden G. Wright, 50 and Edith Bradshaw heirs, 5. Marion County Delegate Robert H. Tennant was a longtime enthusiastic supporter of the Valley Falls project.

To date, development of the park has included 18 miles of winding hiking trails, two pavilions, two parking lots, modern restrooms, picnic tables, a playground, badminton and volleyball court and a horseshoe court. In 1990, the Marion County Commission contributed the park office. The one-mile steep grade from the top of the hill down to the parking lot is a 650-foot decline. Two falls are within 300 feet of each other. A third is 300 feet beyond these and the fourth is half a mile down river from these. Elevation in this one-mile gorge drops 100 feet very quickly. This spectacular event of nature is breathtaking and rare.

Mountain biking is very popular on the park trails so the park sponsors a race every year in April. Drawing bikers from Maryland, Pennsylvania and Virginia, as well as West Virginia, the annual bike race has over 100 participants. The challenging seven-mile course makes it a favorite among bikers. Valley Falls State Park is also quiet refuge for those not seeking excitement. It is special to many in all walks of life.

Rhododendron Trail, once called the old Wheeling Turnpike, leads 2.2 miles downstream towards Hammond. It leaves the river at the boundary line and goes another mile up the hill where it meets the Rocky Trail and the Dogwood Trail. In the old days, the road followed the river to Nuzum's Mill (Hammond). The picturesque mostly trail beside the river makes it popular with the young and old. There was a bridge that crossed Glady Creek but was taken out when the mailman stopped coming this way. It's now gone. Only the cut-stone piers remain. The Rhododendron Trail (3.2 miles) is the longest within the park system. Other trails include: The Deer Trail (2.1 miles), the very steep Red Cardinal Trail (2 miles), Dogwood Trail (.8 mile), Wild Turkey Trail (1.2 miles), Red Fox Trail (.06 mile). During the winter the trails can be used for cross-country skiing.

Swimming and wading was prohibited inside the park boundaries in 1985 because of the dangerous currents above and below the falls. Drownings over the years demonstrated the necessity of the rule that is strongly enforced. In

Turtlehead shaped rock nicknamed "Gilbert Rock" by local senior residents before it became a park in the state park system.

People and Places

downstream into the gorge while dodging room-size boulders? The whitewater sport draws large crowds of sightseers every year.

Whitewater rafting between Valley Falls and Hammond is said to be "intense and aggressive" and described to be like riding a roller coaster. The four swift waterfalls within one mile are unique and very rare. In 1996, whitewater rafting was introduced at the falls. When the water is usually released from Tygart Lake near Grafton, in July and August, the increased level of the river makes the "gorge" an unforgettable experience for a rafter. Tourists always gather to watch this feat. The trips are conducted and closely supervised by professional guides provided by U.S. Raft of Rowlesburg, WV. Rafting trips may be scheduled when water conditions are favorable.

IMPROVEMENTS

In 1989, the Valley Falls State Park Foundation was organized to assist future development of the park. It is a non-profit organization with a 10-member panel comprised of local business leaders who promote the park's activities and raise money for improvements.

In 1974, the West Virginia Legislature appropriated $230,000 for major improvements at Valley Falls. On June 9, 1980 a contract went to Salerno Brothers, Inc. of Shinnston, WV to install water lines, build bathrooms, a water storage tank and a sewage system. The company was paid a total of $178,600.

In 1989, the West Virginia Army National Guard constructed a 20x36 foot picnic shelter. Another pavilion, this one 36x40 foot, was built in 1997. It was partially funded through the sale of hand-painted model boxcars designed by Park Superintendent Ron Fawcett. Each year Fawcett hand paints and details HO gauge scale model railroad cars, honoring historical people, places or events that have taken place in the park or in Marion County. Each railroad car comes with a fact sheet. They are a popular sales item and are for sale in the park office. All profit from the sales goes directly to the funding of projects that improve the park and not to the state. Future development plans for Valley Falls Park include a primitive campground, a visitors' center and a separate road entering the park.

In 1990, the Marion County Commission, Valley Falls State Park Foundation and the Marion County Future Farmers of America, donated a building for the park office and visitors center, valued at $13,000. The park received another grant of $7,500 from the WV Division of Tourism and Parks in that same year for moving the building to its present site and for equipment and landscaping. In 1994, the Legislature appropriated $75,000 for installing electric lines down to the falls area and putting electric in the bathrooms and shelters, and for the installation of a pay telephone. In 1996, the Pleasant Creek Foundation in Taylor County dissolved; it donated a much-needed storage building to the Valley Falls Foundation along with $5,000 worth of tools.

In 1997, the footbridge across the millrace was raised five feet to make the overlook handicapped accessible. That same year, the state funded the construction of another shelter. It was built with in-house labor at a cost of $25,000.

In 1998, park employees built three new footbridges on the Deer Trail, Troop #61 from Boothsville of Mountaineer Area Council of Boy Scouts of America and two WVU student volunteers, working for credit hours. In July 2000, a footbridge was replaced to the horseshoe pit and two new rooms were added to the park superintendent's home. 100 new parking spaces also were added.

Robert E. Harsh was the first resident superintendent for the park in 1965. The superintendent's home is located across the road from the park office and was once the property of the George W. Kirk family. Ron Fawcett, the present superintendent, he was born and raised in Grafton just below the dam. Prior to being named Valley Falls superintendent, he had been superintendent at Pleasant Creek Wildlife Management Area for 17 ½ years.

Improvements to the park are ongoing. As in the days of old, visitors still go to the park to picnic, listen to the birds, and sunbathe on the rocks

Valley Falls State Park Superintendent Ron Fawcett, hand-paints model cars to provide money for park improvements.

or just watch the water roll over the gigantic rocks. In recent years, the park has become a favorite site for weddings due to its spectacular views, which truly reflect the saying "Almost Heaven, West Virginia!

SUPERINTENDENTS OF VALLEY FALLS STATE PARK

Sandstone rock formations leading into the two-mile gorge of Valley Falls. All a part of the Chestnut Ridge anticline. *Courtesy of Blanche Collins.*

Merle Haddox .... 1966 .... who was at the same time Superintendent of Tygart Lake State Park
    Carl Richards .... 1967-1968 who was at the same time Superintendent of Prickett's Fort State Park
    E. D. Dewitt .... 1968-1972. who was at the same time Superintendent of Prickett's Fort State Park
    M. S. Fitzpatrick ...... 1972 .... who was at the same time Superintendent of Tygart Lake State Park
    Robert Harsh .... 1972-1979. First Resident Superintendent
    Thomas Shriver 1979-1981
    John Gygax 1981-1982
    Alfred Dean, Jr 1982-1995
    Ronald E. Fawcett.... 1996-Present

Valley Falls State Park is a scenic wonder and will continue to do so. After eons of high water and erosion, Mother Nature has exposed the spectacular view of the gorge. 1,145 acres of forestland is seeing a second growth of timber on both sides of the river. Tourists can still follow in the footsteps of the Indians and our forefathers who once came here to enjoy the natural beauty of the river.

Many traces of the past have endured in our valley—some perhaps only in the memories of people or in the pages of history. There is still a lot of history to discover about our communities and waiting to be put down on paper. Like the past, the present can easily slip by unnoticed and undocumented unless someone takes the time to do it for future generations.

COFFMAN
2000

Coffman was a small town created by the men who owned and worked at the Winona Mine & Coke ovens. At one time there were 30 ovens in operation with 20 laborers and 20 miners. There was a row of white houses and a row of red houses for the workers. A dirt road from East Grafton Road led down to the town and continued on to Valley Falls two miles

Valley Falls State Park. *Courtesy of Blanche Collins.*

View of the 2.2 mile gorge. CSX Railroad on the left of the river and Hammond Ridge on the right. Fall Hills at the top of picture. *Photo by C. Hamilton.*

downstream.

A great percentage of coking coal was found in West Virginia, and numerous coke plants were located along railroad lines. The dome-shaped ovens at Coffman had an opening where the coal was fed in the top of each one. A tremendous amount of smoke was released into the atmosphere by these ovens.

Today what is left of them can be seen by hiking up the Deer Trail at Valley Falls State Park. The rows of houses are gone but several new homes have been built nearby. The days of the coke ovens are now only an historical fact and their memory is slowly fading with each generation. What's left of them stand as a monument of days gone by that once flourished in our state in coal production.

Valley Falls over looking the Taylor County countryside.

The Winona Coal and Coke Company coke ovens at Coffman are two miles upriver from the falls. The ovens are beside the railroad tracks and were made of red brick. Each oven had a hole at the top where they were fed.

Chapter Four

CHURCHES ON THE RIVER

CHURCH STEEPLES

In this valley,
Each community has a church
The steeple makes it visible,
Way up on its perch.

High above the church so high,
Church steeples reign over all.
They encourage us in our faith,
When the bells give out the call.

Just what would a community be like,
Without a church steeple's guidance?
They represent our love of God,
And deserve all our reverence.

C. Fortney-Hamilton 1998

West Virginia's Lower Tygart Valley River

RELIGIOUS FREEDOM ON THE FRONTIER

In Europe during the 1600's, freedom of religion meant going to the American colonies. It was one of several reasons why people left England where they were not free to worship as they wished. The people of England were supposed to accept the King of England as the head of the church, attend the services, agree to its teachings and give money to its support. Those who did not obey this law, no matter for what reason, were severely punished.

Those who could afford it left England. Those who could not afford passage could strike a bargain with a ship's captain, who would sometimes transport them without cost to them but would collect the price of their passage from someone already in the colonies who wanted to buy their services. Those people arrived as indentured servants who had to repay their debt by working for their benefactors for a certain period of time—usually four to seven years. At the end of their indenture, the servant became a free person. The indenture system worked, except for the blacks that were never released.

After the Revolution, thousands came to America in this way and were welcomed. There was considerable work be done in this new country. Here, when they were at last free, they could take up land of their own. The only land available and cheap enough to buy, however was in the wilderness frontier of western Virginia.

There settlers did not have to pay taxes for the support of the Protestant Episcopal Church (Church of England) and its clergy as in the Commonwealth of Colonial Virginia. For this among many other reasons, settlers began moving westward to the mountains, accepting the hardships and the danger of Indians. This was the only way for some to have relief from those taxes.

When settlers came to the headwaters of the Monongahela Valley, the Baptists, the Presbyterians and Methodists were not far behind. For many years, the Presbyterians and Baptists dominated the frontier. However, due to their circuit riders that went out on horseback into the hills to seek conversions, Methodism became dominant and soon replaced the Presbyterians as first. The Methodists and Baptists became the dominant religion. Other religions on the frontier were the Mennonites, Anglicans, Quakers, Hard-Shell Baptists and German Reformed. Two religious groups were not allowed to immigrate into Colonial Virginia: Catholics from near-by Maryland and the Jews.

Circuit riders made regular horseback visits to preach and administer the sacraments (marriages, death rites, baptisms, etc.) always accepting an invitation to stay overnight with faithful church followers. Their journals tell us they were always welcomed into the homes and never lacked for a good meal during his stay. Being a circuit rider was a tough way of life and they suffered many hardships. Most did not live beyond the age of 40.

After the Redstone Circuit (1783) was established in this area, Francis Asbury (1745-1816) passed through the area several times on his 31 visits to western Virginia. Almost every year from 1789 to 1816, he was in the territory of present West Virginia. During this time he kept a journal. According to it, he made an average of 42 miles daily on horseback. In his notes of 1796, he calls the Tygart Valley the "The Valley of Distress," where many souls needed to be saved.

Asbury was credited for having begun the Circuit Rider system in the frontier wilderness. The circuits provided traveling preachers for the people in outlying areas. Asbury was later appointed Bishop in 1784 and became a legend in the Methodist Church. He died in 1816, 20 miles south of Fredericksburg, VA at age 71. He was laid to rest in Mt. Olivet Cemetery, Baltimore, MD.

From 1800 to 1825, the people, lacking large meeting facilities, took to the woods for camp meetings and revivals. Those campgrounds were well known spots for a hundred years. It was a time of great excitement for everyone who attended—it was an opportunity to socialize as well as to hear the word. The Mon Valley was a famous camp-meeting region.

The Sabbath day was sometimes observed by making neighborly visits to one another's homes, where the Bible was read. They were God-fearing folks who not only helped one another but also held that day sacred. The Sunday visits remain with us today with one exception: most are not accompanied by Bible readings.

1800's EARLY CHURCHES IN MARION COUNTY

The following is a list of Marion County churches and the dates they were built. (These dates were taken from listings already documented by others and from interviews). The roll call gives an insight to the growth of churches of all denominations in Marion County during the 1800's. Many of them were founded earlier when people gathered in homes and schools. Some of the churches no longer exist (or perhaps moved to another location) but they are still listed in order to tell the complete story of the building of religion in this county. This is by no means a complete list. I am sure there were others. M.E. is the abbreviation for Methodist Episcopal. M.P. is the abbreviation for Methodist Protestant. No matter where one lived in the county, there was a church close enough to reach by horse and buggy by the year 1900.

1780	Prickett's Creek Baptist Church
1787	Pitcher M.E. Church at Dakota
1803	West Fork Baptist at Monongah
1803	Quakers' Meetinghouse at Nuzum's Mill (Hammond)
1805	Coon's Run Baptist Church
1812	Gilboa M.E. Church at Levels
1813	Pisgah M.E. Church on Route 73 North to Morgantown
1815	First Presbyterian Church on Jackson Street, Fairmont
1815	St. John M.E. Church at Basnettsville, Fairmont-Fairview Road
1828	M.P. Church at Barnesville near Middletown (Fairmont)
1831	Salem M.P. and M.E. Church at Pricketts' Creek
1833	Hebron Baptist Church on Glady Creek
1833	Mt. Zion M.E. Church on Bunner Ridge
1835	M.P. "Church on the Hill" in Fairmont
1836	Barrackville Methodist Church
1837	First M. E. Church on Washington St., Fairmont (later on Fairmont Ave.)
1840	Monongalia Baptist Church at Plum Run
1841	James Fork M.E. Church near Farmington
1841	Bethesda Baptist Church in Barrackville
1843	Monumental M.E. Church
1844	Hopewell M.P. Church
1844	Boothsville M.E. Church
1844	Worthington Baptist Church
1846	St. Paul Baptist Church (Fairview)
1847	Diamond Street M.E. Church in Fairmont
1850	First Catholic Church in Fairmont
1850	First Baptist Church in Fairmont
1851	First M.P. Church in Fairmont on Market Street
1851	Episcopal Church on Fairmont Avenue
1852	Winfield M.E. Church
1852	Union Church/Walnut Grove M.P. Church
1852	The Temple M.P. Church on Monroe Street, Fairmont
1853	Winfield Methodist Church
1854	Christ Episcopal Church on Washington Street, Fairmont
1854	Catawba M.E. Church
1854	Hoult M.E. Church
1854	Union Valley Baptist at Flat Run near Mannington
1854	First M.E. Church in Mannington
1854	Rhea Cha pel at Watson
1854	Catawba M.P. Church
1855	Worthington M.E. Church
1857	Righter Chapel on Koon's Run
1857	Mt. Nebo Church of Christ on Bunner Ridge
1857	Wesley Chapel M.E., South, Pharaohs Run
1858	Worthington Christian Church (met in the M.E. Church)
1861	Union Baptist Church at Benton's Ferry
1865	Jones Chapel (1st Negro Church in Fairmont)
1865	West Farmington M.E. South
1868	Bethel M.E. Church at Dunkard Mill Run
1868	Fairview M.P. Church on Bunner Ridge

1869	John Wesley M.E. Church (Negro Church in Fairmont)
1870	Calvary Baptist Church at Colfax
1871	Eldora M.P. Church
1871	Dents Run Baptist Church in the Mannington area
1871	Buffalo Methodist Church on Whetstone Run in the Mannington area
1871	First Presbyterian Church in Mannington
1873	Mt. Zion M.E. Methodist near Morgan's Ridge
1873	St. Peter The Fisherman Catholic Church in Fairmont
1873	First United Presbyterian Church in Mannington
1874	Rivesville M.E. Church on Jasper
1875	Baptist Temple in Fairmont on Columbia St.
1878	Levels M.P. Church
1877	Ballah M.E. Church in Grant Town
1881	Willow Tree Baptist Church on Dunkard Mill Run
1883	Hebron Baptist Church on Glady Creek
1883	Flaggy Meadow Baptist Church in the Mannington area
1884	Boothsville M.E., South
1884	Bee Gum Union Church in the Mannington area
1890	Plum Run Church of Christ
1890	Royal Chapel Methodist Church on Parker Run
1892	St. Paul M.P. Church in Watson
1893	Central Christian Church on Walnut at Second Street in Fairmont
1893	First Baptist on Fairmont Avenue
1893	Barnesville or Highland Avenue M.E. Church
1894	Colfax M.E. Church
1895	Wood's Chapel on East Run
1896	Colfax M.P. Church
1896	Evangelical United Brethren Church at Montana Mines
1896	Punkin Center Church of Christ at Fairview
1896	Northern (Beulah) Methodist Church in Baxter
1896	First Baptist Church in Mannington
1897	Fairmont Free Methodist on Morgantown Avenue
1897	Montana Mines M.E. Church

1861—THE CIVIL WAR

A word or two must be said about the Civil War and the Church. When President Lincoln gave a call to arms for brave men, few thought of the bitterness that would eventually affect families, neighbors and fellow Virginians. The slavery issue also would affect the church. Many people did not want to break away from the Old Dominion. The term "brother against brother" was very real right here in our own communities. The social upheaval was felt everywhere. The grocery store, mill, or even at a quilting bee. Here in western Virginia, as throughout the nation, the slavery issue divided relationships—in some cases forever.

In Fairmont, during slavery and before the Civil War, slaves attended church in the gallery of the First Methodist Church on Washington Street. After the war, Negroes built their own Methodist Church. It took a hundred years for the segregated Central Jurisdiction of Methodism to be abolished—in 1965.

Churches of the same denomination were divided; members supporting either the Union or the Confederacy. In 1860, some of the members within the Methodist Episcopal Church did not believe in slavery. They broke away from the main body to create a new doctrine. It became known as the "Free" Methodist Church. It is alive and thriving today. Methodists, Baptists, Presbyterians, as well as other Protestant denominations felt the North-South division long before the war ever started. Divided loyalties meant divided ministers. In some areas, the animosity among the clergy over issues was very fierce. In the South, very early in the war Jefferson Davis refused to exempt the clergy from military duty. One clergyman who fought under General Lee's chief of artillery swore that when a cannon was aimed and fired under his direction, he bowed his head and prayed: " Lord, preserve the soul while I destroy the body".

People and Places

In 1862, Federal Conscription Laws in the North required the clergy to fight. Many went to war as chaplains. The Federal congressional act read, "The clergy stand in the same position as members of other pursuits and professions."

Records show that very few chaplains at the beginning of the war were killed in action, but during the final months of the struggle, numerous chaplains who never used a rifle or carried a battle flag, were killed in action or maimed for life. It might be noted that all chaplains taken as prisoners of war by the South were immediately and unconditionally released. That did not happen to chaplains taken by the Northern armies.

It was hard times for the church as most activities reached an all-time low. It would not be until after the war was over that religious affairs began to show some revival. The bitterness eventually faded; reunions among relatives and friends caused a rise in the church in attendance. New churches of all denominations came into existence.

PLACES OF WORSHIP ON THE TYGART VALLEY RIVER

The following churches are on the Tygart Valley River from Millersville to Valley Falls. They are situated on the east and west banks of the river in Marion County with the exception of one in Taylor County. They are listed by the year in which the church was built.

1804 QUAKERS

The earliest known practiced religion on the Tygart in Marion County was the Quaker faith at Nuzum's Mill (Hammond) below Valley Falls. Officially called the Society of Friends, members practiced their religion within their own settlement, meeting in a log cabin near the river.

The Quaker religion was founded in England by George Fox in 1652. History tells us the name "Quaker" came into being because Fox's voice would "quake" or tremble when he read the word of the Lord. The Quakers look upon their fellowmen as "Friends" because they believe that in the sight of God all men are equal.

Quakers are Protestants who refused to worship in the then established Protestant Episcopal Church. They did not bear arms and were forbidden by their teachings to participate in war, which is why they refused to pay taxes for war. Their rules required marriages to be only between men and women within the society or they were disowned. They always dressed in black, the men removing their hats only to God. Thriftiness, hard work and charity (or good works) were basic standards of Quaker life.

Richard Nuzum (1734-1822) was not a Quaker, when he married Hannah Worrall at age 26. Hannah was a Quaker, who was shunned (or disowned) by the Quakers for marrying a person outside the society. Twenty years and seven children later Richard and his children become Quakers. He advanced to the equivalent of a deacon and kept that position until 1799. Hannah died in 1791.

In 1802 Richard, at 68 years old, sold his land in Pennsylvania and migrated with his seven grown children and their families to the Tygart Valley. He acquired a grant for 1000 acres of land with virgin timber where he developed the community of Nuzum's. By this time, Indian problems were over and soon other Quakers followed. Before long, a sizable community had settled here, worshipping in a log cabin.

At the top of the hill above the settlement, high above flood level, the Society began building a proper church; however, by 1850, it still was not finished due to a gradual decline in membership and the westward migration.

The Nuzums came under the Dunkard influence in the third generation when Albert Nuzum heard the "full gospel" preached for the first time in Thornton, WV. This was very different from the strict silence with prayer that he was used to with the Quakers. He invited Dunkard preachers A. C. Auvil and Zachariah Annon to come to Nuzum's Mill to preach. Services were held in the schoolhouse and Nuzum himself became a Dunkard member. In the face of the decline in the Quaker community, the Nuzum's realized there would be an ultimate need for the maintenance of their cemetery. They decided to offer the church lot to the Dunkards, if they would continue the care of the graveyard that Richard had set aside in 1814.

The schoolhouse had burned down where the Dunkards (Brethren Society) had been meeting, so they decided they were very much interested in the offer. An agreement was made. The unfinished Quaker church lot was deeded to the German Baptist Church of Europe (Dunkard) sometime before 1900. (The exact year is not known. See "Pleasant Hill Church of the Brethren.")

PLEASANT HILL CHURCH OF THE BRETHERN

The German Reformed Church (Dunkards) was already established in the eastern panhandle and the Cheat River area before the Revolutionary War. The Dunkards had slowly moved west to escape slavery and resolve moral issues. Like the Quakers, they refused to bear arms.

Having been deeded the Quaker Church lot and cemetery near Nuzum's Mill before 1900, the old unfinished Quaker structure was torn down and a new foundation begun. Documentation of dates are unavailable. The new church was called the Ross Chapel, named for the Elder J. F. Ross who played an important role in its ministry. He was a teacher, surveyor, blacksmith, farmer, carpenter, cabinetmaker, and broom maker.

In 1922, the church took the name of Pleasant Hill Church of the Brethren and was rebuilt in 1934. It maintains the New Testament as its only belief and follows the New Testament rites of Baptism by triune immersion, feet washing, love feast and communion as part of the Lord's Supper.

Pleasant Hill Church of the Brethern.

Reverend Daniel Webster Kirk ministered to the congregation here off and on for 50 years. He died in 1930 having descended from the pioneer Kirks who settled at Nuzums (Hammond). Kirk and his wife Clara Alice Annon Kirk had ten children and are buried in the Quaker cemetery (Nuzum No. 1).

Other pastors who served here were: Elders Lloyd Wilt, Benjamin Satterfield, George Murphy, Earl Shepler, Henry L. Sanders (1929), John L. Sanders (1934-1944), Selvey Vandergrift, Brooks Vandergrift (1945-47), Silas H. Kirk (1948-62) (the first paid minister); Fred R. and G. B. Clayton (15 months), George W. Kirk, James E. Taylor, Albert Shaver, (part-time in the summer of 1962); Jonas Sines (1961-66) and Edmon Rice (1966-80). The present pastor is Dorman Williams, who came in 1983.

1856 MILLERSVILLE/PLEASANT VALLEY UNITED METHODIST CHURCH

In Millersville, Pleasant Valley and Texas (Colfax), a number of families belonged to the Palatine Methodist Protestant Church in Palatine (Fairmont) but the hardships of winter made traveling very difficult over terrible roads, which stayed that way until spring. In the spring of 1856, William H. Barnes requested that a revival be held in his newly constructed barn. Reverend Jacob B. McCormick held this revival that resulted in the organization of a Bible class.

A plot of ground from the adjoining farms of Mr. Barnes and Isaac Courtney was deeded in 1856 as a site for a wooden frame building to be used for both a schoolhouse and church. It was located within a cluster of trees known as the "The Grove" on Pleasant Valley Road. This building had been in use for seven years when it was destroyed by fire. It was replaced in 1863, at the same location, by a hand-made brick structure. The church served the community for 42 years.

Before West Virginia became a separate state, the congregation supported pay subscription, or pay schools. After statehood this school became the first "free" school in the new state of West Virginia with Miss Emma Griffith as the teacher.

The church and school continued using the same building until 1872 when the school moved to another location. The old structure was jointly bought by the Methodist Episcopal and Methodist Protestant Churches. After many years the building became unsafe and again a new site had to be found for a new church. Some early names associated with the M.P. Church were Barnes, Dodd, Linn, Cochran, Knight, Mundell, Swearingen and Haymond. Associates of the M.E. Church were the Springer, Thomas, Meredith, Koontz, Holt, Satterfield, Miller and Courtney families.

In 1900, the church was declared unsafe. The population of Millersville was growing very rapidly. In 1901, on land donated by J. B. Miller, construction of a new church began at the top of the hill. A church record book dated October 8, 1903 indicates the congregation had $800 in cash and subscriptions with which to build the church, which cost $1,082.26. By the time the building was dedicated on September 3, 1905 the building was debt free. Rev. A. C. Phillips was the first pastor. At least six churches made up the Millersville Charge. One pastor served them all. Walnut Grove and Colfax Methodist Churches were on the Millersville Charge.

Millersville Methodist Church 1905-1958. *Courtesy of Jack Bish*

The church continued to grow and in 1930 when more church school space was needed, the building was elevated for a basement so classrooms and a kitchen could be added in the future. In 1939 the two congregations merged into one. In 1945, a parsonage including four new classrooms was added beside the church. This structure cost $11,500 in 1946. Five years later the congregation remodeled the sanctuary at a cost of $3,000.

Community growth again overtook the church, in 1956. One acre of land on the other side of the highway (I-79) was purchased for $3,000 from Mrs. Lois Cordray on the Pleasant Valley Road. A campaign was launched to construct a new church. A groundbreaking took place in October of 1957. The new building was completed by November of 1958 at a cost of $90,000. Rev. G. G. Wadsworth was the first pastor. The old Millersville Church stood silent until the fall of 1960, when it was dismantled. The bell from the old church steeple was carefully mounted beside the new chapel in 1975.

In 1968, the Methodist and the Evangelical United Brethren churches merged on a national level to form the present-day United Methodist Church.

In May of 1971, under the Reverend "Billy" Helmick, the church became a station church. This terminated the Millersville Charge, which had included Walnut Grove, and Colfax churches. They sold their interest in the parsonage to Valley Chapel. (The old Millersville parsonage had become difficult to maintain so, in 1974, the decision was made to sell it and purchase a house on Lillie Street for $29,000. from Julio Tutalo. Reverend Lehman Channell was the first pastor to live in the Lilly Street parsonage.

Spurred by a congregation willing to commit pledges for over $102,000, church members voted to build an educational wing on the church. Its classrooms were in use by the fall of 1986. A special program for the "Burning of the Mortgage" was held in December of 1992. Their debt was paid in full.

Valley Chapel

West Virginia's Lower Tygart Valley River

A Child Development Center was established in the new facility in 1989. The center provides pre-school and day care programs.

Ministers who served the Millersville Methodist were: A. C. Phillips, J. J. Dolover, J. A. Richmond, S. A. Coffman, O. W. Waters, L. S. Grose, J. B. Feather, A. H. Perkins, W. W. Bragg, A. E. Michael, Thomas Meredith, W. R. Moyer, I. A. Canfield, Thomas McCarty, E. J. Johnson, A. C. Bell, Perry Robinson, Daniel Jones, Gay Feather, E. O. McLaughlin, P. E. DeMuth and G. G. Wadsworth.

Ministers who have served Valley Chapel were: G. G. Wadsworth, O. C. Bunner, Willis Summers, Billie B. Helmick, Lehman A. Channell, Graham Robertson, James Kerr and James Norton.

1858 CALVARY BAPTIST CHURCH
(Inactive)

The Calvary Baptist Church was located one and a quarter miles from the newly finished B&O railroad at Colfax towards the East Grafton Road. Prior to the Civil War, there were no other Baptist churches close by for worship. On April 19, 1858, Elder John Davidson, Thomas Wood and James Wood organized the Calvary Baptist church. Services were held in Holman School. The following families formed its congregation: Job Springer, (d. 1874) was first deacon (his wife was Rebecca): Zadoc and Ruhama (Springer) Nuzum; Richard (Black Dick) Nuzum; Anna Hughes and Sophrania Nuzum. Elder Thomas Wood was the first pastor.

In 1870 John Harr and Zadock Nuzum headed a committee to raise funds for a new church building. Zadock and Ruhana Nuzum gave one acre of land across from Holman School as the site. The land was conveyed to Hun Harr, Jacob Watkins and Charles Hughes, church trustees. They reported in March of that year that $583.00 had been raised. The church building was dedicated as the Calvary Baptist Church on November 5, 1871. Rev. J. B. Solomon delivered the sermon.

Despite a large congregation, the church was closed in 1921 with the building of the Baptist Temple in Fairmont. Members then took their membership and attendance to Fairmont. The Nuzums had stipulated in the original deed that once the property ceased being a church, the property was to go back to the original owner or heirs. In August 1923, the property was sold to A. Glenn Springer from the other heirs. Various members of the Springer family owned the property until 1962, when Arthur and Evelyn Stuart bought it, raised their family on it, and beautifully remodeled the structure as it is today. Many of the old timers in the community say they have fond memories of this church.

Family names appearing on the church rolls are familiar in and around the Colfax community. They are Nuzum, Springer, Harr, Swearingen, Carpenter, Watkins, Hughes, Prickett, Jasper, West, Vandergrift, Reeves, Marshall, Swisher, Knight and Myers.

Some of the pastors who ministered here were Thomas Wood, John A. Heck, J. D. Leachman, E. M. Sapp, T. R. Richards, L. W. Holden and John T. Reynolds.

1861 BENTON'S FERRY UNITED METHODIST CHURCH

In 1861, six years after the completion of the railroad and at the beginning of the Civil War, Sanford B. Hall donated a parcel of land to the community. On this land a structure, which was to serve as a school and a "meeting house," was to be built. The land was deeded to trustees who were chosen by the people of the community. They were Robert Linn, Alexander

Benton's Ferry United Methodist.

204

McAllister and H. C. Morris. There were no conditions or restrictions in the deed so anyone could preach and hold services in the meetinghouse.

The building was used for a subscription school for a while before a new school was built at another site. Then the building was used exclusively as a church. The late Ted Boyles, who grew up at Benton's Ferry, believed one of the bells from the old ferry now rests in the steeple of this church. In 1886, the Baptists called this church the Union Church. Later it was in joint trusteeship with the Church of Christ. Meetings by other denominations were always welcome. The local Methodist Protestants had several meetings here but no organization was formed because Pleasant Valley church was only two miles away.

Reverend Isaac A. Barnes had returned to his hometown in 1920 and later organized a Sunday school for the many children in the area at this church. The Baptists closed down their church services in 1921 and started going to the Baptist Temple in Fairmont. Reverend Barnes was a Methodist Protestant minister who wrote a book on Methodism in 1927, entitled, The Methodist Protestant Church in West Virginia.

After the Billy Sunday revivals in Fairmont in 1921, clubs were organized to continue the evangelistic spirit by holding meetings at various churches. One such meeting was at Benton's Ferry, where many young people were converted. It was decided an established church was needed especially since the Baptists and the Church of Christ no longer ministered here. So in 1924, the church was under the full leadership of the Watson Charge of the Methodist Protestant Conference. Some family names that attended this church were Hawkins, Wilt, Boyles, Linn, Barnes, Rutherford and Griffith.

In 1923, the Church of Christ built their own building on land donated by George W. and Sarah Hull across the river on Route 250 at Hillview. Progress in the county later took this church so they built yet another church close to the county line on Route 250 South near Deerfield Center.

In 1944, a fire destroyed part of the sanctuary of the old church but it was soon renovated. A basement was added in 1951. Then in 1959, Mrs. Daisy Hayhurst left part of her estate to the church, making it possible to enlarge, redecorate and refurnish it.

Church trustees in 1960 were Helen McDougal, Russell Wilt and Joseph Morris. Pastors who have served Benton's Ferry United Methodist Church are: 1925-27, A. W. Lowe; 1927-33, A. L. Nestor; 1933-36, U. R. Hinzman; 1936, B. F. McGee; 1936-40, W. H. Stalnaker; 1940-42, H. C. McCulty; 1942-44, Alfred R. Wallace; 1944-45, George Loar; 1945-47, Walter Bowman; 1947-49, J. B. Rupert; 1949-50, Earl Haywood; 1950-51, Matt Bott; 1951-52, Dale Workman; 1952-56, Donald Goff and 1956-59, W. W. Beckley. 1959-61, Marvin Freed; 1961-62, Charles Eaton, Sr.; 1962-66, Charles Lamb; 1966-67, George Bartholow; 1967-68, Samuel Ryan; 1968-69, T. Leroy Hooper; 1969-70, Allen Ridenour; 1970-72, George Bartholow; 1972, T. Leroy Hooper, 1972-85, Phyllis Harvey; 1985-90, Vance Ross; 1990-91, William Balderson; 1991-94, Dwight Ross; 1994-96, Jeremiah Jasper and 1996, James Norton.

LEVELS METHODIST EPISCOPAL CHURCH

According to Hardesty's History of Marion County, Gilboa Methodist Episcopal Church was the first religious society in Union District. The year was the around 1812. The church was located not far from Sand Bank Road at Levels. Some of the people attending were: Benjamin and Margaret Summers, Ester Davis, Phoebe Kirk, Sarah Leonard, Enoch and Elizabeth Vincent, George Nuzum and Aaron Rogers. Sometime around 1852, a brush fire, created by sparks from an engine on the railroad, set the church ablaze and it was destroyed.

At the close of the Civil War, Bible studies known as Class No. 8 were held in homes under the tutelage of C. Conner, the minister from Diamond Street Methodist Church in Fairmont. Class leader was John Hirons (1829-1893). He and his wife Sally (1825-1914) lived in a log cabin on a 132-acre farm located on the right as you start up the hill towards Levels from Colfax.

Levels United Methodist Church.

Members of the class from Levels and Texas (Colfax) community were; Richard Kirk, Jonathan Kirk, Elizabeth Kirk, Jacob J. Davis, Esther Davis, Elizabeth Davis, James Davis, Emily Davis, Margaret Carpenter, David Carpenter, Joshua Murphy, Mary Yates, Elizy Yates, Benjamin Satterfield, Margaret Hawkins, Elizabeth Satterfield, Enos L. Satterfield, Richard Hall, Rececca Hall, Joshua Shaw, Melissa Irons, James Jenkins, Harriet Jenkins, John Shriver, James Shriver, Thornton Nuzum, and Mercia Nuzum.

After the Civil War, the ME's used the Levels wood frame schoolhouse for their place of worship. Then they built another church near Sand Bank Road but it also burned down. After the fire in 1894, the ME's built a new church at Colfax by the railroad tracks. (See Colfax ME Church).

1812 LEVELS METHODIST PROTESTANT CHURCH

Sometime after a school was built on Goose Creek it was used jointly for a school and a church. Here the Methodist Protestant Church formed and met until 1904 when the building was sold to the Free Methodists. In that same year a church was built on land Job R. Nuzum sold to the trustees. Job Nuzum lived in the red brick home beside the church. The Methodist Conference dedicated the church in 1905.

The congregation consisted of the families of Richard N. Knight, John and James Shriver, and Melissa Irons. Rev. J. J. Phillips was the pastor. He was also pastor at the Colfax MP Church.

In 1967, four needed Sunday school rooms were added. Indoor plumbing with bath rooms and a vestibule were added in December of 1971. The altar in the church was a gift from Colfax M.E. Church when it closed. In September of 2002 Tygart River Mines donated the property across the road from the church for social gatherings. The church continues to grow along with the community. In 1994 a kitchenette was added along with a larger schoolroom in the back.

1875 LAWLER METHODIST EPISCOPAL SOUTH CHURCH
(Inactive)

The Lawler Methodist Episcopal South Church is located on Hammond Ridge on the west side of the river in Taylor County. This church is only a short distance from Valley Falls. In January of 1875, when logging was king, the Lawler family deeded ground for the purpose of erecting a house of worship. The trustees were as follows: John H. Lawler, James Brown, J. C. Wiseman, James Clelland, John Riley and Marseen Smith.

Above: Lawler Church beside the Lawler Cemetery entrance. 1998 Left: Lawler M.E. South Church established in 1875.

People and Places

There are no early records of this church but it is believed that Jehu Lawler was one of the first pastors for which it took his name. It was an active and flourishing congregation until the church at nearby Tappan moved their congregation from that village to the new church at the Janes Memorial Methodist. Because Janes Memorial was so close, Lawler's chapel closed. However, annual services were held to honor the efforts of the people who held sentimental attachment to the church.

In June of 1983 interested friends of the chapel donated funds toward the purchase of the little church when the Methodist Conference sold the property to the care of trustees. In 1998, trustees appointed were William Able, John Keener and John Whitescarver. Families who attended this church were: Tucker, Clelland, Curry, Bennett, Lambert, Riffee, Abel, Shriver, Dadisman, Provance, Scranage, Martin, Nixon, Goodwin, and Lawler.

In 1993, the Open Door Free Will Baptists started leasing the little church from the trustees and put in a movable building for classrooms. Outhouses were still in use here because of the lack of indoor plumbing. By the year 2000 the church had moved on to another site taking their classroom building with them. Reverend James Baker was their pastor.

1894 COLFAX METHODIST EPISCOPAL

The first church in this small, quiet community was the M. E. Church built in 1894 on land willed by John Hirons at his death in 1893 (Will Book 3 Page 129). He is buried in the Hayhurst cemetery on Bunner Ridge. Mr. Hirons, who was a justice of the peace for Union District, and his wife Sally lived on a 132-acre farm that extended to the railroad tracks. They had been attending the Levels M.E. Church when fire destroyed it and another M.E. building there. After the second fire, he felt there was a need for an M.E. church in Colfax. Colfax at this time (1894) was a thriving community with a post office, general store, shoemaker; stream saw mill, school, express agent for the B&O Railroad and a justice of the peace.

The plot of ground he chose was located near the railroad on the main road (Sandy Beach Road) from Levels and so it became known as the 'railroad church.' Like most other country churches in those times, the structure most likely was built by local volunteers. It was completed in 1894; Reverend G. W. White was its first pastor. Sally Hirons attended this church till her death.

Above: Colfax M. E. Church in 1910. Established in 1894. It is now the home of Mark and Brandy Miller on Sandy Beach Road.
Courtesy of Delbert Smith.
Right: 1905 Christmas program inside the railroad M.E. Church.
Courtesy of the Marion County Historical Society.

John and Sally Hirons. *Courtesy of Ila Fortney.*

The church prospered for 45 years. Services were held every two weeks until the ME's and the MP's, united in 1939, when it closed and was sold to Charlie Nuzum in 1939.

It is believed the alter from this church was taken to Levels church where it remains in use. Trustees in 1939 were Hershel Rust, Louis P. Rust and Orville Irons.

In 1945 the property was sold to Delbert and Iretta Smith, who remodeled it for use as their home.

Ministers who served this church were: 1893-94, G. W. White; 1895, W. D. Carrico; 1896-97, Alexander Justice (his post office box was given as Palatine); 1897-99, A. A. Kelley (post office box given as Colfax); 1899-1900, N. L. Bumgardner; 1900-01, J. J. White; 1901, J. F. Deal; 1902-03, W. R. Hennon (P.O. box Fairmont); 1904-05, O. C. Phillips; 1906, Taylor Richmond; 1907, Stephen Coffman; 1908, O. W. Waters; and 1909, J. M. Grose.

1911-13, C.E. Feather (served seven churches); 1914-16, D. H. Perkins; 1917, T.G. Meredith (son of William and Harriet Meredith) served the ministry for 56 years-married Cora Snodgrass) 1918, A. J. L. Curtis; 1919, William W. Bragg (b. 10-6-1888, married Beulah M. Good. They had 3 daughters. Retired in 1938 because of disability); 1920-24, A. E. Michael (served seven churches); 1925-26, T. M. McCarty; 1927-28, W. R. Moyer; 1929-30, I. A. Canfield; 1931-34, E. G. Johnson (served five churches w/ parsonage); 1935-36, A. C. Bell; 1937, Gay Feather and 1938-39, D. W. Jones. In 1939 the unification of the M.E. and the M.P. churches took place.

1896 COLFAX METHODIST PROTESTANT

The following is an account of the history of the Colfax United Methodist Church. As the church historian I have given in-depth details of its growth.

In 1895, Rev. J. P. Varner, the pastor of Marion Circuit, established a preaching place at the Colfax schoolhouse. The school was located on what later would become the Gerald Griffith property on the Colfax road. The old brick church at Pleasant Valley, according to Rev. I. A. Barnes, was declared unsafe; it was abandoned and a class was organized at Colfax in which the members of the old Valley class attended. Members included family names such as Barnes, Linn, Louden, Fleming, Radford. Nichols, Hawkins, Satterfield, Springer, Dodd and Frankenberry.

Members decided to build a proper church under the supervision of Rev. Thomas Ireland in 1896. Land was bought (40 square poles) from Job and Sarah Nuzum and Richard and Jemima Springer for the sum of $50.00 (Deed 108, Page 278, Marion County Court House). No official records were made on the building of this church.

The new Methodist Protestant Church was completed in 1896. The pews and pulpit were donated from the MP Church in Fairmont known as the "old church on the hill". This church moved to a new location known as the People's Temple. Except for the foundation that Rufus Satterfield dug out by hand for the new church in Colfax, it was made entirely of wood. There were three arched double windows on each side with two windows and double doors in the front. A bell tower loomed high above the roof with a large bell to ring every Sunday morning to remind everyone in the valley below that it was the Lord's Day.

The Rev. Benjamin Stout dedicated the little church that also was located on a hill, thus it became known as the "Church on the Hill".

Colfax M.P. Church built in 1896. *Courtesy of Ila Fortney.*

People and Places

Seven years after the completion of the building (1903), plans were already in the making for a parsonage to be built in Colfax. Toward that end, Richard and Jemima Springer sold three acres of their land for that purpose for a small sum to the church board. It was noted at the conference of that year that the Nichols family donated lumber toward the construction project. By 1907, the parsonage was completed with the Rev. J. N. Holt as the first pastor to live there.

Unfortunately, by 1912, the annual West Virginia Conference decided to move Colfax and Levels appointments to the Catawba charge, where they had a parsonage. In 1913, the Colfax parsonage was sold for $1,000.00. Colfax church received $300.00 from the sale. The former parsonage today is the residence of John and Sylvia (Smith) Abel.

Colfax Methodist Protestant Church parsonage as it was being built in 1907.
Courtesy of Beverly (Wilson) Irons

During the late 1930's, the M. P. and the M. E. churches held alternate services for several years until conference unification. The two congregations shared the use of a piano for each of the services, so that meant the piano was taken from one church to the other each week. Services at this time were held twice a month at each church, therefore congregations were made up of almost the same families at each. Sunday School was held, however, every Sunday. By the late 1940's the congregation realized they were outgrowing the church. There were no classrooms and no basement. Many remember the curtains that hung from a wire line that separated the classrooms for Sunday school inside the sanctuary. Again plans for the future were being made.

The Men's Brotherhood planned to build a new church building in 1949. Delbert and Iretta Smith donated land across the road from the existing church as the site. Some of the members of the Men's Brotherhood were Gus Wilson, Cecil Kinty, Delbert Smith, Orville Irons, Guy Taylor, Fred Hawkins, Russell Knotts, Elbert Keener and Charles Huffmaster, who eventually built the church sanctuary that was spearheaded by S.B. Brown, a carpenter. Anna Belle ("Grandma") Nichols was an active early member of the old "church on the hill", and she lived to see the basement of the new church completed. The basement was used for Sunday school classes for a couple of years before the sanctuary was completed. The basement was also used by the Colfax Schools' seventh and eighth grades for classrooms until the new addition to the school was completed. Franklin Cain taught those classes during the 1951-52 term.

Upon completion of the sanctuary new stained glass windows were donated by members of the congregation in honor or in memory of their loved ones. Those members were Fred Hawkins, W. H. Hawkins, Sarah and William Delaney, C. E. "Pete" Keener, Harry O. Nichols, Mr. and Mrs. J. W. "Uncle Web" Fleming, William and Gertie Satterfield, L. Elmer and Charles D. Fortney, Rev. O. E. McLaughlin and David Barnes. The church bell, pulpit and pews were removed from the old church for use in the new one.

In 1953 it came time to hang the new doors in front of the new church. The Men's Brotherhood devoted hundreds of volunteer hours to the new building. Church member Fred Hawkins and Elbert Keener built the front doors of the church that had to accommodate pullbears and caskets. Fred measured the front walk for concrete from May Brothers in Fairmont on a Monday and it was poured on Wednesday. Suddenly on Friday to the shock of the community, Fred died of a heart attack. His funeral was the first for the new church the following Sunday, on December 22nd.

October Homecoming in 1952. Services were held in the basement. Pictured in the front are Fred Hawkins, "Grandma" Anna Belle Nichols, Delbert Smith. Back; Harry Nichols and Web Fleming. *Courtesy of Ila Fortney*

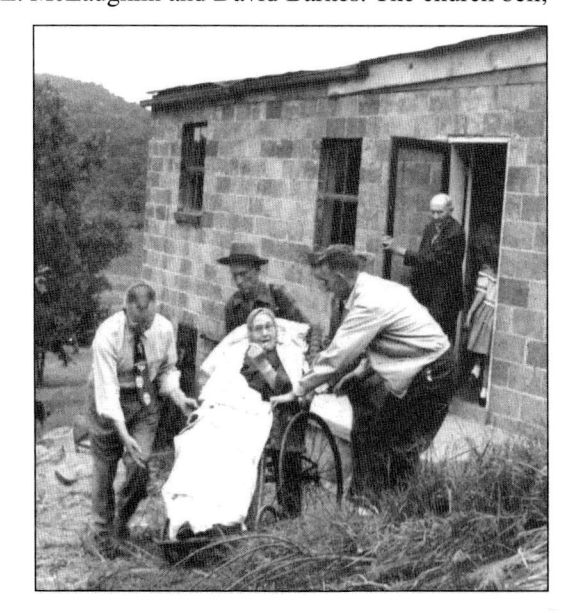

Congregation of the Church on the Hill in 1948. Left to right. Front row: Carolynn Fortney, Richard Keener, Diane Blosser, Louise Mowery, Terressa Herrington, unidentified, unidentified. Second row: Icie Hawkins, Alice Storms, Bobby Wilson, Larry Fortney, Billy Blosser, Joyce and Evelyn Satterfield, Joann Keener holding Linda, Vicki Lynn Wilburn, Flora Boice, Willie Boice and Rev. O. E. McLaughlin. Third row: unidentified, Ila Fortney, Agnes Irons, Cassie Fortney, unidentified, Francis Mowery, unidentified, unidentified, Charles Joe Irons, Jackie Keener, Margarete Wilson. Back Row: Gus Wilson, Elbert Keener, Orville Irons, Sylvia Kinty, unidentified, Barbara Nichols, unidentified, Elizabeth Bice. *Courtesy of Ila Fortney*

Russell Nichols bought the old church property in 1953 and had the church dismantled. Eleven years later in 1964 Russell sold the old church lot back to the congregation. It was deeded to Church Trustees Roy Cottrill, C. D. Smith, Orville Irons and Russell Knotts and used for a parking lot.

The first sermon in the new unfinished church was preached by Rev. O. E. McLaughlin on Sunday, November 8, 1953. (Rev. McLaughlin was earning $70.42 a month that included traveling expenses). Some of the older church members, who had been at the dedication 59 years earlier, gave testimonies.

The adult Sunday school class was called the Robertson Bible Class for its teacher Mrs. "Lovie" Robertson. Her daughter Agnes Robertson-Irons taught the class after Mrs. Robertson became ill and was unable to teach. Ila Fortney followed as teacher of the class until 1996. Jackie Richards is the present adult Sunday school teacher.

The late Rev. Richard Keener and his wife Rev. Alice Keener and Rev. Dwaine Dawson were members of this church when they entered the ministry.

The ladies of the church formed a group called the Ladies Aid in 1936. On their 15th anniversary in 1951 Ila Fortney, then secretary of the group, wrote the following poem.

The present Colfax United Methodist Church built in 1953.

COLFAX LADIES AID (W.S.C.S.)

October 3rd, 1936, fifteen years ago
Three ladies met and plans were made,
To form a group, that was to be
The Colfax "Ladies Aid".

Icie Hawkins, Clara Smith,
And "Grandma" Nichols, too,
Ladies who made those historic plans
A "Ladies Aid", with good works to do.

October 10th, nine more ladies met
With these three, and the Aid was going;
Flora Boyce was elected the President,
Good fellowship they soon were enjoying.

Six more on October 22nd joined the group
Eighteen women now made up the Aid
Years of fine fellowship have made several friends,
Made memories that shall never fade.

They quilted quilts and served at sales,
And sold vanilla too.
They paid the preacher and bought a church rug,
And each paid her ten-cent dues.

Along with the years,
Many changes have come.
Three charter members have gone;
Gertie Satterfield, Flora Boyce, and a friend
  Allie Nuzum.

Some members have moved, are ill or aged,
Six charter members among them.
We miss them and hope they may join us again,
We need them as much as we did then.

Thru the 15 years, nine of the "charters" have
  stood the test,
Always up and ready to do their best.
But old or new, all members alike have made
Whatever our Ladies Aid is today.

Today we do not call it the Ladies Aid,
But the W.S.C.S.
As the Women's Society of Christian Service,
We strive to do our best.

Tonight as we celebrate this anniversary,
We welcome all that have met with us.
A special greeting to the old "charter" friends,
Who are able to be present is a plus.

Eighteen members when the Aid first begun,
Only nine of them meet with us now.
"Grandma" Nichols, you know is ill and can't come,
But as an honorary member takes her bow.

Five old time charter members,
Had their names dropped from the roll.
Four of them have moved away,
To bring the one back in is our goal.

Three out of the eighteen "charters"
Have been called to their heavenly home.
We hope those who are living still,
Will think of us, where e're they may roam.

We are proud of all you members,
And we mean each one of you.
We take this special time tonight,
To say, "May God Bless and Keep You."

By Ila Forney 1951

Members not mentioned were: Goldie Khun, Hazel Nuzum, Susie Knight, Ruth and Alice Storms, Darl Storms, Dale Barnes, Agnes Irons, Annie Davis, Irene Hoskins, Vallie Phillips, Gertie Satterfield, Mrs. A.C. Bell and Mrs. H. K. Rust.

In 1947, the Ladies Aid name was changed to Women's Society of Christian Science (W.S.C.S.). In 1968, the name again was changed to the United Methodist Women. In 1995, the group at Colfax disbanded.

MINISTERS

Dates and notes from the Conference Archives at WV Wesleyan College in Buckhannon, WV and personal notes:

1893-95: J. P. Varner, pastor for the Marion Circuit, who established a preaching place at the Colfax school house (the Griffith house). A class was organized including members from the Pleasant Valley class. His address was Eldora, WV at the parsonage.

1896-97: Thomas W. Ireland, first minister for the new "Church on the Hill" (address was Morgantown.)

1898-99: R. C. Dean (his address was Eldora.)

1900: J. M. Conaway (his address was Eldora.)

1901: W. V. Conference released Rev. Conaway and appointed Rev. Thomas W. Ireland.

1902-05: J. J. Phillips. In 1903, a plot of ground was bought from Richard and Jimima Springer, who were loyal members of the church, for a parsonage at Colfax. During 1904, Rev. Phillips was also the pastor at Levels at their 'new' location after a brush fire was ignited by an engine on the B&O Railroad.

1906: J. P. Varner. The parsonage was well under construction at this time. Lumber was donated by the R. Nichols Lumber Company. The congregation donated labor.

1907-09: J. N. Holt. Reverend Holt was the first pastor to live in the parsonage. He became President of the Pittsburgh & Baltimore Conference in 1913.

1910: G. H. Snyder. (His address was Colfax parsonage).

1911: A. L. Nestor. (His address Colfax parsonage). In 1912, the Annual West Virginia M. P. Conference decided that the Colfax and Levels appointments should be taken from the Marion Circuit and added to the Catawba Circuit. Since Catawba had its own parsonage, the Colfax parsonage was sold. Church received $300.00 from the sale.

1912: J. M. Rhoades. (His address Catawba parsonage).

1913: R. S. Burch. (Catawba.)

1915-17: Sylvester Bennett. (Catawba). Rev. Bennett was released in January of 1917.

1917-18: Paul Riegel. (Catawba). Rev. Riegel was from the Georgia Conference and served six months.

1918-19: J. H. Green. (Watson Circuit; address Watson Parsonage).

1920: J. Rhodes. (Watson).

1921-24: A. W. Lowe. (Watson).

1925-26: A. L. Nestor. (Watson).

1926: Benton's Ferry was added to the Watson Circuit.

1927-32: U. R. Hinzman (1879-1956). Reverend Hinzman and his wife Cora had always liked Colfax and wanted to live there when they retired. They bought a home in the center of town near the railroad but he was unable to be active in the community due to a heart problem. In 1928, under Reverend Hinzman, the retaining wall and driveway to the church were put in at a cost of $1,700. In 1929, Colfax charge was moved from the Catawba Circuit to the Morgantown Circuit. In 1930, Colfax and Benton's Ferry churches received new pianos at a cost of $200.00.

1933-36: B. F. McGee. Due to the untimely death of Reverend McGee on May 6 the Conference appointed Laco J. Lunsford to the circuit until a new pastor could be appointed.

1936-38: H. S. McCulty. The church was on Watson Charge. In 1939, the Colfax Methodist Protestant Church united with the Methodist Episcopal Church at the Annual Methodist Conference.

1939-40: Perry Robinson.

1941-52: O. E. McLaughlin. (1886-1961). Born in Brownsville, Pa. Married Alta Grace Daniels and entered the ministry in 1925. He was the last minister to preach at the "church on the hill" and was the first to preach at the "new" Colfax Methodist Church. He retired in 1957. On November

Front row: Left to right: Marquita Storms, Cassie Fortney, Rev. G. G. Wadsworth and Jackie Richards. Back row: Unidentified and Ronny Irons. *Courtesy of Ila Fortney*

People and Places

13, 1961 he died from complications from an automobile accident. He is buried near his hometown of Elkins, WV. In 1942, the Morgantown District formed the 'new' Millersville Circuit with Colfax, Pitcher, Bethel and Millersville on the circuit. In 1945, a parsonage was built in Millersville. In 1952, Pleasant Valley was added to the Millersville Charge.

1953-56: Phillip DeMuth (His address Millersville parsonage).

1957-60: Golden G. Wadsworth (His address was Millersville). Born July 7, 1891 in Ashley, WV. Married Velma___. They had six children. He was admitted to the WV Conference in 1925.

1960-67: Oscar C. Bunner. (1909-1980). He was born in Shelbyville, WV. and married Mabel Crawford in 1935. They had four children. While serving the Millersville Charge, they lived in the Millersville parsonage. Prior to entering the ministry in 1952, he was an insurance agent. He retired in 1974 as associate pastor at First United Methodist Church in Fairmont. He died at the age of 71.

O. C. Bunner, minister from 1960-1967

1967-69: Willis Franz Summers, address was Millersville. Born in 1916, he married Alicia Doris Sparks in 1946 and had four daughters. In 1968-69, unification with the Evangelical United Brethren Church and the Methodist Church created the formation of the United Methodist Church.

1969-71: Billy B. Helmick (not shown) was born in Gassaway, WV on January 11, 1935. He was the last pastor to live in the parsonage at Millersville. He married Pattie J. Prunty. They had 3 children. He was ordained a deacon in 1963. He died on November 4, 1974.

Willis Franz Summers, minister from 1967-1969.

1971-73: Stephen Graham Engle was born February 15, 1951 in Atlanta, Georgia. In August 1971, he married Beverly Price at Walnut Grove Church. Also in that year, the Colfax/Walnut Grove Circuit was changed to the Walnut Grove Charge. Walnut Grove is the station church. This charge was Reverend Engle's first appointment. Rev. Engle and his wife lived in a garage apartment belonging to Herb and Patty Hawkins behind the Winfield Fire Department sub-station on the Colfax Road.

1973-76: Deloris Lee, born on February 4, 1929 in Fairmont, WV. Daughter of Denzel E. and Thelma T. Rogers Carpenter. She married Robert Edgar Lee in 1947 and had two boys, Robert Earl and Larry Alan. She was the first woman pastor for the Colfax-Walnut Grove charge. Prior to this, she served in the community of Hutchinson.

1976-82: Clarence D. Edman, 1907-1986. The son of Jacob and Minnie Davis Edman of Wood County, WV. He married Lila Mae Collier on October 24, 1943 and had two sons and a daughter. John, David and Sue. The Edmans owned one of the camps on Poplar Island but resided in Rivesville. They are buried in the Nuzum cemetery at Goose Creek.

Stephen G. Engle was minister from 1971-1973.

1982-84: Denise Heater was from Vienna, WV. In December 1981 the Walnut Grove Circuit purchased property for a parsonage at 910 East Park Avenue, in Fairmont for $40,000. Denise was the first pastor to reside in the new parsonage.

1984-2000: Hobart (Bert) Coffman, born 1948. He is the son of Hobart D. and Arlice Moore Coffman of Philippi, W.Va. He married Suzanne Smith Southern, also from Philippi, in 1988 at Walnut Grove Church. They have two children, John and Alex. In 1999, the parsonage was sold to Tom Messenger and Buddy Myers for $90,000 to make way for a new parking lot for a new business complex. The Charge then bought a country cottage on East Grafton Road, known as the

Delores Lee, 1973-1976.

Clarence D. Edman, 1976-1982.

Reverend Hobart "Bert" Coffman, 1984-2000.
Permission to reproduce by United Church Directories,

Howard Garlow house, for $60,000. The house was renovated to meet conference specifications.

2000-2001: Virginia Joan (Gorham) Showalter, 1942-2001 was born in Hartford, Conn. where she earned an accounting degree and later became an ordained First Baptist Minister of the American Baptist Conference in Connecticut. In 1986, she came to Romney, WV as a United Methodist Minister and married Paul Showalter in 1987. She was ordained in the United Methodist ministry in 1992. Showalter and husband were the first to live in the parsonage on East Grafton Road. She died in office from cancer on January 23, 2001 and is buried in Romney, WV.

2001: Due to the death of Rev. Showalter, Lay Speaker James H. Zinn of Fairmont led Sunday services on a temporary basis until the position was filled. In May of that same year, the District Superintendent appointed Zinn to the position. After 35 years with Verizon, he retired and studied to be a Licensed Local Minister in the district. He is married to the former Mary Frances (Teets). They have three children and one grandchild. Zinn has been an active volunteer with the Boy Scouts of America for 30 years.

Virginia Showalter 2000-2001

James H. Zinn 2000-present.

Left: Pictured are left to right are: Gus Wilson, Orville Irons, Reverend Dennis Heater and Cecil Kinty. June 1982
Courtesy of Ila Fortney

1905 NAIN FREE METHODIST CHURCH
(Inactive)

Located in the valley of Goose Creek, this church originated in 1905, when the Union District board of education built a new school. John Wesley Vangilder purchased the abandoned school for the people of Goose Creek for a place of worship, recalling the village of Nain in the Bible that was abandoned and revived by the people of Galilee (Luke 7, Verse 11). Vangilder bought the vacant school in 1905. He and his daughter, Addie, had been holding a class in neighboring homes for several years before they recognized they needed a meeting place. In that same year, trustees for the church, J. W. Vangilder, Sheridan Vangilder and Jacob Martin, bought a quarter of an acre of land across the road from the school from Sarah and Sylvestus Vandergrift for the new church.

Moving the building with a team of horses and a block and tackle proved to be more time consuming than they had anticipated. Darkness settled in before the job was finished so the building sat in the middle of the road overnight. The little church was put on its foundation the next day. Like the people of the biblical town of Nain the people came together to revitalize the building. The church was dedicated as the Nain Free Methodist Church. It flourished with an average of at least 20 persons in Sunday school each week and had a large congregation until the early 1960's, when it was closed for one year. It reopened in 1964 but like so many other country churches, it closed for good in 1969. Then the members either went to the Samaria Free Methodist Church not far away or to the Fairmont Free Methodist Church on Morgantown Ave. in Fairmont. The Samaria church also was named after a biblical village in Palestine.

Today the church is still sitting where it was moved in 1905. It serves as a garage for Dale and Anna Fisher. Some of the ministers who served there were: Boyers Boyce, Brooks Morgan, Rosetta Ullom, Anthony Cantanese, Lester Morgan, Sylvia Boring, Everett McCartney, Warren McDonald, Wayne Carpenter, George D. Carpenter, Tom Jenkins, the Reverends Dotson, Fansler and Gysler. Berle Herron was one of the Sunday school teachers.

Nain Free Methodist Church, at Goose Creek, 1935. From left are members Jimmy Goodwin, Grady Chevuront, Billy Chevuront, Theodore Sypolt, Paul Sypolt, Burl Herron, unidentified teacher, Betty Goodwin (in front of teacher), Myrtle May Vandergrift, Virginia Bittle (sitting on the porch with baby Viola Biddle, Flora Sypolt, Mildred Vandergrift, Judy Chevuront, Helen Chevuront (holding the banner), Gloria Sypolt, Jean Morgan, Helen Morgan, Edna Phillips (holding baby Earl Ray Vandergrift), Hazel Phillips, Ralph Sypolt, Howard Sypolt, Bobby Phillips and Billy Phillips. *Courtesy of Ralph Sypolt.*

1911 ST. ANTHONY CATHOLIC CHURCH

The first St. Anthony Church was erected in Watson in 1911 as a mission to St. Joseph, a national parish for Italians in the area and ministered to by the priests of St. Joseph. It was on the site of the present church. In 1924, the LaSalette Fathers took over the administration of St. Joseph's Parish along with its mission church in Watson.

In time, the Catholic population shifted to the east and south ends of Fairmont where the mission churches of St. Anthony and Immaculate Conception were already established. In 1964, St. Joseph was made into a national parish, so Bishop Joseph Hodges established three new territorial parishes, namely St. Joseph, Immaculate Conception and St. Anthony. As a result of this transition from national parish to territorial parishes, the LaSalette Fathers returned the care of St. Joseph and its mission churches to the Diocesan priests. When Reverend Joseph Dene became pastor of St. Anthony Church in 1964 to 1976, he directed the building of the new St. Anthony now located on Mary Lou Retton Drive. Up from the Tygart Valley River near Muriale's Restaurant the church sits on the old Fox Hills Golf Course.

The solemn dedication of the new St. Anthony church rectory activities building took place on Friday, August 29,1969. The three-part building was erected on a one-acre portion of a five-acre lot at a cost of approximately $260,000. Harold J. Ramsey, a Pittsburgh architect, designed the brick building with its low walls and hipped roofs to blend with the suburban locale.

Pastors who served this new church are: Joseph Dene, 1964-1976; James F. Tierney, 1976-1982 and Eugene A. Schmitt, 1982-1991; John H. Finnell served on a temporary basis from June to December 1991. Pat J. Wash served from December of that year to October 1992. In January 1993, Gary P. Naegele was appointed pastor and is currently serving in that position.

St. Anthony Catholic Church at Watson.

1914 KINGMONT UNITED METHODIST CHURCH

Kingmont United Methodist Church is located across from the community building and post office in the center of town. Near the Tygart Valley River and only two miles by rail from Fairmont, the church has a welcoming appearance created by the decorative double front doors.

Some of the early history of this church comes from Reverend Isaac Barnes' 1926 account of local churches. According to these chronicles, after an earlier attempt to start a class in this coal mining community, Rev. Barnes and Rev. Sylvester Bennett, (who was then pastor of the Watson Charge), organized a class in 1909. They had been requested to hold a revival, which was met with such enthusiasm that the people decided to build a new Methodist Protestant Church. Albert and Lillian Fortney transferred a small piece of their property for the new church. The Rev. Bloomfield, from the Methodist Temple in Fairmont, dedicated the Kingmont church in 1913. Prior to that time, followers had been meeting in each other's homes. Rev. Bennett preached the first sermon. This congregation was added to the Watson Charge with Watson, Benton's Ferry and Colfax. Some of the early families who helped organize the church were Huffman, King, Hillberry, Hunsaker and Fortney.

Kingmont United Methodist Church

Down through the years repairs were done by volunteers. Around 1950, the church was plumbed for gas and the old coal stoves were replaced. Pews were replaced in the 1960's; a new ceiling was installed in 1963, and in 1974 the church was paneled and the cross was put up in the sanctuary. Most of the finances for the improvements came after the death of Hattie Hillberry when a memorial gift was made by daughters and friends. A new roof was put on in 1982; the tower was repaired in 1982, and wall-to-wall carpeting was added in 1983. In 1986, a new furnace replaced the gas stoves, exterior siding was installed, and two new double doors at the entry were replaced.

In 1938-39 the church trustees were: George Hunsaker, Oscar Miller, Randolph Channell, Jesse Belle and A B. Corley.

The Kingmont United Methodist Church is the only church in Kingmont. The foundation was built by hard-working volunteers and still stands strong and firm today. Other ministers who served here were: 1927-33: U.R. Hinzman; 1933-36: Frank McGee, died mid-term in 1936; 1936-40: Henry McCulty, (unification of the Methodist Episcopal and Methodist Protestant churches in 1939); 1940-42: Alfred Wallace; 1942-44: George Loar; 1944-45: Walter Bowman; 1945-47: G. B. Ruppert; 1947-49: Earl Haywood; 1949-50: Matthias Bott; 1950-51: Rev.? Workman; 1951-53: Donald Goff; 1953-56: Warren Beckley; 1957-59: William Marvin Freed; and 1959-61; Charles Jr. Eaton. 1961-64: Paul Lamb; 1965-69: George Barthlow; 1969-70: Allen Padenour; 1970-73: George Barthlow; 1973-80; Wilbur Robinson (lay pastor); 1980-84: Charles Fancher (lay pastor); 1984-85: Phyllis Harvey; 1985-86: Haywood Price; 1986-88: Peggy Scharff, and 1988-96: Paul Fortney (died in 1996). The present minister is Gary Steele.

1914 SARIETTA

The Sarrietta Elementary School was located on the Poplar Island Road, only a stone's throw from the Tygart Valley River. This school was the oldest one-room school in the county when it closed in May of 1951. It was used as a community "meeting house" as well as a place of worship. Reverend Boyers Boyce (1875-1944), a Free Methodist minister, gave sermons here off and on for 30 years. Others who spread the Gospel in the early days here were Rev. Daniel Kirk and Addie Vangilder from Levels. No particular denomination was in honored at this time.

On November 7, 1953 Thurmond Vincent bought the 110-year-old building and grounds when it was sold

Sarrietta Kingdom Heirs Baptist Church on Poplar Island Road. Note the original water pump for the schoolhouse, which is the section with the cupola on the roof.

for taxes on the Marion County courthouse steps for $100. He deeded it over to the trustees of the Sarrietta church at who were at that time John Little, Paul Ables and Joseph Ford. In 1955, Sarrietta Community Church joined the Christ Gospel Missions, Inc., which was an interdenominational organization. Sunday school rooms and gas heating was added in 1958. A vestibule was built on in 1959, and additional Sunday school rooms in 1966. The main entryway is the original schoolhouse.

In 1980, the congregation became affiliated with the Kingdom Heirs Baptist Church. A new sanctuary was built in 1983. Some of the pastors who served here were: Cecil Radcliff, Wayne Vandergrift, Ed Lester, Paul Morrison, Charles Roderick (1955-1998) and Clifford Morgan, who is the present pastor.

Some of the families who attend this church today are Ford, Esultante, Hilling, Vangilder, LeMasters, Love, Huffman, McClone, Gower, Smith, Hern and Cutright.

Time and weather took its toll on the little church so the congregation gathered together and restored and added to the church yet again with the present day chapel. In June 1954 it was dedicated. A. C. Auvil and R. L. Byrd were in charge of the service.

1920 QUIET DELL BAPTIST CHURCH

Submitted by: Mrs. Francis Rudy Swisher

Quiet Dell community is located on Rt. 310 south about six miles from Fairmont. For many years this community had no church. In 1920, Billy Sunday, a nationally known evangelist, came to Fairmont to hold religious services. The members traveled to rural areas where there were no churches and held services. The Billy Sunday Club members were invited to Quiet Dell to lead services in the old school building, which sat on the present site of the Quiet Dell Baptist Church. In the late 1920's, Ethan Vincent held a Sunday Church School in the old schoolhouse. Occasionally, Reverend Albert Ray of the Fairmont Pentecostal Church held revival services here. In 1933-34, the new Quiet Dell school building was erected on a site adjacent to the Basil Rudy farm. It, too, was used for religious services. Mrs. Basil (Mary) Rudy met with the children on Sunday afternoons and instructed them.

Rev. A. C. Bell, an ordained Methodist minister, was called to the community to hold regular worship services in the school in 1935. After his transfer to another church, there were no services for some time. Early in 1945, Mrs. Albert (Marie) Vandergrift contacted Reverend J. B. Sessions, an interdenominational minister of Christ Gospel Mission and the pastor of Grace Tabernacle in Fairmont, and asked his help in organizing a Sunday Church School.

Quiet Dell Baptist Church on East Grafton Road.

Marie Vandergrift was named Sunday school superintendent.

In 1946, the Sunday School's growth led Henry and Gotha Rudy to deed over the property where the old school house had stood for a church, which would be known as the Quiet Dell Community Church. The concrete block building was built in 1947 and paid for by donations and was dedicated on November 9, 1947. Dedicated volunteer workers who gave freely of their time and talents included Albert Vandergrift, Charley Henderson, and Hobert Ingram. Joe Corbin did the excavating for the basement. W. Henry Rudy and Lee Nestor did most of the carpenter work. James Sanders and Wayne Vandergrift laid the stone base for the parking lot. Reverend Brooks Clayton did the wiring. On January 16, 1947 church members voted to become affiliated with Christ Gospel Mission an inter-denominational organization. Rev. Clyde Wright was called as pastor.

The first church service held in the new church building was on the second Sunday in May 1947. When the fellowship moved into the new building, church furniture, decorating and landscaping was needed. Clara Casey headed a successful building fund drive and with money collected worked diligently to accomplish this task.

Christ Gospel ministers who served from 1948-1957 were: June 1948-December 1950, Colmar Nuzum, Jr.; January 1951- December 1951, Baxter Davis; January 1952-May 1953, William Sutfin; May-November 1953, Douglas Rutherford, Interim; November 1953-May 1957, Cecil Radcliff, Jr.

During Mr. Nuzum's pastorate, he and the church board wrote the constitution and by-laws, which were ratified by the fellowship body on May 19, 1950.

On May 28, 1957, church members voted to withdraw its affiliation from Christ Gospel Mission. For about a year, Reverend Joseph D. Billups, philosophy and religion professor at Alderson-Broaddus College in Philippi, served as pastor. The church voted to become affiliated with the American Baptist Convention in 1958. It became a member of the Fairmont Association of the West Virginia Baptist Convention at its annual meeting on August 3, 1958. The church became known as the Quiet Dell Baptist Church. Rev. Gary Bonnell was the first pastor. He served from November 1958 to January 1961.

Other Baptist ministers who have served here: John Kyle, Lon T. Marks, Howard Harper, Clyde Loar, A. J. Dickerson and Durard Estep. Student pastors who were planning to enter the seminary and become full time pastors were Michael Hall, David Allen, Bruce McConihay, Donald Biram, David Burnsworth and John Thomas. Other pastors to the present are Charles Conley, Arnold McIntosh and Gerald Bowman, present pastor.

In a letter from Southern Ohio Coal Company, dated February 13, 1984, to the trustees of the church, it was stated that "Southern Ohio Coal Company intends to mine underneath the premises". An agreement between the church leadership and the coal company was signed by the trustees in April of 1984. The church doors were closed in July 1984. During the reconstruction period, church services were held in a small vacant building owned by the Southern Coal Co., called the "Lodge" on Grassy Run Road. The congregation moved back into the reconstructed building for Sunday Church School and worship on July 20, 1986. A rededication service took place in September with Rev. Donald Biram as pastor.

1949 JEHOVAH'S WITNESSES

In the early 1870's, Charles Taze Russell organized an apocalyptic sect. They were called Russelites, Millennnial Dawnists or International Bible Students. Since 1931, they have been called Jehovah's Witnesses. From the very beginning they have relied on the printed word to win converts and to inspire members. Each Witness is expected to spend at least ten hours a month going door-to-door distributing their *Watchtower* literature. The Witnesses stand apart from civil society by refusing to recite the Pledge of Allegiance, salute the flag, to vote, run for office, serve in our armed forces, or stand for our national anthem.

Fairmont's congregation started in 1912, meeting at various places. They built their first Kingdom Hall on East Park Avenue in April 1949. In 1967, the growing congregation moved to a new building on Country Club Road in Fairmont. By 1990, they had grown in size so much again that they needed a new building. In 1994, the members purchased four acres at the intersection of Route 250 South and Maplewood Drive in Fairmont. Plans for the new Kingdom Hall were made by using the "quick build" plan that is traditional among Jehovah's Witnesses.

Kingdom Hall of Jehovah's Witnesses, on U.S. Rt. 250 south.

Volunteer labor was used with expertise in all aspects of construction, working with congregations from the surrounding areas and states. Working shoulder-to-shoulder, skilled volunteers from all walks of life came together to work for a common goal.

The foundation excavation got underway in July 1995. In August, cement was poured for it and the floor tile was laid on the slab before the building went up.

On Thursday, September 28, 1995, at 7:00 a.m. volunteers began erecting the 5,000 square-foot building that took four days to complete. The women of the church supplied mounds of food for the workers, who worked round the clock on shifts, as is their tradition. The interior walls, air-conditioning, plumbing, electrical work, carpeting, furnishings and landscaping were all finished for 10:00 o'clock Sunday morning in time for their church service.

Kingdom Hall on East Park Ave. in Fairmont. (1967)

Solid mahogany doors lead into the spacious entryway exposing several rooms to the side (such as a kitchen, cloakroom, restrooms, library and auditorium that seats 180 members). Custom-made cabinets house the literature that volunteers use throughout the week in their door-to-door missionary work.

There are 14 elders who serve as unpaid ministerial servants and who teach their theological ministry school once a week. Following the Bible's example, the governing body of the church sends out traveling volunteers to distribute Bible related literature on a regular basis. Their meetings are open to the public.

Left: Laying the slab and tile on the foundation of Kingdom Hall one month before construction, July 1995. Right: Beginning of the actual construction on Thursday, September 28, 1995 at 7:00 am *Courtesy of Kingdom Hall of Jehovah's Witnesses.*

Left: Workers laying the roof on Thursday. Right: Laying the brick on Friday afternoon. *Courtesy of Kingdom Hall of Jehovah's Witnesses.*

1964 FIRST SOUTHERN BAPTIST

Southern Baptist Church at Pleasant Valley.

The Southern Baptists came to Fairmont in 1964. Starting families were Charles and Joyce Irons and family of Colfax, Mr. & Mrs. Donnie Morrison and family and Mr. & Mrs. David Nyberg and family. They invited pastors Charles Young and Bob Brown from Morgantown to come to Fairmont and hold services. Early meeting places were at the boardroom of the Community Bank and Trust and at the Y.W.C.A. in downtown Fairmont for several years before enough funds were raised to purchase a building on 409 Market Street in 1971. The congregation grew very rapidly. The building next door was bought by the church when it became available in order to add Sunday school rooms.

It was decided to build a much bigger church in 1981. Property was purchased on Nicki Street off Pleasant Valley Road near Fairmont. Southern Baptist volunteers built the new church from local and surrounding communities. Today this church has a very large membership; Jeff Street is its present pastor. Others who have served as pastors include: Bobby Bowen, Charles Whitlock, James McGoldrich, David Anderson, Russell Talley, John Andes and David Ivy.

1971 GALILEAN BAPTIST CHURCH

The Galilean Baptist Church first began meeting at the Colfax Community Building on Sunday, August 8, 1971. Two weeks later, 38 charter members began holding services in the home of the pastor, Rev. Timothy Amundson, at Hillview on Rt. 250. Amundson served for eight and one-half years.

On February 28, 1972 the church was recognized as a duly organized Fundamental Baptist Church and was voted into the West Virginia Fundamental Baptist Association. In the spring of 1972, the church applied for membership in the General Association of Regular Baptist Churches but due to an oversight was not voted into membership until 1973. The church is also a member of the state Freedom Baptist Fellowship.

On May 24, 1972, members voted to purchase four lots on which to build a church on Lanham Drive in White Hall. While the land was being cleared, plans also

Galilean Baptist Church at White Hall.

were being made for construction. A groundbreaking was held February 25, 1973 and two days later, construction began. The first service took place in the new building on Mother's Day, May 13, 1973 and the dedication held on Sunday afternoon, August 5, 1973.

Since then the church has grown and several improvements were made. Additional land was purchased, and an architect engaged to draw up plans for an addition to the building. As funding became available these plans were utilized.

Galilean Baptist Church has a strong Women's Ministries organization, an active Teen Ministry, Vacation Bible School. and sponsors Summer camp trips.

Many of the members of the church have been called to fulltime service as pastors and missionaries. Many of its young people have gone on to Christian colleges, high schools and grade schools in the area.

Ministers who have served Galilean Baptist Church;

August 5, 1971 to February 10, 1980; Pastor Timothy Amundson.

June 29, 1980 to September 28, 1986; Pastor Mark Peterson.

October 1986 to June 1987; Interim Pastor Robert Clater.

June 1987 to April 30, 1995; Interim Pastor Robert Lemon.

June 1987 to April 30, 1995. Interim Pastor Don Matheny.

September 1995 to July 1996; Pastor Doug Packard, who started in August 1996 and is the current pastor.

1985 PLEASANT VALLEY CHURCH OF CHRIST

A new setting with new life began for this church when it moved to Pleasant Valley in 1985. This congregation began in 1870 when members met in each other's homes. In 1890, land was deeded over to the site of their first church on Columbia Street in Fairmont. The congregation met there continuously for 95 years. In 1983, a feasibility committee began studying the possibility of expansion. Twenty-three new sites were looked at before a decision was made to buy the former Mellon-Stuart building on Pleasant Valley Road.

Renovation work was mostly done by men of the congregation. It included design, electrical and plumbing work. The completed structure has an auditorium that accommodates 225 people, Sunday School rooms, a library, nursery, four offices, foyer, vestibule and cloakroom. A parking lot was paved for 26 cars and graveled for another 70.

A formal dedication was held June 2, 1985. Frank Higginbotham, a minister from Chester, West Virginia, was the keynote speaker. Building tours were given after the program.

Over the years, the various men who have served as preachers include: Harry Bennett, 1953-Frank Higginbotham, Bill Daines, Bob Cooper, Clarence Rice, Don Jarrett, Amos Orrison, Don Summers, David Epler, Jim Smith, Steven Eddy, Darrell Toothman, and Earl Stevens, the current evangelist.

Pleasant Valley Church of Christ.

1990 FAITH REFORMED PRESBYTERIAN CHURCH

The Faith Reformed Presbyterian Church is located on Sunnyview Lane in Pleasant Valley. It began on January 14, 1990. The history of the local church began in the mid-to-late 1970's when several families became concerned that their denomination was straying away from the historic foundation upon which it was built. By early summer of 1989, the number of concerned families had grown to approximately 30. At the families' request Reverend Harold C. Kelly of New Martinsville, West Virginia came to Fairmont to provide information about the Presbyterian Churches of America, a young, fast-growing denomination that began in 1973, seeking to be "true to the scriptures". The new local congregation had their first service on August 6, 1989 at the Jesus Outreach Church of Living Waters on Country Club Road in Fairmont. The Reverend Kenneth G. Robinson ministered to this new congregation.

During the next five months, Reverend Robinson preached on Sundays and Reverend Kelly led the mid-week Bible study, which prepared men to be examined for the office of elder and deacon, as well as to educate the membership. During this time, evening services were held at the Youth Center of the Free Methodist Church on Morgantown Ave. in Fairmont.

On Sunday, January 14, 1990, a Commission from the New River Presbytery of the Presbyterian Church of America came to Fairmont and organized the Faith Reformed Presbyterian Church into an individual church. At this time there were 62 charter members and 18 children. The congregation elected three elders: Frank Deli, William Floyd and James Mohr and five deacons: Robert Drake, James Hayhurst, Steven Mohr, Kenneth Pearson and Frank Snider, Jr. Reverend Robinson has been its only pastor.

A vacant church building was bought in Pleasant Valley on March 1, 1990, with the first church service the following Sunday. After extensive remodeling to the church a service of dedication was held on June 3, 1991.

Faith Reformed Presbyterian Church in Pleasant Valley.

Chapter Five

CEMETERIES

SACRED SOIL

*Sometimes hidden in the woods,
Old graveyards have a certain charm.
They speak to us of loved ones,
Who are forever out of harm.*

*No longer to worry about taxes,
Sickness and death.
Their legacy is told on the headstone,
After they have taken their last breath.*

*Far off the beaten path,
Sometimes kept neat as a pin.
But most often found in disarray,
Which I feel is a sin.*

*Old graveyards reveal past history,
Tombstones tell it all.
They have gone on to their eternal reward
When our Father makes the call.*

By: C. Fortney-Hamilton 1997

Graveyards

The path to tracing family history usually leads to the graveyard, a place most people do not want to talk about or visit for one reason or another. Graveyards create an atmosphere of sorrow and sadness. Unless there are personal ties, most of these burial grounds are avoided or not given much attention. However, I find graveyard browsing fascinating. Each one reflects the social history of a community— telling us ethnic backgrounds, religious beliefs and even suggesting the economic conditions of the people buried in them. It goes without saying that some are more interesting than others but the vital information historians and genealogists need more often than not starts there.

Modern cemeteries are landscaped like and even called gardens. Their "mow-over" markers offer no evidence of family relations or of the personality of the person buried there. They simply tell us that he or she lies beneath, was born in a given year and died in another. This is very different than the older graveyards with their grand monuments.

Country graveyards started out as family plots on the farm. A child would die and the family buried the body on the farm. As the land changed hands, the site may or may not have continued in use as a burial ground. Most often it became larger and connected to a local church for community use.

However, most of the cemeteries along the Tygart Valley River were separated from the nearest church. They were usually on ridge tops or upper slopes. There is one case where a cemetery is in a valley. Some of them had no road leading up to them. According to local folklore, graveyards high on a hill were supposed to have made it easier for the soul to reach heaven.

In my wanderings through the Tygart Valley River cemeteries, I found most in excellent condition. Some were far off the beaten path but still cared for while others were hidden under years of neglected growth. Some were large, some were small, and there is even a lone single grave marked only by a flagstone on the east bank of the river near the old Mundell Ferry landing. During the early days of 1800, this was the stagecoach route to the ferry. Could it have been one of those passengers? We'll never know who it was or how the person died.

Gravesite found by Alice (Glasscock) Swick at her childhood home place near Mundell's Ferry landing. 1997

Tombstones

Tombstones tell us considerable information. Written in Italic or Roman they were meant to teach the living as well as pay homage to the dead. Usually, they give the specific dates of birth and death, family relationship, and sometimes their station in life, such as, soldier, biker, father or mother and often some insight into the community's past and their financial background. Many graves of children gave evidence of epidemics and childhood diseases. Marking a grave benefits coming generations. During the nineteenth century it was a common practice to omit the birth date. In those instances, I had to subtract from the death date when it gave the year, month and day. In my research, I found several tombstones with no death date and had to resort to researching courthouse records. In some instances, when the last person in a family died often there were no provisions for having the tombstone engraved and was left blank. In other examples, the stone carver misspelled a word, which created confusion in doing research. Sometimes a tombstone referred to wives as Mrs. John Brown with no name of her own while others had their own stone. Names on tombstones can be very colorful and are very rare today. Very seldom will names such as Ebenezer, Elijah, Enoch, Ezra, Jeremiah, Silas, Alpheus, Claudius and Zacheus appear on modern day tombstones.

Interesting epitaphs are scattered through all of the cemeteries. They speak eloquently about their thoughts, how they lived, sometimes how they died, and how they were regarded. Some were touching and some were amusing.

Descriptive carvings on a tombstone reveal what words could never say and are interpreted as:

Calla Lilies	a symbol of purity, the flower of the Virgin
Ivy	remembrance and regeneration
Weeping Willow	sorrow
Lambs	innocence (usually for children)
Buds	renewal of life
Arches	victory in death
Flying Birds	flight of the soul
Hosta	eternal resting place
Roses	brevity of earthly existence
Bugles	resurrection and the military
Hearts	soul in bless; love of Christ
Tree Stumps	cut down early in life
Bells	tolling for the dead
Hourglass	the sand (life) ran out

During the 1800's, death was considered as the Gateway to Heaven. The older arch-shaped headstones suggested easy passageways through which the soul would travel on its journey, while others actually had fingers pointed toward heaven. Attitudes toward death were much more serious than today. Reading the tombstones is interesting. I skimmed only the surface of the art and would have liked to have taken more time to study them. It is easy to understand how superstition has surrounded them.

Since West Virginia does not produce any granite or marble, tombstones were and still are brought in from out of state. Local talented stonecutters have traditionally done the engraving. They were artisans who were influenced by beliefs, trends and traditions of the day. Most of the early stone carvers were men who made their livings as woodcarvers, masons, or leather workers. They did stone carving only when hired by a family who had a death.

The older monuments are easily detected from the newer ones. Some were initialed in the corner by the stonecutter. Allison Fleming (1814-1871) was one of those stonecutters. He would either leave his mark with AF or A. Fleming at the bottom of the tombstone. Allison Fleming learned the trade at age 14 and later had a large marble worker's shop in Fairmont. I found one or more tombstones carved by him in almost all of the cemeteries I visited. In some cases he used local slate because it was economical. Sometimes he would hand chisel the shape out and take it to the actual gravesite where he would then engrave it. Those same tombstones today have stood the test of time. They are still in very good condition, very legible and have withstood the ravishes of almost two centuries. Tombstones made of other material during the same period have deteriorated and are hardly legible.

A study was made by Thomas Meierding, a geographer at the University of Delaware, on the rates at which tombstones weather. His study found that tombstones in polluted cities weather at a rate two-to-ten times faster than tombstones in the surrounding countryside. Nowadays, acid rain adds to the speed-up of deterioration.

In the old days, families who could not afford a proper headstone used fieldstones, sometimes engraving them. They scraped or hand chiseled them as best they could. All the graveyards I visited had some gravesites marked this way. This was a hint of how the economy was in the neighborhoods for the common folk where services and materials were either unavailable or unaffordable.

I have included the WPA readings that went up to 1938-39 and the number of unmarked gravesites they found at that time. Some of the unmarked sites were probably once marked with a wooden cross which in time deteriorated. Therefore, names and dates were lost.

And some there be which have no memorial;
who are perished, as though they had never been.

In the yard of a homeowner on the west bank of the Tygart Valley River near Scout Island is a tombstone with the last name of Linn barely visible on it.

Burial Traditions

During the 1800's bodies were not embalmed which meant burial could not be delayed very long. There were no funeral parlors. The family washed and dressed the dead at home and they were placed in bed or in the parlor for viewing. Close friends and relatives stayed up all night with the body. Neighbors would send in mounds of food for the many visitors that dropped in to pay their last respects. In a time when houses were scattered over hundreds of acres this was an opportunity for neighbors to exchange the news of the community.

Some old-time burial customs for graveyards are still practiced. For instance, most funeral directors have kept the Egyptian custom of burying the dead facing the East just as our ancestors did two centuries ago. Why do we do this, you ask? It has been prophesized that Christ will return from the direction of the rising sun (East) and the dead shall rise and walk to meet him to the everlasting life.

Grave digging was done by what were referred to as gravediggers. They were men who were usually paid good money because most did not want to do it. Tall men were preferable. Tradition in some families required a friend of the family or a close relative to dig the grave. This can still be found true still today. It was a hard and fast rule that graves were only to be dug on the day of the funeral. If work was started before that day, some part of the labor was delayed until a few hours before the funeral. It was believed by superstition that a man who digs a grave and does not stay to see it filled and covered was marked for an early death.

Sample of an obituary of 1916.

The tradition of a non-stop funeral procession to the gravesite is now state law. It has always been considered bad luck if a procession had to stop for any reason en route to the graveyard. Sometimes a police escort is used to lead the procession through the red lights and stop signs. A state law now prevents a driver of a car to merge into a funeral procession.

Coffins

During the 1800's, timbering was the major occupation in the Tygart Valley. Sawmills were located up and down the river. The base of a white oak tree was considered the very best grade of oak. This cut was used for building coffins. (It became known as "coffin oak"). The wood had to be without knots, windshakes, heavy sap or stains, and was very much in demand. Loggers would send these choice logs on their journey down the river to Pittsburgh where loggers could get a better price. After the railroad arrived they were shipped by rail. As a result of the extensive logging, most of the large coffin oak trees were gone by 1900.

Coffins were built locally by a carpenter, cabinetmaker or furniture store employee. They were made of pine, poplar, and chestnut or of the very best which was oak. Sometimes they were body shaped, but most often oblong that was painted black. Vaults were unheard of. In those days coffins cost a dollar a foot. People believed in ashes to ashes and dust to dust and would have considered it folly to attempt to preserve a body once the soul had gone. When the coffin was covered with dirt it eventually deteriorated and the soil above would sink. A walk through a very old cemetery offers plenty evidence of that.

I can recall one superstition from an early age to NEVER walk on a gravesite or impending doom would surely come your way. I learned later that this was due to the sinking of the grave. Many amusing tales have been handed down about people sinking into graves.

Some of the loveliest beauty spots in West Virginia are in the cemeteries—places the average tourist does not see. Each cemetery has its own story to tell. My research began at the junction of the Tygart Valley and West Fork rivers and went upstream to just beyond Valley Falls. Cemeteries are on both sides of the Tygart. There are directions about how to find them, a brief description and history of each one.

People and Places

Cemeteries

In 1936, the Historical Records Survey Project was a part of a nationwide program that was instituted in West Virginia under a branch of the Works Progress Administration (WPA) believing that cemetery readings were a valuable part of our state archives. The following readings are from the historical records survey Project that was a part of a nationwide program that was instituted in West Virginia in April 1936. They were updated with the co-operation of Carpenter and Ford Funeral Home in Fairmont and my own research. Record includes the number of unmarked gravesites for each cemetery.

Key to codes:

(d) daughter	RW - Revolutionary War
(s) son	CW - Civil War
(w) wife	WWI - World War I
(h) husband	WWII - World War II
(ts) twin son	K - Korea
(td) twin daughter	VN - Vietnam
(v) veteran	

1852 SAMUEL LINN CEMETERY
(Benton's Ferry)

In Union District, located off I-79. Take the Kingmont exit to Benton's Ferry; turn left just before the bridge, turn right at the Y in the road and keep right. The name of this cemetery is on a sign at the entrance. There is a chain link fence surrounding the entire graveyard, which is in excellent condition and well kept. It is still being used today with burial sites available.

Samuel and Anzy Linn donated the one and one-half acres of land on a knoll that was a part of their farm.

Samuel, son of William Linn of Glady Creek, was born on September 22, 1789 on Patterson Creek, in what is now Mineral County, WV. His family settled at Glady Creek on the Tygart Valley River in 1804. There he met and courted Anzy Reese, daughter of George and Nancy Reese, also of Glady Creek. They were married on December 26, 1822. In 1835, they moved to Benton's Ferry where Samuel built a log cabin. Here they farmed and reared nine children. It is here that they spent their entire life. Samuel died Aug 15, 1852 of typhoid fever. His wife selected a spot on the farm by a pine tree where she wanted him to be buried. He was the first person to be buried in the cemetery. Anzy lived to be 92 years old when she died in 1893. She was laid to rest beside her husband.

Many outstanding citizens of Benton's Ferry are buried here. Reverend Isaac Barnes kept the cemetery's records until his death in 1944. This cemetery is also his final resting place. Walking the graveyard, I found not far from the entrance the marker for my seventh and eighth grade school teacher, George R. Jefferson. He was an educator for many years in Marion County. Not far from him is a tombstone with this popular epitaph. It reads:

Remember, friend, as you pass by,
As you are now, so once was I.
As I am now, you soon will be.
Remember, friend, and pray for me.

The following is a list of those known to this author who are buried here:

SAM LINN CEMETERY

Name	Birth	Death	Relationship
B., E. M. on fieldstone	NO DATES		
B., N. J. on fieldstone	NO DATES		
B., S. on fieldstone	NO DATES		
B., T. W. on fieldstone	NO DATES		
Bainbridge, Edgar Linn	1879	1926	(h) Emma J
Bainbridge, Emma J.	1886	1973	(w) Edgar L.
Bainbridge, James E.	1855	1933	(h) Margaret
Bainbridge, John R.	1902	1961	
Bainbridge, Mamie V.	?	12-02-1895	(d) J.E. & M. L.
Bainbridge, Margaret L.	1859	6-26-1909	(w) James E.
Bainbridge, Mary E.	?	11-25-1895	(d) J. E. & M.L.
Bainbridge, Raymer L.	1926	1926	(s) Edgar & Emma
Barnes, Abraham H.	1784	1872	(v) Spanish/American
Barnes, Dale Nelson	1921	6-17-1996	(h) Betty (v) WWII
Barnes, Frank R.	1887	1972	
Barnes, Frederick N.	1882	11-15-1960	(h) Lena D. (v)WWI
Barnes, Isaac A. (Rev.)	1857	1944	(h) Maggie A.
Barnes, Issac N.	1823	1880	(h) Margaret
Barnes, Lena D.	1899	6-01-1990	(w) Frederick N.
Barnes, Lena Linn	1881	1892	
Barnes, Maggie A.	1860	1957	(w) Issac A.
Barnes, Margaret Linn	1916	1930	
Barnes, Martha A.	1894	1956	
Barnes, Mary A.	?	11-30-1858	(W) Abraham
Barnes, Sarah	?	9-02-1850	(w) William H.
Bartholow, Bessie Ellen	1904	11-26-1989	
Bartholow, Evelyn P.	1923	3-11-1995	(w) Reverend George W.
Bartholow, Hazel J.	1903	5-24-1995	(d) Oliver & Alice
Bartholow, George W.	1920	1-24-1988	(h) Evelyn P. (Cox)
Bartholow, Lawrence	1946	12-28-1994	(s) Geo. & Evelyn
Blair, Patsy E.	1834	11-30-1924	
Bleigh, Howard V.	1919	1958	(h) Zelda N.
Boyce, Quentin J.	1984	7-14-1984	(ts) William & Debra
Boyles, Cora B.	1895	1970	(w) George W.
Boyles, George W.	1892	1952	(h) Cora B.
Brenneman, Lawrence	1916	1982	(h) Rhoda M.
Brenneman, Rhoda M.	1904	1980	(w) Lawrence
Brue, Mary L	?	3-09-1877	(w) Arthur
Butler, Earl	1922	1977	(v) WWII
Canfield, Hanning B.	1926	10-04-1991	(h) Helen (v) WW II
Canfield, Randy B.	1949	2-13-1951	(s) Hanning & Helen
Carlin, Charles Jr.	1917	1979	
Carpenter, Betty	1929	6-12-1986	(w) George A.
Cherry, Della	1860	1949	
Christy, Donald E.	1934	8-04-1984	
Christy, George	1893	10-23-1967	(h) Gertrude (v) WW I
Christy, Gertrude (Harris)	1901	4-29-1992	(w) George
Christy, Jennie	1867	1914	(w) Jesse G.
Christy, Jesse G.	1863	1910	(h) Jennie
Clark, Authur Carl	1906	10-21-1974	
Clark, Ira Herschel	1913	7-10-1979	(v) WW II

Sam Linn Cemetery at Benton's Ferry; established in 1852.

Clelland, Carroll E.	1898	1984	(h) Rilla L.
Clelland, Janet Ann	1926	3-05-1987	
Clelland, Rilla L.	1897	1977	(w) Carroll E.
Closson, Joseph P.	1920	1-25-1985	(v) WW II
Collins, Sarah Ellen	1884	1956	
Conley, Alberta M.	1929	12-12-1993	(w) F. Franklin
Conley, Fletcher F.	1885	6-26-1966	(h) Alberta (Heston)
Cowell, Charles S.	1870	1933	(h) Dorcas A.
Cowell, Clarence	1906	3-11-1908	(s) C. & D.
Cowell, Dorcas A.	1881	1959	(w) Charles S.
Cowell, Loretta G.	1922	1943	'Daft"
Cox, Earnest	1908	1985	(s) James & Omay
Cox, Omay (Thayer)	1878	1961	(w) James
Cox, Opal	1909	7-13-1982	
Cox, Ruby	1915	6-25-2000	(d) James & Omay
Cox, Russell T.	1912	12-27-1992	(s) James & Omay
Cox, William T.	1921	1986	(s) James & Omay
Dalton, Hough J.	1910	1973	(h) Mary Alice
Dalton, Mary Alice	1914	5-08-1993	(w) Hough J.
Dalton, Rickey Lee	1946	1969	(s) Hough & Mary
Deleruyelle, Annette V.	1917	3-20-1985	(w) Fernand Joseph
Deleruyelle, Joseph M.	1947	6-26-1990	(ts) Fernand & Annette
Deleruyelle, Phillip Anthony	1947	7-10-2003	(ts) Fernand & Annette
DeVault, Florence M.	1914	3-2-2003	(w) Paul E.
DeVault, Paul E.	1914	2-18-2000	(h) Florence M. (Hickman)
Dodd, Benjamin	1817	2-14-1907	(h) Elizabeth
Dodd, Clarence A.	1887	11-01-1934	(h) Lovie M.
Dodd, Clarence E.	1899	5-25-1981	(h) Nellie Jane
Dodd, Elizabeth	1823	5-30-1870	(w) Benjamin
Dodd, Harvey E.	1868	1936	(h) Lena
Dodd, Howard W.	1922	1944	(v) WWII
Dodd, James T.	1835	4-11-1911	(h) Martha J.
Dodd, Lena	1875	1957	(w) Harvey E.
Dodd, Lovie M.	1891	1967	(w) Clarence A.
Dodd, Martha J.	1839	1926	(w) James T.
Dodd, Nellie J	1899	7-18-2001	(w) Clarence E.
Drake, Addie M.	1891	1965	(w) Henry J.
Drake, Henry J	1890	1958	(h) Addie M.
Drake, Ida B.	1864	1957	(w) William B.

Drake, Richard W.	1916	1988	
Drake, Rose Mae	1894	1967	(w) William "Tude"
Drake, Wilbur Lee	1922	3-06-1923	
Drake, William M.	1861	1927	(h) Ida B.
Drake, William "Tude"	1894	1954	(h) Rose Mae
Dunn, Margaret	1823	1910	(w) Owen
Dunn, Owen	1819	1907	(h) Margaret
Durrett, C.C.	NO DATES		(h) Geneva
Durrett, Erma (Wilt)	1893	1973	(w) Travis V.
Durrett, Geneva B.	1872	5-29-1926	(w) C.C.
Durrett, Travis V.	1906	1979	(h) Erma (Wilt)
Emery, Lewis C.	1892	1980	(h) Katherine
Evans, Donald	?	9-15-1929	
Falkenstein, Leo E.	1918	9-11-1990	(h) Eleanor (v) WWII
Falkenstein, Scot	1964	10-06-1964	
Fast, Audra (Dixon)	1908	1986	(w) David V.
Fast, Franklin D.	1935	8-25-01	(s) David & Audra
Findley, Alston Gordon	1898	1979	(h) Mary Ida
Findley, Mary Ida	1900	1955	(w) Alston
Fortney, Lorina (Infant)	1910	7-10-1910	(d) Geo. & Catherine
Fortney, Albert H.	1884	1948	(h) Lillian I.
Fortney, Anna(Yates)	1879	1922	(2nd w) William S.
Fortney, Catherine H.	1878	1936	(w) George
Fortney, Eli H.	1857	5-30-1933	(h) Mary (Rowe)
Fortney, George F.	1875	5-26-1936	(h) Catherine H.
Fortney, Goldie G.	1912	?	(w) William B.
Fortney, Lela M.	1906	1919	(d) Joseph & G. Edna
Fortney, Lillian Irene	1884	1969	(w) Albert H.
Fortney, Mary Margaret	1849	4-14-1919	(w) Eli
Fortney, Robert Lee (twin)	1908	4-23-1913	(s) Geo. & Catherine
Fortney, William B. (twin)	1908	2-09-1990	(h) Goldie
Fortney, William S.	1873	2-02-1940	(h) Annie
Foster, Celia	1894	1963	(w) James Ray
Foster, James Ray	1887	1963	(h) Celia
Fulaytar, Steve, Jr.	1921	7-01-1995	(h) Irene (Griffith)
Glaspell, Melissa M.	1973	7-07-1973	
Goddard, Elizabeth	1889	6-22-1938	
Gower, Charles E.	1920	12-02-1990	(v) WWII
Gower, Dee	1923	1987	
Gower, Earnie	NO DATES		
Gower, Harvey D.	1956	1-28-1989	
Gower, James W.	1898	2-08-1976	(h) Nellie
Gower, John	1861	1930	
Gower, Joseph Anthony	1966	12-01-1971	(s) Larry & Pam
Gower, Nellie L.	1899	4-22-1965	(w) James W.
Gower, Pam	1950	1992	(w) Larry
Gower, Patricia M.	1923	1925	
Gower, Patty Ann	?	10-17-1937	
Gower, Ray F.	1900	7-27-1953	
Gower, Roger Alan	1955	1988	
Gower, Ruth R.	1904	7-28-1987	
Gower, Sarah Virginia	?	10-17-1935	
Gower, William, Jr.	1931	1931	
Grimes, Edmond	1888	1965	
Grugg, Annie	1892	1976	
Hall, George L.	1858	1939	(h) Martha
Hall, Jordan	?	6-02-1855	(V) CW

Name	Born	Died	Relation
Hall, Martha F.	1865	1923	(w) Geo. L.
Hansford, Alice May	1872	1963	(w) Oliver T.
Hansford, Oliver T.	1851	3-16-1937	(h) Alice May (Davis)
Hatzel, Thelma (Piggott)	1909	12-01-1993	(w) Wilbur
Hawkins, Martha Lee	1922	3-16-1926	(d) Martin & Mary
Hawkins, Martin Lee	1888	1970	(h) Mary "Katie"
Hawkins, Mary "Katie"	1887	1975	(w) Martin Lee
Hayhurst, B. Nelson	1876	1952	(h) Daisy E.
Hayhurst, Daisy E.	1883	1959	(w) B. Nelson
Hayhurst, Margaret J.	1853	6-06-1936	(w) Sanford
Hayhurst, Sanford	1851	12-29-1917	(h) Margaret J.
Heiskell, E. Helen	1867	1944	(w) John J.
Heiskell, John J.	1868	1929	(h) E. Helen
Herzer, Pamela Ruth	1946	11-01-1946	(d) Fred & Ruth
Heston, Daniel P.	1939	4-11-1994	(h) Katherine (West)
Heston, Katherine Irene	1943	5-07-2000	(w) Daniel P.
Hickman, Alfred E.	1928	1980	
Hickman, Alice	1901	1947	(w) John
Hickman, Glenn Delmar	1940	9-27-1947	(s) Paul & Thelma
Hickman, Hazel E.	1896	10-18-1954	(w) Thomas M.
Hickman, James J.	1944	1959	
Hickman, James W.	1922	7-01-1942	
Hickman, John	1900	1952	(h) Alice
Hickman, Paul L.	1918	2-23-1955	(v) WWII (h) Thelma
Hickman, Thomas M.	1892	11-22-1977	(h) Hazel
Hillberry. Burchie L.	1883	1950	(h) Hattie
Hillberry, Cora M.	1875	1942	(w) James
Hillberry, Hattie	1886	1974	(w) Burchie L.
Hillberry, Irene L.	1909	2-28-1988	(v) WWII
Hillberry, James1868	?	1945	(h) Cora
Holland, Margaret	1828	1904	(w) Barnes & Holland
Hughes, Hattie B.	1875	5-21-1938	
Hughes, John N.	1830	1883	(h) Margaret
Hughes, Margaret	1838	1919	(w) John N.
Hughes, Mollie	1881	1881	(d) John & Margaret
Hughes, Rosa M.	1874	1874	(d) John & Margaret
Hull, Amy Lester	1889	1911	(1st w) Nelson Brooks
Hull, Anna	1828	4-01-1913	(2nd w) Nelson
Hull, Clara Ella	1897	1962	(3rd w) Nelson Brooks
Hull, George W.	1859	3-11-1934	(h) Jennie & Sarah
Hull, Ida J.	1867	1938	(w) Samuel B.
Hull, Jane	?	10-04-1878	(w) John
Hull, John	?	6-10-1869	(h) Jane
Hull, Nelson	1825	9-22-1910	(h) Anna
Hull, Nelson Brooks	1891	1976	(h) Amy & Clara
Hull, R. Jennie	1858	11-05-1908	(1st w) George W.
Hull, Samuel B.	1861	1951	(h) Ida J.
Hull, Sarah F	1861	11-10-1951	(2nd w) George W.
Jackson, Sophia	1905	1985	
Jefferson, George R. Sr.	1912	1984	(h) Mildred
Jefferson, Mildred M.	1912	11-23-1992	(w) George R. Sr.
Johnson, Anthony S.	1793	2-02-1865	
Johnson, Edith	1906	1969	
Johnson, John	1894	1973	
Johnson, Ruth	NO DATES		
K., P. J.	NO DATES		
Kendrick, Annie	?	6-06-1904	

Name	Birth	Death	Relation
Kendrick, Elijah L.	1856	10-21-1910	(h) Mary E. (Kisner)
Kendrick, George E.	1881	1946	(h) Mary
Kendrick, Mary (Kisner)	1882	1967	(w) George E.
Kendrick, Mary Etta	1861	11-06-1937	(w) Elijah L.
Kendrick, William L.	1909	8-15-1986	
Kerns, Steen Ernest	1929	11-12-1993	(s) Howard & Gladys
Kramer, (Infant)	?	4-15-1938	(d) Charles B.
Langley, Albert	1866	1908	(h) Sarah J.
Langley, Sarah J.	1878	1916	(w) Albert
Ledsome, Fairy Lee	1932	10-01-1991	(w) Virgil H.
Ledsome, Russell	1900	4-09-1957	(h) Stella
Ledsome, Stella	1909	1945	(w) Russell
Ledsome, Virgil H.	1926	7-22-1993	(h) Fairy Lee
Lewis, Anna L.	1898	1988	(w) Walter C.
Lewis, Walter C.	1894	2-10-1978	(h) Anna L. (v) WWII
Lewis, Walter J.	1927	11-25-1927	
Lewis, William R.	1920	11-27-1920	
Linebaugh, Frank	1886	4-26-1951	(h) Rebecca
Linebaugh, Rebecca	1880	10-27-1954	(w) Frank
Linn, Anzy	1801	3-18-1893	(w) Samuel
Linn, Bessie A.	1884	12-28-1889	(d) H.R. & M.G.
Linn, Dessie	1864	1945	(w) Lewis A.
Linn, Edith M.	1913	10-15-1991	(w) George R.
Linn, Elizabeth	1825	1900	(w) William
Linn, Elizabeth J.	?	1-10-1858	(d) R. & R.
Linn, George B.	1860	12-19-1934	(h) Ida
Linn, George R.	1910	11-30-1977	(w) Edith M.
Linn, George W.	1906	1961	
Linn, Gibson	1860	1946	(h) Virginia E.
Linn, Golie	1885	4-16-1893	(s) L.A. & Dessie
Linn, Gordon D.	1894	2-14-1978	(h) Millie R.
Linn, Herbert E.	1908	7-20-1969	(h) Ruth (v) WW II
Linn, Hiram O.	1895	6-01-1956	(h) Sina (v) WWI
Linn, Hugh R.	1840	3-03-1899	(h) Maria E.
Linn, Ida M.	1868	12-03-1938	(w) George B.
Linn, Ivy M.	1871	1955	
Linn, James R.	1913	3-23-1962	
Linn, John D.	1901	1975	(h) Winifred A.
Linn, John M.	?	3-27-1871	(s) R. & E.
Linn, Katherine L	1866	1945	
Linn, Larry Lee	1948	7-03-1992	(h) Connie (Fancher)
Linn, Lewis A.	1856	15-1904	(h) Dessie
Linn, Maria E. (Thomas)	1843	7-13-1899	(w) Hugh R.
Linn, Mark Allen	1953	6-29-1970	(s) Lloyd & Emma
Linn, Martha A.	1850	1918	
Linn, Mary A.	1943	8-30-1943	
Linn, Mary L.	1925	10-17-1993	(d) Hiram & Sina
Linn, Mary L.	1871	12-29-1885	(d) H.R. & M.E.
Linn, Mary S.	1878	1947	(w) Sanford O.
Linn, Millie R.	1902	12-30-1975	(w) Gordon D.
Linn, Phoebe Jane	1869	3-10-1938	
Linn, Rachel A.	1834	8-04-1888	(w) Robert
Linn, Raymond E.	1932	1-06-1951	
Linn, Robert	1827	12-06-1910	(h) Rachel A.
Linn, Robert G.	1869	1953	
Linn, Ruth B. (Cox)	1920	12-02-1992	(w) Herbert E.
Linn, Samuel	1789	8-15-1852	

Linn, Sanford O.	1929	?	
Lorshbaugh, Margaret	1868	1921	(w) Harmon G.
Lukins, Billie Jo	1982	4-12-1993	(d) William & Linda
Lunceford, Julia	1876	1904	
Manning, Lucy	1863	1927	
Martin, Geraldine F.	1927	1942	
Martin, James	1905	1952	(h) Sina M.
Martin, Sina M.	1902	1983	(w) James
Mason, Charles W.	1918	1-24-1974	(h) Nellie V.
Mason, Nellie V.	1917	12-15-1976	(w) Charles W.
McAllister, Alexander	1818	7-19-1907	(h) Nancy
McAllister, Anza	1857	1932	
McAllister, Elizabeth	?	5-14-1882	(w) John
McAllister, Hugh R.	1863	1959	(h) Jennette F.
McAllister, James	?	1888	(s) John
McAllister, Jennette F.	1869	1951	(w) Hugh R.
McAllister, Nancy	1830	1-17-1912	(w) Alexander
McAllister, Nettie I.	1865	11-01-1914	
McCord, G. Thomas	1904	1-02-1978	(h) Wilda G.
McCord, Wilda G.	1909	10-29-1981	(w) G. Thomas
McIntyre, Albert	1886	1963	
Merrill, Austin A.	1910	10-29-1972	
Merrill, Dennis A.	1941	3-13-1942	
Merrill, Pearl	1904	1936	
Miller, Carrie E. (Reese)	1891	6-01-1971	(w) Harland W.
Miller, Doris Ann	?	2-24-1918	
Miller, Elisha W.	1869	1939	(h) Mary Ellen
Miller, Fernie B.	1907	1978	(h) Kathleen I.
Miller, Harland J. (Pete)	1920	5-02-1986	(s) Harland W.
Miller, Harland W.	1891	4-06-1975	(h) Carrie (Reese)
Miller, Kathleen I.	1912	1988	(w) Fernie
Miller, Mary Ellen	1871	1958	(w) Elisha W.
Moran, John O.	1877	1967	(h) Pearl
Moran, Pearl	1886	1921	(w) John O.
Morgan, Charles E.	1858	1937	
Murphy, Virgie	1907	8-19-1987	
Musgrave, Polly	NO DATES		
Newell, Paul T.	1913	12-01-1973	(h) Pauline
Newell, Pauline	1917	6-19-1982	(w) Paul T.
Nixon, Rachel A.	1867	1914	(w) Thomas B.
Nixon, Thomas B.	1871	1-16-1932	(h) Rachel A.
Oiler, Harold	NO DATES		
Oiler, Minnie May	1893	1943	
Oiler, Pauline	?	3-07-1938	
Parrack, A. Jean	1921	19-1982	
Parrack, Ebert L.	1907	2-28-1977	
Pearson, Mary (Wilson)	1909	1972	(w) William M.
Pearson, William M.	1909	1964	(h) Mary (Wilson)
Powell, Earley J.	1895	10-18-1983	(h) Eva E. (v) WWI
Powell, Eva E.	1897	1981	(w) Earley J.
Prince, Arthur	1896	1947	(h) Nellie C.
Prince, Nellie C.	1889	1971	(w) Arthur
Prince, Paul Edward	1926	11-25-1961	
Provance, Joseph H.	1856	10-01-1935	(h) Nicia A.
Provance, Nicia A.	1852	1940	(w) Joseph H.
Radford, A.S.	1833	11-09-1917	(v) CW (CSA)
Radford, John D.	1852	?	(h) Louisa E.

Radford, Louisa E.	1856	1929	(w) John D.
Radford, Kenneth S.	1915	7-25-1917	
Radford, Louisa E.	1856	1929	(w) John D.
Reese, Barbara Jane	1931	4-29-1934	
Reese, Carrie E.	1937	8-21-1937	
Reese, Carrie Watkins	1868	12-22-1935	(w) Robert E.
Reese, Delmar C.	1909	1969	
Reese, G.W.	NO DATES		(v) CW
Reese, Gerald B.	1897	1947	(h) Hazel B.
Reese, Hazel B.	1898	1975	(w) Gerald B.
Reese, Margaret	1866	?	
Reese, Nettie Ann	1902	1946	(w) William E.
Reese, Robert E.	1869	8-30-1944	(h) Carrie (Watkins)
Reese, Sallie C.	1886	1940	
Reese, Samuel E.	1860	5-08-1920	(s) C.W. & M.H.
Reese, Steven W.	1963	12-04-1988	
Reese, Thomas J.	?	10-07-1919	
Reese, Ula (Bond)	1895	6-10-1975	(w) William A.
Reese, William A.	1887	2-02-1954	(h) Ula (V) WW I
Reese, William E.	1899	1981	(h) Nettie Ann
Rice, Grover	1887	1912	
Rice, John	1847	1924	
Rice, Mary	1860	1945	
Ritchey, Vernon R.	1892	4-15-1969	(v) WW I
Rowand, Mary A.	1860	3-12-1936	(w) Thomas L.
Rowand, Thomas L.	1865	1941	(h) Mary A.
Rowand, Loucillea	1908	9-09-1917	(d) C. & L.
Rowand, Mary E.	1904	1-02-1905	(d) C. & L.
Rush, George W.	1903	4-19-1976	(h) Minnie
Rush, Minnie (Shoemaker)	1901	4-02-1978	(w) George W.
Saffle, R. Elizabeth	1889	12-29-1961	(w) William H.
Saffle, William H.	1886	10-31-1953	(h) R. Elizabeth
Satterfield, Gertie R.	1884	1949	(w) William R.
Satterfield, Glenn	1920	8-10-1991	
Satterfield, Nancy L.	1936	1991	
Satterfield, William R.	1881	1953	(h) Gertie
Schmidt, Bonnie Marie	1949	1988	
Schooley, Thelma A.	1884	1950	
Shoemaker, Mary M.	1878	1940	(W) William S.
Shoemaker, William S	1847	3-31-1930	(h) Mary M.
Shorter, Betty J.	1925	4-11-1925	
Shorter, Edward L.	1929	4-11-1997	(h) Ada Helen (Frye)
Shorter, Helen L.	1924	6-23-1924	
Shorter, Norma (Holt)	1906	4-04-1945	
Shumaker, (Infant)	1937	5-12-1937	(s) R.C. & S.G.
Shumaker, Infant)	1943	1-17-1943	Owen & Pearl
Shumaker, Anna May	?	8-31-1937	
Shumaker, Earnest W.	NO DATES		Infant
Shumaker, Elsie May	1904	1973	
Shumaker, Elvira J. (Mason)	1876	1957	(w) Harry E.
Shumaker, Harry E.	1875	1950	(h) Elvira J.
Shumaker, Margaret B.	1877	1963	(w) Wesley J.
Shumaker, Owen	1937	9-18-1938	
Shumaker, Owen C.	1911	1974	(h) J. Pearl
Shumaker, Rena Marie	1902	8-05-2003	(d) William & Mary (Miller)
Shumaker, Roy David	1928	1928	(s) R.C. & S.G.

People and Places

Shumaker, Wesley J.	1872	1954	(h) Margaret B.
Simmons, Francis B.	1908	1935	
Simmons, June E. (Drake)	1928	9-09-1997	(w) Troy L.
Simmons, Troy L.	1926	7-10-1974	(h) June E.
Smith, Agnes	1842	1917	(w) James A.
Smith, James A.	1860	1917	(h) Agnes
Stahl, Fred R.	1929	1975	(v) Korea
Stahl, Jodi Lee	?	9-24-1969	
Stahl, Violet	1903	1986	
Stanley, Esther (Barnes)	1896	1982	(w) Morgan
Stanley, H. Musgrave	1914	1981	(h) Elinore Janes
Stanley, Michael B.	1941	1977	(v) Viet Nam
Stanley, Morgan Bert	1896	4-01-1970	(h) Esther (v) WW I
Summers, Howard P.	1917	8-18-1995	(h) Elma May
Swisher, Cora Ann	1896	1930	(w) William E.
Swisher, Rena Marie	1902	8-05-2003	(d) William & Mary Miller
Swisher, Sonny	1940	1985	
Swisher, Waunita G.	1923	1965	
Swisher, William E.	1890	1960	(h) Cora Ann
Tennant, Enos	1860	1935	(h) Mary E.
Tennant, Lula J.	1900	1979	
Tennant, Mary E.	1861	1928	(w) Enos
Thomas, J. Edna	1890	4-26-1911	
Tibbs, Marvin Eugene	1924	1-14-1990	(h) Vanda 'Jean'
Tibbs, Mary Jo (Vanda)	1926	12-29-1998	(w) Marvin
Vance, Clara B.	1863	1944	
Vance, Elizabeth M.	1875	1940	
Vance, Emma O.	1868	9-09-1956	(w) J.W.
Vance, Isabell	1831	12-22-1909	(w) John R.
Vance, J.W.	1865	12-14-1904	(h) Emma
Vance, James P.	1893	3-23-1893	(s) J.W. & Emma
Vance, John R.	1828	11-28-1914	(h) Isabell
Vance, Martha N.	1860	1947	
Vandervort, Helen	?	10-19-1888	(w) James A.
Vandervort, Jamie	?	1888	(s) James & Helen
Vincent, Deby	1909	1955	(h) Grace
Vincent, Fiberious	?	5-21-1938	
Vincent, Grace	1910	19?	(w) Deby
Vincent, Mildred L.	1917	1918	
Vincent, Sarah Helen	1862	1960	
Vincent, Ulha Spider	1882	1962	
Vincent, Wilbert	1904	8-19-1972	
Ware, Judy	1939	1941	(d) Remley & Elba
Ware, M. Elba	1917	7-25-1978	(w) Remley H.
Ware, Remley H.	1914	8-21-1967	(h) M. Elba
Ware, Ryan Thomas	1984	7-23-1984	
Watkins, Alice M.	1873	1960	(w) Harvey H.
Watkins, Harvey H.	1880	1964	(h) Alice
Watkins, Mildred P.	1911	7-10-1986	(w) Ray
Watkins, Ray	1907	1976	(h) Mildred
Welch, Charles E.	1880	1961	(h) Goldie
Welch, Doris J.	1928	1986	
Welch, Gilbert H.	1909	5-07-1938	
Welch, Goldie M.	1883	1980	(w) Charles E.
Welch, Jesse M.	1891	1960	(w) John M. Jr.
Welch, John M., Jr.	1883	1966	(h) Jessie M.
Welch, John, Sr.	1855	1941	(h) Lida Jane

Welch, Lida Jane	1859	1940	(w) John, Sr.
Welch, Opal L.	1913	7-11-1995	(d) John & Jesse
West, Arthur Leroy	1928	2-04-1981	
West, Betty J.	1930	1977	(w) Charles R.
West, Carl	1904	1979	(h) Flossie
West, Dorsey F.	1894	1947	(h) E. Blanche
West, Dorsey, Jr.	1919	1954	
West, E. Blanche	1902	1962	(w) Dorsey F.
West, Etta Pearl	1925	1945	
West, Eugene G.	1934	7-08-1984	(h) Dorothy Mae
West, Flossie	1906	1981	(w) Carl
West, Goldie Marie	1912	1-12-1948	
West, James L.	1866	1947	(h) Susan B.
West, Marcus Ray	1984	1984	
West, Marion W.	1923	11-16-1975	(v) WWII
West, Susan B.	1872	1944	(w) James L.
West, William H.	1913	8-07-1975	
Westley, Nancy	NO DATES		
Westley, Thomas	?	5-06-1852	
Whitehair, Dora	1894	1965	
Wilk, Charles F.	1902	3-20-1986	(h) Lucille
Wilk, Lucille C.	1903	5-07-1980	(w) Charles F.
Wilson, Ada T.	1886	1964	(w) Charles C.
Wilson, Charles C.	1881	1968	(h) Ada T.
Wilson, Emma Margaret	1910	1917	(d) C.C. & Ada
Wilson, Jeston, Jr.	1923	7-25-1966	(v) WWII
Wilson, John R.	1845	1920	(h) Mary A.
Wilson, Mary A.	1955	1906	(w) John R.
Wilson, Nancy A.	1808	1887	(m) John R.
Wilson, Nellie G.	1880	1940	(w) William W.
Wilson, Sybil	1882	1973	
Wilson, William W.	1879	1953	(h) Nellie G.
Wilt (Infant)	1947	10-11-1947	(s) Henry & Mary
Wilt, (Infant)	1945	8-24-1945	(s) Henry & Mary
Wilt, Eva A.	1888	1964	(w) Russell D.
Wilt, Jesse W.	1892	1921	
Wilt, Lloyd W.	1872	5-30-1930	
Wilt, Lola (Hartley)	1877	1946	
Wilt, Russell D.	1887	1961	(h) Eva A.
Wilt, Walter R.	1880	1921	
Work, Elizabeth	?	1905	(w) J.A.
Work, J.A.	1825	3-05-1909	(h) Elizabeth
Work, Jacob	?	2-14-1872	(h) Margaret
Work, James	1824	1880	(h) Rebecca
Work, Madge	1907	12-11-1983	
Work, Margaret	?	2-06-1872	(w) Jacob
Work, Rebecca	1826	2-21-1905	(w) James
Work, Sarah	1819	2-27-1888	(w) William
Work, Wattman W.	?	4-25-1885	
Work, Wesley	1863	1936	
Work, William	1820	1-25-1888	(h) Sarah
Yates, Infant	1910	?	(d) J.C. & D. M.
Yates, Charles E.	1905	1959	(h) Frances V.
Yates, Daisy Mae	1887	?	(w) John C.
Yates, Frances V.	1920	1965	(w) Charles E.
Yates, John C.	1882	1944	(h) Daisy Mae
Yates, Nola May	1908	11-11-1920	(d) J.C. & D. M.

People and Places

1961 REST HAVEN MEMORIAL GARDENS

Situated in Grant District, this modern cemetery can be found on US Rt. 250 South not far from exit 132 off I-79 at White Hall in the area known as Hillview. It can easily be seen from the interstate. The late Leon Lowther started this cemetery on the hillside in 1961 when he bought the Glenn Wilt farm. His daughter, L. Lesley Lowther is the present owner.

The entrance plaque reads:

"Lives are commemorated—deaths are recorded—families are reunited—memories are made tangible—and love is undisguised. This is a graveyard.

"Communities accord respect, families bestow reverence, historians seek information and our heritage is thereby enriched.

"Testimonies of devotion, pride and remembrance are cast in bronze to pay warm tribute to accomplishments and to the life—not the death—of a loved one. The cemetery is homeland for memorials that are a sustaining source of comfort to the living.

"A cemetery is a history of people—a perpetual record of yesterday and a sanctuary of peace and quiet today. A cemetery exists because every life is worth living and remembering—always."

A praying hands monument will greet you as you enter. At the top of the drive is the Tree of Life Circle. The grounds are attractively maintained and are perpetually kept. A special fund to insure this perpetual care and maintenance comes from money set aside from the sale of every lot. All headstones are flush to the ground; urns are available for cut flowers. This is characteristic of this region's modern cemetery.

The view overlooking the Tygart Valley Bridge and I-79 is worth the drive up into the cemetery. The real prize in this cemetery is the beautiful poem on the backside of the praying hands monument as you leave. It reads:

> **The kiss of the sun for pardon,**
> **The song of the birds for mirth.**
> **One is nearer God's heart in a garden**
> **Than anywhere else on earth.**
>
> *Dorothy Frances Bloomfield*

Rest Haven Cemetery was established in 1961, on Rt. 250.

This graveyard has twelve unmarked graves. Call the office for information and burial records. Grave sites are available at this writing.

1836 JOHN LINN CEMETERY
(White Hall)

This small hilltop cemetery in Grant District is off Rt. 250 South, past the mall behind the Fabric Shop. Walking to the top of the hill is required. This cemetery is very overgrown; the markers are barely visible in warm weather. Mine subsidence has disturbed some of the graves. It is no longer in use as a cemetery. According to WPA readings done in 1938, there are 15 unmarked graves. Monuments can be found peaking their way up through the brush and vegetation.

John Linn was the son of Samuel and Anzy Linn from Benton's Ferry. He was born September 18, 1833 and married Rachel Powell in 1856. They had 10 children. He was a leading laymen in the Methodist Protestant Church and a farmer all of his life. In Mr. Linn's 1899 will he specified burial here upon his death. "… buried in the family cemetery located on his farm". (Will book 3 Page 305). No monuments were

John Linn born Sept. 18, 1833; died 1899.

237

John Linn Cemetery at White Hall, WV, established in 1836. It is no longer being used as a graveyard.

marked LINN. Stones may have been vandalized or could have been just wooden crosses that deteriorated over the years. Perhaps his is among the 15 unmarked graves that the WPA workers discovered.

The cemetery was established in 1836 when the William Hall family owned the property and their infant daughter Arah Jane died at age 10 months and 18 days. She was buried in the tradition of those days and laid to rest on top of the hill on the family farm. The property was later sold to the Linn who sold lots to community residents. In June 1896, Linn sold lots to T. L. Tucker, Samuel P. Nixon, Samuel Nixon, Jr., Calder Bice and James Lanham (Deed 75/Page 415). The cemetery today still remains on private property. It is sometimes referred to as one of the Nixon cemeteries. Burial listing is as follows:

JOHN LINN CEMETERY

Name	Birth	Death	Relationship
Bice, Elizabeth	1849	6-12-1886	(w) Calder
Dean, Anzy Bell	?	?	(d) Rev. R. C & M. M.
Dean, Paul	1898	2-07-1899	(s) Rev. R. C. & M. M.
Dean, William H.	?	5-05-1866	(s) W. H. & N. Dean
Hall, Arah Jane	?	12-07-1836	(d) William N.
Hall, Elizabeth	(age 61)	6-12-1856	(w) Wm. N.
Hall, I.A.	1839	1915	
Hall, John C.	(age 25)	8-13-1844	
Hall, M.R.	1842	1923	
Hall, Thomas	(age 37)	7-24-1858	(s) Wm. & Elizabeth
Hall, William N.	(age 87)	4-27-1884	
Hall, William J.	(age 3)	10-05-1836	
Hartley, John A.	1828	5-04-1901	
Lanham, (Infant)	1906	1906	(ts) Wm. & A. L.
Lanham, (Infant)	1906	1906	(td) Wm. & A. L.
Lanham, James	1912	7-20-1898	(h) Malinda
Lanham, Malinda	1824	3-13-1911	(w) James Martin
Martin, Anne	(age 1 year, 1 month)	9-11-1853	(d) Geo. J. & R. E.
Martin, Thomas H.	(age 1 Year)	3-23-1860	(s) Geo. & R. E.
Nixon, Bernetta	(age 1 year, 1 month)	8-18-1891	(d) S. & D.
Nixon, Catharine	(age 29)	6-30-1883	(w) Samuel
Nixon, Harriet V.	(age 33)	10-14-1884	(w) Sylvanias
Nixon, Lucinda	?	6-25-1875	(w) Samuel
Nixon, Samuel P.	1813	7-15-1907	(h) Lucinda & Cathy
Nixon, Sylvanias	1846	7-16-1897	(h) Harriet V.
Reese, Mary E.	(Age 1 mo. 25days)	08-21-1866	(d) Samuel & M. F.
Reese, Mary F.	(Age 29)	07-06-1870	(w) Samuel L.
Reese, Lillian	1873	05-27-1873	(d) Samuel
Reese, Samuel L	(age 69)?	10-27-1908	(h) Mary F.
Rutherford, Charles W.	1882	07-09-1907	
Tucker, Charles L.	1864	06-29-1889	(s) T. L. & A. M.
Tucker, Clara B.	1868	06-22-1895	(d) T. L.& A. M.
Tucker, J.H., Jr.	1810	01-22-1890	(f) Thaddeus L.
Tucker, Thaddeus L.	1840	06-29-1909	(h) Ann (Provance)

VINCENT CEMETERY
(Coal Bank Road)

This quiet community's cemetery is located atop Vinegar Hill. Take Route 250 South, go past the Mall to the Colfax Road and turn right. Make a left on Coal Bank Hill Road. At the top of the hill turn left. Immediately on the left is the entrance gate that is kept shut. The cemetery is at the top of the hill after going through the entrance gate.

The cemetery began with the death of a two-year-old child in 1835 and is surrounded by a chain link fence. In the right corner is a tall white pine. The center has an old hydrangea bush grown into a lovely tree, typical of the older graveyards. Sitting near the pine tree, listening to the whispers, I was impressed with the serenity and neatness of this cemetery. There was a feeling of peace, faith and love. The view to the east is superb as it overlooks the valley where so many valley residents have their roots.

Vincent Cemetery on Vinegar Hill, established 1835.

In the back two stones made of slate rock cannot be missed when browsing here. The stones are typical of the early 1800's. One of them reads:

> In Memory of
> John N. Vincent
> Who departed this life
> May 3rd 1835
> Age 2 Years 1 day
>
> AF (Allison Fleming 1814-1871)

Note the stonecutter's mark in the lower right hand corner. It is the earliest headstone. Folks of the older generation say this cemetery also contains the unmarked graves of Native Americans.

When the WPA took cemetery readings in 1939 the Vincent Cemetery had 40 unmarked gravesites; 20 have since been identified. Early records indicate that the land on which the cemetery is located was a part of the Thomas Little farm; that portion of land was sold to Charles H. Vincent. Vincent sold it to Cephas Lanham, who in 1902 signed the cemetery over to a board of trustees for a community cemetery (Deed 109-319).

Today strict rules and by-laws govern the cemetery. Its officials have an annual summer meeting to discuss issues concerning it. The cemetery is solely supported by donations from family members and friends and is maintained by volunteer labor. It is watched closely by family and loved ones. The following is a list of those known buried there:

VINCENT CEMETERY
Coal Bank Road

Name	Birth	Death	Relationship
Barniak, Frank	1912	1999	(v) WW II
C. C. A.	NO DATES		
C, Elizabeth J.	NO DATES		
Campbell, James E.	1925	12-18-1996	(h) Mary Lu (v) WW II
Carpenter, Ida Virginia	1882	1943	(w) Ott
Carpenter, Ott	1875	1967	(h) Ida
Clark, Charles W.	1885	1964	(h) May
Clark, May G.	1890	1972	(w) Charles W.
Copen, Dora (Hunt)	1917	1-08-2001	(w) James R.
Copen, James R.	1916	1980	(h) Dora
Copen, Willa	1951	1998	
Criss, Calder	1855	1889	(h) Elizabeth
Criss, Cora A.	(1 mo.)	6-02-1883	(d) Calder & E. J.

Name	Birth	Death	Relation
Criss, Delia M.1892	1-05-	1898	(d) William & E. C.
Criss, Elizabeth	1860	1883	(w) Calder
Criss, Mary J.	1888	11-10-1896	(d) William & E. C.
Cristy, Cecil	1936		
Cumpston, Glen H.	1898	1956	(h) Minnie
Cumptson, Minnie B.	1895	1965	(w) Glenn
Currey, Shearle E. (Ice)	1903	12-12-1987	
Eby, Opal A.	1911	1954	
Fisher, Charles E.	1935	1937	
Fleming, Carrie	1881	2-21-1975	(d) Edgar & Mary
Fleming, J. Wilbur (Web)	1864	9-05-1958	(h) Iva (s) Edgar & Mary
Fleming, S. Iva	1877	1936	(w) J. Wilbur (Web)
Freeman, Julia Ann	1911	1937	(d) Charles & May Clark
Freeman, V. Carlton	1910	1950	
Griffith, Charles L.	1881	2-15-1942	(s) Orlando & Sarah
Griffith, Cora D.	1878	1960	(w) Hiram
Griffith, Hiram L.	1871	10-21-1930	(s) Orlando & Sarah
Griffith, Lawrence E.	1912	1971	(s) Charles & Maggie
Griffith, Lena B.	1908	10-07-1910	(d) Charles & Maggie
Griffith, Maggie M.	1887	1966	(w) Charles L.
Griffith, Orlando	?	2-15-1912	
Griffith, Prudy K.	?	1-02-1915	(d) Orlando & Sarah
Griffith, Sarah A.	?	10-07-1907	(w) Orlando
Griffith, Thomas E.	?	5-06-1916	(s) Orlando & Sarah
Gump, Lloyd L.	1908	1981	(h) Pauline
Gump, Pauline	1908	1966	(w) Lloyd L.
Hartley, Anna V.	1872	1959	(w) John W.
Hartley, Charles M.	1871	12-16-1913	
Hartley, Earl F.	1894	1932	(s) Thomas & Sarah
Hartley, John W.	1869	1940	(h) Anna V.
Hartley, Lizzie B.	1867	4-08-1912	(d) M. & H.
Hartley, Opal E.	1904	2-29-1907	(d) John & Anna
Hartley, Sarah F.	1845	1924	(w) Thomas A.
Hartley, Thomas	1845	7-11-1913	(h) Sarah) (v) CW
Hartley, Thomas A.	1893	1928	(s) Thomas & Sarah
Hartley, William H., Sr.	1941	6-02-1999	(h) Terry (Harbarger) (v) WW II
Hewitt, Charles W.	1920	2-18-1983	(h) Texel E.
Hewitt, Lizzie B.	1920	4-08-1912	
Hewitt, Junior	1942	12-06-1942	(s) Charles & Texel
Hewitt, Texel E.	1923	5-14-1988	(w) Charles & Mary
Hunt, Charles D.	1895	1967	(h) Mary R.
Hunt, Grace	1938	6-19-1938	(d) Charles & Mary
Hunt, Lettie Elva	1929	10-21-2000	(w) Charles Dale
Hunt, Mary R.	1900	1982	(w) Charles D.
Hunt, Pearl Marie	1924	7-22-1984	(w) Robert Issac
Ice, Fred G.	1904	2-25-1920	(s) James & Mary
Ice, James R.	1857	1944	(h) Mary E.
Ice, Liddie	1886	1898	(d) James & Mary
Ice, Mary E.	1863	1953	(w) James R.
Ice, Ollie M.	1880	1898	(d) James & Mary
Imes, Kenneth Allen	1957	12-22-1957	(s) Kenneth & Marling
Irons, Dora	1856	1925	(w) Joseph
Irons, Elizabeth S.	1891	1965	(w) James B.
Irons, Glenda R.	1958	1959	(d) Glenn & Beverly
Irons, Glenn R. (Bud)	1939	11-25-1991	(h) Beverly (Wilson)

Name	Born	Died	Notes
Irons, James B.	1891	1954	(h) Elizabeth (Shaver)
Irons, Kenneth (Infant)	?	1940's	(s) W. Hubert & M. E.
Irons, Larry (Infant)	?	1940's	(s) W. Hubert & M. E.
Irons, Mary Elizabeth	1917	9-19-1992	(w) William H.
Irons, William Hubert	1916	6-09-1992	(h) Mary (Enright)
Keener, Fred	1883	1957	(h) Ivy
Keener, Ivy	1874	1958	(w) Fred
Little, Anna V.	1854	1934	
Little, Britta L.	1898	1965	(w) E. Brooks
Little, E. Brooks	1889	1949	(h) Britta L.
Little, Harry C.	1876	1946	(s) Anna
Little, Ida J.	1884	6-09-1967	(w) John E.
Little, John E.	1880	1-10-1977	(h) Ida J.
Little, Sanford B.	1873	2-04-1930	
Lowther, George D.	1900	12-15-1965	(v) WWII
McCelland, Elizabeth E.	1924	10-31-1995	(d) Scott & Sigrid V.
McCelland, Kelland	1965	1999	(s) Elizabeth
McDonald, Elizabeth	1882	1960	
McLaughlin, Audrey V.	1913	1985	(w) Glenn
McLaughlin, Glenn F.	1918	1981	(h) Audrey
Moore, Fannie A.	1911	3-24-1996	(w) Walter A.
Moore, Mary Alice	1942	10-14-1942	(d) Walter & Fannie
Moore, Walter A.	1908	1964	(h) Fannie (Vincent)
Mundell, Joanna	1831	10-15-1895	(w) William B.
Mundell, William B.	1823	7-05-1899	(h) Joanna
Musgrave, Mary Ethel	1909	10-24-1988	(Vincent)
Parrish, E. Yvonne	1959	1978	(d) Charles & Lettie Hunt
Roby, Ballard B.	1882	1960	(h) Cynthia A.
Roby, Cynthia A.	1879	1971	(w) Ballard
Rutherford, Albert L.	1947	1999	(v) Vietnam
Rutherford, Lawson E.	1946	1946	
Sargent, Eliza I.	1869	1914	(w) E.J.
Shaver, Annie	?	1-26-1908	(d) William & Annie
Shaver, Annie M.	1875	1948	(w) William A.
Shaver, Ben F.	1899	3-04-1954	(v) WW I Air Corps
Shaver, Birchinal	?	1902	(s) William & Annie
Shaver, Edgar C.	1899	1891	
Shaver, Hezekiah	1827	2-08-1909	
Shaver, Howard G.	1913	2-27-1978	(s) William (v) WWII Army
Shaver, James	1861	1931	(h) Margaret Ann
Shaver, Lillian	?	3-08-1912	(d) William & Annie
Shaver, Margaret Ann	1856	1939	(w) James
Shaver, Pearl	?	1912	(d) William & Annie
Shaver, William A.	1869	1959	(h) Annie M.
Shaver, William H.	1893	12-11-1925	(s) James & Margaret
Shorter, Cecil	1905	1966	
Shorter, Robert	1956	1956	(s) Cecil & Nellie
Shorter, William	1954	1954	(s) Cecil & Nellie
Smallwood, French Hazel	1891	2-02-1895	(s) James & Laura
Smallwood, James W.	1865	1941	(h) Laura
Smallwood, Jay J.	1895	1906	(s) James & Laura
Smallwood, Laura A.	1868	1952	(w) James W.
Smith, Harry O.	1916	1985	(h) May L.
Smith, May L. (Rader)	1921	11-28-1992	(w) Harry
Springer, Cora O.	1873	1962	(w) William H.
Springer, William H.	1869	1954	(h) Cora
Stottlermire, Earnest	1908	1991	

Toothman, Lewis H.	1942	1991	
Vincent, Beatrice M.	1912	1942	(w) Walter
Vincent, Carl	1904	1974	(h) Pauline
Vincent, Catharine L.	(Age 16)	8-10-1845	
Vincent, Clara Olive	1859	11-07-1909	(w) E. F.
Vincent, Cora	1870	11-26-1873	(d) Edgar & Nettie
Vincent, Delbert N.	1907	1913	(s) Walter & Sarah
Vincent, E.F.	1858	8-23-1891	(h) Clara
Vincent, Edward	NO DATES		
Vincent, Edgar C.	1837	6-05-1883	9s) William
Vincent, Edward (Rev.)	1783	1868	(h) Rebecca
Vincent, Effie F.	1885	8-15-1964	(w) Virgil E.
Vincent, Ellenora	1856	1889	
Vincent, Elsie			NO DATES
Vincent, Freeman			NO DATES
Vincent, Florence J.	1890	5-27-1920	(d) Thomas & Luana
Vincent, Floyd T., Jr.	1951	9-01-1951	(s) Floyd & Lillie
Vincent, George W.	1894	5-24-1900	
Vincent, Hannah	1835	1912	(w) Edger
Vincent, Issac	1851	1934	
Vincent, Isaac L.	?	4-28-1934	(v) 5th WV Cav. CW
Vincent, Isaiah	1850	1916	
Vincent, Ivy	NO DATES		
Vincent, James R.	1865	4-23-1894	
Vincent, James W.	1921	12-21-2000	(s) Virgil & Effie (v) WW II
Vincent, Jennie Belle	?	189?	(d) C.M.
Vincent, John F.	1860	10-9-1900	
Vincent, John N.	(2 yr.1 day)	5-03-1835	(s) William
Vincent, Joseph	?	1892	
Vincent, Lawrence J.	1890	1920	
Vincent, Leah Grace	1922	10-28-1923	(d) Sigrid & Scott
Vincent, Leona A.	1881	1949	(w) Marion H.
Vincent, Luana	1871	1955	(w) Thomas
Vincent, Luther E.	?	3-02-1853	(s) S. W. & M.
Vincent, Mable O.	1887	8-20-1888	(d) M.A & E. L.
Vincent, Mamie A.	1889	1981	(d) Luana & Thomas
Vincent, Marion H.	1874	1956	(h) Leona
Vincent, Mary	1868	1936	
Vincent, Mary	1911	1914	(d) Marion & Leona
Vincent, Masel	1894	8-05-1895	
Vincent, Molly	NO DATES		
Vincent, Nettie	1877	12-05-1877	(d) Edgar & Hanna
Vincent, Nora	1913	1918	(d) Marion & Leona
Vincent, Olive	1856	1899	(w) E.F.
Vincent, Pauline	1912	6-23-1989	(w) Carl
Vincent, Polly	1848	1937	
Vincent, Raymond E.	1930	1932	(s) Walter
Vincent, Rebecca	1793	1875	(w) Edward (Rev.)
Vincent, S. W.	(Age 32)	1-16-1865	
Vincent, Sarah A.	1827	10-14-1909	(w) J. S.
Vincent, Sarah O.	1886	1929	(w) Walter
Vincent, Scott	1898	1977	(s) Thomas & Luana
Vincent, Sigrid G.	1901	12-20-1992	(w) Scott (Sapp)
Vincent, Sylvester	NO DATES		
Vincent, Thomas	1867	1935	(h) Luana
Vincent, Thomas F.	1927	3-29-1986	(s) Scott (v) WWII
Vincent, Virgil E.	1893	5-13-1963	(h) Effie

Vincent, Walter	1872	1946	(h) Sarah O. McGinnis
Vincent, Walter	1907	1956	
Vincent, William	(age 78)	5-15-1880	
Vincent, Charles A. (Gus)	1908	3-29-1993	(h) Marguite M. (Fleming)
West, Alice	NO DATES		
Wilson, Mary Marguite	1911	6-01-1984	(w) Charles A.
Wilt, Mattie J.	1887	1951	(w) Wayman F.
Wilt, Wayman F.	1885	1951	(h) Mattie J.

1850 DODD CEMETERY
(Pleasant Valley)

This little cemetery may be found in Union District off the Pleasant Valley Road by going up the hill beside Valley Chapel Church. At the Y, turn to the right. It is situated on the very top of the hill in a grove of trees. It is in the middle of a pasture on private property belonging to the Bob Stemple family. There are three huge crosses near the site which can be seen from the Interstate. They were put up by the late Bernard Coffindaffer of West Virginia, who spent over a million dollars of his money for the project as his way of spreading the gospel. They can be seen all along I-79 in West Virginia.

Three crosses overlooking Pleasant Valley near Dodd Cemetery that was established in 1850.

The cemetery has had several owners since its beginning. The James Thomas family owned the property when the first burial took place. In 1812, when Thomas sold the property to John A. Hughes, he reserved a lot for a cemetery with a 10-foot wide road leading up to it. There are 13 marked Thomas family graves. 1850 is the earliest headstone date. Some of the 25 unmarked graves probably are also Thomas's.

The cemetery got its name from James T. Dodd, who owned the property and surrounding land at the time when cemeteries had to have a name. This was between the years of 1883-1912. It has had several owners after the Dodds sold the property in 1912.

The cemetery is no longer used as a burial ground. It is in poor condition, and some of the headstones broken. A lone, very old arborvitae tree shades some of the gravesites. In some cases, the birth dates could not be read because of prolonged exposure to the elements.

The panoramic view overlooking Pleasant Valley and Colfax is breathtaking. Looking south from the top one can see the church in the valley of Colfax. Valley Chapel Church in Pleasant Valley can be seen by looking to the North. It is understandable why this site was chosen for a burial ground. Mountain top graveyards were a tradition in the old days and are appreciated today.

During the 1800's the original Morgantown-Bridgeport Pike came by here to the Tygart Valley River, where there was a ferry. The locals called it the Mundell Ferry road.

Except for the unmarked gravesites the following is a list of those laid to rest here.

DODD CEMETERY
(Pleasant Valley)

Name	Birth	Death	Relationship
Bainbridge, David	(Age 61)	12-23-1869	(s) E. & M. J.
Bainbridge, Minerva	(Age 25)	6-22-1856	(w) J. E.
Barnes, Estella	(Age 9 mos.)	5-21-1883	(d) J. W. & I. M.
Brand, Elizabeth	(Age 29)	7-02-1858	(w) William

West Virginia's Lower Tygart Valley River

Brand, Clarence	?	2-22-1887	(s) J. R. & L.
Brand, J. R.	(Age 31)	9-06-1889	
Brand, Jessie R	1-20-1890	10-31-1889	(d) J. R. & A. L.
Cox, Guy L. A.	4-02-1880	2-23-1897	(s) Thos. & Deborah
Dodd, Thomas (baby)	11-20-1889	11-28-1890	(s) J. E. &H. R
Harr, Martha	(Age 23)	9-17-1870	(w) John
Harr, Willie R.	?	6-14-1869	(s) J. M. & Martha
Harr, India A.	(Age 13)	4-25-1877	(d) John & Edith
Haught, Margaret	10-15-1854	2-14-1890	(w) Henry
Haught, John N.	?	5-28-1883	
Hughes, John N.	(Age 53)	??-28-1883	(h) Mollie
Hughes, Mollie	1-15-1881	1-15-1881	(w) John N.
Hawkins, Alex		NO DATES	(cw) Co. F.12th WV Infantry
Hawkins, Arthur G.	5-10-1872	3-12-1873	(s) Alex & O. J.
Hawkins, Edward E.	1-23-1874	3-15-1875	(s) Alex & O. J.
Holt, Rex Thomas	(Age 58)	1-11-1870	
Plymale, Dorthie	(age 35)	11-03-1935	
Prickett, Louiza E.	(Age 31)	4-07-1874	(w) Meredith
Prickett, Meredith	1-01-1838	12-01-1920	(s) Nathan
Thomas, Matilda		?12-21-1850	(d) Rich & H.
Thomas, Samuel F.	10-03-1879	1-16-1882	(s) R. F. & M. J.
Thomas, R.F.	?	11-29-1880	
Thomas, Richard	(stone broken)	1-05-1879	Age 75
Thomas, Nancy	(Age 15)	4-25-1853	
Thomas, Ann M.	4-23-1835	6-28-1905	(w) William G.
Thomas, William G.	(Age 32)	4-02-1865	
Thomas, James W.	(Age 17)	6-13-1880	(s) W. G. & A. M.
Thomas, John E.	(Age 26)	11-04-1890	(s) W. G. & A. M.
Thomas, Hanna	(Age 55)	4-06-1865	(w) Richard
Thomas, James A.	7-26-1872	3-06-1897	(s) R. F. & M. J.
Thomas, Martha	12-23-1872	3-23-1874	(d) J. H. & M. E.
Thomas, Nettie E.	(Age 21 days)	8-20-1863	(d) J. H. & M. E.
Shoemaker, James	1-05-1898	5-11-1914	
Shoemaker, J.W.	NO DATES		(cw)Co. H. 10th WV Infantry
Springer, Sweden	(Age 45)	10-30-1876	
Springer, James H.	4-29-1863	12-29-1899	
Wilson, John J.	10-25-1812	2-09-1895	

1816 COLFAX CEMETERY
(Nuzum No. 2)

Located in the heart of the Colfax community, this small cemetery is very close to the Tygart Valley River. Originally called the Springer Graveyard, this cemetery began with the burial of John Springer (1756-1816) who owned most of the valley surrounding present-day Colfax. According to Springer history records, his wife Barsheba (Merrifield) died forty years later in 1859 and is buried beside him. Both graves are unmarked. Legend has it that Indians are also buried here. In 1890, this property was sold to Zadoc and Ulysses Nuzum. It continued as a burial ground.

Before the Baltimore & Ohio Railroad came through, there was a deep ravine directly beside the cemetery. When the railroad workers started their grading in the early 1850's, the ravine was filled in with the excess dirt. At that time, there was no county road by the cemetery, which meant plenty of room for burials. However, by 1902, with the construction of the Colfax Bridge, the county put a road in beside the graveyard leading to the bridge. In 1928, another county road was completed directly in front of the cemetery, which shortened it. Today there is less than a half-acre for burials. A very old, huge maple tree is in the center of the graveyard.

In September of 1901, the Nuzum heirs, who were: Staats, Manassa, Job S. and Sarah M., deeded the property over to the community for use as a public cemetery (Deed book 109/Page 147). W. C. Malone, Job S.

Nuzum and P. M. Carpenter were named as the trustees. The cemetery was called the Colfax Cemetery but it is referred to as the Nuzum No. 2.

The river flows directly in the back of the cemetery. Before the Grafton Dam was built in 1939, this site was on flood level and was under water during the 1888 flood. An unusual tabletop tombstone, also in the back, will catch your eye. On it is written;

Colfax Cemetery (Nuzum No. 2) established 1816.

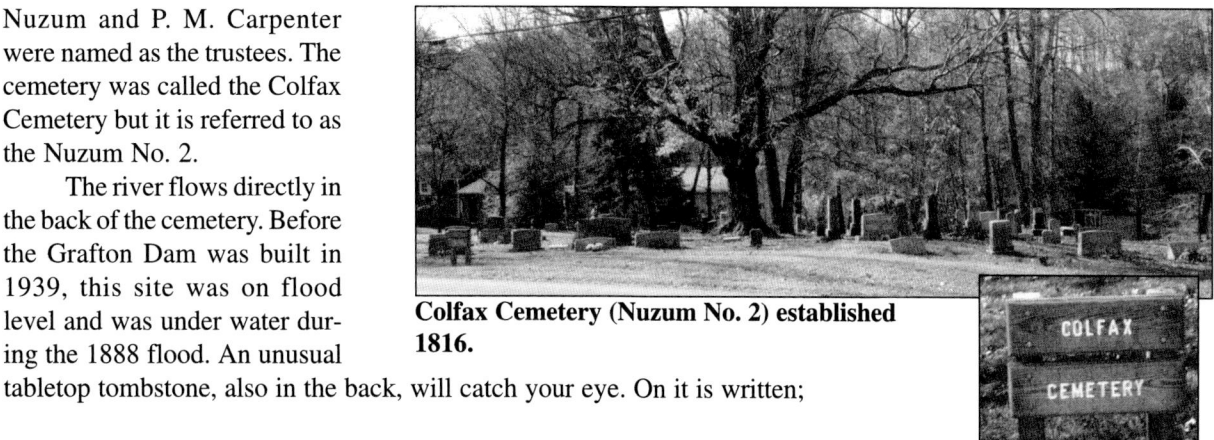

"Sacred to the memory of Phebe Nuzum
who was born October 26, 1797
and departed this life March 8th 1852
Age 54 years
4 months
19 days"

Phebe was the third child of John Springer and the first wife of Richard (Black Dick) Nuzum of the third generation. They had three daughters and six sons who were all in the Civil War and survived. (See Communities on Hammond).

The late Russell Nichols (1888-1974) is buried here as is his wife Pearl Jacobs (1890-1966). They both grew up in Colfax. Russell built the first camps on the river at Colfax when he was 16 years old and later developed Poplar Island with six other camps. He was a telegrapher for the B&O Railroad. He became Sheriff of Marion County in 1941 to 49. He was widely known for his success in buying and selling real estate throughout the county. The couple were members of the Colfax Methodist Church.

Also laid to rest here is Joseph Springer who was also a telegrapher for the B&O Railroad, and worked the towers between Grafton and Fairmont. He became president of the Telegraphers Union and moved to Chicago. He requested to his family that when he died, he wanted to be buried in the Colfax Cemetery because it was his hometown and close to the railroad that he loved so much. He died in 1970 and was buried there. In 1974, his fourth and last wife decided she wanted him closer to her, so she had his body exhumed and reburied in Chicago, Illinois. One year later, five-month old Daniel Cordray, Joseph's great grandson, was buried in the empty plot.

In August 1861, at the call for good strong men to fight for the Union Army, George W. Fleming, 18, enlisted. Local rebels attempted to hang Fleming. Shortly after this ordeal he contacted a deadly disease and knew he faced death. He requested that he be sent home to Texas (Colfax) to his hometown to die. The Army agreed. He was brought home by train and died on June 10, 1863. His grave is in the back of the cemetery with half of a military headstone. The other half is missing. For more about George W. Fleming's story, see Civil War Stories.

Family members and friends oversee the care of the cemetery. David Nuzum, Jr. is chairman of the board of trustees. The grounds are maintained solely by donations and are neatly kept. According to WPA readings taken in 1939, there are 53 unmarked graves in the Colfax Cemetery. According to early reports from the older folks there are several unmarked graves of Native Americans.

The following is a list of those known to be laid to rest here:

COLFAX CEMETERY

Name	Birth	Death	Relationship
Ball, Ellis William	1902	1947	
Barker, Mary M.	1865	1944	(w) William R.
Barker, William R.	1863	1951	(h) Mary M.
Barnes, Affie	1867	11-07-1941	(w) George W.
Barnes, Carrie W.	?	1-31-1897	(w) Samuel W.

Barnes, Charles H. (Infant)	1900	3-15-1900	(s) Geo. & Affie
Barnes, George W.	1863	1-01-1935	(h) Affie
Barnes, Glen W.	1889	5-11-1913	
Barnes, Hilda Maxine	1918	3-17-1918	
Barnes, Jerry	?	5-04-1933	
Barnes, Samuel W.	1854	4-28-1917	(h) Carrie
Blosser, Betty (Nichols)	1919	3-14-1984	(w) William (Bill)
Boyles, Charles E.	1918	3-15-1918	(s) G. W. & C.X.R.
Carpenter, Asahel B.	1866	4-14-1906	Single
Carpenter, Carl H.	1886	5-21-1903	(s) W. W. Carpenter
Carpenter, Catherine	1845	8-22-1931	(2nd w) Thomas W.
Carpenter, Clarence H.	?	7-17-1880	(s) J. & L. J.
Carpenter, Hattie V.	1905	1905	
Carpenter, Hazel B.	1897	8-08-1898	(d) P. M. & Z. B.
Carpenter, Josephine	?	12-30-1883	(w) J. L.
Carpenter, Thomas W.	1840	4-02-1903	(h) Sarah & Catherine
Cordray, Daniel Joseph	2-27-1975	7-20-1975	(s) Joseph & Martha
Cordray, Isaac Campbell	3-12-1980	3-12-1980	(s) Joseph & Martha
Fleming, Bessie E.	1888	4-13-1960	(w) Charles E.
Fleming, Charles E.	1883	11-10-1965	(h) Bessie E.
Fleming, Edgar W.	1837	11-04-1900	(h) Mary E.
Fleming, Elizabeth	?	9-02-1873	(w) Geo. W.
Fleming, George W., Jr.	1844	6-10-1863	(s) Geo. & E. (v) CW
Fleming, George W., Sr.	?	9-02-1873	(h) Elizabeth
Fleming, Maggie	1867	2-05-1870	(d) J. W. & S. A.
Fleming, Mary E.	1840	7-02-1893	(w) Edgar W.
Fortney, G. Madeline	1905	6-25-1999	(d) Geo. & Affie Barnes
Fluharty, Laura	1901	1968	
French, Clara V.	1862	5-25-1952	(w) Issac N.
French, Issac N.	1872	1942	(h) Clara
Gallahue, William	1875	12-24-1893	(s) C. A. & M. J.
Gallahue, Joseph M.	1858	11-03-1898	
Hammond, William N.	1933	2002	(h) Mary Lou (Arnett)
Harr, Ashel	1804	5-05-1887	
Hawkins, Bobby	1927	1-04-1927	(s) W. Fred & Icie
Hawkins, Icie G.	1893	11-25-1978	(w) William Fred
Hawkins, William Fred	1891	11-19-1953	(h) Icie (Nichols)
Herrington, Terressa	1917	5-08-1996	(w) Frank
Herrington, Dr. Frank H.	1905	8-20-1960	(h) Terressa (Hawkins)
Hoffmaster, Charles D.	1880	8-31-1955	(h) Velma L.
Hoffmaster, Dorothy E.	1922	1924	(d) Charles & Velma
Hoffmaster, Velma L.	1901	12-23-1980	(w) Charles D.
Hunter, Dona Jean (Infant)	1929	1929	(d) Vance & Ruth
Hunter, John Wayne (Infant)	1933	1933	(s) Vance & Ruth
Hunter, Mary Eloise (Infant)	1947	1947	(d) Vance & Ruth
Huster, Harry E.	1921	4-20-1999	(h) Lysbeth (McCullough)
Irons, Agnes	1903	2-10-1994	(w) Orville
Irons, Orville H.	1904	1-09-1987	(h) Agnes (Robertson)
Jasper, Addie May	(2 yr. 7 Mo.)	1-29-1870	(d) W. R. & Nancy
Jasper, Charles E.	(Age 6 Mo.)	2-17-1870	(s) W. R. & Nancy
Jasper, Jennie S.	(Age 2 Mo.)	2-08-1882	(d) W. R. & Nancy
Jasper, Nancy J.	1845	12-13-1882	(w) W. R.
Jasper, W. R.	NO DATES		(h) Nancy J.
Keener, Betty Joan	1922	12-18-1922	(d) Pete & Sybil
Keener, Jack Edward	1933	5-03-1933	(ts) Pete & Sybil
Keener, Jerry Barnes	1933	5-03-1933	(ts) Pete & Sybil
Keener, Mary Judith	1934	7-04-1934	(d) Pete & Sybil

Name	Born	Died	Relation
Knight, Infant	1939	3-15-1939	(d) Allen & Mable
Louden, Beradine O.	?	1909	(d) L. C. & M. M
Louden, Charlotte G.	1844	4-04-1919	(w) Geo. W.
Louden, G. F.	1876	12-13-1898	(s) G. W. & C. G.
Louden, George W.	1844	8-18-1918	(h) Charlotte (v) CW
Louden, Minnie M.	?	8-15-1873	(d) Geo. & Charlotte
Malone, Ellen E.	1839	12-03-1883	(1st w) William C.
Malone, James F.	1872	11-09-1883	(s) William & Ellen
Malone, Mary (Shriver)	1850	7-29-1936	(2nd w) William C.
Malone, Rosa E.	1880	5-15-1898	(d) William & Ellen
Malone, William C.	1840	1932	(h) Ellen & Mary C.
Martin, Lettie	1839	11-01-1904	Single
McCullough, Clyde T.	1896	8-08-1987	(w) Henry
McCullough, Henry M.	1889	10-19-1958	(h) Clyde T.
McKinney, Gertrude	1890	7-12-1891	(d) L. H. & E. M.
McMahan, George W.	1907	4-09-1972	(s) Peter & Clara
Miller, Dorris Ann	1919	1919	
Mowery, Arkie F.	1912	1-13-1988	(h) Dorothy M. (Taylor)
Mowery, Donzil E.	1928	6-08-1949	(s) Orville & Hazel
Mowery, Dorothy M.	1913	12-05-1991	(w) Arkie F.
Mowery, Lorene	1931	5-10-1935	(d) Arkie & Dorthy
Mundell, Charles N.	1873	11-4-1918	(h) Dolly G.
Mundell, Dollie G.	1881	1954	(w) Charles N.
Murphy, George E.	1874	7-08-1951	(h) Nina
Murphy, Nina (Springer)	1878	1-26-1959	(w) George E.
Nichols, Anna Belle (Campbell)	1868	1-05-1952	(w) Hiram L.
Nichols, Harry O.	1896	1-31-1965	(h) M. Grace
Nichols, Hiram L.	1866	2-15-1946	(h) Anna Belle
Nichols, Jannettie	1831	4-28-1907	(w) Valintine
Nichols, Lillian Pearl	1904	7-25-1904	(d) Hiram & Anna Belle
Nichols, M. Grace (Barnes)	1891	2-18-1924	(w) Harry O.
Nichols, Pearle Irene (Jacobs)	1890	12-10-1966	(w) Russell
Nichols, Russell	1888	7-17-1974	(h) Pearle)
Nichols, Valintine	1826	6-09-1901	(h) Jannettie
Nichols, William C.	1920	9-09-1994	(h) Betty (Longfield)
Nuzum, Allen W. Jr.	1928	1929	
Nuzum, Betty Jean	1921	1921	
Nuzum, Clara A.	1862	4-13-1899	(w) Manasseh
Nuzum, Deborah	1872	1952	(w) Job R.
Nuzum, Howard E.	1899	8-03-1899	(s) Manasseh & C. A.
Nuzum, Job R.	1865	10-30-1933	(h) Deborah
Nuzum, Job S.	1843	1924	(h) Sarah M
Nuzum, Manasseh	1853	5-03-1918	(h) Clara A.
Nuzum, Phoebe Y.	1797	3-08-1859	(w) Richard B.
Nuzum, Richard B.	1795	04-30-1887	(h) Phoebe Y.
Nuzum, Sarah M.	1860	8-20-1918	(w) Job S.
Nuzum, Staats M.	1858	2-16-1904	(w) Cornelia
Nuzum, Zadoc J.	1862	5-27-1952	single
Prahl, Sheila Anne	1937	5-29-1997	(w) James
Sandon, Louis S.	1874	2-20-1896	
Satterfield, Austin Ambrose	1876	12-19-1944	(h) Idella V.
Satterfield, Enos L.	1853	5-15-1916	(h) Nancy A.
Satterfield, Idella V.	1875	2-25-1962	(w) Austin A.
Satterfield, J.M.	1883	5-30-1912	
Satterfield, Nancy A.	1858	11-09-1924	(w) Enos L.
Satterfield, Russell F.	1900	11-08-1943	(s) Austin & Idella
Satterfield, Wyona C.	1906	3-18-1912	(s) Austin & Idella

Name	Born	Died	Relationship
Shorter, Robert L.	1923	1924	
Shorter, Ruth K.	1916	11-30-1916	
Springer, Brady	(Age 5 mo.)	12-01-1874	(s) Zacheus & C.
Springer, Christianna	1847	7-06-1920	(w) Zacheus
Springer, Jane	?	4-02-1877	(w) Dennis
Springer, Jemima	1851	2-13-1914	(w) Richard
Springer, Matilda	?	10-15-1873	(d) Zacheus & C.
Springer, Pearl E.	1898	1921	(Mason)
Springer, R. T.	(Infant)	5-09-1869	
Springer, Richard	1845	10-27-1913	(h) Jemima
Springer, Zacheus	1842	2-12-1915	(h) Christianna (v) CW
Stuck, Infant	1931	1931	(s) Geo. & Ernestine
Summers, Ruth Ann	?	2-09-1937	
Thomas, Elisha	1812	12-30-1894	
Thomas, Sarah J.	1821	2-24-1895	
Thorne, Edward S., Jr.	1920	2-18-1998	(h) Joan (Hawkins)
Travis, Charles W.	1876	1956	(h) Florence B.
Travis, Ernest L.	NO DATES		(v) Span. Am. War
Travis, Florence B.	1872	2-25-1945	(w) Charles W.
Travis, Howard E.	1899	11-13-1921	(s) Charles W.
Vincent, Alice L.	?	11-05-1864	(d) E. & H.
Waite, Cindy	NO DATES		

1841 BOYCE-CLARK CEMETERY
(Colfax)

Name	Born	Died	Relationship
Boyce, Samuel	5-15-1783	4-13-1841	(h) Mary (Stines)
Clark, Martha	NO DATES		
6 Unmarked Graves			

This small burial ground is on the old Shaw family property in Union District at Colfax, one and one-half miles from Rt. 310 South near the Colfax Road, no longer in use and lost somewhere in the woods. In fact, if it weren't for the WPA readings in 1939 and other local historians who also made notes, its existence would be unknown. At one time, the graves were marked with fieldstones with the exception of two. One headstone read S.B. and another Martha Clark. According to WPA readings there are six other unmarked graves.

In December of 1997, I went in search of this place. Many old timers told me it was there and where it was, but I could not find it. I did find the high point of the property where one could look out over Guyses Run valley. Judging from the other graveyards that I had visited, this would have been the perfect site but there were no tombstones.

The tombstone marked S. B. could only have been that of Samuel Boyce. According to the Boyce family history, Samuel was born May 15, 1783 in Fayette County, Pennsylvania. He married German-born Mary Stines, and together they had 11 children: John F. Boyce (1808-1883) married Mary Peters; Elizabeth Boyce (1809-1884) unmarried; Clementine; William Boyce (1811-1890) married Catherine Rogers; Mary Boyce (1815-1910) married Joseph Carder and Archie Rogers; Katherine (1819-?) married Henry Williams; Samuel, Jr. (1820-1866) married Mary Vandergrift; Isaac (1822-1878) married Rebecca Poe; Francis (1825-1910) married Lucinda Fancher; Henry (1825-1910) married Triphenia Poe, Michael (1827-?) married Phoebe Ann Murphy.

The family settled, sometime after 1820, on a farm on Guyses Run near Springer's Bend (Colfax). When Samuel died, on April 13, 1841, he was buried on the farm at the top of the hill behind their homestead. This is the same year his son Samuel, Jr., would marry Mary Vandergrift (See Vandergrift Cemetery).

After the death of Samuel Sr., the family homestead burned down. Mary (Stines) Boyce sold the property to the Shaw family who built another house on the Boyce's foundation. Mary Boyce moved to a farm on Glady Creek and then to a farm on Cherry Run. Later in her advanced years she made her home with her two sons, Isaac

People and Places

and William. She died in 1879 at the age of 97 and is buried in the Lake Cemetery on Bunner Ridge, Marion County. In recent years, a portion of the old Boyce property was sold but the small cemetery remains somewhere on Shaw property. Mary Boyce had two other two sons, Michael who fought for the Confederacy and Samuel, Jr., who fought for the Union. This was truly a house divided.

This writer could find nothing about Martha Clarke. It is believed she may have been a relative of the Vandergrift family. She remains a mystery.

VANDERGRIFT CEMETERY
(Colfax)

This abandoned cemetery can be found one mile from Rt. 310 South on the Colfax Road. Turn left at the Fire Station Road. The cemetery is on top of the hill on the right. There is no road to it only a wide path. The 70x70 foot lot was fenced in at one time but is now lying on the ground. In 1938, the WPA recorded 21 unmarked graves. The earliest stone reads 1866 but the graveyard could have been started much earlier.

According to their family history, the Vandergrifts were Dunkards who came to Virginia (now WV) from Pennsylvania. Ebenezer and Phoebe had a homestead on a large farm between Goose Creek and Guyses Run.

Samuel Boyce, Jr. is buried here. He was born in Greene County, Pennsylvania in 1820. He and Mary Vandergrift were married in May of 1841. Samuel, Jr. was a veteran of the Civil War. His discharge papers read, "Age 41 years, 6 feet high, dark complexion, blue eyes, dark hair, occupation - Farmer". He was discharged on July 9, 1862 and died 4 years later, in 1866.

In their 25 years of marriage, Samuel and Mary had 10 children. They were: Ebenezer 1843-1878, who married Elizabeth VanGilder. Their children were Boyers Boyce, who became a minister and Viola (Hayhurst, Curry). Two infants died. Phoebe Jane married John Mundell. They had six children. Isaac married Havannah Morgan and had 12 children. Mary Elizabeth married Joshua Hawkins and had 11 children. Sarah married Dr. Newt Wattonhad and had five children. Eliza married Elias Satterfield and had eleven children. Virginia married Frank Satterfield and had eight children. Cristia Olive married Andrew Joseph Utt and they had 19 children. Samuel remained unmarried and died at age 65. Joanna married Reverend John Wesley VanGilder and had eight children.

Mary Elizabeth Boyce married Joshua Hawkins. They lived on the Hawkins family farm on Bunner Ridge, later moving to the Vandergrift property. Their children were: John born ?; Charles, born 1874, married Mary Satterfield; William, born 1875, married Eliza Ann Huffman; Samuel, born 1879; Edward married Leona Kincaid; Henry, born 1882, married Delia Huffman; Mary, born 1884, married Charlie Martin; Harry, born 1887, married Ona Nutter; Andrew, born 1888, married Ada Lake; Sarah, born 1890, married Walter Reynolds and Ebenezer, born 1894, married 1st Ruth Giles, 2nd Isabella Ford.

Charles owned the property in 1886. He farmed and had a small dairy. The cemetery did not survive property ownership changes and is no longer being used as a burial ground. Mother nature has re-claimed it.

Below Left: Vandergrift Cemetery established in 1866. Right: Tombstone of Samuel Boyce, Jr., Civil War veteran.
Courtesy of Linda Kitner

VANDERGRIFT CEMETERY

Name	Born	Death	Relationship
Boyce, Mary (Vandergrift)	1824	11-26-1902	(w) Samuel, Jr.
Boyce, Samuel, Jr.	1820	4-01-1866	(h) Mary (v) CW Co. C, 6th WV Inf
Hawkins, Joshua E.	1850	4-19-1920	(h) Mary Elizabeth
Hawkins, Mary Elizabeth (Boyce)	1847	1-06-1944	(w) Joshua E.
Hawkins, Samuel	1879	9-05-1899	(s) Joshua & Mary
Martin, Fay	?	1912	(s) Charlie & Mary
Martin (Hawkins)	NO DATES		
Vandergrift, Grant	?	3-16-1870	3 yrs., 1 Mo., 13 days
Vandergrift, John	1829	1862	(v) CW 1st W.Va. Lt. Art

John Vandergrift enlisted in the Union Army on August 16, 1861 and was assigned to Company C, sixth Regiment Infantry. He died in November 1862 in Grafton, WV of disease.

1840 LITTLE CEMETERY
(Sarrietta)

Thomas Little Cemetery established in 1840.

Located in Grant District off U. S. 250 South past Middletown Mall. Turn left on Colfax Road, and travel one mile to Poplar Island Road. Go two-tenths of a mile to the private driveway of Homer Currance on the left. Cemetery is on the Currance property. Owner requests that you ask permission. It is no longer used for interment. WPA readings of 1939 show 15 marked and 19 unmarked graves here.

The earliest headstone, dated 1840, is that of Rachel, wife of Thomas Little, Sr., but there could have been others before this date. Indians are buried here. Rachel was 76 years old when she died and was buried on the home place. Rachel's maiden name was Nixon, daughter of Jonathon Nixon and was a widow with four children before she married Thomas Little.

Thomas Little, Sr. was born in England in 1765; he emigrated to America with three older brothers. He is reportedly a Revolutionary War veteran, who was a private in a Pennsylvania Legion although he would have been only 11 years old when the war began and was 16 years old when the actual fighting stopped. Records show he was still entitled to 200 acres of land for his service.

Marion County records indicate there were several surnames of Little in the area prior to the late 1800's. They included a John and Adonijah, (who was killed by the Indians), Stockley, and Absolum. All of them were traders with the Indians. Legend has it that Absolum once swapped enough material for a dress and a dress pattern for 400 acres of land.

These listings were found in Monongahelia County Survey Book No. 1, Absolum Little, Sr., 400 acres on both sides of Glady Creek in 1776. From Survey Book No. 4: Henry Warsal settled very early on the Tygart Valley River on 400 acres. He sold his acreage to Absolum Little in 1776 with river frontage at the "fish pot". It is a reasonable assumption that Absolum Little could have been a relative of Thomas Little even though no records were kept.

In 1806, John Tyler, Esquire, Governor of the Commonwealth of Virginia, presented to Thomas Little by virtue of a Land Office Treasury Warrant No. 3775, a 190-acre tract or parcel of land bearing the date January 22, 1806. This was 15 years after the last Indian attack in this area. The land was described as "lying and being in the county of Harrison, and drains of the "Tyger's" Valley River". Later Thomas purchased several hundred acres more and settled on it.

During this period, Rachel Nixon Sparks and her husband, George moved from the Boothsville area to what is now known as Levels, which is just across the river from Poplar Island. The couple and their four children lived in a log cabin George had built for his family.

One winter night before retiring, Mr. Sparks stepped outside the cabin. When he failed to come back inside, his family went out to look for him and found his tracks in the snow. A short distance from the cabin, the footprints ended abruptly. No other tracks were found, either human or animal and no cries for help were heard. George was never seen again.

A year or so after the disappearance of George Sparks, it seems that Thomas Little, a bachelor living alone in his cabin across the river, told someone, "God preserve my soul, that woman can't raise them kids over there all by herself." So he hopped into his boat and rowed over to the east side of the river to the Sparks cabin and brought Rachel and her four children to live with him. At this point in her life, it probably didn't take much persuasion to convince the young widow to take a new husband. Thomas Little reared the Sparks children as his own and the couple had four more children. Two of which were born before they made the 1808 journey on horseback to the Harrison County Courthouse to get married.

Thomas Little, Sr. died six months after his oldest son, Thomas Allen, and ten years after his wife, Rachel. Their three tombstones stand out among all the others. All three were cut from the same stone quarry, which was on the Little property and probably engraved at the gravesite. The stone cutter was A. Fleming, who engraved his mark on the tombstones. Note the way the word "body" is spelled on the headstone:

> Here lies the boddy of
> THOMAS LITTLE
> husband of R. Little
> DIED
> Sept. 27th. 1851
> In the 86th. Year
> of his age
> AF

Thomas A. Little III died at the age of 22 years 2 months and 2 days. He worked for the B&O Railroad and his tombstone has a railroad lantern engraved on the back.

The farm stayed in the Little family for generations. Sections of the farm were slowly sold and what was left was purchased in 1930, by Thomas Richie, who later sold it to Russell Nichols. Mr. Nichols sold 40 acres to Lt. Col. Homer and Ann Currance in 1964, and they built a new log home almost in the same spot as Thomas Little's. During the summer of 1997 Boy Scout Troop #10 from the Baptist Temple cleared off the small cemetery and put up a split rail fence as an Eagle project. A historical marker was put up that included the history of the small graveyard. Way to go, scouts! Bless you.

A huge red-oak tree once stood by the graveyard but died in 1985 and had to be cut down. All that is left today is its stump that measures five feet across. A Department of Natural Resources forest officer said it had to have been at least 500 years old. Oh, the stories it could tell!

The following is a list of those buried here:

LITTLE CEMETERY

Name	Birth	Death	Relationship
Gallagher, Harry Brooks	1909	11-16-1912	
Gallagher, Nile William	1910	6-07-1910	
Little, Delia A.	?	1-31-1858	(d) Thomas A. & Kahziah (Kiz)
Little, Georgie	NO DATES		
Little, Hattie J.	1893	7-30-1904	(d) George & Ann
Little, Lewis	?	7-25-1868	
Little, Lewis O.	1877	7-19-1888	(s) Geo. & Ann
Little, Mary E.	1865	1-19-1874	(d) Lewis & Phoebe
Little, Rachel	1764	8-03-1840	(w) Thomas, Sr.
Little, T.A.	1874	12-18-1896	(s) Thomas A., Jr.

Little, Thomas, Sr.	1765	9-25-1851	(h)Rachel)
			(v)Revolutionary War
Little, Thomas Allen	1814	3-06-1851	(s) Thomas & Rachel
Prickett, John L.	?	11-23-1860	
Swearingen, John S.	?	2-01-1855	
Vincent, Cassandra Jane (Little)		NO DATES	(w)Freeman Vincent
			(d) Jane Little
Vincent, Mary A.	?	5-05-1860	

1903 SMALLWOOD CEMETERY
(River Run Road)

Smallwood Cemetery on River Run Road. Established in 1903.

The Smallwood Cemetery in Grant District is located on private property. Take Rt. 250 past Middletown Mall and turn left on River Run Road. At the Y turn to the left, and go six tenths of mile. Cemetery is on the left in the back of the Burl Smith property.

In 1888, John H. and Margaret Smallwood purchased a farm. It would be here that their son Everett D. Smallwood died and his parents would lay him to rest. As more deaths occurred within the family, this portion of the property was set aside for their burial ground. The graveyard has continued to grow and remains in use today. Surrounded by woods on a gentle slope, it has been well taken care of and is very neat. The setting is quiet and pleasant. In the center, shading a few gravesites is a large native rhododendron. Five World War II veterans are buried here. Two are marked with bronze plaques.

Name	Name
Mallard Haze Corbett	Charles L. Smallwood
West Virginia	Tec 5 U.S. Army
S1 USNR	World War II
World War II	1925-1982
1918-1963	

Others in
SMALLWOOD CEMETERY

Name	Birth	Death	Relationship
Corbitt, Alma M.	1921	1975	(w) Mallard
Corbitt, Mallard Haze	1918	4-06-1963	(h) Alma M. (v) WWII
Cox, Anna Delcie	1905	6-17-1978	(w) Lester
Cox, Lester Lee	1896	2-10-1938	(h) Anna
Cox, Lester Lee, Jr.	1935	13-1935	(s) Lester, Sr. & Anna
Huber, Daniel H.	1918	5-11-1982	(v) WWII
Mathews, Mildred Myrtle	1914	1935	(w) William
Metz, Betty Elizabeth	1926	11-06-1926	(d) Ulric & Hazel

Metz, Hazel W.	1908	3-11-1980	(w) Ulric & Hazel
Miller, Alma Pearl	1895	1954	(Smallwood)
Smallwood, Alma Edith	1905	9-29-1948	(d) Harry & Julia
Smallwood, Alma M. (Abel)	NO DATES		
Smallwood, Chad Michael	1973	10-25-1973	(ts) John E.& Pamela
Smallwood, Charles L.	1925	9-11-1982	(h) Garnett (v) WWII
Smallwood, Clara R.	1930	1-20-1992	(w) Russell, Jr.
Smallwood, Claude E.	1895	1906	Killed in the mines.
Smallwood, Claude E.	1917	9-24-1938	
Smallwood, Crystal Dawn	1973	10-25-1973	(td) James E. & Pamela
Smallwood, Everett D.	?	1-28-1903	(s) John & Margaret
Smallwood, Garnett E.	1924	7-14-1997	(w) Charles L.
Smallwood, Glenn R.	1893	10-14-1965	(h) Ethel, Alma (Abel) & Phyliss
Smallwood, John H	1843	1-31-1924	(h) Margaret
Smallwood, Lewis C.	1866	1948	(h) Minnie
Smallwood, Margaret	NO DATES		(w) John H.
Smallwood, Minnie M.	1873	1943	(w) Lewis C.
Smallwood, Rufus Glenn	NO DATES		(h) Alma
Smith, Earl L.	1908	5-26-1995	(h) Viola Virginia
Smith, Harriet Ann	1951	7-13-1951	(d) Harry & Waneta
Smith, Harry Lee	1929	7-15-1988	(h) Julia Waneta
Summers, Norma J.	1933	1987	(w) James
West, Violet R.	(Huber)	1919	1990

SHRIVER CEMETERY
(Levels)

Above: Shriver Cemetery established in 1814. Fig. 19 Inset: Unique tombstone of Claude Motter. It is made of Hammond Brick material.

This cemetery is in Union District. From East Fairmont, take Route 310 south to Crossroads and then turn right. Shriver Cemetery is in the middle of Tygart Mine Property. Turn left at the Tygart Mine entrance. The guard will stop you and ask your business. Access will not be denied. Cemetery is hidden behind a gob pile. When permission to enter has been granted, take the second road on the right. I was told by the guard I might have to dodge monster trucks that were covering-up a gob pile at the time. I saw none and safely entered the one lane cemetery road, reserved in a deed for cemetery use.

Cemetery parking is limited. Many years ago legislation was passed requiring fencing around graveyards because of wandering livestock, however, the gateposts and original fence that once surrounded the cemetery is all that remains. In excellent condition, the cemetery there is very neat with beautiful old yucca plants in the older section of the graveyard.

Off center in the grounds, there is a graceful hemlock tree adding to the landscape. A birdbath under the hemlock caught my eye. Upon closer observation I found the engraving for Claude A. Motter who died in 1925. He was the son of Will Motter, who worked at the Hammond Firebrick Company. He made this birdbath out of the light colored firebrick clay and had it engraved for his son's monument.

John and Mary Shriver settled on the Tygart Valley River in 1800. John was born 1753 in Germany and Mary who was much younger, was born in Maryland where they lived until moving to Virginia. Five children were born to them in Maryland; the first was born when John was in his forties. In 1814, John died and was buried on their farm, which was the beginning of the Shriver Cemetery. Mary's grave is not marked.

One of the oldest legible tombstones was that of Mary Shriver. She died in 1851. The stonecutter again initialed his work: A.F. (A. Fleming). Some of the tombstones are facing the east while others face the west.

Shortly after the death of John an unidentified man was found floating in the river. He was buried near John in one of the oldest cemeteries along the river.

John and Mary's children were: Jacob, who married Anna Bunner; Susannah, who married Thomas Gorsuch; Samuel, who died a young man; Daniel, who married Lavina Nuzum, daughter of "Black Dick" Nuzum, and John, who married Jane Nuzum, daughter of John Nuzum of the Nuzum's Mill settlement.

Jacob (died 1873) and Ann (died 1887) Shriver bought 222 acres of land near his home place on the river in 1843. They had two sons: John, who was a mechanic, and James, a blacksmith. Jacob, John (died 1857) and James (died 1891) and their families are buried here. The land stayed in the Shriver family for 99 years, when it began being slowly sold off.

The cemetery was deeded to a board of trustees separate from the rest of the property that now belongs to Southern Ohio Coal Company. It is still in use as a cemetery today. WPA readings indicate there are 42 unmarked graves. Here is a list of those known to be laid to rest here.

SHRIVER CEMETERY

Name	Born	Death	Relationship
Anderson, George W.	1857	1939	(h) Mary R.
Anderson, John A.	1886	1970	
Anderson, Mary R.	1870	1951	(w) Geo. W
Bacon, Nancy Freeman	1863	1942	(d) Issac Parsons
Biddle, Enos M.	1856	1884	
Burnsworth, Omar R.	?	1966	(h) Ora
Burnsworth, Ora L.	?	1980	(w) Omar
Canfield, Alma E.	1906	1964	
Canfield, John	1876	3-17-1970	(h) Mary
Canfield, Sarah Jane	1884	10-28-1957	(w) John
Clayton, Judith	1935	1989	(d) Ruth Keller
Fetty, Lillian Gertrude	1904	1-21-1906	
Freeman, Charles Ray	1927	11-10-1957	(s) Georgia Freeman
Freeman, Frank D.	1898	7-30-1963	
GIRL	?	1957	
Graves, Walter Earl, Jr.	1960	7-12-1963	(s) Walter & Lorraine
Griffith, Ernie	1883	1972	(h) Lily
Griffith, Lily A. Martin	1883	1967	(w) Ernie
Hansford, Nancy Ellen	1858	5-19-1890	
Hawkins, Roberta K.	1936	12-17-1998	
Hawkins, Isaac	1820	3-19-1866	
Hicks, Bessie	1889	1980	(w) Charles
Hicks, Charles	1897	1968	(h) Bessie
Ingram, Charlotte M.	1890	1970	(w) John W.
Ingram, Emma Beryle P.	1910	1947	(w) Holbert
Ingram, Holbert F.	1909	12-25-1983	(h) Emma
Ingram, John W.	1880	1961	(h) Charlotte
Irons, Charles	1817	4-07-1897	(h) Malissa

Irons, Charles R.	1885	1-27-1903	(s) Charles & Malissa
Irons, Goldie A.	1900	10-15-1901	(d) Joseph
Irons, Joseph	1855	5-11-1936	(s) Charles and (h) Nanna
Irons, Malissa (Shriver)	1830	9-16-1903	(w) Charles
Irons, Nanna E.	1863	4-07-1897	(w) Joseph
Keller, Ruth Esther	1916	1995	(d) Jessie & Bessie Weaver
Keener, Boyd "Rat"	1897	12-23-1964	(h) Elsie Varie
Keener, Clyde Russell	1891	1954	(s) Martin & Lamina
Keener, Elsie Varied	1890	3-09-1972	(w) Boyd
Keener, Howard Martin	1899	1983	(s) Martin & Lamina
Keener, George F.	1948	1986	
Keener, J.C.	1813	6-25-1896	
Keener, Lavina	1870	2-23-1951	(w) Martin
Keener, Lona May	1890	1960	
Keener, Martin A.	1864	11-05-1903	(h) Lavina
Keener, Mary Ann	NO DATES		(w) Joseph
Keener, Novella I.	1903	1975	(w) Howard M.
Kiger, Jessie A.	1898	1898	(s) Samuel
Kiger, Samuel B.	1876	1901	(Father)
Knight, Clarence Junior	1933	11-15-1933	23 days old
Knight, Eliza A.	1855	5-15-1930	(s) Robert
Knight, Isaac W.	1919	2-10-2001	(h) Lucille
Knight, Ivan Neal	1933	11-15-1933	
Lemmon, Mathias Dilworth	1851	9-27-1853	(s) Jacob & Nancy
Linn, Sarah S.	1831	7-28-1869	(w) B.
Martin, Eldora D.	1878	1962	(h) Grace M.
Martin, Grace M.	1890	1968	(w) Eldora
Martin, Sarah V.	1881	1936	(d) Joseph & Mary Keener
Martin, William F.	1892	1-30-1957	(v) WWI
Motter, Claude A.	1900	9-10-1925	(s) William & Nannie
Motter, Claude Wilbert	1904	7-17-1970	
Motter, Nannie M. (Knight)	1882	1908	(w) William J.
Motter, William J.	1863	1940	(h) Nannie M.
Peterlin, Jeremy	1997	2002	(s) Danette Shorter
Phillips, Vallie Irons	1888	1-06-1981	(d) Joe Irons
Pratt, Daisy E.	1907	1968	(w) Cecil J.
Pratt, Cecil J.	1906	1957	(h) Daisy E.
Poling, Dorothea Elaine	1936	1939	(d) Henry & Juanita
Poling, Harry G.	1910	1940	(s) Oscar & Hattie
Poling, Hattie D.	1888	1963	(w) Oscar
Poling, Joseph Michael	1949	1960	
Poling, Mary M.	1852	11-14-1937	(w) Stephen
Poling, Stephen	1845	4-04-1932	(h) Mary
Poling, Oscar E.	1884	1969	(h) Hattie
Potter, Davey L.	1935	4-05-1982	
Robinette, Charles W.	1948	1948	(s) James & Mary Agnes
Satterfield, Ely	1829	1901	(h) Emily
Satterfield, Emily J.	1831	10-01-1897	(w) Ely
Shaw, Sarah A.	1830	3-29-1860	(w) B.
Shorter, Lewis G.	1912	8-06-1980	(v) WWII
Shorter, Norma (Holt)	1907	1945	(w) William
Shorter, Paul R.	1979	6-05-1985	
Shriver, Anna	1798	2-21-1887	(w) Jacob
Shriver, Henry	1853	12-18-1908	
Shriver, Ingabe	1827	3-19-1908	(w) James
Shriver, Jacob	1796	2-17-1873	(h) Anna
Shriver, James	1820	6-19-1891	(h) Mary C.

Shriver, John	1754	4-18-1814	(h) Mary
Shriver, John	1806	6-20-1885	(h) Jane
Shriver, John C.	1854	1-07-1857	(s) J. & M.
Shriver, John, Jr.	1823	1-23-1895	(h) Matilda
Shriver, Jane (Nuzum)	1809	9-24-1889	(w) John
Shriver, Helen	1866	3-05-1868	(d) J. & L.
Shriver, Mary C.	1823	8-31-1851	(w) James
Shriver, Matilda	1826	2-23-1900	(w) John, Jr.
Shriver, R. L.	1861	4-18-1880	(s) John & Matilda
Shriver, Sarah	1863	10-09-1869	(d) J. & L.
Shriver, Virginia	1860	10-12-1863	(d) J. & L.
Smell, Margaret	1826	12-14-1893	(w) A. P.
Stackhouse, Ambreanna D	1990	6-10-1991	
Stackhouse, Dorothy L.	1905	1977	(w) Virgil
Stackhouse, Edward G.	?	8-15-1942	"Buck"
Stackhouse, Kenneth E.	1934	6-01-1994	(v) Korea
Stackhouse, Virgil Lee	1907	10-05-1970	(h) Dorothy L
Simmons, John T.	1873	2-17-1918	(h) Nettie
Simmons, Nettie Alice	1880	5-08-1965	(w) John T.
Summers, Virgil Lee	1952	1952	(s) Harold & Bessie
Vincent, D.W.	1829	2-02-1912	
West, Thomas W.	1902	1982	(h) Georgia
West, Georgia B.	1903	9-01-1970	(w) Thomas
Williams, Charles H.	1887	3-16-1910	
Williams, Dessie M.	1883	12-02-1883	(d) W. L. & A. C.
Williams, Kate	1851	1927	
Williams, William	1854	12-06-1898	
Willis, Delphia Merle	1904	1953	Mother
Willis, Lawrence H.	1938	1-10-1992	(h) Theresa
Yannoff, Jim	1880	6-15-1972	Immigrant

1814 NUZUM NO. 1

To find this graveyard from East Fairmont, take Rt. 310 South to Crossroads and turn right towards Goose Creek. Turn left at the next intersection at the sign to the Church of the Brethren. The cemetery is beside the church on two acres of land reserved by Richard Nuzum, which he conveyed from his original grant in 1814 for use of a graveyard. The deed stipulated that no one be refused burial in it. Formerly referred to as the Dunkard Cemetery, it is still used as a burial ground.

Just as the name implies, Pleasant Hill is indeed a pleasant hill. Traditionally landscaped like the most older graveyards with ancient arborvitae (Tree of Life) trees, it has the perfectly quiet, country setting beside the white

The Nuzum Family Historical Society mounted this bronze plaque beside the cannon in 1965 at the Nuzum No. 1 Cemetery.

Above: Nuzum No. 1 Cemetery was established up on the hill from Nuzum's Mill in 1814. Later the Church of the Brethren was built beside it. Inset: A plaque placed by the Nuzum Historical Society naming the cemetery.

church building. A large, very old maple tree shades a large portion of the middle of the graveyard. The Nuzum Family Historical Society placed the two well-preserved Nuzum gristmill stones on the grounds as a reminder of the beginning of the town of Nuzum's Mill.

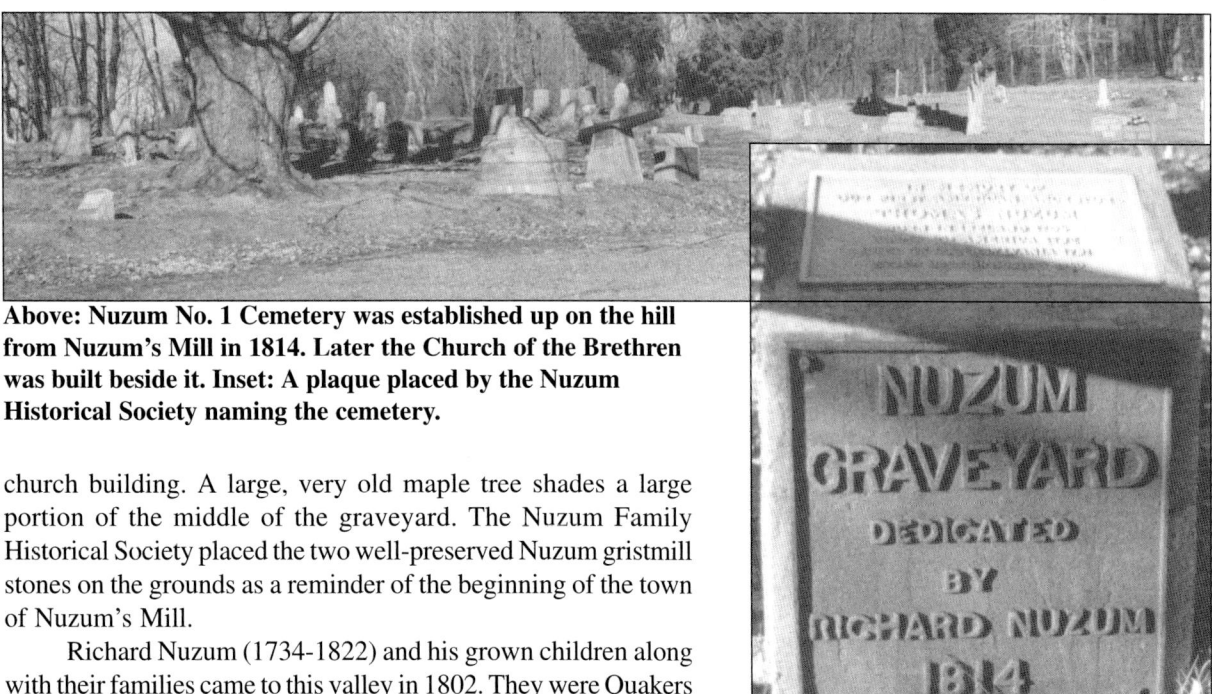

Richard Nuzum (1734-1822) and his grown children along with their families came to this valley in 1802. They were Quakers with strict beliefs. Richard's sons (John, a millwright, and William), erected the first mill on the lower Tygart Valley River. It was rebuilt and remodeled several times by John. Beside the original millstones is a Civil War cannon that serves as a memorial to all the military veterans buried here. It was presented to the Trustees of the Nuzum Cemetery by Rufus A. West from Morgantown, on September 10, 1939. Trustees at that time were Charles W. Vandergrift, Clarence Nuzum and Clifford C. Herron.

Thomas, the family's patriarch and father of Richard, died before 1791. Richard's wife, Hannah, (?-1791) also died before the move in 1802. Richard lived for 20 years in his new settlement; long enough to see the town of Nuzum's Mill grow. In 1822, Richard, in ill health, may have been living with his grandson and wife, "Black Dick" and Phoebe Springer of Texas (now Colfax). Richard died in 1822 and according to *The Nuzum Family History*; Richard was buried in the Springer Graveyard (now the Colfax Cemetery) at Texas (now Colfax). No markers are found for him but he probably was buried in an unmarked grave like his good friend, John Springer.

Off to the side of the cemetery is a huge red oak tree that must be at least 300 years old. Here, sort of hidden from the entrance, is a headstone that would attract immediate attention even without mention. It is an attractive black granite portrait tombstone that is a fine example of modern stone cutting technology with tombstones. It marks the grave of David "Big Dave" Cumpston 1957-1994 (April 28) who died in Texas as a result of a motorcycle accident. A picture of Fortney's Mill (one of his favorite places) in Preston County, WV is etched on the front of it along with a depiction of the state of Texas and the poem, "Foot Prints", on the back. A motorcycle is etched beside the mill.

NUZUM NO. 1 CEMETERY

Buried in front of the church

Name	Birth	Death	Relationship
Hannah Mabel Vandergrift	1895	4-11-1974	(w) Huey D.
Huey D. Vandergrift	1896	2-13-1953	(h)Hannah(v) WW I

Here is the list of those known by this author that are buried in the cemetery.

Armstrong, Avis M.	1905	1990	(w) Edward F.
Armstrong, Edward F.	1887	1961	(h) Arvil M.
Barniak, Lewis	1903	1986	(h) Mary

Barniak, Mary	1904	1988	(w) Lewis
Bartholow, Arthur E.	1922	1-26-1998	
Bartholow, Kathleen J. (Collins)	1933	8-03-1988	
Baughman, Brenda K.	1946	1984	
Bean, Martha Florence	1894	6-08-1925	(w) C. E.
Bower, Jacob	64 years old		
Bowman, Martha	1828	6-07-1900	
Boyce, Anna Marie	1930	4-29-1998	(w) Chester
Boyce, Emily	?	4-18-1938	
Boyce, Lester Lee	1932	11-11-1932	(s) Herman
Boyce, S. E.	1861	1926	
Brannon, Laura Ethel	1884	1949	
Bulleck, Steve	1907	2-12-1966	(v) WW II
Carpenter, Clara	1908	1908	(d) C. C. & M. E.
Carson, Victoria France	1869	1947	
Cheuvront, Hazel	1905	2-07-1992	(w) Raleigh R.
Cheuvront, Raleigh R.	1904	1976	(h) Hazel (Goodwin)
Cheuvront, Ruby	?	6-24-1938	
Collins, Charles L.	1906	1974	(h) E. Florence
Collins, Charles, R.	1906	1974	(h) Florence (Henderson)
Collins, Gertrude B.	1890	1977	(w) John W.
Collins, Howard	1915	1917	
Collins, John W.	1880	1979	(h) Gertrude B.
Collins, Kathleen	1929	1970	(w) Virgil
Collins, Kenneth	1913	1924	
Collins, May P. (Rice)	1932	1984	(1st w) Robert Lewis, Sr.
Collins, Robert Jr.	1965	1981	(s) Robert & May P.
Collins, Robert Lewis	1928	1-06-1996	(h) May & Peggy
Collins, Theadous Gean	?	9-16-1937	
Collins, Virgil	1917	11-15-1989	(h) Kathleen (v) WW II
Cottrill, Edward	1902	1965	(h) Laura
Cottrill, Laura Gay (Bowyers)	1906	11-04-1993	(w) Edward
Cumpston, Captolia N.	1870	1955	(w) Harrison L.
Cumpston, David G.	1957	4-28-1994	(h) Tammy (Schumaker)
Cumpston, Earl J.	1901	6-02-1960	(h) Mussetta Gum (v) WW II
Cumpston, Fay Harrison	1903	3-26-1961	(h) Martha Jewett
Cumpston, Harrison L.	1867	1935	(h) Captolia N.
Cumpston, Martha Jewett	1908	2-22-1086	(w) Fay Harrison
Cumpston, Patricia Y.	1953	12-30-1969	
Curry, Helen	?	8-07-1922	(d) Clyde & Anna
Danley, James	NO DATES		(v) C W
Danley, Jonathan J.	1837	9-25-1922	(h) Rosezilia
Danley, Rosezilia	1857	10-05-1913	(w) Jonathan J
Davis, Donald L.	1972	7-25-1972	
Davis, Elsa A.	?	5-10-1884	(d) W. & H.
Davis, Emily	1838	5-05-1881	(w) Wesley F.
Davis, Essa K.	1893	1913	(d) John & Hannah
Davis, Fletcher	1921	1921	(s) Ira & Ida
Davis, George A.	1888	1892	(s) John & Hannah
Davis, Hannah J.	1865	1933	(w) John E.
Davis, Hannah Ruth	1899	1963	(d) John & Hannah J.
Davis, Ida H.	1891	1960	(w) Ira N.
Davis, Ira N.	1887	1963	(h) Ida H.
Davis, John E.	1865	1933	(h) Hannah J.
Davis, Kathryn L.	1909	1910	(d) John & Hannah
Davis, Martha	1902	1975	
Davis, Phoebe A.	1892	1892	(d) John & Hannah

Davis, Regina E.	1926	6-28-1976	(w) Lewis E.
Davis, Roy, Jr.	1936	11-25-1996	(h) Hazel (Brown)
Davis, Violet	1913	1913	(d) Ira & Ida
Davis, Wesley F.	1836	?	(h) Emily (v) C W
Delany, Earl R.	1899	1965	
Dexter, Grace	1907	1908	
Dodson, Larry Sean	1967	1967	
Dodson, Steven Michael	1958	6-06-1964	
Downey, Alfred	NO DATES		(v) C W
Edman, Rev. Clarence D.	1907	1986	(h) Lila Mae (Collier)
Edman, Lila Mae	1920	6-01-2001	(w) Clarence D.
Elder, Sue Ellen	1951	?	(d) David & Mildred
Falls, Chester W.	1920	11-04-1974	(h) Leona
Falls, Floyd D., Sr.	1943	1991	
Falls, John Lee	1948	10-12-1957	
Falls, Leona M.	1920	3-08-1991	(w) Chester
Falls, Melvin	1890	12-20-1980	(h) Rosie E. (v) WW I
Falls, Rosie E.	1896	1-25-1969	(w) Melvin
Fast, Chester	1910	6-12-1995	(h) Ruby
Fast, Ella	1891	1973	(w) Henry J.
Fast, Henry J.	1890	1941	(h) Ella (Hayes)
Fast, Ruby	1915	11-22-1992	(w) Chester
Fast, William R.	1920	1979	
Fetty, Charles O.	?	1-11-1927	
Fetty, Charley H.	1910	11-19-1912	
Fetty, Dessie R.	1878	10-20-1918	(w) J. O.
Fetty, Garnet M.	1906	5-28-1906	
Fetty, J.O.	1877	1-06-1939	(h) Dessie M.
Fluharty, L. Dale	1927	1987	(h) Virginia G.
Ford, Delbert C.	1913	1979	
Garlow, Alfred E.	1832	8-27-1891	(h) Nancy
Garlow, James W.	1849	4-05-1908	(v) CW
Garlow, Nancy	1838	3-28-1901	(w) Alfred
Gilmore, J. Ray	1906	1988	(1st h) Lillian F. Kirk
Goodwin, Brooks N.	1909	1962	(h) Edith A. (Lewis)
Goodwin, Charles	1933	4-29-1933	
Goodwin, Edith A.	1905	1-30-1995	(w) Brooks N.
Goodwin, Kenneth Lee	1932	4-22-1980	
Goodwin, Myrtle M.	1876	1962	(w) William L.
Goodwin, Scott Allen	1965	5-06-1986	(s) Edsel & Pauline
Goodwin, William L.	1875	1965	(h) Myrtle M.
Griffie, Thomas	1822	12-14-1909	
Griffith, Flemand	NO DATES		(v) Indian War
Griffith, Gerald F.	1906	6-01-1995	(h) Nondise Opa
Griffith, John A.	1888		(h) Mary A.
Griffith, Mary A.	NO DATES		(w) John A.
Griffith, Nondise (Boyce)	1910	11-12-1980	(w) Gerald F.
Griffith, William G.	1930	1932	(s) Gerald & Nondise
Grivich, George	1892	1976	
Gum, Mussetta (White)	1926	1975	(w) Earl Cumpston
Haddix, Claude E.	1900	3-23-1924	
Haddix, George O.	1892	1976	(h) Nettie & Rosanna
Haddix, I. Mable	1918	1919	(d) F. R. & D. M.
Haddix, John Oscar	1892	3-11-1998	(v) W W II
Haddix, June A. (Martin)	1923	4-23-2001	(w) Lloyd E.
Haddix, Minnie G.	1920	1985	(w) Walter
Haddix, Nettie N.	?	1924	(1st w) Geo. O.

Name	Birth	Death	Notes
Haddix, Rosanna	1908	1981	(2nd w) Geo. O.
Haddix, Walter B.	1916	3-28-1992	(h) Minnie (Jenkins)
Haddix, William Max, Jr.	1957	1-29-1957	
Hadix, Mabel	1912	1913	
Hager, Charles M.	1874	1939	(h) Martha V.
Hager, Martha V.	1877	1939	(w) Charles M.
Hair, Albert D.	1876	1940	
Hair, Inez	1880	1954	
Hall, Elisha	NO DATES		(v) C W
Hall, Lester E.	1871	1902	
Hall, Mariah H.	?	9-20-1834	
Hall, Martha (Nuzum)	1859	1924	
Hall, William H.	1855	8-29-1891	
Hannah, John N.	1878	1970	(h) Mary M.
Hannah, Mary M.	1879	1958	(w) John N.
Hannah, Violet S.	1902	1973	(w) Walter M.
Hannah, W. M. Rev.	1850	9-28-1936	
Hannah, Walter M.	1906	1945	(h) Violet S.
Hayes, Clay Allen	1963	5-10-2002	(s) Donald & Karen
Hayes, Opal Belle	1914	2-02-1993	(w) Chester (Ott)
Helsley, Elhannon	1856	1922	(h) Rebecca M.
Helsley, Rebecca M.	1865	1947	(w) Elhannon
Helsley, Sarah (Nuzum)	1868	1924	
Henderson, H. H.	NO DATES		(v) C W (Union)
Herron, Amanda L.	1897	1979	(w) James L.
Herron, B. Dexter	1872	1945	
Herron, Bernard Earl	1901	1903	
Herron, Helen	1860	1947	(w) Marion L
Herron, Helen Prodan	1924	10-06-1986	(w) Jack B.
Herron, James C.	1895	1918	(v) WW I
Herron, James L.	1896	12-16-1969	(h) Amands L.
Herron, Joe	1929	1929	(s) James & Amanda
Herron, John	1923	1923	(s) James & Amanda
Herron, Marion L.	1860	1936	(h) Helen
Herron, Noraine O.	1893	1973	
Herron, Robert Eugene	1928	7-27-03	(s) James & Amanda
Herron, Stella Jane	1872	1968	
Hite, Bruce	1854	1931	(s) George & Hulda
Hite, George M.	1817	1907	(h) Hulda
Hite, Hulda F.	1829	4-06-1903	(w) Geo. M.
Hite, J. Otis	1865	1896	(s) George & Hulda
Hoffman, Hershel L.	1927	2-14-1934	(s) O. L. & K. A.
Hoffman, Katherine A.	1906	1976	w) Orva L.
Hoffman, Orva L.	1907	1983	(h) Katherine A.
Holden, Ellsworth I.	1919	1959	(h) Elta L.
Holden, Elta L. (Fast)	1917	7-27-1992	(w) Ellsworth & Valatine
Hughes, Hester	1883	9-07-1934	
Ingemanson, Eric	1905	4-09-1965	
Jacobs, Patty L.	1970	1970	
Jacobs, Pearl B.	1933	1984	
Jenkins, Augusta M.	1884	?	(w) Gideon R.
Jenkins, Gideon R.	1877	1957	(h) Augusta M.
Jenkins, James W.	1853	1918	(h) Josephine (v) CW
Jenkins, Josephine	1860	?	(w) James W.
Jenkins, Mary A.	1883	10-11-1974	
Keener, Basil B.	1895	6-12-1978	(v) WW I
Keener, Elizabeth K. (Lizzy)	1896	1975	

Kelley, Vernon E.	1906	1929	
King, Dalton Ryan (Infant)	1999	6-13-1999	(s) Richard & Lisa
Kinkaid, Alice	1871	1915	(w) Charles
Kinkaid, Guy	NO DATES		(v) WW I
Kinkaid, Nettie E.	1893	12-05-1898	(d) C. M. & A.
Kirk, Bertha E.	1911	4-04-1989	(1st w) Silas H.
Kirk, Clara Alice	1874	1953	(w) Daniel W.
Kirk, Daniel Webster Rev.	1857	1930	(h) Mary M. & Clara
Kirk, Dorothy Dare	1903	8-25-1991	(w) George W.
Kirk, Enoch M.	1862	1926	
Kirk, George W.	1900	12-30-1985	(h) Dorothy Dare
Kirk, George Webster	1885	1890	
Kirk, Howard E.	1933	5-29-1933	
Kirk, John E.	1892	1892	
Kirk, Joseph	1889	1889	
Kirk, Lillian Gilmore	1915	?	(w) J. Gilmore & Silas
Kirk, Mary Jane	1886	1890	
Kirk, Mary M.	1859	9-12-1889	(1st w) Daniel W.
Kirk, Silas H.	1912	?	(h) Bertha & Lillian
Kirk, William Avery	1921	8-13-1921	
Kirk, William Job	1888	1890	
Knight, Carrie	1881	1941	(w) Nelson
Knight, Clifford C.	1908	2-11-1973	(v) WW II
Knight, Edny R.	1896	1896	
Knight, Hazel	1900	4-01-1900	
Knight, Henry G.	1864	1955	(h) Phoebe
Knight, Jennie	1882	1925	
Knight, Nelson,	1875	1961	(h) Carrie
Knight, Phoebe I.	1870	1910	(w) Henry G.
Knight, Robert F.	1858	3-31-1928	
Knight, S. C.	1853	12-05-1911	
Knight, Sarah H.	1855	2-08-1919	
Knight, Virgle M.	1914	1958	
Leonard, Bernard F.	1816	7-17-1906	(s) Gardiner & Sarah
Leonard, Gardiner	1771	1851	(h) Sarah
Leonard, Sarah	1777	1851	(w) Gardiner
Lewis, Charles R.	1877	1901	
Lewis, Harriet J.	1852	1901	
Lewis, William H.	1842	1907	
Martin, Frank	1894	1978	(h) Gertrude
Martin, Gertrude	1893	1975	(w) Frank
Martin, Judith Kay	1948	1958	
Martin, Rodney Paul	1972	4-17-1972	(s) Earl & Lois
Martin, William F.	1917	4-02-1997	(h) Beatrice F.
Mason, John	1835	2-26-1857	(h) Sarah J (Hite)
Mason, John W.	1837	3-05-1924	
Mason, Owen	1872	7-04-1895	
Mason, Sarah J.(Hite)	1868	9-10-1880	
Mason, Sarah J.	1844	4-14-1919	
McCauley, Gay O.	1891	1942	
McHenry, Inza	1915	1963	
McNemar, Ova May	1878	1937	
McNemar, Benjamin	1874	1950	
McNemar, Iva	1877	1937	
Metro, Vera P.	1917	1984	
Metro, Virginia	1954	1954	
Miller, Kermit R.	1952	1974	(h) A. Lorraine

Name	Birth	Death	Relation
Miller, Mary Frances	1881	1951	(w) William Isaac
Miller, William Isaac	1864	1951	(h) Mary Frances
Moran, Howard	1916	1982	
Morgan, Archie	1844	1923	(h) Eliza (v) C W (Union)
Morgan, Edna	1900	7-02-1913	(d) C. & S. F.
Morgan, Eliza	1857	1929	(w) Archie
Morgan, Lawrence C.	1918	6-07-1997	(h) Nola (Williams)
Morgan, Mary C.	1876	5-26-1907	(w) Harry
Morgan, M. Nola	1922	9-16, 2001	(w) Lawrence C.
Morgan, Opal M.	1904	3-14-1905	(d) Harry & Mary C.
Morgan, Thomas M.	1882	9-30-1910	
Motter, Charles F.	1907	1978	(h) Delphia I.
Motter, David Lee	1930	1930	
Motter, Deloris June	1939	1939	
Motter, Delphia I.	1910	1991	(w) Charles F.
Motter, Frederick O.	1937	6-28-1937	
Motter, Thomas	1874	1957	
Nickols, George	?	4-23-1923	
Nickols, John Williams	?	1852	
Nickols, Malisa	?	7-29-1932	
Norris, Chapman W.	1873	10-05-1944	(h) Nancy Jane
Norris, L.	1889	7-17-1897	
Nancy Jane	1860	10-04-1940	(w) Chapman W.
Norris, W.H.	1894	4-16-1894	
Nuzum, Alpheus	?	7-31-1862	(s) R. B. & Phebee
Nuzum, Amelia E.	1824	10-06-1896	
Nuzum, Ann A. (Smell)	1855	7-05-1938	(2nd w) Winfield
Nuzum, Banks	1856	1-17-1914	(h) Ida
Nuzum, C. D. Dent	1872	5-02-1939	(h) Ora
Nuzum, Charles A.	1894	1918	
Nuzum, Clarence	1878	8-16-1964	(h) Minnie
Nuzum, Cynthia	1811	1836	
Nuzum, David Owen	?	3-13-1890	
Nuzum, Dennis	NO DATES		(h) Harriet (v) C W
Nuzum, Dessie Lynn	1882	12-07-1970	
Nuzum, Edna Louise	?	4-03-1931	
Nuzum, Edwin T.	1843	?	(h) Lucy (v) C W
Nuzum, Enos L. Jr.	1861	1944	(s) Enos, Sr. & Sarah
Nuzum, George	1774	1-06-1867	(h) Ruth
Nuzum, Harriet	?	3-20-1870	(w) Dennis
Nuzum, Ida	1853	1905	(w) Banks
Nuzum, Jane	?	10-12-1815	
Nuzum, Job	NO DATES		(v) C W (Union)
Nuzum, John S.	1819	8-20-1901	(v) C W
Nuzum, Joseph M.	1807	3-15-1832	
Nuzum, L. N.	NO DATES		(v) Army
Nuzum, Lucy J.	1842	7-24-1898	(w) Edwin J.
Nuzum, Martha Jane (Kirk)	1840	1883	
Nuzum, Mercia	1825	1915	
Nuzum, Minnie Linn	1885	11-19-1937	(w) Clarence
Nuzum, Olive J.(Barnes)	1849	8-14-1884	(1st w) Winfield
Nuzum, Ora (Shriver)	1875	10-21-1954	(w) C. D. Dent
Nuzum, Richard B.	1860	10-08-1896	(s) T. & S.
Nuzum, Ruth	1784	12-30-1824	(w) George
Nuzum, Sam R.	1915	1955	
Nuzum, Sarah Wilt	1848	1918	(w) W. F.
Nuzum, Synthia	?	8-06-1836	

Name	Born	Died	Notes
Nuzum, Thomas	1824	3-05-1890	(v) C W
Nuzum, Thomas A.	?	9-26-1880	
Nuzum, Thornton M.	1819	1915	
Nuzum, Tillie	1815	12-31-1880	(d) Thomas & Helen
Nuzum, W. F.	1847	9-05-1899	(h) Sarah Wilt (v) C W
Nuzum, Warrack	1814	?	
Nuzum, William R.	1871	1896	
Nuzum, Winfield S.	?	8-08-1895	(h) Olive & Ann
Peyton, Ruth	1904	1985	
Phillips, Clarence Okey	1934	3-30-1935	
Phillips, Rosa Z.	1907	1978	(w) Truman E.
Phillips, Truman E.	1901	1962	(h) Rosa Z.
Postlethwait, Eula	1916	4-19-1992	(w) Ford & Chester
Powell, John	?	1852	
Powell, Margaret	?	1861	(w) Joseph
Powell, William	NO DATES		(v) C W
Reese, Marjorie Dale	1911	10-12-1911	5 Mo. old
Reynolds, Howard A.	1915	9-19-1915	
Reynolds, James Robert	1888	1908	
Reynolds, Joel B.	NO DATES		(v) C W (Union)
Reynolds, Mary J.	1845	1928	
Riley, Myrtle	1882	1955	
Riley, William C.	1882	1955	
Rogers, Ralph	1913	1984	
Root, Lillie D.	1908	1977	(w) Orpha W.
Root, Orpha W.	1905	1978	(w) Lillie D.
Ruse, Marjorie Dale	1911	10-12-1911	
Rush, Mary S.	1907	1-24-1993	(s) Daniel & Grace
Rutherford, Ann	?	5-29-1891	
Rutherford, John Evan	NO DATES		(v) C W
Rutherford, Marcus	NO DATES		(v) C W
Sanders, Aaron O.	1878	1952	(h) Zoe O.
Sanders, Benton Lee	1934	1935	(s) Glenn &Wilma
Sanders, Charles W.	1923	6-05-1990	(s) Fred & Cordia
Sanders, Cordia B.	1911	1975	(w) Lawrence D.
Sanders, Fred R.	1896	1972	(h) Jesse (Nuzum)
Sanders, Glenn E.	1907	10-09-1998	(h) Wilma P. (Stuck)
Sanders, Hattie	1870	1953	(w) Lawrence
Sanders, James A.	1912	9-06-1993	(h) Delphia (Herndon)
Sanders, Jane	?	1892	(w) John
Sanders, Jessie C.	1900	1977	(w) Fred R.
Sanders, John E.	1872	1952	(h) Mary A. (Nuzum)
Sanders, John L., Jr.	1944	3-28-1970	(v) Viet Nam
Sanders, John L., Sr.	1891	1980	(h) Naomi (v) WW I
Sanders, Lawrence	1866	1955	(h) Hattie
Sanders, Lawrence D.	1903	4-09-1994	(h) Cordia B. (Hanna)
Sanders, Mark R.	1969	1969	(s) Earl D.
Sanders, Mary E.	1906	1906	(d) Lawrence & Hattie
Sanders, Naomi K.	1903	1985	(w) John L., Sr.
Sanders, William Keith	1932	1943	(s) Lawrence
Sanders, William R.	1905	10-23-1970	
Sanders, Wilma Pearl	1908	1985	(w) Glenn E.
Sanders, Zoe Ola	1885	1977	(w) Aaron D.
Sanders, Zoe Ola	1928	1-14-1930	
Satterfield, M. A.	?	3-28-1899	
Satterfield, William C.	1925	12-20-1959	(v) WW II
Shaffer, Charles W.	923	12-20-1959	(h) Dorotha

Name	Born	Died	Relation
Shaffer, Dorotha M. (Haddix)	1933	3-10-1994	(w) Charles W.
Shaw, Brushrod	1816	1904	(h) Sarah
Shaw, Emily Jane (West)	1839	3-25-1874	(w) Joshua
Shaw, Harriet A.	1841	9-03-1925	(d) Isaac Holman
Shaw, Harry	1913	?	
Shaw, Joshua	1829	5-26-1910	(h) Emily (v) C W
Shaw, Samuel	1796	1841	(v) C W
Shaw, Sarah	1819	1949	(w) Brushrod
Shaw, Sylvester A.	1855	7-01-1930	(s) Joshua
Shaw, Willie	?	2-13-1872	(s) J. & E. J.
Sheranko, Amanda L.	1981	9-13-1990	(d) David & Margo
Sheranko, Davis A.	1950	5-12-1996	(h) Margo (Jenkins)
Shields, Ellen F.	1904	1972	(w) Frank D.
Shields, Frank D.	1904	1955	(h) Ellen F.
Shorter, Frank E., Sr.	1917	3-18-1991	(h) Ada Pearl (Rushton)
Shorter, Frank, Jr.	1945	3-11-2002	(s) Frank & Ada Pearl
Sinclair, Anna G.	1879	1943	(Lewis)
Sinclair, Edith J.	1912	1976	
Sinclair, Charles Howard	1938	6-14-1939	
Skidmore, Eulace	1921	1964	
Skidmore, Pauline	1921	1966	
Springer, Ruth J.	NO DATES		(w) John J.
Starcher, Fred W.	1914	1963	(h) Lillie M.
Starcher, Lillie M.	1919	1980	(w) Fred W.
Stone, James Ray	1931	2-13-1970	(v) Marines
Surtees, (Unknown)	1850	?	(w) John T.
Sutphin, Lawrence L.	1923	12-25-1967	(v) WW II
Sutphin, Richard	1947	4-30-1976	
Sypolt, Paul E.	1927	4-16-1992	(h) Doris J. (Gower)
Sypolt, Selvey Ted	1928	1-02-1993	(h) Martha (Hawkins)
Tenney, Alva	1892	11-20-1965	(h) Vera (v) WW I
Tenney, Vera May	1896	1976	(w) Alva
Thomas, Earl E.	1895	7-12-1895	
Thomas, Gabbie	?	3-20-1893(d) George A.	
Thomas, George E.	1859	1-14-1934	(h) Serepta A.
Thomas, James Beryl	1905	3-31-1974	
Thomas, Sally	?	4-15-1891'	(d) George A.
Thomas, Serepta A.	1865	8-31-1928	(w) George A.
Thompson, Algustis	?	12-02-1934	78 yrs.
Thompson, Bert	1900	1920	
Thompson, Clarence	1902	1902	
Thompson, Mary B.	1868	1960	
Thompson, William P.	1845	1939	
Vandergrift, Calvin	1843	1940	(v) Army
Vandergrift, Albert D.	1899	5-06-1980	(h) E. Marie (Collins)
Vandergrift, Alice Minn	1908	10-24-1989	
Vandergrift, Bertha Belle	1924	9-22-2002	(w) Wayne A.
Vandergrift, Boyd M.	?	8-21-1904	(s) M. & S.
Vandergrift, Charles W.	1873	1943	(h) Effie L.
Vandergrift, E. Marie (Collins)	1901	5-10-1971	(w) Albert D.
Vandergrift, Edna Mae	1934	2-27-1934	
Vandergrift, Effie L.	1872	1965	(w) Charles W.
Vandergrift, Francis D.	1887	1961	
Vandergrift, Gilbert	1887	1959	
Vandergrift, Hannah M.	1895	4-11-1973	(w) Huey D.
Vandergrift, Harley L.	1882	1911	
Vandergrift, Harve	1872	1941	(h) Nellie

Name	Birth	Death	Notes
Vandergrift, Hattie	1870	1939	
Vandergrift, Huey D.	1896	2-13-1953	(h) Hannah (v) WW I
Vandergrift, Issac U.	1893	6-20-1916	
Vandergrift, Iva Mae	1877	1949	(w) Leonard
Vandergrift, James A.	1880	1962	
Vandergrift, John C.	1888	1962	
Vandergrift, Leoda	1887	1965	(w) Nezer
Vandergrift, Leonard	1872	1941	(h) Iva Mae
Vandergrift, Leonard	1910	4-17-1955	(v) WW II
Vandergrift, Margaret E.	1851	4-18-1915	(w) Calvin
Vandergrift, Marshall	1844	11-02-1930	(v) C W (Union)
Vandergrift, Martha F.	1863	1915	(w) William G.
Vandergrift, Mary A.	1869	1954	(w) U. Grant
Vandergrift, Maude	1890	1940	
Vandergrift, Nellie	1883	?	(w) Harve
Vandergrift, Nezer	1878	1943	(h) Leoda
Vandergrift, Phillip A.	1932	7-11-1955	(v) W W II
Vandergrift, Robert	1897	2-10-1973	(v) WW I
Vandergrift, Sarah	1854	12-23-1907	(w) Sylvestus
Vandergrift, Selvey G.	1876	1965	(h) Viola M.
Vandergrift, Sophia	1859	1936	
Vandergrift, Sylvestus	1849	7-18-1905	(h) Sarah
Vandergrift, U. Grant	1867	1931	(h) Mary A.
Vandergrift, Viola M.	1878	1958	(w) Selvey G.
Vandergrift, Virgil	1883	1965	
Vandergrift, Wayne A.	1927	2-03-1996	(h) Bertha (Williams)
Vandergrift, William G.	1848	1937	(h) Martha F.
VanGilder, Blanche	1897	11-22-1998	
Voyle, Aultie G.	1899	?	(w) William J.
Voyle, Philip R.	1917	1980	(h) Addie L.
Voyle, William J.	1892	1963	(h) Aultie G.
Wade, Wilda M.	1955	4-26-1958	
Walters, Floyd A.	1927	1990	
Welch, Clyde A.	1898	9-12-1980	(h) Ellen D. (v) W W I
Welch, Ellen D.	1909	10-27-1985	(w) Clyde A.
Wells, Margaret	NO DATES		(w) Joseph O.
West, Armanda	1828	8-12-1875	
West, Evelyn M.	1919	1965	
West, John	1823	7-22-1893	
Williams, Susan D.	1865	1940	
Wilmoth, Richard	1930	1979	
Wilt, W.L. F.	1847	9-05-1899	(v) C W (Union)
Wilson, Arthela	1875	11-06-1911	(w) B. F.
Wilson, Benjamin Franklin	1872	09-05-1899	(v) Army

Taylor Cemetery behind the Nuzum Cemetery. It was established in 1972.

1860 TAYLOR CEMETERY

Beyond the Nuzum No. 1 Cemetery, way in the back behind wire fencing is another small cemetery. A statue of a horse stands beside one of the gravesites. Undoubtedly indicating that the person buried here loved horses.

Situated on Taylor property, the burial ground takes its name from the family. It overlooks the Nuzum No. 1 Cemetery. When I visited here in the fall of 1997, there were seven gravesites in need of care. It is still used as a burial ground.

Name	Birth	Death	Relationship
Bright, Victoria	1973	1973	Infant
Smith, John I.	1919	1993	(h) Mary L.
Smith, Mary Lou	1923	1978	(w) John I.
Taylor, Alma Marie	1939	1989	(w) Fred
Taylor, Cory Scott	1992	11-10-1992	(s) Randy & JoAnn
Taylor, Harry J.	1889	1972	(h) Lizzie S.
Taylor, Lizzie S.	1907	1987	(w) Harry J..

Nuzum No. 3 Cemetery at Williams Crossroads near Rt. 310. It was established in 1860 by Hiram Nuzum.

NUZUM NO. 3
(Williams Crossroads)

This cemetery is located six and one half miles from East Fairmont on Rt. 310 towards Grafton. Turn right on the Williams Crossroads Road to the top of the hill. Turn left at the driveway of the Weaver residence. The poorly kept cemetery is behind the house on private property. There is no trace of the fence that once surrounded it. Four huge, very old arborvitae trees are still thriving there.

Measuring about 30x30, the older part was established in 1860 with the death of the infant daughter of Enos L. and Sarah (Tatterson) Nuzum. The site was chosen to overlook the Nuzum farm and was used strictly as a private burial ground for the Nuzum family.

The DeMary graves are off to the side of the burial ground. It is enclosed within in a new chain link fence and kept locked. The well-kept area is reserved for the DeMary family. This graveyard's appearance is quite a contrast to the older part. Pete and Nancy DeMary owned a grocery store in Rivesville for many years and they were former owners of the farm on which the cemetery is located. When the property was sold, a right-of-way for entry was reserved.

The following names of the Enos Nuzum family were taken from the 1870 U.S. Census Book.

Enos L. Nuzum, Sr.	58 years old	Farmer
Sarah	38	Housewife
Calvin	21	Son
Henry Clay	20	Son
Hiram	17	Twin son
Agustus	17	Twin son
Matilda	15	Daughter
Martha (Mattie)	14	Daughter
Enos, Jr.	9	Daughter
Sarah	2	Daughter

One stone I found interesting in the tall dried weeds was the tombstone of Nimrod Helsley. He was a volunteer in Company E., First W. Va. Infantry in the Union army during the Civil War. No dates were legible on the tombstone, but the insignia of a Civil War veteran could be determined. Nimrod married Elizabeth (last name unknown) and they had five children. After the death of Elizabeth, Nimrod married Sarah Nuzum, youngest daughter of Enos and Sarah Nuzum. It would have been a May/December marriage as he would have been much older than she. She is buried in Nuzum No. 1 cemetery.

Enos L. Nuzum, Sr. sold small portions of his farm after the death of his wife Sarah in 1880. He sold 55 acres to his son Enos, Jr. in 1885. Family names of those who owned the farm at one time are Williams, Vangilder, Leeson, DeMary and currently Gary and Barbara (Linn) Weaver.

Those known to be laid to rest here are;

NUZUM NO. 3 CEMETERY

Name	Birth	Death	Relationship
DeMary, G. Pete	4-27-1894	2-15-1994	(h) Nancy (Colarusso)
DeMary, Nancy	8-25-1902	2-02-1996	(w) G. Pete
Hensley, Elizabeth	2-19-1829	11-01-1900	(1w) Nimrod
Hensley, Nimrod	1831	?	(v) C W (Co. E., 1st W.Va. Artillery)
Nuzum, Calvin	9-27-1848	11-05-1872	(s) Enos & Sarah
Nuzum, Enos L.	1812	1895	(h) Sarah (Tatterson)
Nuzum, Hiram H.	4-04-1853	4-03-1860	(ts) Enos & Sarah
Nuzum, Infant	4-09-1860	4-09-1889	(d) Enos & Sarah
Nuzum, Matilda	10-05-1855	4-30-1883	(d) Enos & Sarah
Nuzum, Sarah	6-07-1831	7-26-1884	(w) Enos L.

1808 WILLIAM LINN CEMETERY
(Rock Lake)

William Linn Cemetery established in 1808 at Rock Lake.

To find this quaint little cemetery from East Fairmont, go out East Grafton Road south towards Grafton. Turn right onto Rock Lake Road, and go one mile to the lake. Turn right, cross the bridge and take the second dirt road on the right. It is called the William Linn Cemetery road. When you reach the three-way fork, go straight ahead up the hill. The cemetery is on the right.

Bronze plaque placed on the grave of William Linn by the Morgan Morgan Chapter of the DAR.

WILLIAM LINN

One William Linn of Irish birth,
    Who lived near Belfast town,
Desired to roam o'er this old earth,
    And get to himself renown.

So packing up his earthly stores,
    His wife and children three,
He crossed the "pond" to American shores
    Where men are all born free.

In Mexico he made a pause,
    To see what it was like;
He didn't like the "Greaser" laws,
    So he took a Northward hike.

In Pennsylvania's genial clime,
    He found his first new home.
He meant to live here all the time,
    And thought no more to roam.

But Uncle Sam had need for men,
    To fight the British foe.
So he bid farewell to home, and then
    To the battle fields did go.

But when the war-clouds lifted high,
    And peace once more did reign,
And men no more were called to die,
    He returned to his home again.

But discontent now filled his mind,
    And he longed once more to roam,
So he left his acres all behind,
    And sought a Virginia home.

'Mid Hampshire's hills he stopped awhile,
    Where Patterson's Creek waters flow,
But not for long did these hills beguile,
    And he was soon once more "on the go."

Old Monongalia's charms he sought,
    And thence he made his way,
On Glady Creek a farm he bought,
    And was here content to stay.

This William Linn, of Irish birth,
    Loved honesty and truth.
He was a man of sterling worth;
    An example for all of our youth.

His home was a place of delight,
    To those who its comforts would share;
The latchstring hung out day and night,
    And strangers were made welcome there.

Poem written by Margarett Virginia Hull in 1932. She was the daughter of John Wesley and Sarah Hull of Benton's Ferry. She wrote the book *Genealogical History of the family of William Linn*.

This peaceful burial spot was established in 1808 with the death of pioneer William Linn, who was the progenitor of the Linns along the Tygart Valley River in Marion County. Born January 30, 1734, he came from near Belfast, Ireland. There he married Agnes (her last name is not known). The Linns decided to emigrate to America, we find them first in Mexico in 1771. They lived in Mexico City for a time. Then their names are recorded in Westmoreland County, Pennsylvania, where on September 8, 1777, William took the oath of allegiance as a private in Pennsylvania's First Regiment during the Revolutionary War. He is recorded to have served in Lt. Isaac Miller's Company, First Battalion, Seventh Company, beginning on March 28, 1778.

Children of William and Agnes: Mary, born 1765, married and moved to Ohio; Jane, born 1767, married and moved to Ohio; Adam, born 1769-1771; Adam II, born 1772; Nancy born 1775 (died in childhood), and Margaret, born 1782 (died in infancy).

Some time after Margaret's birth, Agnes died. William is next found living on Patterson's Creek (now

Mineral Co., WV) in 1788. He had remarried—this time to Isabella Gibson, who also was Irish. They had seven children together: John (1786-1856) married Polly Cooper; William (1787-1862) married Elizabeth Henderson; Samuel (1789-1852) married Anzy Reese in 1822. They moved to Benton's Ferry in 1835; Hugh (1799-1861) married Polly Reese; Gibson (1801-1891) married Tabitha Reese; Anna married Henry Tucker; Sarah Ann (Sallie) married William Henderson.

In 1804, William and Isabella and their family settled on Glady Creek in the Tygart Valley, Monongalia County, Virginia, near what is now Rock Lake. Part of the land probably was awarded to him as a reward for having served in the Revolutionary War. The last Indian attack had been five years past so it was safe enough to start clearing the land for farming and building a log cabin. On December 23, 1808, they were preparing to move in to their new log home when William Linn died. He was buried on this pleasant knoll overlooking his farm known as the "Billy Linn" farm in the valley below. In 1979 Owens Illinois Glass, whose large factory was in Fairmont, owned the farm. It closed down in 1982.

This little cemetery is by far the oldest one on the Tygart Valley River in Marion County. I found the beauty and the charm of the countryside, just as I am sure William did, as the perfect setting for a man to settle in. It is sad that he only had four years to enjoy it before he died.

The Col. Morgan Morgan Chapter of the Daughters of American Revolution in Marion County (of which I am a member) put a bronze plaque for valor on Mr. Linn's grave as a reminder of his service in fighting for independence of our country. Honoring our ancestors means more than just remembering them. It means living up to the standards they set.

Two matching tombstones bearing the "gates to heaven" images are those of Samuel and Lavinia Linn who are buried side by side. Each has a different epitaph. In the back of the graveyard is the older section where fieldstones were used as markers. Some had initials. The WPA readings taken in 1938 recorded 24 flagstones, many of which were not legible. All of the tombstones are facing the east, as tradition dictates. A barbed wire fence surrounds the burial ground with a 12 ft. gate at the entrance. Family members maintain the grounds.

Stonecarver William T. Blue from Grafton carved the stone of Polly Linn, wife of Hugh Linn. He signed his name at the bottom as artisan.

Pioneer William Linn probably would be proud of his family for providing burial grounds. His son, Samuel, donated land in Benton's Ferry for a cemetery. Samuel's son, John Linn, donated land in Grant District for another family site, not to mention the three other Linn cemeteries on the upper part of Glady Creek.

WILLIAM LINN CEMETERY

Name	Birth	Death	Relationship
Linn, (Infant)	1886	2-27-1886	(s) Samuel & Lavinia
Linn, A. (Infant)	1863	1863	(s) Samuel & Lavinia
Linn, (Infant)	NO DATES		Mother: Nora Linn
Linn, Nora	NO DATES		
Linn, Andy(Infant)	NO DATES		(s) George
Linn, Blanche Anna	1910	3-23-1911	(d) John & Gibbie
Linn, Cynthia Isabella	1883	1908	
Linn, Edward Marion	1840	5-26-1916	
Linn, Ethel Virginia	1909	6-17-1910	(d) John K. & Gibbie
Linn, Gibbie Rebecca (Neal)	1873	1-20-1956	(w) John Keys
Linn, G.	1833	?	
Linn, Gibson	1801	1-15-1891	(s) William & Isabella
Linn, Hugh	1799	7-29-1861	(h) Polly
Linn, Ida May	1926	5-11-2000	(w) William Carl
Linn, Isabella (Gibson)	1761	2-24-1834	(2nd w) William, Sr.
Linn, Isabella	?	3 yrs old	(d) Gibson & Tabitha
Linn, John Keys	1868	4-26-1949	(h) Gibbie
Linn, John	NO DATES		(s) Gibson & Tabitha
Linn, Lavinia (Spicer)	1840	10-17-1910	(w) Samuel L.
Linn, Mary (Holbert)	1820	2-?-1890	(w) William H.

Linn, Mary Elizabeth	11-05-1873	1875	(d) Samuel & Lavinia
Linn, Matilda (Williams)	NO DATES		(d) John Williams
Linn, Michael Gibson	1889	7-10-1919	
Linn, Nancy	1884	1-14-1973	(w) Edward Leroy
Linn, Nancy Y.	1834	7-25-1853	(d) Hugh & Polly
Linn, (Infant)	NO DATES		(d) Nora Linn
Linn, Polly	1803	12-12-1873	(w) Hugh
Linn, Samuel L.	1836	12-15-1910	(h) Lavinia
Linn, S.	(Infant)	NO DATES	(s) Gibson & Tabitha
Linn, Tabitha (Reese)	1811	5-26-1873	(w) Gibson
Linn, William Aril	1912	5-07-1993	(h) Ida May (Henderson)
Linn, William	1734	12-23-1808	(h) Isabella (v) R W
Linn, William Harrison	1844	6-23-1922	(h) Elizabeth
Morgan, Howard O.	1910	4-15-1928	(s) Thomas & Nancy
Nixon, Brady R.	1916	8-03-1991	(h) Norma L (v) WWI
Shriver, (Infant)	NO DATES		Mother: Leslie Shriver
Vincent, Edward M.	1840	5-26-1916	(h) Nancy
Vincent, Jennie J.	1866	2-21-1869	(d) Edward & Nancy
Vincent, Mary A.	1864	3-06-1870	(d) Edward & Nancy
Vincent, Nancy (Linn)	1837	11-27-1867	(w) Edward M.

1823 SAMUEL LINN CEMETERY

(Rock Lake)

Samuel Linn Cemetery at Rock Lake. Established in 1823.

The place where Samuel and Elizabeth Linn and their family are buried can be located by taking the East Grafton Road to the Valley Falls turnoff. It is on the hill behind Bruce Kirk's Body Shop on the left just before you get to the Rock Lake sign.

Sam Linn was known as "White Sam" because there were so many Sams in the Linn family. The others were called Black Sam and Red Sam. White Sam was the son of John and Betsy (Rudy) Linn. Being the son of William, who came from Ireland, he inherited a portion of land from his father's original tract, where he and his wife Polly (Cooper) raised their family.

When John and Polly's eight-year-old daughter, Hannah, died in 1823, they buried her on the family farm. She was the first to be buried in the family plot up on the hill. Two years later, White Sam was born and stayed on the family farm for the rest of his life even after he married Elizabeth (Betsy) Rudy. The Rudy family came from Germany in 1804, and did not live far away. According to the book, *Genealogical History of William Linn*, Betsy's grandfather, Henry Rudy, Sr. is reported to have worked for two years to pay for his passage to America. Legend has it that White Sam Linn owned a nice apple orchard, which supplied delicious cider to the neighbors for 25 cents a gallon.

The second person to be buried there was Polly in 1852 and then John four years later, in 1856. They were the beginning of the family cemetery up on the hill.

Sam and Betsy had 11 children. Four of them died as infants or in adolescence, and of course, they were buried on the farm. Sam's youngest son, Hiram, never married and saw to it that his mother and father were buried in the same tradition. Hiram continued to live on the old homestead with his three unmarried sisters: Polly, Harriet and Sarah Ann.

Hiram, born in 1869, was a successful businessman and prominent man in the community. He was vice president of the Taylor County Bank (in Grafton) and was the Linn family historian. In 1923, he sold one acre of land to the Union District Board of Education for a school. It was located at the top of the hill from Valley Falls. He traveled to and from Grafton by train. He died in 1937.

White Sam's daughters, Polly, Harriet and Sarah Ann, lived their entire lives on the family farm. They are all buried up on the hill.

SAMUEL LINN CEMETERY

Name	Birth	Death	Relationship
Linn, Cyrus	1856	3-16-1856	(s) Sam & Elizabeth
Linn, John L.	1850	6-16, 1851	(s) Sam & Elizabeth
Linn, Hannah	1815	7-08-1823	(d) John & Polly
Linn, John	1786	9-29-1856	(h) Polly
Linn, Polly (Cooper)	1792	4-24-1852	(w) John
Linn, (Infant)	1856	1856	Sam & Elizabeth
Linn, Polly	1857	1-18-1937	(s) Sam & Elizabeth
Linn, Hiram R.	1869	1-14-1937	(s) Sam & Elizabeth
Linn, Henry L.	188?	5-?? -1892	(s) Sam & Elizabeth
Linn, Samuel (White Sam)	1825	10-27-1912	(h) Elizabeth (Rudy)
Linn, Elizabeth (Betsy)	1832	3-15-1915	(w) Samuel
Linn, Harriet E.	1870	4-13-1955	(d) Sam & Elizabeth
Linn, Sarah	1861	7-12-1952	(d) Sam & Elizabeth

LAWLER CEMETERY
(Taylor County)

Lawler cemetery is in Taylor County below Currey Ridge towards the river. From Marion County, go south on US Rt. 250 3.4 miles and turn left on Meetinghouse Road. Drive another six tenths of a mile and you will come to the Lawler Church. The cemetery is directly across from the church. It is fenced in and has an extra wide gate. Very old hemlocks shade the entrance of the cemetery.

Seeing this graveyard for the first time I wondered then and still do, why the gravesites of Basha and Perry Sanders are completely covered over with concrete. I was also attracted to a black wrought iron fence that surrounded two members of the Wiseman family and was fascinated by the tombstone of Elizabeth Lawler, who died in 1884. Her well-preserved headstone was engraved on local slate by Willhide B. Blue of Grafton.

Lawler Cemetery in Taylor County. Established in 1856.

N. T. and Elizabeth A. Lawler donated land for the Methodist Episcopal South Church in 1875. The cemetery began when their daughter, Elizabeth, died in that same year. The church and the cemetery are symbolic of the song "Church in the Wildwood".

In 1983, the Methodist Conference sold the church to trustees, who keep the cemetery in excellent condition. It is still used as a burial ground for the families whose ancestors once attended the church. Those known to be buried here are:

LAWLER CEMETERY
(Taylor Co.)

Name	Birth	Death	Relationship
Abel, F. Marion	1882	1973	(h) Lizzie
Abel, Hallie	1875	1949	(w) James L.
Abel, Inez B.	1912	1983	(w) Lloyd
Abel, James L.	1871	1946	(h) Hallie
Abel, Lizzie (Shriver)	1883	1960	(w) F. Marion
Abel, Lloyd	1907	1980	(h) Inez
Abel, M. Kate	1934	1989	(w) Bill
Abel, Sarah A.	1843	1904	(w) Stephenson

Name	Born	Died	Notes
Abel, Ronald Cory	1987	11-19-1987	
Abel, Stephenson	1839	1932	(h) Sarah
Abels, James	1851	1943	
Anderson, George F.	1861	1916	
Anderson, Roy G.	1890	1-27-1902	(s) Geo. F. & M. G.
Bennett, Celia	1842	1-20-1903	(w) Claudius
Bennett, Claudius	1843	4-06-1920	(h) Celia
Clark, Carl	1910	10-20-1984	(h) Bertha H.
Collins, Judith Lynn	?	10-07-1980	Infant
Currey, Cordelia E.	1876	3-08-1899	(w) Elihu
Currey, Ida E.	?	7-09-1893	(w) Elihu
Currey, Lizzie	1859	8-27-1913	(w) Louis
Currey, Martha E.	1847	2-15-1887	(w) Silas
Currey, Silas	1824	4-12-1907	(h) Martha E.
Davis, Charlotte	?	3-03-1901	
Davis, Elizabeth	?	1899	
Dollison, Dorothy Ashba	1917	8-19-1984	
Dollison, James R.	1939	5-04-1989	(v) U.S. Air Force
Hall, Nancy F.	1839	1899	
Hall, Laura	1883	8-08-1911	
Hall, Luther	1882	5-30-1907	
Holt, Horatio N.	1829	?	(h) Margaret
Holt, Margaret	1833	6-15-1906	(w) Horatio
Hume, Harry	1850	10-27-1912	
Hume, Mary	1850	10-27-1912	(w) Perry
Hume, Perry	1846	1911	(h) Mary
Janes, Caroline	1854	7-22-1911	(w) W. B. Janes
Keener, Earl	1886	10-08-1902	(s) Geo. & Sarah
Keener, George	1855	1929	
Keener, Katherine	?	3-19-1917	(d) J. S. Keener
Keener, Sarah	1858	1925	(w) George
Kepner, Garron Brittie	1870	1959	(w) William A.
Kepner, John Davis	1872	1952	
Kepner, William A.	1856	1929	(h) Garron
Lambert, Annie D.	1870	1952	
Lambert, Ernsel F.	1894	1985	(s) Annie
Lambert, Joseph	1861	4-06-1922	
Lambert, Joseph L.	1836	6-10-1905	(h) Sarah (Morgan)
Lambert, Laura V.	1862	1-18-1926	
Lambert, Minta L.	1895	1-26-1943	(d) Joseph
Lambert, R. Burl	1892	8-17-1929	(s) Joseph
Lambert, Rachel (Morgan)	1846	1933	(w) W. P. Lambert
Lambert, Sarah	1830	?	(w) Joseph L.
Lambert, William P.	1844	1920	(h) Rachel (v) C W
Lawler, Robert	1878	7-02-1893	Twin brother
Lawler, Carrol R.	1903	3-13-1906	
Lawler, Catharine	1823	1916	(w) Jehu
Lawler, Elizabeth	?	10-14-1875	
Lawler, Elizabeth A.	1839	3-07-1894	(w) N. L. Lawler
Lawler, Flossie	1896	3-24-1898	
Lawler, Gideon M.	1852	7-06-1929	
Lawler, Hattie	1882	7-04-1889	
Lawler, Henry R.	1847	1-01-1925	
Lawler, Rev. Jehu H.	?	8-26-1884	(h) Catharine
Lawler, J. M.	1888	9-07-1889	
Lawler, Martha G.	1904	3-02-1906	
Lawler, Martha J.	1852	1-20-1888	(w) J. M. Lawler

Lawler, Mary	1855	1-08-1913	
Lawler, Mary C.	1862	1937	
Lawler, Polly Hannah	1882	2-23-1926	(w) Wilber Cook
Lawler,	1878	?	(Twin brother of Bert)
Lawler, Wilber Cook	1880	2-01-1935	(h) Polly
Linn, ?	?	6-30-1887	(d) J. W. Lynn
Linn, ?	?	4-03-1887	(d) J. W. Lynn
Linn, J.W.	?	5-05-1935	(h) Sarah (Lawler)
Linn, John	1859	1930	(h) Nancy J.
Linn, Nancy J.	1857	1939	(w) John
Linn, Sarah	?	3-31-1910	(w) J. W.
Martin, Bird C.	1880	1955	
Martin, Eli Homer	1849	1923	(h) Rebecca
Martin, Rebecca (Lawler)	1855	1932	(w) Eli
Martin, Roy J.	1886	1960	
Martin, Willie Earnest	1882	1942	
Mason, Benjamin F.	1847	5-15-1907	(h) Helen
Mason, Helen M.	1856	?	(w) Benjamin
Mauller, Floyd S. 1906	?	9-05-1907	(s) George & H. E.
Mauller, George B.	1866	7-27-1934	(h) Hannah
Mauller, Hannah E.	1869	1942	(w) George B.
Mauler, Lena M.	1906	8-03-1906	
Mauller, Troy	1916	12-16-1916	(s) George & H. E.
Rutherford, A.G.	1865	5-27-1903	
Rutherford, J.J.	1836	1-03-1909	
Rutherford, James	Infant	11-13-1931	
Rutherford, Josephus	1867	11-08-1936	
Rutherford, Mary J.	1842	9-15-1932	
Sanders, Basha	1852	1922	(w) Perry G.
Sanders, Perry G.	1858	1924	(h) Basha
Severe, Mary Ann	?	11-26-1926	(d) Hayward & Pearl
Shaver, Anna K.	1892	1979	
Shaver, Helen	?	8-19-1924	
Shaver, Orel B.	1893	1979	
Shriver, Burl	NO DATES		
Shriver, Eliza J.	1863	1931	(d) Samuel
Shriver, Elizabeth R.	1842	1920	(w) Samuel
Shriver, Lindsay	1862	11-25-1910	(s) Thomas
Shriver, Samuel W.	1835	1917	(h) Elizabeth R.
Spaskley, Florence	1862	1917	
Springer, Alpheus	1812	4-11-1894	(h) Mary A. (v) C W
Springer, Bashaba	1852	11-20-1893	(d) Alpheus & Mary
Springer, Mary (Griffith)	1824	4-29-1907	(w) Alpheus
Springer, Fletcher	Infant	8-28-1922	(s) Wilbur & Emma
Springer, Hannah V.	1871	1900	
Springer, Jennie	1878	1957	
Springer, Job	1866	1953	
Springer, Virginia	?	7-13-1900	
Taliaferro, Mary	1875	1923	
Tucker, Drusilla	1819	2-15-1887	(w) Harrison
Wagner, Nina	1892	1914	
Wiseman, Infant	1900	12-04-1900	(s) L. J. & Z. A.
Wiseman, Infant	1916	5-02-1918	(s) L. J. & Z. A.
Wiseman, James C.	1833	11-12-1921	(h) Julia
Wiseman, Julia A.	1840	?	(w) James C.
Wiseman, Rella	?	8-31-1894	(d) G. W. & J.

The history of any cemetery is written in stone, one name at a time, one stone at a time. Sadly, the passage of time and vandalism threaten many of our old cemeteries. Many good works are going on in reclaiming some of them. The historical significance of cemeteries and the sanctity of human remains are all the more reasons for us to remember to protect and preserve gravesites. They are our heritage.

Chapter Six
Local Civil War Stories

THE NORTH AND THE SOUTH

*John Brown's Raid in '59,
Failed in the attempt.
Slavery was the issue,
Much to his contempt.*

*Unrest ran rapid through out the land,
Till cannons began to fire.
Then our nation was ripped apart,
By men that we admire.*

*With a call to arms in '61,
The troops were on the move.
Philippi saw the first land battle,
As many were to prove.*

*Pruntytown in '62,
Saw the first slaves freed.
Six months afterward,
Western Virginia proclaimed to secede.*

*"Stonewall" Jackson was for the South,
In charge of the Valley Campaign.
Fifteen months later in '63,
Was shot down by his own domain.*

*In '64 Grant was in charge,
Of all Union forces.
General Lee and the South,
Were running out of sources.*

*The battlefields took their toll,
When the two Generals met.
The '65 surrender came,
Appomattox we won't forget.*

C. Fortney-Hamilton 1999

West Virginia's Lower Tygart Valley River

THE BLUE AND THE GRAY

It is thought that 623,000 men died during the Civil War. Countless physical wounds went untreated and the mental wounds lingered a lifetime. So tragic was the Civil War that friends and neighbors could never get over the emotional trauma. After the fighting was over, hiding one's true feelings became a common practice so everyone could get along with each other. The hurt and anger was only skin deep and stayed there for the next two generations. The emotional turmoil was salved through the church; after the war more people practiced their faith.

The issue of slavery started it all. Some of the families in our valley kept slaves but most could not afford them. The Johnsons, Martins, Nixons, Watsons and Nuzums all owned slaves. Other slave owners are listed in the census books. They show that in 1860, there were 18,371 slaves in all of Virginia. Most of those were in the eastern portion of the state. The point here is that western Virginia did not have as much at stake over the issue of slaves as our mother state did.

Virginia, the most important state in the Confederacy, seceded from the Union in the spring of 1861. During this period, Fairmont was a Confederate point since the officers and officials of Marion County were southern sympathizers. By 1863 when the Jones Raid took place, the town had gone pro-Union; the sympathizers had either left town or were keeping quiet.

In the early days of the war Marion County residents were divided. The county had the well-trained Company A, 31st Regiment under Andrew "Stonewall" Jackson's command, which was called the "Marion Grays." Some of the family surnames whose men joined up were Ashcraft, Atkinson, Busey, Cooper, Davis, Danley, Evans, Griffith, Hull, Jolliffe, Kerr, Morgan, Martin, Mumford, Nixon, Nay, Hess, Roberts, Nichols, Prunty, Rider, Steele, Straight, Shaver, Rutherford, Stewart, Tennant, Toothman, Vincent, Wright, Wilson, West, Henderson, Hall, Blakenship, Tucker, Carpenter, Ross, Stringer and Arnett. This regiment suffered many casualties. The county also had a local pro-Union volunteer group known as the "Home Guards" who were part-time soldiers, as well as the First WV Infantry that fought at Philippi. This pitted local men against local men.

One month after Virginia seceded from the Union, T. Bailey Brown enlisted in the Union Army. On that same day, May 22, 1861, he was shot and killed at Fetterman. He became the first Union soldier to be killed in the Civil War and the first to be laid to rest in what later became the Nation's first National Cemetery in Grafton. This conflict brought the war to our back door. Twelve days later on June 3, 1861 further upriver, the town of Philippi experienced the first land battle of the war. The North had triumphed by safeguarding the railroad that both sides coveted. Activity on the railroad between Grafton and Fairmont increased in the fall of 1863 when the War Department in Washington decided to transport 20,000 soldiers and their equipment to Chattanooga, TN as reinforcements. It was the first time in history that railroads became an important part in warfare. The increased traffic along the Tygart Valley River did not go unnoticed.

The B&O Railroad was the most important east-west rail line near Washington D.C. and it was used to transport supplies to the troops. When the people of western Virginia let it be known that they wanted to form a separate state, President Lincoln was most eager to sign the proclamation. Not only would it be the 35th state in the union, but it also meant that the Union would control the B&O Railroad.

The Ohio River and the Mason-Dixon Line were borderlines separating the North from the South. The railroad ran along the Tygart Valley River from Beverly to Grafton and beyond towards the Mason-Dixon Line. The rails from Grafton to the Ohio River, finished in 1857, became another vital link in who was to win the war.

For folks in the Tygart Valley life went on. One by one the young men left their families and farms to volunteer for the cause they felt was right. Those who did not but felt that slavery needed to be abolished helped in a way that never got recorded in the history books.

Slaves trying to escape their southern owners to freedom in the north became such a dangerous undertaking that those who helped them were sworn to secrecy. To those who helped in so many different ways the routine became known as the "Underground Railroad." In actual fact though, the railroad was not used by escaping slaves except in the later years of the war. On those few occasions in this area, the railroad was secretly used because it was the fastest mode of travel that went due north towards the Mason-Dixon Line to freedom.

Slavery was critical to the South. Plantation owners depended upon slave labor to raise their crops for market. Slaves, who tried to make a break for freedom, increased, in the 1840's. They wanted to escape to the North to make their way to Canada and freedom. People who helped them were mostly whites. They were called "Agents." It was dangerous for anyone of either color to help them for they would have been severely punished if caught. Harboring a fugitive slave was against Federal laws that were favorable to the south. So "Safe Houses" where slaves could hide on their way North could be found almost anywhere, but under a cloud of secrecy. They became known as "stations" along the route to freedom.

In 1850, the new Fugitive Slave Act made all blacks, even free blacks in the north, subject to be returned to slavery in the South. Freed slaves were then being put back into slavery, thus activity on the "Underground Railroad" increased. Many of its tales and legends originated right here in the Tygart Valley.

THE SLAVE AUCTION

In this day and age, it is very hard to comprehend how local outstanding citizens could have been believers in human bondage. Owning slaves was considered a status symbol to some. The Civil War was on and southern slave owners needed money. The slave traders saw their chance to make some easy money by buying slaves cheaply and driving them to a more prosperous area. They had what they called Public Auction Sales or commonly known as the Slave Market. In Vol. 12 of the *Norman Kendall Scrapbooks*, Mr. Kendall writes of at least two fattening slave pens that were located on the west end of the old bridge on U.S. Rt. 50 crossing the Tygart Valley River at Fetterman. Here unfed, starving slaves were impounded and fed to good condition in order for them to bring a high price at auction. Slaves were also sold here.

Illustration by Jackie Richards. 1999.

Strange as it may seem to us today, good people were great believers in slavery. According to the same article by Norman F. Kendall he reported that in June of 1845 a prominent citizen advertised four of his good "thoroughbred" young slaves for sale. Two boys and two girls. The boys were said to be strong and intelligent. The girls were said to have light complexions with fine well made-bodies and bright happy minds. The notice related how men could well afford to buy them for special service. The boys were bought for $750 each. The girls were $997 each; one went to a wealthy citizen in Harrison County and the other to a leading citizen in Barbour County.

The largest and last slave auction held in this valley was near the Baptist Church in Pruntytown in June of 1862. Seventy-seven slaves were brought from Winchester, Virginia over the Northwestern Turnpike (now Rt. 50) all tied together with a large rope thrown over the saddle horn of the slave driver. There were 57 males and 20 females.

Very little was documented about this sale; however, one account was penned by Daniel Morris, editor of Pruntytown's newspaper and a southern sympathizer. On this particular day, being too busy himself with his duties at the newspaper, he sent his nine-year-old son, Homer, to the sale with instructions to relate to him afterwards what had transpired. Upon young Homer's return, he explained how the slaves were bought cheaply in southern Virginia and brought to northern Virginia to be sold at a public auction. According to the newspaper article a platform was built for the special occasion and the auctioneer, a southerner, explained why the American flag was draped around it. It was to show "their devotion to the constitution."

The frightened Negroes were huddled together near the platform. The auctioneer mounted the platform and made a strong speech praising slavery saying, "God's way of lifting the drudgery and burdens of the white man." One by one, they were put on the "uppenblock" starting with the best of the lot first, then auctioned off. There was no regard for families as husbands and wives and children were separated. The article continued to say, the crying and screaming among the slaves was heart wrenching and could be heard all over Pruntytown. Some of the bidders even asked to see teeth and their mouths were yanked open like that of a horse. The bids rose well over the thousand-dollar mark. Homer told of the sly whispers through the crowd as the auctioneer pointed out the capabilities of the young women.

The human barter continued until all of them were sold to prominent men from Marion, Taylor, Monongalia and Barbour counties. The total sales came to $41,788. and paid for in cash. One "good looking yellow girl" brought in the highest bid of $1,695. When it was over, the slaves were claimed by their new masters and the separation screams began anew. Homer Morris told his father that if he were ever able to vote, he would never vote for slavery.

This was the last slave auction held in this valley. It wasn't long before General James A. Mulligan, U.S. Army, arrived with his forces and placed his men in position overlooking Pruntytown and Grafton. All Southern sympathizers, including Homer's father, fled southward. The Federal troops were in charge but slavery continued until the famous words of President Lincoln were put into effect. "All persons held as slaves…shall be then, thenceforward, and forever free." The slaves from the Pruntytown auction were reunited on January 1, 1863 after the Emancipation Proclamation went into effect on September 22, 1862. Under this action slaves were freed only in those regions controlled by the northern armies. The Pruntytown slaves were the first in the Union to be released. Six months later West Virginia became a state. Slavery was abolished forever in 1865 when it became a part of our Constitution as the Thirteenth Amendment. Lincoln was among the first to see that this country could not stand half-slave and half-free.

A Ghost Story

Folklore abounds almost in every family tree. The following tale was presented to Ruth Ann Music, author of *The Telltale Lilac Bush. How Kettle Run Got Its Name* is fiction but I firmly believe that legend and folklore are sometimes based on fact.

PARTICULARS: The setting for this tale begins at the mouth of Kettle Run on the west side of the river where it empties into the Tygart Valley River at Benton's Ferry. The run begins on top of the hill next to U. S. Rt. 250 at White Hall and drops in elevation very quickly to the river. At the foot of what is now Vinegar Hill is a log cabin called "The Log." Directly across the river from the log cabin is a cemetery, and the railroad.

As the tale goes, Yankee soldiers would help bring escaping slaves down Kettle Run and hide them in the log cabin until it was safe to cross the river. When they did, they would follow a drain (Copper Hollow) to the other side of the river and one step closer to freedom.

One night while a dozen or more slaves were waiting for safe passage down the deep ravine, a band of rebel raiders found them, shot them all dead and cut off their heads. They placed the heads in a copper kettle, which they left on the riverbank while they went back for the bodies.

Meanwhile, the master, who lived in the log cabin, found the kettle of heads and took them across the river to the cemetery where they were buried in a long, narrow grave.

After that, "the heads began looking for their bodies." The tale relates that on a still, dark night, from an upper window in the log cabin, pairs of small, bright lights (eyes) could be seen marching down Copper Hollow to the river, where they would cross over and disappear up Kettle Run. However, only people living in the log cabin could see the lights and then only from a small attic window that overlooked the river.

The facts are these:

1. The setting, on Vinegar Hill with the log cabin and Kettle Run, are all factual places. Kettle Run was named before the Civil War. This could indeed be how Kettle Run got its name.

2. The ravine across the river does lead up to the railroad tracks, although it has never been named or referred to as Copper Hollow. (After 1852 it is believed the railroad was actually used as an escape route).

3. It was whispered that the "underground railroad" did operate in the area and resulted in small raids during the Civil War.

4. The log cabin at the mouth of Kettle Run is still called "*The Log*" today.

5. Benjamin Linn, who did not believe in slavery, lived in *The Log* during the Civil War. His log cabin could easily have been a "safe house" for slaves.

6. There are several unmarked graves in the Linn Cemetery across the river.

7. Mutilation was not unheard of, when escaping slaves were caught.

And YES, the folks who have lived in the log cabin since the Civil War have seen strange lights coming across the river at night but only from a small attic window facing the river. One of the more recent owners boarded up the window...and the lights have not been seen since. Although...some say on moonlit nights...the sparkling waters of the Tygart will give you second thoughts.

THE RAIDERS

On April 29, 1863, 21 days before West Virginia became a state, Fairmont and the surrounding communities were raided. The "Jones Raid", (as it became known in local history books), was conducted by General William Ezra Jones from southern Virginia. Jones was the ranking officer but the plan was devised by General John D. Imboden of the Confederate army. Jones was described to be one of the "worst dressed officers" for the South, according to comments in the book *Civil War Curiosities*. It said Jones and his troops were unshaven and usually dressed in blue overalls, homespun shirts and coats. Looking every bit the part of raiders because they had no semblance of uniforms. Ten days before they arrived in Fairmont they received new uniforms.

The raiders took Morgantown. The town surrendered to the rebels without even a return shot. The invading rebels had three goals in western Virginia. The first was to stop the statehood movement; the second was to destroy the B&O Railroad, its bridges and trestles, and the third was to obtain supplies and recruit troops. General Robert E. Lee was planning an invasion of Pennsylvania and needed men, horses, grain and food.

In Fairmont, one of their objectives was to destroy the B&O train bridge that spanned the Monongahela River there. Within one hour of entering Fairmont, the Confederates were in complete control and men were working to bring down the bridge. It was a three-span iron structure, 615 feet long and reportedly the most expensive bridge on the railroad. Tubular columns of cast iron rested on hand-cut stone piers, which supported the superstructure. The Confederates poured blasting powder into these tubular columns but even though the demolition expert was skilled, his method proved defective. Instead of catapulting the bridge into the river as expected, the explosives did no damage. Ensuing charges of powder also failed. General Jones then ordered the wooden parts of the bridge burned. After this order was completed, the rebels tried again. This time the explosive proved effective. By nightfall, the last of the spans laid in the river.

> **'Old Bob' Finds Way Back Home to Die**
>
> FLEMINGTON, Va., Apr. 10, 1863 — It's no empty thing when you talk about "horse sense."
>
> During the Jones-Imboden raid near Grafton, the Bailey family at Flemington hid all their horses on a hill overlooking the house, leaving only "Old Bob" in the stable. The Baileys figured no one would bother the old, sickly, swayback horse. But they were wrong; the soldiers took him.
>
> Months later "Old Bob" came limping home; they had turned him loose and he found his way back to the Bailey barn where he died.

Article found in the *Norman Kendall Scrapbooks* in the Genealogy Room at the Fairmont Public Library.

After the news of the attack on Fairmont was finally received in Grafton (delayed because the telegraph lines and poles were torn down), a small battalion of Union troops was sent out by train aboard flatcars to help protect the B&O train bridge, but of course they were too late. The iron railroad bridge was destroyed. Within four months after the Jones Raid on Fairmont, a temporary pontoon bridge was built just above where the old one had been. Light train traffic was maintained until construction of a "new" railroad bridge on the same piers was finished.

Word spread about the "raiding rebels" to the surrounding communities. Farmers hid their horses, livestock and valuables in hideouts hoping they could not be found. Col. A. W. Harmon was in charge of capturing livestock. His troops drove hundreds of horses and cattle from Kingwood to Fairmont, passing through White Day Creek, the Bunner Ridge area, Winfield and Colfax. Farmers on Piney Run hid their stock in caves until Harmon's 12th Virginia Cavalry passed through. Raiders combed the countryside for new horses. Scarcely a village or community within a radius of ten miles escaped their plunder. When the raiders left East Fairmont the horses and cattle were driven across the river at the fords of Texas (Colfax), Mundell's Ferry and Benton's Ferry. At the McAllister farm in Grant District, near today's Middletown Mall, the McAllister's hid their horses in a deep ravine on Vinegar Hill. They were never found. Fairmont owners of fine horses were forced to give them up in exchange for nags that were completely worn out. Eleven exceptional horses were taken from the Watson family.

The cattle and horses were driven to the Confederate lines in the Shenandoah Valley from Philippi to Beverly then on to Staunton, VA. The Jones-Imboden raid captured an estimate of more than 3,000 cattle and over 1,200 horses. It was the largest drive of livestock ever to pass through western Virginia. Union forces did nothing to stop them. They were taking refuge in the mountains.

Texas (Colfax), another community split in loyalties, was searched many times by both sides looking for rifles to be used in the war. Landowners and farmers hid their best rifles even after being warned not to. Many slept with their rifles in their straw tick mattresses till it was safe to bring them out.

Illustration by Jackie Richards, 1999.

As a result of the Jones raids in western Virginia, the statehood movement could not be stopped. There were 18,408 votes for statehood and 481 against when it came time to vote. Jones failed to destroy all the B&O Railroad bridges (except the ones around Fairmont) as planned, but he was successful in stealing money, livestock, food, boots, clothing, blankets and anything of value for supplies. When the Confederates left, they took with them one million dollars worth of valuables from the surrounding region. Quite a loot from just plain folk who didn't have much.

The following is a true story from *Recollections* by Judge H.C. McDougal. This is a true Civil War story about neighbor against neighbor.

In March of 1862 the two Barker brothers, who lived upriver near the railroad tracks near what later became known as Shrivers Flat, belonged to the Confederate forces. They captured Private George W. Fleming near his parents' farm near Texas (Colfax). George had entered the service in August of 1861 as a volunteer in the Sixth Regiment, Company A of the Western Virginia Infantry. His captors took him up the railroad tracks and twice hung him by the neck, but were too drunk to finish their terrible deed and Fleming escaped.

When the news arrived at McDougal's headquarters in Fairmont, a squad of 20 men was sent up the Tygart Valley River to hunt down the Barkers. When they arrived at Texas, the community had made the Barker brothers prisoners of war. (The residents knew where to find them and had made a citizens' arrest). The men were then turned over to the squad and were on their way back to Fairmont when the Barkers started to run to escape. When the squad caught up with them the Barkers were found dead on the B&O Railroad tracks.

The ordeal of 18-year-old George W. Fleming proved fatal; he died from shock and complications from disease three

The Irons homestead was built on the same foundation as the original log cabin where Civil War soldiers target practiced with their livestock. This house was also destroyed by fire in 1989. *Courtesy of Delbert Smith. 1960*

months later. On June 18, 1862, he was laid to rest not far from his home in the Springer graveyard (Colfax Cemetery).

Charles Joe Irons of Colfax related the following story to me. It has been handed down in the Irons family for several generations and is worth sharing. It depicts the life in a small, quiet community along the railroad during the Civil War.

Troop trains passed through the rural communities on the river quite often during the war. The solders aboard seemed to enjoy target practicing at livestock on the farms. It didn't matter if it was the north or the south; chickens were their favorite targets.

One afternoon between Poplar Island and Texas (Colfax) a troop train passed the isolated log cabin homestead of the Irons family. Malissa Irons sat in her rocker on the front porch of her home holding a baby in her lap. The soldiers began shooting at a rooster running across the yard. Bullets tore at the grass and splintered the wood along the front of the cabin. Through some miracle neither was hit during the volley of fire. With God's grace they both lived to tell about it.

The Irons log cabin burnt down from a chimney fire towards the end of the 1800's and a new structure built on the same foundation. When the new house was being built, the family made sure each room had two outside doors in it for fire escape purposes. This house was vacant when it mysteriously burned to the ground in 1989.

This true story comes from the book *The Barnes Family in West Virginia*.

Silas Barnes, son of Abraham and Mary Barnes, married Sarah Ann Mundell (daughter of William Bailey Mundell of Mundell's ferry); they lived by the railroad not far from the ferry. In 1861, at the beginning of the war, Silas enlisted in the Union army. While he was away their home was raided by the rebels. Sarah was shot in the arm while trying to escape. Her arm was split from elbow to wrist. Silas, sick himself in a Parkersburg hospital, received word to return home. He remained home and stayed there until Sarah started to recover.

Military picture of Silas Barnes.

When he returned to his command one day late, he was arrested for desertion for being one day late and sent to headquarters for a court martial. Fortunately his papers passed over the desk of Col. Larkin Pierpont, a brother to Governor Francis H. Pierpont.

The Barnes and the Pierpont families lived on opposite sides of the Tygart Valley River and as boys, they had been playmates. Silas grew up in the area where the Pump Station Road is today in Pleasant Valley. Silas had not recognized Col. Pierpont but Pierpont had recognized Barnes' name. After he had told his story about the raid on his home and the shooting of his wife, Pierpont destroyed the desertion papers. He made new ones certifying that Silas was returning from furlough and was on his way to join up with his command.

Later in the war, Silas Barnes was in the battle of Winchester, Virginia where he was taken prisoner again and imprisoned. After two months as a prisoner, he was released along with some others as part of an exchange program. He again returned to his regiment and served safely until the end of the war.

The Bloody Six

Many wild stories resulted from the Civil War like the true tale of Rev. James Clelland. Six members of the Union Home Guards, led by Captain Pole Altop, killed his good friend and neighbor Mr. Ashcraft. These guards were known locally as the "Bloody Six." There had been no reason for the killing except that the six men were reported to be drunk and had set out to terrorize the area. After the murder of Mr. Ashcraft, the guards moved on to the log cabin where Rev. Clelland and his 18-year-old son, George lived.

Altop demanded to know why George was not in the Union army, then ordered father and son to turn and run toward the cabin. Knowing if they ran, they would be shot in the back, Rev. Clelland reasoned with Altop and persuaded the guards to move on without killing them. Happenings such as this in the valley were commonplace during the war.

Vincent's Escape

Thomas Vincent was a known Southern sympathizer and lived on Vinegar Hill, up from Benton's Ferry. One night in 1862, the Union Home Guards visited his house and were going to arrest him. There was an argument and Mr. Vincent went upstairs where he blew a horn from a window, hoping to call friends. The guards fired a shot at Vincent and wounded his wife instead. Vincent escaped by jumping out of an upstairs window and ran.

He joined up with the Confederate Army and learned later that his wife had been shot during the incident. While secretly traveling home to visit her he was shot and killed. Mrs. Vincent died 19 years later.

Chapter Seven

ORIGINAL LOG CABINS ON THE RIVER

RUGGED BEAUTY

First they had to clear the land,
All around was timberland.

Cabins were built for protection,
All hand made every section.

The notching and chinking were precise,
The cut stone chimney made it real nice.

Log cabins of old were built to last,
They all have tales of the past.

Carolynn Fortney-Hamilton 1999

ORIGIN OF LOG CABINS

As our pioneer forefathers moved westward across the Appalachian Mountains, the art of building log cabins came with them. At the start, it was the only form of building in this area. They provided exceptional shelter from the howling winter winds and from the drenching spring rains but they were most prized for the protection they provided from the savage Indians. Bullets and arrows could not penetrate their thick walls. Our forefathers probably felt fortunate to have such homes.

When the first colonists arrived in North America, they did not know how to build a log cabin. They lived in makeshift shelters. In 1638, Swedish settlers built the first log homes in Delaware. The Swedes had been building log cabins in their native country for centuries. In 1710, German pioneers built the first cabins, barns and smokehouses in Pennsylvania. Ten years after that, those same pioneers began moving into the backcountry of the Appalachian Mountains, where they used the same method—using the forest trees to their advantage. By the time the Revolutionary War started, settlers were building log cabins all through the wilderness of western Virginia.

During the 1800's, there were many such cabins situated along the Tygart Valley River. Traces of them still can be spotted along the roadside or next to open fields and in the woods although most of the log cabins were replaced when sawmills made it easier to build a home out of clapboards. The log homes then became hay barns, animal shelters or outbuildings. Some still exist today.

Evidence of old log cabins reveal several clues; indications such as a lone chimney which remains standing, hand-cut foundation stones; perhaps daffodils blooming in the middle of nowhere, a lonely old lilac bush or apple trees growing in formation as though planted that way.

The whereabouts of some of the old log cabins were recorded in family histories while still others will remain a mystery. This chapter is devoted to the log homes along the Tygart—the ones that have withstood the ravages of time and continue to give us pleasure just by being able to look at them.

A log cabin was not easy to build and not everyone knew how to build them in the beginning. Most of our pioneers had very few tools to work with except for a broad ax. All the materials for the floors, walls, foundations, and chimneys could be made from local natural materials joined together without nails. There were several styles in which they were built.

One of the biggest myths about a house made of logs is the classification of a "cabin." According to present-day experts on historical log architecture refer to a log dwelling as a cabin only if it meets certain criteria. The "cabin" was usually only one or one-and-a- half stories high and measure less than 20 x 20 feet square. Anything over those standards should be called a log house.

In 1828 Andrew Jackson was elected President of the United States. He was born and raised in a log cabin. The frontier people, familiar with this mode of pioneer living, were sympathetic with him and their vote swayed the election away from the plantation owners and the wealthy merchants in the east. Abraham Lincoln, who had humble beginnings, wrote in his autobiography that he and his father built and lived in several log cabins during his boyhood.

Three types of logs were used: round, hewn on both sides, and squared. Mud, clay or moss or even a combination of all three was used to chink the cracks. Rough-wooden shingles, also cut from logs, were used on the roof. The floor, if there was one, was made of split logs laid side by side. In the days of virgin timber, pioneers made an entire door from one slab of timber. The chimney was usually made of cut sandstone taken from the fields. Our forefathers came from modest means but how proud they must have been when their home was finished!

With camera, pad and pen in hand, I went on a log cabin expedition along the Tygart. It took me several weeks tracking them all down, interviewing the owners and taking lots and lots of pictures. I was amazed at how many I came up with and enjoyed every minute of it. Each log home had a story to tell by its own workmanship. Some were very, very old while still others were the modern versions. I counted over 20 modern log homes along the river.

Today the fine art of building a genuine log cabin rests only in the minds of those who have carried on the tradition from earlier generations. First hand knowledge is rare. The following are some fine examples of that lost art.

SAM LINN LOG HOME
Benton's Ferry

The Sam Linn log cabin at Benton's Ferry can be traced back to 1836. Sam Linn was the third son of pioneer William and Isabella (Gibson) Linn of Glady Creek. He married Anzy Reese of Glady Creek and moved to Benton's Ferry in 1835. Here in 1836 he built his log cabin for his wife and growing family. They lived in a small house not far away while the log home was being built. Samuel and Anzy were both Primitive Baptists.

Sam was a hard-working farmer. According to family genealogy, he spoke few words but always kept them. Samuel and Anzy had nine children: William (Billy), Mary (Polly), George (who in later years lived in the log cabin); Nancy, Isabella, John, who later lived across the river at White Hall (see Cemeteries); Sarah Ann, Margaret and Hugh R, who in 1882 operated a store near the railroad tracks.

Backdoor view of the Sam Linn cabin as it looked in 2001.

Sam died of typhoid fever the year the railroad came through in 1852. He had lived in his log home for 17 years. He was buried on the family farm and was the first to be buried in what is known as the Sam Linn Cemetery. Anzy lived to be 92 years old. She had a healthy life except for her hearing, which was destroyed when lightning struck the cabin and burst her eardrums. She died in 1893 and is buried beside her husband.

The home stayed in the Linn family until 1910 when George Lilley bought it. He sold it in 1935; it has had three other owners since.

The two-story structure is built in the Scotch-Irish style with a front and back door (not all log homes had back doors.) Inside on one wall is a beautiful fireplace made of cut fieldstone. There is another on the second floor. A front porch was added at some point in its history. Judging from early pictures, a back porch was added even later. The two very old pines in the back of the home were perhaps planted by old Sam himself.

Scotch-Irish style homes were always rectangular in shape. Their main distinquishing feature was the front and back doors. According to medieval Scottish legends, two doors were required so that in bad weather, cows could be brought in for milking and led out the back door after it was finished.

Today the Linn log home is 164 years old and has passed the test of time. Currently, it is owned by Robert and Marilyn Ice, who use it as a rental property. It has been well preserved and is still as beautiful as it probably was when it was first built.

Front view of the Sam Linn cabin as it looked in the 1930's. It was built in 1836 at Benton's Ferry.

"THE LOG"
Benton's Ferry

One of the oldest log cabins still standing on the Tygart has had several additions over the years but retains the look of pioneer days. This log home is at the foot of Vinegar Hill on Camp Road in Grant District, Benton's Ferry. This beautiful home has been called "The Log" ever since the Civil War. It was built of heavy hand-hewn logs and has withstood several floods.

The original cabin was built in the Scotch-Irish style with two floors, a fireplace on each level, front door and back doors and windows all around the home.

The first addition to the cabin was made in the 1920's by then - owner John Y. Hite (part-owner of the Kingmont Mine). This addition is still the main entry, and was built of hand-hewn logs similar to those in the original structure. The logs for this addition including a back porch were brought in from another log cabin site. It was carefully reconstructed. It is difficult to detect the old from the new. This cabin was the first camp on the lower Tygart Valley River.

In the 1950's, under the ownership of Louis and Murine Baron, there was a second addition. The log became a residence again. Fieldstone was used on the lower level, which became a two-stall garage. Hand-hewn logs were used to build the second floor over the garage. Large picture windows were added in the back to allow a panoramic view of the river. The chimney and fireplace are original; they are in the center portion of the original home.

This property has had eleven different owners since 1869. It is not known for sure who built the original portion but I believe it was Benjamin Linn since his family was very knowledgeable about building log homes. Sam Linn built his cabin just across the river in the same styling. In 1869, the Benjamin Linn estate included 11 acres at this site.

According to his death certificate, Benjamin Linn was the son of Robert and Catherine Linn. He was born in Monongalia County, Virginia in 1820. The 1860 census lists Benjamin (39) and Sarah (28), his wife, as farmers. At that time they had three children: Ann C., 4, Robert B., 2, and Jacob, 1.

Six years after the Linns sold "The Log", they moved to what is now Pleasant Valley. In 1876 at the age of 57, Benjamin Linn died of typhoid fever. There have been two additions to the original structure. The north side addition was built in the early 1920's when John Y. Hite was the owner. He added two floors and a porch, all built from old logs relocated from another log cabin.

In the 1950's, Louise & Murine Baron owned the home. They made the second addition on the south side. Again using logs from other sites, a two-stall garage and upper floor were added. Today *The Log* is a year-round residence for Bob and Janene Hurst. They have preserved its beauty and rich heritage.

"The Log" as it looked in the early 1920's after the first addition. *Courtesy of Bob and Janene Hurst.*

This view of the orginal section of the log cabin shows the chimney made of local fieldstone.

Back view of the "The Log" facing the river. Note the original structure in the middle section. *Courtesy of Bob and Janene Hurst.*

Clelland Log Cabin
River Run

Rev. James Clelland came here from the Cheat River and Ice's Ferry area, where he was an early settler in 1769. By 1843, land records for Marion County show James Clelland owning three parcels of land that included 382 acres on River Run. He is buried on the hill behind his cabin in the Janes Memorial Cemetery on US Rt. 250 south (see Civil War Stories).

It is believed the cabin was built sometime between 1790 and 1810 because this was when settlers built their chimneys on the inside of the cabin, the idea being that it kept more heat in. Only the front of the cabin can be seen from the chain-link fence that surrounds it. The old structure and chimney is clearly visible. Besides the cabin, there are several log outbuildings and a stone cellar for food storage in the side of the hill on the property.

The Clelland cabin was built between 1790 and 1810 on River Run Road near the Marion-Taylor County line. It is listed on the National Register of Historic places.

This fascinating log cabin in Taylor County can be found six-tenths of mile from US Rt. 250 on River Run Road on the South Fork of River Run. A large meadow is in front of the cabin where it rests on a hillside on a fieldstone foundation. River Run gently flows through the bottom in front of the cabin, which is on private property but can be seen from the road.

Over its 200-year-long existence, the cabin has undergone many changes. It is made of hand-cut logs notched so that they fit very tightly. A passageway between the kitchen and the main room was added in the 1800's. Original inhabitants had to go outside to get from the kitchen to the rest of the cabin.

It is on the National Register of Historic Places. For more about the family who lived there (see Chapter Six.)

THE HONEYMOON CABIN
Sarrietta

This little one-room cabin, on the Colfax Road coming from US Rt. 250, was built when Thomas Little, Jr. married Eliza Harr in the early 1930's. Eventually, they had a family of nine children so probably, they did not live there very long. When Amos and Juliann (Pearse) Little were first married, they also started their married life in this cabin. Amos was the second son born to Thomas and Rachel Little, who owned the property overlooking the river.

Few people could recognize it now. The cabin is located on the left, high on the knoll across from the Poplar Island Road intersection where it crosses Fall Run. There is no indication that there is a log home underneath the white exterior siding.

Thomas, Jr. and his father Thomas, Sr. died within six months of each other in 1851 (see Cemeteries). Thomas Jefferson (TJ) Little (Thomas, Jr.'s third son), owned the cabin when it was sold to Thomas A. Hartley in 1883. TJ Little married Mary McCallister and they had three daughters.

The original one-room cabin measured 21x15. It had a cut-sandstone fireplace on the north side. The original entryway and the two window wells measure 16 inches in depth. Over time, three rooms were added in back and the fireplace was removed. Wood siding was added to the exterior walls which were later white washed. More recently, white siding was added. There is a hand-dug basement.

The wide front porch is not the original but one similar to it. In the early years, a backporch was added to create more space. The inside of the house has been remodeled, leaving no reminders of the logs underneath except at the entrance and in the deep window wells.

The Hartleys lived in it for awhile before they rebuilt across the creek. He bought the mill down by the river in January of 1888. It was swept away in a flood six months later. Several Hartleys are buried in the Vincent Cemetery, which means the family lived in the community for quite some time. The Hartleys sold the property to the Lanham family and 10 years after that, it was acquired by Jesse Nixon. In 1920, the Vincent family became owners. They kept it for 15 years before selling it to the Griffith family.

The county road used to pass right in front of the cabin before the WPA cut a new road below it by Fall Run. The Griffith driveway was once the old county road. Fall Run is written as such on many of the old deeds. It was named for the beautiful 15-foot falls at the bridge crossing over the run in front of the cabin. The creek quickly drops in elevation and empties into the Tygart.

The Honeymoon Cabin overlooking Sarietta. It was built in the early 1830's.

White siding conceals the cabin, which is at least 150 years old.

It is interesting to note that Homer and the late Anne Currance built a modern log home near the same site as the original Thomas Little, Sr. log cabin, which is gone now. The Little Cemetery is located nearby.

One wonders how many old cabins could be found under clapboards or siding? There could be a forgotten one near you.

THE TUCKER CABIN
At White Hall

The Thaddus L. Tucker cabin can be found very easily on U.S. 250 south at White Hall. Located on the corner of the street that takes you to White Hall School, at first sight this beautiful cabin can take your breath away. Local residents who pass the home several times a day undoubtedly wonder about its origin.

Thaddeus L. Tucker, who purchased 35 acres of land from William N. Hall, built this attractive roadside cabin in 1875. Thaddeus and his wife Ann (Provance) had two children when they moved into the house. He lived the rest of his years in this cabin, died at the age of 68 in 1909 and is buried beside the rest of his family in the John Linn Cemetery not far from his home (see Cemeteries).

It is built of four-sided hand-hewn logs that were dovetailed notched in all four corners. The skillful axmanship can be detected even from the road. There are two rooms downstairs and a set of narrow stairs that go to the two rooms upstairs, commonly called the loft. Both downstairs rooms have a front and back door. This is known as the Saddlebag design, which was used for early log cabins. Their main feature was a large fireplace, made of local fieldstone, in the center of the home. To the passer-by the only exterior evidence of a chimney is the smokestack on the roof. In the early days the fireplace was the only source of heating and cooking so there were hearths on both sides of the chimney, upstairs and down. In the front of the house there is a hand-dug water well with fieldstones neatly placed around it. A lantern was permanently affixed at the top of the well to light the night.

The Tucker cabin is located on U.S. 250 south at White Hall. It was built in 1875 by Thaddeus Tucker.

Original flagstone water well in front of the Tucker log home in White Hall.

Front view of the Thaddeus L. Tucker cabin.

This log home remained in the Tucker family until 1924. Since then it has had six other owners. Additions to the home over the years, such as three porches and a kitchen, have not detracted from its character. The original structure has undergone some major repairs in recent years. Some of the logs have been replaced

Windy and Steve Cutlip, who appreciate its history, now own and live in the log home. They have kept the pioneer character of the home inside and out. It proudly overlooks the constant steady stream of traffic in front. This historic log home has been a significant landmark for over 125 years and is still going strong.

OTHER INTERESTING LOG HOMES

In my search for log cabins along the river, I discovered many log homes, most of which were the modern versions sold mostly in kits by dealers. One entire housing development just inside the Taylor County line on U.S. Route 250 was made up of them.

One new log cabin unique in craftsmanship is the Williams' cabin near the river. Brent Williams built his cabin from trees cut down at the site. The four-sided logs were not hand-hewn but were cut by more modern methods. As a hobby using the simple plan our ancestors used long ago, he started the structure in 1990 that includes an upper loft, huge cut-stone fireplace and a cozy front porch. Measuring 18x24 ft. and 13 logs high it is like looking at a page out of the history books. Williams, who uses the cabin for a workshop, continues his work. He has added an extra room.

Another log structure withstanding many, many years of durability is on the Rock Lake Road to Valley Falls. On the right, this very old structure once belonged

Familiar landmark on the Rock Lake Road to Valley Falls. This barn was originally built by Samuel Linn, an early settler in the area.

to Samuel Linn and probably was built before the Civil War. It has survived the elements of time and still is being used as a shelter for horses. It is currently owned by Gerald and Donna Musgrove, who live on the property.

In 1938, Chester and Maude Berry of Fairmont decided to build a log home in the country at Colfax for their large family. Making the design himself and with the help of some local neighbors, Chester bought logs taken from behind the Grafton Dam before the area was flooded. They were purchased from a logging concern hired to remove the trees during construction. The poplar logs were delivered to the building site where the bark was removed and logs cut again into the proper size. Each log was creosoted twice before being chinked in place with cement. The six-room home has pine tongue-and-groove flooring throughout the house and has handmade solid oak entry doors. Still boasting of country charm, it became the home of their son, the late Wesley and his wife, Mildred Berry of Colfax.

Edwin Nuzum had a log building built at the same time as the Berry home at Colfax. It was also built of logs taken from behind the Grafton Dam. In 1938, the structure became the "The Homestead Inn," a restaurant operated by Nuzum and known for fine home-cooked meals. Doris Barnes, who had an A.B. Degree in Home Economics, was the cook. She married Edwin Nuzum in 1940. Mr. Nuzum ran the family dairy across the road with his father, Faye, and later operated Nuzum Contracting Company. The restaurant was closed around 1942. It became a rental property before it was sold. Both of these eye-catching buildings (homes) can be seen from a car on the Colfax Road.

Today there are numerous modern log homes scattered along the river and across the state. Some have been relocated from other sites, reconstructed and updated. This ancient form of housing is still pleasing to the eye and still in demand. There is something about a log building that reaches out to many of us. They beckon us to come in and take a step back in time.

Log home constructed from cut logs taken from behind the Grafton Dam during its construction. It was built by Chester and Maude Berry of Colfax in

The Williams workshop cabin off the Colfax Road. Building began in 1990 and has been an ongoing project.

Log dwelling built by Edwin Nuzum in 1938 for a restaurant. It was called "The Homestead Inn."

The Tygart Valley River is no longer as free flowing as it was when our pioneers came up the river. We can no longer drink freely from its waters as they did. Those of us who know and love the river must stand guard against the river-killers who are slowly ruining its splendor and beauty–not only for future generations but for ourselves.

BIBLIOGRAPHY

Balderson, Walter L. *Fort Prickett Frontier and Marion County.* Publisher unnamed. 1976.
Barnes, Rev. I. A. *The Methodist Protestant in WV.* Mennonite Publishing House, Scottsdale, PA. 1926.
Barnes, Rev. I. A. *The Barnes Family In West Virginia.* Mennonite Publishing House, Scottsdale, PA. 1920.
Bittinger, Emmett F. *Allegheny Passage, Churches & Families, West Marva District Churches of 1752-1990.* Pennobscot Press, Camden, Maine. 1990.
Bonner, J. William. *The Baptist Temple History.* Morgantown Printing & Binding Company, Morgantown WV 1975.
Callahan, James Morton. *Semi-Centennial History of WV.* Semi-Centennial Commission. 1913.
Conley, Phil. *History of the Coal Industry.* Education Foundation, Inc., Charleston, WV, 1960.
Core, Earl. *Monongahalia Story I, II, and III.* McClain Printing, Parsons, WV. 1974.
Davis, Dorothy. *History of Harrison County.* McClain Printing, Parsons, WV. 1970.
Dunnington, George A., *History and Progress of the County of Marion, West Virginia,* George A. Dunnington Publisher, Fairmont, WV, 1880, Reprinted by Morgantown Printing and Binding Co., Morgantown, WV, 1992.
Fitzpatrick, John C., *The Diaries of George Washington Vol. 1 1748-1770.* Houghton Mifflin Company, Boston and New York. 1925.
Garrison, Webb. *Civil War Curiosities.* Rutledge Hill Press, Nashville, TN. 1994.
Harrison County Bicentennial Committee. *Harrison County A Bicentinnial Album 1784-1984.* Walsworth Press, Inc.1985.
Hennen, Ray V. *WV Geological Survey County Report of 1913 for Marion, Mon. and Taylor Co.* Wheeling News Litho Co. 1913.
Hinds, Lynn Boyd. *Broadcasting the News: The EarlyYears of KDKA-TV.* The Pennsylvania State University Press, University Park, PA. 1995.
Hull, Margarett Virginia. *Genealogical History of the Family of William Linn.* Mennonite Publishing House, Scottsdale, PA. 1932.
Hupp, J. C. *A Short History of Diamond Street Church-Fairmont, WV.* Banner Printing Company, Parkersburg, WV. 1951
Jacobs, G. Walker. *Stranger Stop & Cast an Eye.* The Stephen Green Press, Battleboro, Vermont, 1972.
Koon, Thomas and Oce Smith. *Marion County, West Virginia.* The Donning Company, Virginia Beach, VA. 1995.
Lough, Glenn. *Now and Long Ago.* Morgantown Printing & Binding Co., Morgantown, WV, 1969. Reprinted McClain Printing Co., Parsons, WV. 1994.
Marion County Historical Society. A *History of Marion County.* Walsworth Publishing Co., Marceline, Missouri. 1985.
Methodist Ministers of the West Virginia Conference, The Methodist Publishing House, 1964.
Nuzum, David G. *Nuzum Family Genealogy,* McClain Printing Company, Parsons, WV. 1983.
Daniel Ried, Robert D. Linder, Bruce L. Shelly & Harry S. Stout. *Dictionary of Christianity in America.* Intervarsity Press, Downers Grove, Ill., 1990.
Spevock, Frank. *Memories of Yesterday.* Yates Printing, Fairmont, WV. 1965.
Spevock, Frank. *Memory's Lane.* Yates Printing, Fairmont, WV. 1975.
Spevock, Frank. *45 years of Diary Notes 1947-1992.* Color Craft Printing, Charleston, WV.
Summers, Festus P. *The B&O Railroad in the Civil War.* G. P. Putnam, New York. 1939.
Taylor County Historical & Genealogical Society. *Images of America Taylor County.* Arcadia Publishing, Charleston, SC. 2000
Watson, J. O. *Marion County in the Making.* Press of Meyer & Thalheimer, Baltimore, MD. 1917.
White Day Watershed Association. *The History of White Day Creek.* Published by the White Day Watershed Association. 1997.
Woodall, Ronald. *The Log Cabin: Homes of the North American Wilderness.* Dai Nippon Printing Co., Tokyo, Japan. 1978
WV Heritage Foundation. *West Virginia Heritage. Vol. 1.* James Comstock, Richwood, WV.
Wyckoff, Jerome. *Geology, Our Changing Earth through the Ages.* Golden Press Publishing, New York, NY, Western Printing & Lithographing. 1967.

OTHER RESOURCES

Fairmont Times, Tom Koon. March 11, 1998.
Fairmont Times, Church Histories. William J. Wilcox.
Fairmont Times, E.E. Meredith. April 26, 1953.
Fairmont Times, Tom Koon. January 22, 1998.
Fairmont Times, Eleanor Carson. May 10, 1951.
Fairmont Times, E.E. Meredith. *Do You Remember* articles
Golden Seal Magazine. Fall 1986. *Kingmont* by Norman Julian.
Manuscript of *The Little Family,* Author unknown.
Maps from *"Marion and Monongalia Counties".* D. J. Lake & Co. 1886.
One Hundred Twenty-Nine Years of History, Diamond Street United Methodist Church, Bicentennial Issue, 1776-1976.
Personal Diaries of Della Satterfield. 1926 to 1945.
Personal Diaries of Iretta Smith. 1945 to 1985.
Personal Manuscript of *The History of Taylor County,* Vol. I, Prepared by Charles Brinkman, 1986
The Grafton Sentinel Articles
The Grafton Press, Articles by Norman F. Kendall
The Robert Files Family Genealogy
The Personal Scrapbooks of Norman F. Kendall, Marion County Genealogical Club.
Taylor County in Profile, a publication of the Taylor County Genealogical & History Society, winter 1995
West Virginia, A Quarterly Magazine, Article by Ross Johnston, Published by the State Department of Archives and History, Charleston, WV, October 1953.
West Virginia State Gazetteer & Business Directories. WV Dept. Of Archives & History. Charleston, WV.
The West Virginia Review, Lawrence Rollins, Editor, Mathews PTG. & Company, Charleston, WV, 1937
Wonderful West Virginia Magazine article by Kenneth L Carvell.
Margaret Files of Cleveland, Texas and Lois Jowers Dealy of Daphne, Alabama. *The History of the Files Family*
Beverly Hopkins, Erie, Pennsylvania, *The Fettermans*

Index

A

Able
    Guy 158
    Hallie 192
    William 207
Adams, Patricia 73
Addison 186
Adelphia 135
Adena Culture 12
Alcorn, John Roy 192
Alderson-Broaddus College 186
Algonquin Indians 12
Allegheny River 11
Allender, Mr. 151
Altop, Captain Pole 282
American Railway Express Company 87
Annon, Zachariah 201
Antioch 43, 61
Apple Valley 93
Arbogast, Terry 172
Armstrong, Hattie Davis 171, 174
Arnett
    Lily 151
    Louise 73
Ashby, Mabel Groves 190
Atha Chicken Farm 129
Atha,
    P. C. "Bud", Jr. 129
    V. P., 171
Atkin Work farm 84
Augusta County 14, 67
Autistic Training Center 128
Auvil,
    A. C. 201
    Myrtle 190
Auxiliary, Women's 74

B

B&N Railroad Company 63
B&O Railroad 276, 279
Baker,
    Edith 157
    James 207
Baker's Curve 62
Baker's, Stark L. Mill 13
Balderson,
    Estel 73
    Ethel 153
    Walter 13, 23, 70, 72, 92, 118, 153, 176, 190
    William 205
Ballah M.E. Church 200
Baltimore and Ohio (B&O) Rail Road 34
Baptist Temple 200
Barker,
    David 35, 114, 151
    Elizabeth 104
    John 48
    Rawley 36
Barlett,
    Jean 173
    Rebecca (Johnson) Springer 103
Barnes,
    Abraham 70, 71, 89
    Abraham and Mary 35
    Asenath 71
    Charles "Bailey" 130
    Dale 136, 211
    Dale (Winnie) and Clarence 144
    David 209
    David, Genevieve and Bailey 144
    Doris 137, 290
    Ed 18
    Genevieve 119, 136, 147
    George 156
    Hubert "Hez" and Charles "Bailey" 130, 131
    Isaac 216, 227
    Jacob 68, 70
    Linn, Annalore and George 147
    Mary Ann 71
    Mill 114
    Peter T. 24, 71, 131
    Rev. Isaac A. 70, 89, 205
    Sarah 68
    Silas 281
    Silas and Sarah 35
    Store 131
    The Family in West Virginia 281
    William 71
    William H. 202
    William, Sr. 68
Barnesville or Highland Avenue M.E. Church 200
Barnsville 67
Baron, Louis and Murine 286
Barrackville Methodist Church 199
Bartholow, George 205
Bartlett, Jean 190
Batten, Joseph 103
Batton,
    Janet, Karen, "Kookie", Sylvia and Wayne 145
    Sylvia 136
    Wayne and Sylvia 131
Beaty, Emaline 68
Beckley, W. W. 205
Bee, Asa 86
Bee Gum Union Church 200
Belkeep, Fred 111
Bell,
    A. C. 204
    Mrs. A.C. 211
    Rev. A. C. 217
Belle, Jesse 216
Belmear, Geraldine 136
Bennett,
    Betty 73
    Sylvester 216
Benny's Cut 61, 154
Benton,
    James T. and a Mordecai 86
    Thomas Hart 86
Benton's Ferry 24, 35, 38, 41, 42, 43, 45, 48, 58, 61, 62, 74, 85
Benton's Ferry Bridge 87
Benton's Ferry Schools 92
Benton's Ferry United Methodist Church 205
Berry,
    Chester 137
    Chester and Maude 290
    Faye C. 176
    Mildred and Wesley 145
    Wesley and wife Mildred 137
    Willa 151
Bethel M.E. Church 199
Bethesda Baptist Church 199
Beverly 13
Bice,
    Cassie Fortney and Elizabeth (Fortney) 141
    Elizabeth 128, 136
    Elizabeth (Fortney) 128, 153, 158
    Elizabeth and Fred 142
    Fred 48, 126, 134
Biddle,
    Ingle 192
    Robert 48
Bide-e-Wee 18
Big and Little Falls 182
Billy Sunday Club 217
Bishop,
    George M. 92
    Jacob 48
    Will 87
black gold 78
black-powder explosives 182
Blacksville 63
Blake, Joetta Fisher 128
Blankenship,
    Jessy (Chuck) 111
    Mike 111
Bloody Six 282
Blue, The Ridge Lunch 95
Blue, Willhide B. 271
Bluemont Cemetery 186
Boice,
    Curtis 173, 190
    Francis 48
    William (Willie) 38, 48, 122
Bond, Linda 73, 82
Boone, Grace 174
Booth,
    Carol 73
    James 17, 101
    John 17
Booths Creek 101
Boothsville 67, 132
Boothsville M.E. Church 199, 200
Boothsville School 94
Bott, Matt 205
Bowman, Walter 205
Bowyer, Lane 111
Boy Scout Troop #10 252
Boy Scouts of America Troop 4 18
Boyce,
    Boyers 216
    Curtis 158
    Flora 211
    Nellie L. 81
    Samuel 248
    Samuel, Jr. 249
    Willie" 61
Boyce-Clark Cemetery 248
Boyers, Jonathon 182
Boyles,
    Dr. 76
    Edna Brown 190
    Ted 87
Bradshaw,
    Edith 192
    John 36, 40, 170, 184, 185, 189, 191
Bragg, W. W. 204
Brand, Kenneth 100
Branson, Lois Beckner 112, 128
Brett,
    I. A. 170
    Thomas I. 167, 169
Brown,
    James 173, 190, 206
    T. Bailey 276
Buckhannon and Northern Railroad Company 63
Buckhannon River 14
Buffalo Methodist Church 200
Bunner,
    Anna 254
    Irene 176
    John 103
    Joseph L. 103
    O. C. 204
Bunner Ridge Post Office 169
Burgreen, Belle Hartley 94
burial customs 226
Burns, Richards 48
Burnt Cabin Run 16, 101
Byers, Andrew 35
Byrd, Senator Robert C. 136

C

Cain, Franklin 126, 128
Calvary Baptist Church 200, 204

Camp Victoria 189
Canfield, I. A. 204
Canfield, Olive Davis 158
Canning Hotel 189
Canning, Sarah (Bradshaw) 189, 191
Canton Bridge Builders Company 109
Capitol High School 76
Carder, Ms. 73
Carolina 84
Carpenter and Ford Funeral Home 227
Carpenter,
    Bernice 176
    David 206
    James 136, 176
    James J. 128
    Karen 176
    Margaret 206
    T. M. and Florence 94
    W.W. 178
    Watson 151, 157
    William and Margaret 35
Carr,
    Harry 112
    Patrick 26
    Rosby 41
Carroll, Charles 34
Carrrone, Alphonse 192
Carunchia, Joe 84
Catawba Indian War Path Trail 13, 132, 181
Catawba M.E. Church 199
Catawba M.P. Church 199
Cather, Elsie Dale Little 151, 171, 190
Cathers, Lawrence 21
Cattafesta, Guy J. 81
Causey, Henry D. 80
Cayuga 12
Cecil 29
Central Christian Church 200
Century Cable 135
Cervo,
    Iva 73
    John 81, 82
Chalfant 173
Chaney, Joe 151
Channell, Lehman A. 203, 204
Channell, Randolph 216
Chapman, Carol 82
Charles Curry 100
Cheat Mountain 12
Cheat River 13
Cherokee Falls 13
Cherokee Valley 13, 181
Chesapeake & Ohio Canal 34
Chesapeake & Ohio Railroad 62
Cheuvront,
    A. 171
    William 48
    Pearl 151
Chicago World's Fair 167
Chidester, Jennie 173
Christ Episcopal Church 199
Christen, Anna 104
Christie, Hyson 151
Church of the Brethren 157
Church on the Hill 208
Civil War 200, 276
Civil War Curiosities 279
Clarke, Martha 249
Clarksburg tunnel 184
Clayton, Cora 174
Clayton, Pauline Satterfield 190
Clelland, James 206, 287
Clelland Log Cabin 287
Clelland, Rev. James 282
Clevender, Orval 190
Clinton, Ida 106
Cochran,
    Alcinda 173, 190
    James 72
    Nathaniel 101
Coffey, Jack 149
Coffindaffer, Bernard 243

coffins 226
Coffman 43, 196
Coffman, S. A. 204
coke ovens 196
Col. Morgan Morgan Chapter 269
Colfax 17, 42, 43, 44, 45, 49, 61, 73, 90, 101, 103, 104, 105, 106, 108, 110, 111, 112, 114, 115, 117, 118, 119, 120, 121, 122, 123, 124, 125, 126, 128, 129, 130, 131, 132, 134, 135, 136, 137, 139, 148, 150, 152, 153, 156, 157, 158, 161, 163
    Brick Company 121, 125
    Bridge 11, 22, 23, 24, 25, 28, 101, 108
    Cemetery 104, 244, 245
    Community Association 130
    Elementary School 112, 128
    Grocery Stores 131
    Ladies Aid 211
    M.E. Church 200, 208
    M.P. Church 200
    Post Office 114
    Public Service District 135
    School 124, 125
    Schuyler 105
Collins,
    Albert and Blanche 153
    John 158
Colony of Virginia 14
Community Educational Outreach Service Clubs 136
Community, The Association 130
Company A, 31st Regiment 276
company store 81
Conn, J. P. 121
Connellsville B&O branch 34
Conner,
    C. 205
    Patty 128
Construction camps 38
Conturo, Mary 150
Cook, John J. 123
Coon's Run Baptist Church 199
Cooper,
    Polly 269
    Hollow 278
Cordray,
    Daniel 245
    Ezra 106
    Martha 176
    William Ezra 108
Core, Earl 114
Corley,
    A B. 216
    Jesse 100
Cornstalk, Chief 154
County, Marion Commission 130
Courtney,
    Isaac 35, 72, 202
    Sarah and Isaac 72
Cove Run 29
Credit Mobilier Scandal 105
Creek, George's 68
Criss, Henry 80
Cristy, Mike and Misty 161
Cross Roads 183
Crossroads 23
Crouser, D. J. and Minnie 158
Crown American Corporation 98
CSX 62
Cumpston , David "Big Dave" 257
Currance, Lt. Col. Homer and Ann 251, 288
Currens, John 94
Current, Grace 128
Curry,
    Alfred 97
    Annie 158
    Asby 173
    Jonah 173
    Mary Giles 173, 190
    Mattie 158
    Wade H. 92

Curry's General Store 95, 97
Curtis, Fay 153

D

Daddisman,
    Miss 94
    Samuel 173, 190
Dalton, James C. 111
Daniel, Morrow 169
Daughters of American Revolution 269
David Morgan Bridge 99
Davidson, John 204
Davis ,
    Franklin and Jane 35
    Anna 140
    Annie 211
    Charles B. 94
    Elizabeth 206
    Emily 206
    Ester 205, 206
    Hattie 157
    Jacob and Ester 35
    Jacob J. 206
    James 206
    James T. 94
    Joseph 101
    Martha 82, 128, 158, 171, 176
    Mary 128
    Rufus 171
Dawson, Dwaine 210
Day, Scott 94
Daylight Saving Time 137
de, Baron Bulan 183
de Bulan, Sarah Constantine 182
de, Marquis Lafayette 185
Dean, Alfred, Jr 194
DeBalski, Mary 73
Deer Park, Maryland 185
Delaney, Sarah and William 209
Delawares 101
Deli, Frank 222
DeMary, Pete and Nancy 267
DeMayo, Barbara 73
DeMuth, Phillip 204, 213
Dents Run Baptist Church 200
DeVito, Tom and Patricia 161
Dewitt, E. D. 194
Diamond Street Methodist Church 199, 205
Dicken, Ed 70, 119
Dickinson, Joseph 163
Dietz, Gertrude 153
Dinwiddie, Governor Robert 14
Dodd,
    Alza 70
    Cemetery 243
    Elzy 35, 105
    James T. 71, 243
    Rebecca 103
Dollison, Ralph 134
Dolover, J. J. 204
Donald, Alma 73
Dragich, George 76
Drake, Robert 222
Duckworth, Orvilla 153
DuMont, Allen B. 134
Dunkard Cemetery 256
Dunkard's Bottom 13
Dunmore, Lord John Murray 154
Dunmore's War 154
Dunnington, George A. 38

E

Early, Sandra 100
East Branch of the Monongahela River 13
East Fairmont High School 75
East Fairmont Junior High 76
East Side Utility Company 156
Eastern Associated Coal Corp 162
Eaton, Charles, Sr. 205
Eddy, Alice Storms 142

Eddy, James E. 135
Edwards, David 101
Efaw,
    Earnest 48
    Tommy 48
Elder, Jasper 158
Eldora 12
Eldora M.P. Church 200
Elkins 12
Elliott, Ron 135
Elmer, L. 209
Elsey, L E. 30
Emancipation Proclamation 278
English, Minnie 128
Environmental Energy Engineers 135
Episcopal Church 199
Erie Canal 34
Evangelical United Brethren Church 200
Evil Sprit Falls 181

F

Faber, Harry 106
Fairmont & Beverly Turnpike 99
Fairmont
    Free Methodist Church 200, 214
    Municipal Airport 77
    State College 120
Fairmont Times 164
Fairview M.P. Church 199
Fall Run 18
Falls, Richard 16, 101
Falls, Valley Public Service District 69
Fancher Family photo 143
Fansler, Steve 100
Fantasia, Nick 82, 91
Farm Women's Club 136
Farmer Brown's Market 97
Farmington 84
Faulkner, Charles H. and Olive 178
Faust, J. W. 94
Fawcett, Ronald E. 193, 194
Feather, Gay 204
Feather, J. B. 204
Fetterman 36, 183
Fetterman ,
    George and Hannah (Plummer) 182
    Captain William Judd 183
    Gilbert L. B. 185
    Sarah B. 36
    W. W. and Sarah 37, 182, 185
    Wilfied B. 188
Field Creek 15
Files Creek 13
Files,
    Margaret 13
    Robert 13
First Baptist Church 199, 200
First Catholic Church 199
First M.E. Church 199
First M.P. Church 199
First Presbyterian Church 199, 200
First Presbyterian Church of Fetterman 184
First Southern Baptist Church 220
First United Presbyterian Church 200
First WV Infantry 276
Fisher, Joetta 112, 176
Fitzpatrick, M. S. 194
Five Mile House 98
Flaggy Meadow Baptist Church 200
Fleming,
    Mr. and Mrs. J. W. "Uncle Web" 209
    Allison 225
    Charlie and Wilbur 146
    Ed 106
    Edgar 110
    George W. 280
    John, 106
    Mary (Smith) 148
    Mathew 105
    Mathew L. 35
Fleming School 94

Flesher, Betty Grimes 173
Fletcher, Patty Resetar 128
Floyd, William 222
Fluharty,
    Dale 123
    Joe 48
Foot Prints 257
Ford,
    Ruse 48
    Standish 182
    Wilma 73
Forshey, John 151, 152
Forshey's Levels 17, 151, 182
Fort Edwards 101
Fort Fetterman 183
Fort Kearny 183
Fort Prickett Frontier and Marion County
    13, 23, 70, 118
Fort Wilson 154
Fortney ,
    Ila, Carolynn and Charles (Larry) 142
    Albert 82, 216
    Charles and Nancie 135
    Charles D. 119, 209
    Elba 149
    Elizabeth 126
    Elmer 48
    Hugh 149
    Ila M. (Dubay) 111, 112, 118,
        119, 120, 127, 130, 131, 135, 136,
        188, 210
    L.E. 106
    Lillian 216
Fortney/Kinty railroad crossing 114
Fortney's Mill 15, 257
Four States 84
Francis Asbury 198
Frankenberry,
    Miles 117
    William 117
Frankman Field 77
Frankman, Samuel J. (Sam) 77
Frank's Aviation Flight School and Banner
    Towing S 77
Franks, Marvin 77
Frederick Snare Corporation 29
Freed, Marvin 205
French and Indian War 13
French Indians 14
French, Mamie 122, 136
Frew, Sam 182
Friends For the Restoration of Guyses 161
Ft. Le Bouef 14
Fugitive Slave Act 277
Fuller, George Warren 69
Fulton, John C. 121

G

Galilean Baptist Church 220
Gallahue,
    John 108
    P. S. 105
Gandee, Kent 76
Gardi, Vincenzo, 123
Garlow,
    Jemima 104
    Tillie 115
Garrett, John Work 185
Gaskins, Nancy 178
Gates, Thomas J. 192
Gateway Market 97
Gath Post Office 173
Genealogical History of William Linn 270
General Paving Contractors 135
Gerkins, Nellie L 81
Ghost House 189
Ghost Story 278
Gilbert Rock 191
Gilboa Church 152
Gilboa Methodist Episcopal Church 199, 205
Giles, Dorothy 125

Gillespie, Elizabeth 158
Gist, Christopher 14
Glade Fire Brick Company 165, 170
Glady Creek 15, 179
Glenn K. Little Store 18
Goff,
    Donald 205
    Nathan 192
Goode, Jemima Hayhurst 128, 153
Goodwin,
    Edsel 48
    Mattie Curry 190
    William 158
Goose Creek 17, 156
Goose Creek School 157
Gordon Martin Store 137
Gorsuch, Thomas 254
Graftin 36
Grafton 36
Grafton Dam 85
Grafton, John 36
Grafton-Fairmont Gas Company 121
Grant, Ulysses S. 105
Gray, David 182
Great Cannaway 14
Great Catawba Indian Warpath Trail 101, 156
Great Cunnaway 14
Gregg, Samuel 163
Greippe, Charles 192
Griffith,
    Emma 82, 92, 202
    Gerald and Nondise 140
    Janice 126
    Mary 103
    Nondise 126, 136
    Orlando 150
Grose, L. S. 204
Gulf of Mexico 11
Guyses Run 22, 103
Gwynn's Falls 34
Gygax, John 194
Gypsies 134

H

H. B. Huffman Coal Company 95
Haas, Gwendolyn 128, 171
Haddix,
    George 158
    Oscar 48
Haddox, Merle 194
Hale, Lenora 151
Half-King 14
Hall,
    Allen 71
    Florence 153
    Jordan 71
    Mary Ann 71
    Mattie Morgan 157, 176
Hall Mill 151
Hall,
    Rececca 206
    Reynear 35
    Richard 206
    Sanford B. 89, 92, 150, 204
    Susie 151
    Thomas and Rebecca 71
    William 238
Halleck Road 118
Hamilton,
    John E. 159
    Sally (Peterson) 95
Hammond 16, 61, 163
Hammond,
    Bill and Mayr Lou 142
    E. R. 165
Hammond Fire Brick Company 165, 175
Hammond,
    James Brett 166
    James S. and Elizabeth (Brett) 166
    James B. 165
Hammond Ridge 173

Hammond Ridge School 173
Hampton Valley 156
Haney, William 182
Hanway, Samuel 182
Harbert, Goldie 153
Hardman,
    John 181
    L. 43
Harman, Lester H. 81
Harmon's 12th Virginia Cavalry 279
Harper, Hoyt 174
Harpers Ferry 14, 67
Harr,
    A.P. 94, 153
    Alice 68
    Eliza 287
    Harry 178
    Hun 204
    John 104, 204
    R. E. 178
    Zimri 35
Harrington, Deborah 128, 176
Harris,
    Jane 103
    John 106
Harrison,
    Benjamin 67
    William Henry 15
Harsh, Robert E. 193, 194
Hartley, Thomas A. 287
Harvey, Phyllis 205
Hauge, Andrew 100
Hawkins,
    Isaac and Margaret (Irons) 116
    A C. 48
    E. L. 106
    Emma 116
    Fred 116, 131, 209
    Henry 24
    Icie (Nichols) 143, 211
    Joshua 249
    Margaret 206
    Opal Tatterson 171
    Pearl 18, 116
    Thomas 169
    W. Fred 122
    W. H. "Peg" 61, 106, 116, 118, 131, 209
    William "Peg" and Susan 18
Hawkins-Wilt, Kathleen 137
Hayes,
    Wanda 192
    William 48
Hayhurst,
    Charles 148
    Daisy 205
    David and Tabatha 179
    Howard 137
    James 222
    John, 110
Hayhurst Mill 28
Hayhurst,
    Orlando 78, 88
    Ruth and Levi 144
    William 48
Haymond, Thomas 34
Haywood, Earl 205
Hebron Baptist Church 199, 200
Heck, John A. 204
Helmick, Billie B. 204
Helmick Foundry 90
Helmick, Reverend "Billy" 203
Helsley, Nimrod 267
Henderson,
    Andrew 171, 174
    Elizabeth 269
    Ethel 126, 136
    Margie McKinney 190
    William 269
Henry, Governor Patrick 182
Hepburn Railway Act 37
Herron,
    Basil 153, 171

Berl 176
Berle 214
Beryl 153, 158
Charles 176
Clifford C. 257
J. D. 70
Lynn 171
Marion L. 117
Martin A. Keener and Marion 121
Mary Vangilder 153, 176
Hewitt,
    Ben 48
    Beulah 126
    Mary Jean 128
Hi-Way, The Shoppe 95
Hill, Greg, Clifford, Crystal and Margie 143
Hinebaugh, Frank O. 81
Hinzman, U. R. 205
Hirons,
    John 205, 207
    Sally 207
Historical Records Survey Project 227
History and Progress of the County of Marion, WV 38
History of the Family of William Linn 87
Hite,
    George M. 159, 169
    John Y. 286
    P. G. 80
    Peter Yost 79
    Rolfe M. 80
    Samuel R. 80
Hobert, Rosa 151
Hodges, Bishop Joseph 215
Hoffmaster,
    Charles 125
    Albert (Abe) 141
    Michael 48
Holden, L. W. 204
Holman, Isaac 124, 184
Holsberry, Meryl Berry 174
Holt,
    Charlie 48
    Mrs. Lester 176
Home Guards 276
Homemakers Club 74, 130
Homestead Act of 1779 103
Homestead, The Inn 137
Honeymoon Cabin 287
Hooper, T. Leroy 205
Hoover, Myra 174
Hopewell M.P. Church 199
Horn, Jacob 13, 181
Horn Papers 181
Horn, W.F. 12
Hoskins, Irene 211
Hoult Locks & Dam 167
Hoult M.E. Church 199
Hoult school 12
Hoult Town 67
How Kettle Run Got Its Name 278
Howe, Nan 151
Howell, Abraham A. 105, 115
Hoyland, Donna 176
Huffman, Harry 95
Huffman mine 95
Hughes,
    Anna 204
    Charles 204
    Thomas 150
Hull,
    George W. and Sarah 205
    John Wesley 86, 87
    Rev. John and Jane 86, 177
    Sarah Ann. 86
Hull School 177
Hungry Man Hill 84
Hunsaker,
    Estyl Balderson 125
    George 216
    Robert 81

Hunt,
    Charles 48
    Robert, Jr. 48
    Robert, Sr. 48
Hunter,
    Dale 38, 48, 61, 119, 130
    Dale, Eileen, Eric and Phyllis 141
    Ruth 136
    Vance 48
    Vance, Ruth and Patty 143
Hunter-Vincent, Phyllis 126
Hurst, Bob and Janene 286
Hustead, William 173
Huster, Harry and Lizbeth 145

I

Ice,
    Frederick 101
    Robert and Marilyn 285
    William B. 109
Ice's Mills 38
Idamay 84
Imboden, General John D. 279
Industrial, National Recovery Work Act 28
International Bible Students 218
Ireland, Thomas 208
Irish 37, 38
Irish, The Patch 38
Irons,
    Agnes (Robertson) 118, 128, 136, 211
    Charles 35, 105
    Charles Joe 39, 118, 281
    Dale 141
    Gail 173
    Glenn 149
    Glenn and Hubert 149
    Henry 103
    Hubert 149
    Icie Dora (Fleming) Vincent 117
    James Dale 139
    Joseph 106, 117, 121, 122, 137, 139, 154
    Joyce, Jill and Charles Joe 141
    Melissa 206, 281
    Orville 117, 118, 149, 208
    Orville and Agnes 147
    Pearcy Phillips 35
    Ronnie, Willa, Glenn and Gary 147
    Vallie 150, 151, 171, 173
    Willis 106, 122, 131
Iroquois Nation 12

J

J. R. and Susie Knight 137
Jackson, Andrew "Stonewall" 105, 276, 284
Jacobs,
    Dana 118
    Fannie (Bennett) 118
    Luther 118
    Pearl 118
    Sara 118
James Fork M.E. Church 199
Janes, Mary Linn 92
Janes Memorial Methodist. 207
Jarrett,
    Charles 82
    Dave 84
    William 81
Jasper,
    Jeremiah 205
    Nancy 115
    W. R. 106
    William R. 115
Jefferson, George R. 89, 128, 227
Jehovah's Witnesses 218
Jenkins,
    Harriet 206
    James 206
Jesus Outreach Church of Living Waters 222
Joe Morgan 100
John Linn Cemetery 237

John Nuzum 164
John Wesley M.E. Church 200
Johnson,
    Charley S. 35
    Colonel J. J. 114
    E. J. 204
    G. A. 106
    George "Granddaddy" 131
    John 70
    John L. 121
    Margaret 103
    Mr. 151
    Nola 173
    Ross 192
    Ross Bradshaw 191
    Samuel 122
Jolliff,
    Jacob 114
    Joseph 12
Jones Chapel 199
Jones,
    Daniel 204
    General William Ezra 279
    Omer 174
Jones Raid 114, 279
Jones-Imboden raid 280
Julian,
    Angelina 171
    Nick 77, 84

K

Kate Griffith 52
Kaufman, Lester 123
KDKA 134
Keener,
    Alice 210
    Barbara Nichols, Sybil and Pete 146
    Ben 135
    C. E. "Pete" 209
    Dwayne 190
    Elbert 131
    James and Dot 135
    Jimmy, James, Dot, Lillian, Tiny and Chuck 146
    John 207
    Martin A. 106, 131
    Pete 134
    Ralph 158
    Richard 210
    Sybil and Pete 131
Kelly,
    Alma 153
    Anna 149
Kendall, James 151
Kendall, Norman Scrapbooks 277
Kenner, Elbert and Marsilete Keener 142
Kerr, James 204
Kettle Run 89, 278
Khun, Goldie 211
King, Ben 78
King George III 14
King Station 78
King,
    Thomas Durn 77
    Vanden 176
King-Mill Valley Public Service District 74
Kingdom Heirs Baptist Church 217
Kingmont 43, 74, 77
Kingmont Community Building 83
Kingmont Improvement Association 83
Kingmont TV Cable Company 84
Kingmont United Methodist Church 216
Kings Ferry 114
Kings Station 28
Kinty,
    Cecil 48, 123
    Jerry 111
    Sylvia 136, 143
Kirby, Joan 176
Kirk,
    Clara Alice Annon 202
    Daniel 216
    Daniel Webster 202
    Elizabeth 206
    George Washington 190, 193, 202
    Jonathan 206
    Phoebe 205
    Richard 157, 206
    Silas H. 202
Kirk's Ferry 157
Klepfel, John H. 173
Knight,
    Charles 'Doc' and Suzie 123, 143
    Isaac 28, 153, 158
    Mac 48
    Orlie Cheuvront 152
    Richard and Josinah 157
    Richard N. 206
    Robert 106
    Susie 211
Knights of Columbus 43
Knotts,
    Clara Boice 190
    Dorothy 136
Knott's Radio Repair 134
Knotts,
    Russell 134, 135
    Russell and Dorothy 144
Knottsville 114
Koon's Run 84
Kovach, Joe 93
Ku-Klux-Klan 134
Kyre, Pearl (Smith) 148

L

LaDonne, Tony 119
Lake, Fay 174
Lake Floyd 179
Lake,
    John 174
    John L. 178
    Kingery K. 179
Lamb, Charles 205
Lance, Irene and 'Pop' 143
Lanham, Cephas 239
Lantz, Jim 123
Laratta, Therese 73
LaSalette Fathers 215
Late Adena 12
Latrobe, Benjamin 36
Lavorata, Chris 112, 128
Lawler Cemetery 271
Lawler Church 16, 190
Lawler,
    Jehu 207
    John H. 206
Lawler Methodist Episcopal South Church 206
Lawler,
    Mortimer 173, 190
    N. T. and Elizabeth A. 271
    Truman 173, 190
    Willis 104
    W.T. 128
Leachman, J. D. 204
Leah Swearingen 115
LeDonne, Tony 70
Legg, Paul 111
LeMasters, Thelma 72
Leonard,
    Gardner 163
    Sarah 205
Lester, Ed 217
Levels 49, 151
Levels Methodist Episcopal Church 205
Levels M.P. Church 200, 206
Levels Methodist Church 49
Levels Road 156
Levels school 153
Levi Springer Homestead 102
Lewis County 11
Lewis,
    Edith 158
    Mary Stanley 125
Liberty Coal & Coke Company 158
Liberty Mine 17, 156
Lick Run 15
Lietzell, Lawrence 121
Lightner, Ann 73
Lilley, George 285
Lincoln, Abraham 284
Linn,
    Benjamin 286
    Benny & Junior 48
    Brady 169
Linn Cemetery 67
Linn Chapel 190
Linn,
    George 48
    Gordon 48
    Hiram 190
    Hugh R. 87, 88, 92
    Hugh W. 86
    James 178
    John 237
    Lawrence 176
    Lloyd 48
    Lucy 174
    Margaret 89
    Mary 72
    Nancy 89
    Olive Virginia 82
    Robert 89, 204
    Sam 178, 286
Linn, Sam log cabin 285
Linn,
    Samuel 35, 88
    Samuel ("White Sam") and Betsy (Rudy) 177
    Samuel and Anzy 227, 237
    Samuel Gideon 87
    Samuel L 178
Linn School 173
Linn,
    Viola 151
    William 35, 190, 227, 268
Lipscomb, Mike 48
Little,
    Absolum 182
    Absolum, Sr 250
Little Cemetery 250, 253
Little, David J. 150
Little Family History 108
Little,
    G. K. 18, 48
    Josephine (Merrifield) 148
Little Kanawha Syndicate 63
Little Kennaway 102
Little,
    Kenneth 173, 190
    Marceline 148
    Mark W. 115
    T. J. 94
    Thomas Allen and Eliza (Harr) 115
    Thomas, Jr. 287
    Thomas Sr 105, 106, 250
    William 115
    Zimri 18
Loar, George 205
Log Cabin Hill 73
log cabins 284
Log, The 90, 93, 286
Long,
    Emma 122
    Ethel 158
    John 111
Lord Dunmore's War 103
Lost Run 16, 101
Louden,
    George W. 49
    Glenn 12, 101, 164
Loughridge, Bessie 190
Louman, Mary Lou 82
Love, Alice 151
Lowe, A. W. 205

M

M.P. "Church on the Hill" 199
Madaria,
    C. A. 131
    Charles 116
    Charles R. 115, 116
    George and Margaret (Pierpont) 115
    Charles 106
Mallonee, Tim 70
Malone, Henry 43
Mangos 12
Manley, Mary Catherine 14
Maple Lake 179
Marion County 12
Marion County Commission 193
Marion County Future Farmers of America, 193
Marion County's Poor House 83
Marion, Francis 67
Marion Grays 276
Marshall University 128
Martin,
    Avis 174
    Brooks 173
    Dorrie 158
    Eliza 94
    Gordon C. 131
    Guy "Pappy" 137
    Jacob 214
    Joe 180
    Mary Linn and Avis 73
    Willie 151
Martinka Coal Company 160
Martinka Mine 17, 45, 156, 160
Martray, Carl 128
Mason,
    Carl 192
    Clem N. 189
    Dick 151
    Helen 173
    John 173
    Kate 178
    Pearl 192
    Ronald 192
Mason-Dixon Line 101, 276
Mason's Landing 42, 62
Massawomees 12
Mathey, Madge 176
Maze, Ron 131
McAllister,
    Alexander 89, 205
    Granville 151
    John and Jane (Work) 89
McAlpin 99
McCallister, Mary 287
McCarty, Thomas 204
McClelland, James 92
McClure, Willa 151
McCormick, Jacob B. 202
McCullough, Elinor 176
McCulty, H. C. 205
McDaniel, Hannah 102
McDonald,
    Eddie and Emma 125
    John 149
    Juanita 149
    Martha 149
    Ray 149
    Raymond 149
McDougal,
    Harold 89
    Helen 205
    Judge H.C. 280
McGee,
    B. F. 205
    Manassah 103
    Owen 173
McGraw, John T. 37
McIntire, William 100
McKenny, Christina 104
McKinney, Luther Haymond 104
McLaughlin, Rev. O. E. 204, 209, 210
McVicker, Daisey 190
Meetinghouse Run 16
Meierding, Thomas 225
Mellett, John 86
Meredith camp 22
Meredith Construction Company 90
Meredith,
    E. E. 164
    Myrtle Hill 157
    Russell 21
    Thomas 204
Merrifield,
    Bathsheba (Bashy) 102, 103
    Josephine 149
    Richard 103
    Samuel 103
Michael,
    A. E. 204
    Earl 157
    Earle 125
    Grace 82, 174
Michaels, Ray 173
Middletown 67
Middletown Investment, LLC 100
Middletown Mall 84, 90, 98, 100
Middletown-Wheeling Turnpike 181
Millennnial Dawnists 218
Miller,
    Arthur and Mabel 147
    Cecilia 176
    Cora 151
    Dennis 72
    Jesse 35
    John Bunyon 68, 70
    John Bunyon, Jr. 68
    Joseph 68
    Lawrence 174, 189
    Oscar 216
    Rymer 67, 68
Millersville 41, 68, 74
Millersville School 73
Millersville/Pleasant Valley United Methodist Church 202
Mineral Contracting Corporation 135
Ministers,
    Colfax Church 212
    Kingmont United Methodist Church 216
    Colfax Methodist Episcopal Church 207, 208
    Conference Archives at WV Wesleyan College 212
    Galilean Baptist Church 221
    Millersville Methodist 204
    Nain Free Methodist Church 214
    Pleasant Valley Church Of Christ 221
    Quiet Dell Baptist Church 218
    Valley Chapel 204
Mission Farms on Glady Creek 148
Mitchell, Dave 111
Moatsville 29
Mohawks 12
Mohr,
    James 222
    Steven 222
Mollahan, Congressman Alan B. 136
Mollahan, Robert H. 100
Monkey Wrench Hollow 83, 84
Monongah 84
Monongah Municipal Water Works 84
Monongah Road 12
Monongahela
    Lake 11
    Railroad Company 63
    River 11
    Valley 198
    Valley Traction Company 137
    Baptist Church 199
    County 15
    Railroad 63
Monongalia Story I 114
Monongalia Valley 102
Montana Mines M.E. Church 200
Monumental M.E. Church 199
Moonshine stills 184
Moore, Arch, Jr. 99
Moore, Chester 178
Moran Family photo 144
Moran, Stella 128, 190
Morgan,
    Brenda 73, 82
    Clifford 217
    Ellsworth 153, 157
    Frank 125, 156, 157
    Horatio 104
    Jay 100
    Joan 73, 82
    Mollie Morris 157, 174
    Morgan 102
    Naomi 125, 128, 136, 157, 174
    Oliver P. 103
    Stephen 101
    Uriah 103
    W. E. 173
    Willa 73
    Zackwell 102
Morgan's Fort 157
Morgantown 114
Morgantown & Bridgeport Pike 99
Morris,
    Daniel 277
    H. C. 89, 205
    Homer 278
    J. Claude 73
    oseph 205
    Molly 125
Morris Park 70, 73
Morrison, Paul 217
Morrow, Daniel L. 169, 170
Morrow, Vernon 173
Motter,
    Claude A. 254
    Jerome (Pete) C. 159
    Olive Mason 171
    Will 254
Mound Builders 12
Mountain Gate 100
Mountaineer Area Council in Marion County 18
Mountaineer Area Council of Boy Scouts of America 193
Mowery,
    Betty 136
    Hazel 137
    Hilda 136
    Janice 136
    Orval 180
    Orville 131
Moyer, W. R. 204
Mt. Nebo Church of Christ 199
Mt. Zion M.E. Methodist 199, 200
Muddy, The 13
Mulligan, General James A. 278
Mundell,
    Benjamin 108
    Ben 151
    Ben F. 94
    Janet 73
    William B. and Rebecca 35
    William Bailey 108
Mundell's Ferry 86
Muriale's Restaurant 83
Murphy,
    George 202
    Joshua 206
Musgrove, Gerald and Donna 290
Music, Ruth Ann 278
Mustacchin, Lorena 128
mustard gas 122
Myers,
    Ella 177, 178
    S. 106

N

Naegele, Gary P. 215
Nain Free Methodist Church 214
National Cemetery, Grafton 276
National Road 34
National, The Archives 81
Nelson, John "Net" Nuzum 171
Neptune, Virginia 158
Nestor, A. L. 205
New Canaan 135
Newton, Gwendlyln 176
Nichols Addition 123
Nichols,
    Billy 28
    Clarence and Harry 149
    Grandma" 211
    Harry 122
    Harry O. 209
    Hiram 48
    Russell
        18, 118, 122, 123, 125, 156, 210, 245
    Russell and Pearl 140
    Ruth 131
    Valentine 110
Nickols, Rick 111
Niehaus, Mildred Rudy 153
Nixon,
    Elias 94
    Harmon 94
    Jesse 94
    John 94
    John and Minerva 98
    John G. 94
    Jonathon 94
    Joshua 151
    Robert P. 94
    Ronald 98
    Samuel 94
    Samuel P. 70
Nixon School 94
Nixon, Thomas B. 179
Northern (Beulah) Methodist Church 200
Northwestern Virginia Railroad 36
Norton, James 204, 205
Now & Long Ago 12, 101, 164
Nunnally, Gladys and Tom 142
Nuzum No 1 Cemetery 257
Nuzum,
    Ulysses 120
    Agnes McKinney 190
    Albert 167
    Allie 211
    "Black Dick" 164
    Charlie 208
    Clarence 257
    David 76, 111, 135
    David and Helen 161
    Doris, Linda Faye and Edwin 145
    Edwin 290
    Elenora ("Nora") 97
    Elizabeth 163
    Enos 67, 267
    Enos L., Jr. 174
    Fay and Oda 137
    Faye 137
    Flora 176
    George 163
    Hazel 211
    II, David and Joanne 161
    James 103, 163
    Jane 254
    Jane Shriver 35
    Job R. 206
    Joel 35, 164
    Joel ("Dode") 173
    John 163
    Lavina 254
    Mercia 206
    Miner 178
Nuzum No. 1 Cemetery 257
Nuzum No. 3 267
Nuzum,
    Oda and Faye 146
    Phoebe 163
    Richard 67, 103, 163, 201
    Richard (Black Dick) 103, 164, 204
    Richard B. 35
    Ruth 103
    Sarah 115, 117, 163
    Sophrania 204
    Staats 117, 121, 131, 132
    The Family History 257
    Thomas 163
    Thomas and Elizabeth 163
    Thornton 206
    Ulysses 115
    William 163
    Z. & Son 106
    Zadoc 103, 120, 125
    Zadoc and Ruhama (Springer) 204
    Zadoc and Ulysses 244
    Zadock 204
Nuzum's Mill 16, 35, 40, 41, 56, 67, 164
Nuzum's Mill Post Office 169
Nuzum's Mill-Hammond post office 169
Nuzum's Mills 150
Nuzum's Run 16

O

Oakland, Maryland 37
O'Donnell, Earl 82
Ohio River 11
Oiler,
    Julia and Floyd 149
    Charles 131
    Charlie 118
Ol' Engine No. 44 43
Onderko,
    Mike 84
    Steve 84
O'Neal, Nancy 71
Oneidas 12
Onondagas 12
Open Door Free Will Baptists 207
Orange County 14, 67
Orders Construction Company 111
Orr, Henry 174
Osburn, Kenny 48
Osburne, Patricia 153

P

Paddy Hands 48
Palatine 67, 114
Palatine Knob 12
Palatine Methodist Protestant Church 202
Palmer, Christine 128
Parkeson, Thomas 181
Parkinson, Joseph 12
Parrick,
    Allison 157
    Cecil 157, 174
Parrish, Glenn 21, 140
Parrott, Ely & Hurt 135
Pastors,
    Benton's Ferry United Methodist Church 205
    Calvary Baptist Church 204
    First Southern Baptist 220
    Sarrietta Church 216
    St. Anthony Catholic Church 215
Patch, The 38
Patterson, Phillip 104
Peabody Coal Company 160
Pearson, Kenneth 222
Pebble Beach 24
Pence, Gene 73
Pendergast, Madeline Motter 158
Pentecostal, Fairmont Church 217
Perkins, A. H. 204
Pettijohn, William 182
Pettyjohn 67

Pettyjohn, John 67
Pettyjohn Trading Post 114
Phillips,
    A. C. 203
    Betty 73
Phillips Coal Company 88
Phillips,
    Margaret Bailey 128
    Ms. 73
    Rev. J. J. 106, 206
    Vallie (Irons) 139, 140, 153, 211
Piercy,
    Charles S., Jr 81
    Pat Lindsay 81
Pierpont, Col. Larkin 281
Pierpont, Governor Francis H. 281
Pigott, George 100
Pinchgut Hollow 24, 133
Pisgah M.E. Church 199
Pitcher M.E. Church at Dakota 199
Pittsburgh 12
Pizatella Realtors 18
Pleasant Creek 29
Pleasant Creek Foundation 193
Pleasant Hill Church of the Brethren 202
Pleasant Valley 70, 74
Pleasant Valley
    Church Of Christ 221
    Community Building 75
    Community Educational Outreach 74
    Homemakers Club 74
    chool 72, 73
    town council 75
Pleasantville 102
Plum Run 15
Plum Run Church of Christ 200
Poe, Edgar 190
Police, William 84
Poling, Andy 81
Polsley, Jacob 114
Polsley's Mill 114
Poplar Island 18, 43, 61
Porter,
    James 165
    James M. 165
    Jasper M. 165
    John 165
Potter, Don 192
Powell 43, 61
Powell Bottom 154, 157, 159
Powell Coal & Coke Company 159
Powell,
    John 157
    Margaret 35
    William 105
    William B. 35, 157
Prahl, Sheila, Sharon and Jim 143
Preston County 35
Price, Goldie 174
Prickett,
    Ann 102
    Jacob 101, 102
Prickett's Creek 164
Pricketts' Creek Baptist Church 199
Prickett's Fort 15, 67, 101
Prickett's Post 101
Prunty,
    Nancy (Shaver) 148
    Paul 90, 180
    William Lee 91
Pruntytown 16, 36, 183, 278
Pruntytown Grade School 190
Puffenbager, J. R. 43
Punkin Center Church 200
Pyecha, Andy and Betty Jo 22

Q

Quaker Society 163
Quakers 201
Quakers' Meetinghouse 199
Quiet Dell 16, 178

Quiet Dell Baptist Church 217
Quiet Dell School 174

R

R. Nichols Lumber Company 122
Radcliff, Cecil 217
Radford, Larney 151
raiding rebels 279
Railing Brothers 123
railroad church 207
Railroad Express 88
Ray, Albert 217
Realty Development Company 179
Recollections 280
Red, Chief Cloud 183
Redstone Circuit 198
Reed,
    Clark 151
    John 182
    Joseph, Jr. 173
    Joseph, Sr. 190
    Richard, Jr 190
Reese & Hammond Fire Brick Company 166
Reese,
    Anzy 88, 227, 269
    Charles 112
    Fanny 173
    George and Nancy 227
    Matty 178
    Polly 269
    Samuel 192
    Tabitha 269
Reese-Hammond Fire Brick Company 165
Reid, H. 43
Rest Haven Memorial Gardens 237
Revolutionary War 14
Rexroad, Margaret 74, 136
Reynolds,
    Jane 76
    John T. 204
Rhea Chapel 199
Rice, Edmon 202
Richards,
    Carl 194
    Henry 135
    Jackie 210
    T. R. 204
Richardson, William 173, 190
Richie, Thomas 251
Richman, Karen Donner 73, 128
Richmond, J. A. 204
Ridenour,
    Allen 205
    Christine Gainer 128
Rider, I. L. 92
Righter Chapel 199
Riley, John 190, 206
riots 38
Ritchie, David 123
River Run 18
River Run School 151
Rivesville 67, 102
Rivesville M.E. Church 200
Rivesville Power 137
Roades, Maryln 119
Roanoke River 14
Roberson, Will 151
Robertson,
    Agnes 126, 151
    Charles W. and Lovie 21
    Graham 204
Robertson Island 21, 22
Robertson,
    Lovie 210
    Mr. 158
Robertson-Irons, Agnes 210
Robey, Irene 82
Robinson,
    Christopher 71
    John 111
    Kenneth G. 222

    Lizzie 171
    Louise Lambert 190
Robinson Mine 70, 71
Robinson, Perry 204
Robinson Run 24, 132
Rock Lake 178, 180
Rock Lake Club 179, 180
Roderick, Charles 217
Rodriquez, Steve 176
Rogers,
    Aaron 205
    Edith 174
    Edyth 190
    Edythe Baker 128
    John M. 188
    Masel 128, 176
Roosevelt, Franklin D. 28, 61
Rosbby's Rock 41
Ross Chapel 202
Ross,
    Charles 190
    Dwight 205
    Lucinda 104
    Vance 205
Rowland, Ronald 26
Royal Chapel Methodist Church 200
Rudy,
    Basil and Mary 175
    Henry 169
    John 170
    Mary Poe 174
    Rem 174
Run, Mill 68
Rupert, J. B. 205
Rural Free Delivery (RFD) 88
Rush, C. M. 43
Rushton, Albert and Hazel 147
Russelites 218
Russell, John A. 94
Rust,
    Carrie 148
    Hershel 208
    Louis P. 208
    Mrs. H. K. 211
Ruston,
    Hazel 136
    Tom 48
Rutherford, Beatrice and Goldie 149
Ryan, Samuel 205

S

S&D Grocery 178
Sabo, Debra 73, 82
Salem M.P. and M.E. Church 199
Salerno Brothers, Inc. 193
Salt Lick Creek 102
Sam Linn Cemetery 228
Samaria Free Methodist Church 214
Sam's Club 100
Samuel Linn Cemetery 271
Sanders,
    Earl 48
    Fred 158
    Henry L. 202
    John 104
    John L. 202
    Lawrence 154, 158
    Lawrence, Jr. 158
Sandy Beach 21
Sandy Eagle Ball Field 77
Sapp, E. M. 204
Sapps Run 94
Sarrietta 18
Sarrietta church 217
Sarrietta School 94, 150
Satterfield,
    Benjamin 202, 206
    Dave 174
    David 157
    Elizabeth 206
    Enos L. 206

    Etta 136
    Gerry 126
    Gerry and Junie 145
    Gertie 211
    Gladys 126
    Hattie 106
    Junie and Gerry 135
    Martha 158
    Mildred 176
    Russell "Junie" 130
    Sweden 157
    William and Gertie 209
Sayers, Roxie McKinney 190
Sayre, Charles 48
Schmidt, L.D. 73
Schmuck, Emmet 48
School No. 8 94
Schoolcraft, Carol 73
Scott, Marie 176
Scout Island 18
Scouts 136
scrip 81
Scritchfield, Mark 77
Securro, Nancy 128
Sedera, Paul 73
Seneca 12
Seneca Trail 13
Sertees, John 40
Sertees, Phyllis 171
Shackleford, Lucie Holbert 125
Shaffer,
    Glenn 75
    Henry 156, 158
    Minta 189
    Harvey 189
    Nellie and Howard 149
Shaver,
    Albert 202
    Delphia 151
    John 49, 148
Shaw,
    Harry 164, 184
    James 128
    Joshua 106, 159, 170, 206
Shawnees 12, 101
Shea, Ila 128
Shepler, Earl 202
Shinnston Water Treatment Plant 84
Shiveley, Philip 151
Shorter,
    Ada Pearl 136
    Charles L. 106, 131
Shrieve,
    Thomas 179
    Deborah 136
Shriver Cemetery 253, 254
Shriver,
    Jacob 35, 105
    Jacob and Anna 152
    James 206
    John 154, 206
    John and James 206
    John and Mary 21, 254
    Lloyd 173, 190
    Ned 173
    Thomas 194
Shrivers Flat 280
Shrivers's Run 21
Shuman, Nerva 158
Simmons,
    Benny 84
    Tobe and Nettie (Shriver) 152
Sines, Jonas 202
Sines, Margaret Mae 169
Sioux Indian nation 183
Sipe, Carolynn Janes 128, 158
Six Nations 12
Sixth Regiment, Company A of the Western Virginia 280
Skarzinski, L. D. and Misty 161
Slamick, Teresa 73

Slave Market 277
Smallwood Cemetery 253
Smallwood,
    Everett D. 252
    John H. and Margaret 252
Smith & Porter Company 165
Smith,
    Allen 111
    Clara 211
    Col. James K. 183
    Delbert 18, 61, 134, 135
    Delbert and Iretta 145
    Earl Herndon 44
    Eldon "Smuck" 61, 148
    Frank 151, 159
    Joseph L. 151
    Judy and Junior 146
    Kathy, Bob, Bill, Sylvia and Mitchell 145
    Lewis 165
    Marseen 206
    Mary and Darrell 149
    Mrs. Eldon (Clara) 149
    Robert 94
    Rosa 151
Snider, Frank, Jr. 222
Snowden, W. J. and Son 167
Snyder,
    Bernice 158
    Lillian B. 92
Society of Quakers 163
Solomon, J. B. 204
Southern Ohio Coal Company 160, 168
Sparks,
    George 251
    Rachel Nixon 251
Spottswood, Alexander 14, 67
Spriggville 173
Springer,
    Alpheus 103
    Bathsheba 103, 104
    Dennis 103
    Drusilla 102, 103
    Edith 104
    Eliza 104
    Elizabeth 103
    Hannah 103, 104
    James 104
    Jane 103
    Job 103
    John 104
    John J. 103
    Levi 102
    Levi Cornelius 104
    Lucinda 103
    Malinda 103
    Nancy Ann 103
    Paulina 103
    Phoebe 103
    Reason T. 103
    Richard 104
    Roanna 103
    Ruhama 103
    Swedon 103
    Sylvanus H. 104
    Zacheus 104
    Zadock 102, 104
Springer, Amos 102
    Andrew 169, 170
    Benjamin 102
    Christopher 101
    Dennis 102, 115
    Dennis, Jr. 102
    Dorothy 102
    Druscilla 102
    Firman and Viola (Swearingen) 125
    Glenn 204
Springer Graveyard 104, 244
Springer, Hannah 102
    Humphrey 102
    Jacob 102
    Job 102, 114, 120, 204
    Job and Rebecca 35

    John 101, 102, 103, 120, 244
    John and Drusilla 114
    Joseph 245
    Josiah 102
    Levi 102
    Nathan 102
    Nellie Raikes 125
    Pauline 176
    Phoebe 102, 257
    Ruhama 120
    Scott and Brady 131
    Swedon and Lucinda 116
    Uriah 102
    William F. 106
    William Firman 116
    Zadoc 102
Springer's Bend 24, 104
Squires Run 15
St. Anthony Church 215
St. John M.E. Church 199
St. Paul Baptist Church 199
St. Paul M.P. Church 200
St. Peter The Fisherman Catholic Church 200
Staats, David 103
Staggers, Mary Ellen 125
Stalnaker, Douglas 111
    Linda 73
    Robby 111
    W. H. 205
    Windal 111
Stanley, Bell E. 151
    Karen 73
    Lillian 82
    Mabel 73, 125
Stansberry, Lem 174
State Rt. 310 132
steam engines 41
Steel,
    James 170
    John 170
    Mrs. John 170
    Ralph 97
Stemple,
    Bob 243
    Boyd 48
    Boyd and Locia 141
Stevens, Mildred and Henry 131
Steward, Louis 190
Stewart, Beverly 73
Stickley, C.W. 100
Stillwell, Minnie Cole 190
Stines, Mary 248
Stonehouse Hollow 29
Stoops, Don 128
Stor, Marquita, Bill, Allison, Darlana and Christe 141
Storms,
    Ruth and Alice 211
    Bill 48
    Darl 141, 211
Stout, Benjamin 208
Straight,
    Charles 69
    Grace Kinsey 125
    J. J. 175
Strum, Minnie Davis 174
Stuart, Arthur and Evelyn 204
Summers,
    Benjamin and Margaret 205
    Linn 48
    Willis 204
Sunday, Billy 205
Sunfish Rock 21
Superintendents, Valley Falls State Park 194
Swearingen,
    Brent 156
    Florence 178
Swearingen School 125
Swearingen, Viola 116
Swisher, Francis Rudy 128, 217
Sycamore Island 18

T

Taggart House 14
Tarazell 18
Tatterson, Opal 153
    Ruby 158, 171, 174
    Sarah 35
Taylor Cemetery 266
Taylor,
    Guy and Ollie 137, 146
    James E. 202
    John 67
    Mark 120
    Ollie 136
Teachers,
    Quiet Dell School 174
    Colfax School 125
    Goose Creek School 157
    Hammond Ridge School 173
    Hammond School 171
    Hull School 177
    Levels School 153
    Linn School 190
    "New" Quiet Dell School 175
    Powell School 158
    Sarrietta School 151
    Valley Falls School 189
Telltale, The Lilac Bush 278
Tennant, Burley 70, 119
    Delegate Robert H. 192
Terra Alta 35
Texas 43, 105
Texas Station 106
The Temple M.P. Church 199
Thickson, Thomas 151
Thomas,
    B.F. 87
    Columbus 92
    Emma C. 92
    Emma F. and B. F. 85
    George 106
    James W. 71
    Lucinda 103
    Maria E. 88
    Richard 35, 72, 105
    Richard and Hannah 35
    Sarah 103
    William M. 92
Thompson, Ada Saunders 171
Thorn, Joan 126
Thorne,
    Ed 142
    Joan 131
Thorne's Grocery 131
Three Forks Creek 15, 34
Tillett, Pearl 136
Times, Fairmont 172
Times/West Virginian 70
Tobrey, Cathy 73
Tomahawk Rights 101, 154
Toothman, A. G. 176
    Arlie 82
    Harriet 95, 97
    Richard 100
Town Hill Road 157
Town, Scab 84
Track Foremen 48
Train Wrecks 52
trestles 39
Trinity Assembly of God Church 12
Triune 118
Tucker cabin 288
Tucker, Dolice 173
    Henry 269
    John, Jr. 94
    John, Sr 94
    Jr., John and Mary 94
    Lemuel 190
    Mason 173
    Phoebe 103
    Thaddeus 288
    William 173, 182

Tunnel Hollow 16, 164, 165
Turtle Creek 14
turtle rock 24
Tuscarawas 12
Tygart City 85
Tygart Dam 27
Tygart, David 13
    Elizabeth 13
Tygart Lake State Park 30
Tygart River Mine 16, 160, 162, 206
Tygart Valley Brick and Tile Company 123
Tygart Valley Mall 100
Tygart Valley River cemeteries 224
Tygers River 181
Tyler, John 250

U

U.S. Army Corps of Engineers 22
Uffington 99
Unclaimed Civil War Medal list 86
Underground Railroad 277
Union Baptist Church 199
Union Church/Walnut Grove M.P. Church 199
Union Home Guards 282
Union Mission 148
Union Valley Baptist 199
United Methodist Women 211
Upper Mingo 12
US Geological Survey 22
US Route 250 132
Utt, Vicki 128

V

Valentine, Ada 151
Valentine's Day Flood in 1884 27
Valley Bend 148
Valley Bend School 148
Valley Bridge 183
Valley Falls 16, 42, 43, 61, 181, 184, 191
Valley Falls Hotel 184
    Post Office 169
    Postmasters 188
    School 189
    State Park 15, 178, 192
    State Park Foundation 193
    Explorers 13
Valley, The of Distress 198
Valley Volunteer Fire Department 74
Van Braam, Jacob 14
Vance, Jim 111
Vandalia Foundation 37
Vandalia Redevelopment Corporation 37
Vandergrift, Brooks 202
Vandergrift Cemetery 249
Vandergrift, Charles W. 18, 257
    Ebenezer 157
    Effie 141
    Mary 249
    Selvey 202
    Sylvester 157
    Tim, D.D.S. 141
    Wayne 217
Vangilder, Addie 216
    Buck" 131
    John Wesley 214
    Phillip 169
    Sheridan 214
    Wesley 157
VanMeter, Archie and Lillian 178
Varner, Rev. J. P. 208
Veach, Thomas 86
VF Tower 62
Victor, Dave 189
Victory Farm Women's Club 136
Vincent,
    A. J. 170
    Arthur 118
    Beatrice 118
    Bernice 118
Vincent Cemetery 239

Vincent,
    Charles H. 239
    E. L. 170
    Edward 104
    Effie (McCord) 118
    Ethan 217
    G. A. 170
    Glen 171
    Henry 170
    James 118, 139
    Joanna 108
    Mamie 151
    Marquerite 169
    Pam 128
    Thomas 282
    Thurmond 151, 216
    Virgil 118
    Virgil (Punk) 117
Vinegar Hill 90, 93
Virginia & Pittsburgh Coal & Coke Company 79, 95, 160

W

Wadsworth, G. G. 204
Wal-Mart 100
Wallace, Alfred R. 205
Wallas, Bill 111
Wallman, Dwillia 176
Walsh, J. J. 37
War, Revolutionary 68
Washington, George 14
Washington's Diaries Vol. I 14
watch houses 49
Watchman's Ghost 49
Waterford 14
Waters, O. W. 204
Watkins,
    Glen and Junior 149
    Jacob 204
    Ralph 70, 119
Watson, James O. 164, 169
Waynesburg 63
WDTV 134
Weaver,
    Gary and Barbara (Linn) 267
    Steve 77
Wel, Lillian 94
Welk, Layman 149
Wells Fargo 87
Wesley Chapel M.E 199
West Augusta 15
West Augusta County 67
West Branch of the Monongahela 13
West Farmington M.E. 199
West Fork Baptist 199
West Fork River 12, 29
West, Rufus A. 172, 257
West Virginia Army National Guard 193
West Virginia Baptist Convention 218
West Virginia Gazetteer 80, 106
WV Sportsmen and Firearms Association 156
Westerman, Charlotte 189
White Day 114
White Hall 90, 93, 94, 100
White Hall School 151
White Hall's Red Roof Inn 12
White,
    Ike 22
    Reverend G. W. 207
Whitescarver,
    C. H. 192
    George 37, 186
    George M. 185
Whitescarver Hall 186
Whitescarver, John 207
Whitewater rafting 193
Wickwire, John, Sr. 15
Wickwire Run 15
Wickwire's Ford 182
Wile, George W. 71
Willard, Daniel 37

Willard Hotel 37
Willeytown 67
William Linn Cemetery 268
William Work 183
Williams,
    Blanche 125
    Brent 289
Williams' cabin 289
Williams Crossroads 173
Williams,
    Dorman 202
    Han 174
    Hans 178
    M. 123
    Parris 126
    Samuel 36
    T. B. 106, 121
Williamsport 183
Willis, Loftis 137
Willow Tree Baptist Church 200
Wilmouth's Ford 63
Wilson, Ada DeMoss 190
    Benjamin 154
    Colonel 184
    Elza 151
    Frank 178
    J. R. 170
    Margaret, 126
    Margarete and Gus 146
    Mrs. Annie (Boice) 144
    Rita 158
    Willis 174
Wilt, Beatrice Stanley 128, 153
    Eleanor 73
    Lillian 148, 151
    Lloyd 202
    Ruby 149
    Russell 205
Wimer, Belle 157
Windsor Camp 18
Winfield M.E. Church 199
Winfield Methodist Church 199
Winfield Volunteer Fire Department 180
Winter, Beulah 82
Wise, Governor Bob 180
Wiseman, Joseph C. 35, 206
Wiseman, Marshall 190
Wood,
    James 204
    John 18, 154
    Thomas 204
Wood's Boat House 94
Wood's Chapel 200
Woods, Paul and Eloise 25
Work, J. A. and William 183
Workman, Dale 205
Works Project Administration 126
Works Projects Administration 22, 132
Worrall, Hannah 163, 201
Worthington 67
Worthington Baptist Church 199
Worthington Christian Church 199
Worthington M.E. Church 199
Wright,
    Glenden G. 192
    William J. 80
WV State Gazetteer 87
WV University Homemakers Club 136

Y

Yates 29
Yates, Elizy 206
    Farrel 190
    Mary 206
Youth Center of the Free Methodist Church 222

Z

Zinn, Alice Springer 125, 157
Zollinger, Maxmillian A. 169, 171

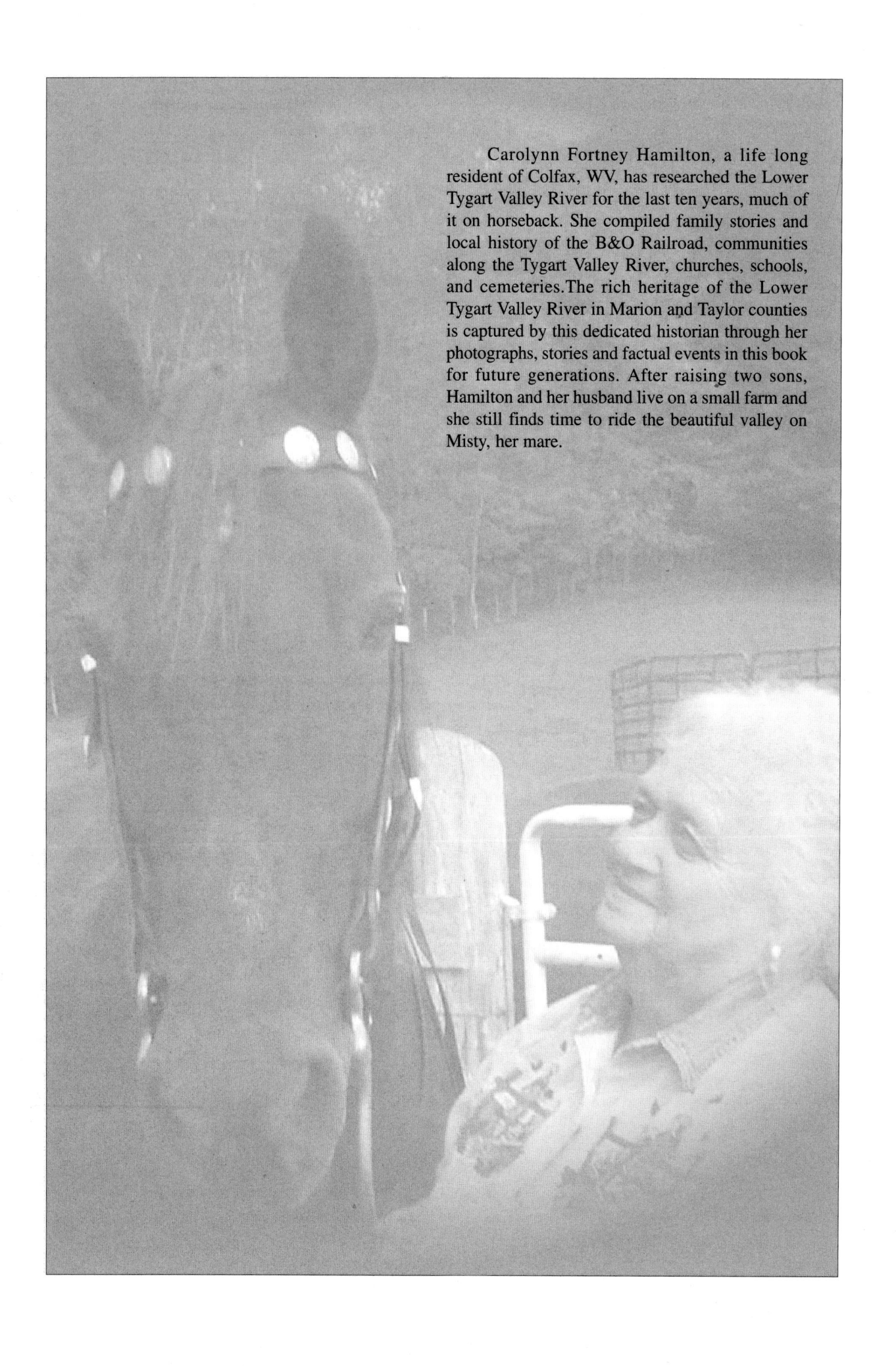

Carolynn Fortney Hamilton, a life long resident of Colfax, WV, has researched the Lower Tygart Valley River for the last ten years, much of it on horseback. She compiled family stories and local history of the B&O Railroad, communities along the Tygart Valley River, churches, schools, and cemeteries. The rich heritage of the Lower Tygart Valley River in Marion and Taylor counties is captured by this dedicated historian through her photographs, stories and factual events in this book for future generations. After raising two sons, Hamilton and her husband live on a small farm and she still finds time to ride the beautiful valley on Misty, her mare.